EVERYTHING SHE TOUCHED

THE LIFE OF RUTH ASAWA

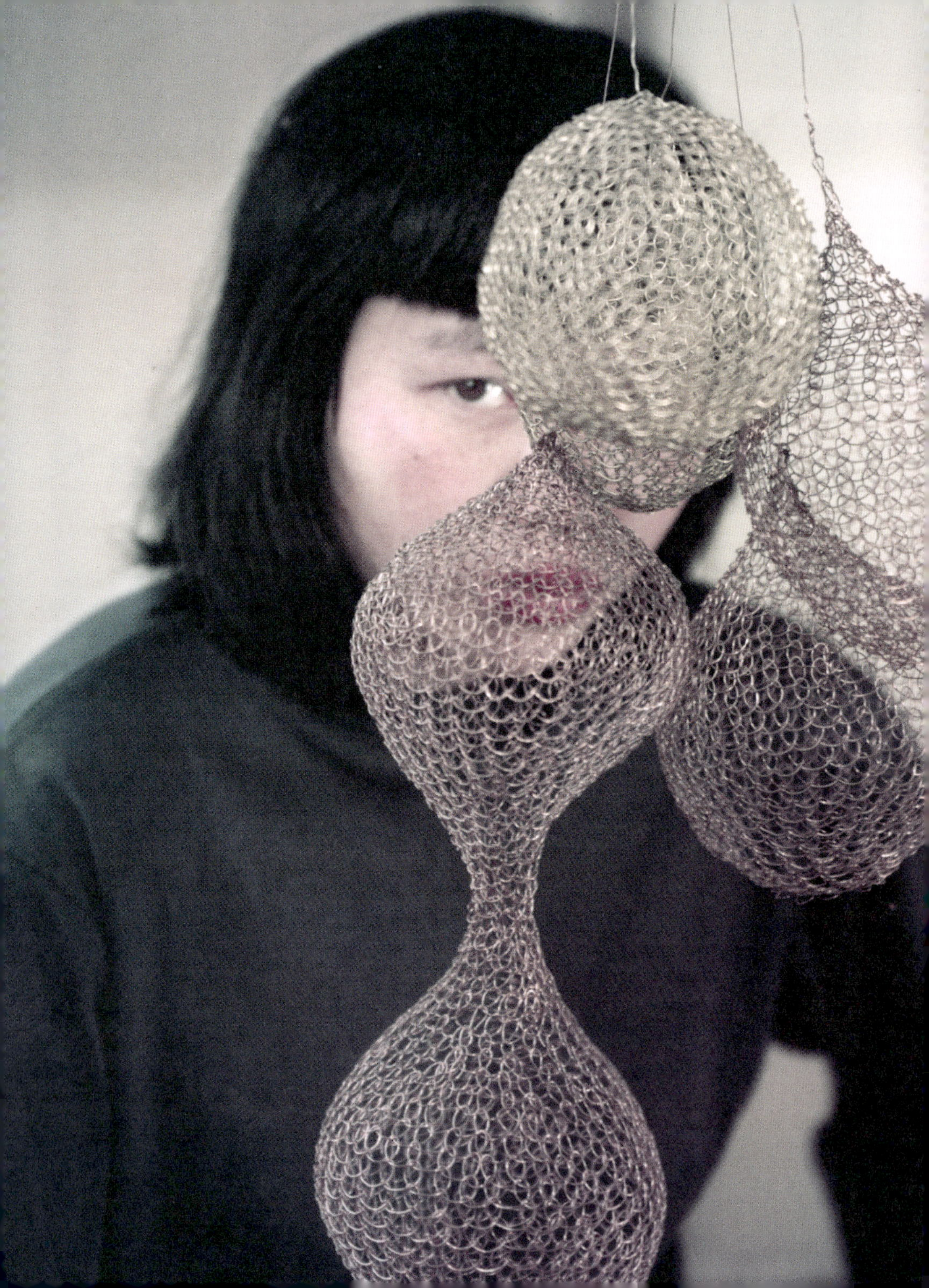

EVERYTHING SHE TOUCHED

THE LIFE OF RUTH ASAWA

BY MARILYN CHASE

With a new foreword by Jonathan Laib,
director of David Zwirner Gallery

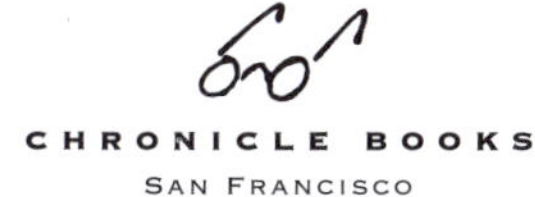

CHRONICLE BOOKS

SAN FRANCISCO

First Chronicle Books LLC paperback edition published in 2025.
Originally published in hardcover in 2020 by Chronicle Books LLC.

Foreword copyright © 2025 by Jonathan Laib.
All other text copyright © 2020 by Marilyn Chase.
Photographs copyright © 2020 by the individual licensors.
All rights reserved. No part of this book may be reproduced
in any form without written permission from the publisher.
Page 316 constitutes a continuation of the copyright page.

Library of Congress Cataloging-in-Publication Data
Names: Chase, Marilyn, 1949- author.
Title: Everything she touched : the life of Ruth Asawa / by Marilyn Chase ; with a new foreword by
Jonathan Laib, director of David Zwirner Gallery.
Description: First Chronicle Books LLC paperback edition. | San Francisco : Chronicle Books, 2025. |
Includes bibliographical references and index.
Identifiers: LCCN 2024036810 | ISBN 9781797232645 (paperback)
Subjects: LCSH: Asawa, Ruth. | Sculptors--United States--Biography. | Japanese American
sculptors--Biography.
Classification: LCC NB237.A82 C49 2025 | DDC 730.92 [B]--dc23/eng/20240916
LC record available at https://lccn.loc.gov/2024036810
The Library of Congress has cataloged the original edition under ISBN 978-1-4521-7440-2.

Manufactured in China.

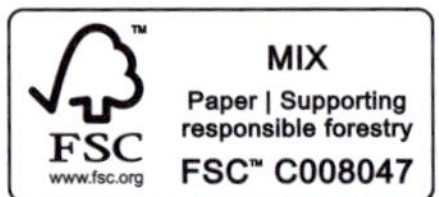

Design by Stella Kim and Kristen Hewitt.

Cover photograph: Ruth holding one of her early looped-wire sculptures, 1951.
Photograph by Imogen Cunningham.

10 9 8 7 6 5 4 3 2 1

Chronicle books and gifts are available at special quantity discounts to corporations, professional associa-
tions, literacy programs, and other organizations. For details and discount information, please contact our
premiums department at corporatesales@chroniclebooks.com or at 1-800-759-0190.

Chronicle Books LLC
680 Second Street
San Francisco, California 94107
www.chroniclebooks.com

CONTENTS

FOREWORD

It is early October 2023, and I am surrounded by more than one hundred of Ruth Asawa's mesmerizing works on paper. This posthumous exhibit at the Whitney Museum of American Art is the artist's first proper survey of drawings. It is a long-awaited institutional tribute to her graphic works, which are arguably the conceptual source from which all of her visual art stems. Though best known for her suspended sculpture in wire (linear, looped forms that are both volumetric and transparent), Asawa also created line drawings that are obsessively executed and intensely rendered. In a 1963 lecture Asawa gave about her mentor Josef Albers, she said, "We deal with a visual world. Our job is the seeing world, our insight into life. The eyes behind the eyes are the decisive ones, so the outer eye is merely a tool that we must sharpen by every means so that the inner eye is free to express itself." With her eyes wide open, Asawa kept her hands constantly busy, recording the delicate edges of a cherry blossom or the fine creasing within the folds of a baby's puckered cheek. She kept her tools sharp.

Like most people who have been fortunate enough to experience Asawa's masterful sculptures firsthand, I was immediately entranced. It was 2008, and I couldn't believe that her reputation did not extend from the West Coast to New York. I set out to help correct that oversight, initially as a New York–based auction specialist in postwar and contemporary art and now as a senior director at David Zwirner Gallery. It has been the highlight of my career to help Asawa receive the respect and attention that she has long deserved.

My challenge was to instate Asawa as part of American art history; the solution I found was to realign Asawa with her better-known artworld contemporaries, Louise Bourgeois and Philip Guston, each of whom had held multiple solo exhibitions at the same Peridot Gallery in New York where Asawa showed in the 1950s. The initial success of this initiative came, rather unusually, through auction, as that was the platform that was available to me at the time. Staging auctions of Asawa's work uncovered a deep reserve of significant public interest that led to an East Coast exhibition in 2013, Asawa's first in New York City in over fifty years. Asawa herself was able to enjoy this success before she passed away that August. Ten years on, her lesser-known drawings now cover the walls of one of New York's most prestigious art museums; her place in history is now cemented, and yet her reputation continues to grow as more people encounter the work and become aware of her incredible talent.

Marilyn Chase is a fellow traveler in Asawa's universe. Chase is, to my knowledge, the first researcher to thoroughly review Asawa's complete papers held at the Stanford University Archives. This research was only one facet of her multiyear project, an obvious labor of love, perfectly suited to a writer with proven skill in historical reporting. Asawa's story is wrapped up in the history of a world at war, of prejudice and discrimination, and ultimately of the rewards of a life lived fully in the arts, while also immersed in her family and community in San Francisco. Chase lays bare the facts of this brilliant artist's life and creates a narrative that helps contextualize Asawa's profound accomplishments.

Jonathan Laib
Senior Director, David Zwirner Gallery
2024

AUTHOR'S NOTE

When I walked into the Whitney Museum of American Art on an autumn evening in September 2023, the air shimmered with a sense of overdue celebration. Almost ninety-eight years after her birth, the late artist Ruth Asawa was having an unprecedented moment. It was a reception honoring her first-ever solo museum exhibition in New York City. The preview crowd was taking in *Ruth Asawa Through Line*, a display of works selected from her prolific daily drawing practice, which encompassed many media: graphite and ink, water color and oil, prints and folded paper, copper and tin. Amid this explosion of her lesser-known works were placed, here and there, a few of her signature wire sculptures. They acted as elegant signposts in this enchanted terra nova.

As Asawa's biographer, I savored the excitement of that night in lower Manhattan. Since the 2020 publication of the hardcover edition of this book, I had given scores of book talks to diverse readers: art lovers, book club members, museum docents, and gallery groups, as well as people honoring World War II history and Japanese American incarceration camp survivors. Binding them together was the sense of wonder that Asawa's life and works inspire. Their hunger to know her story overcame the fact that the global COVID pandemic forced some of us to gather remotely over our computers instead of in person to explore her gift for making art and celebrating life despite hardships that dwarfed our daily challenges. While leading a revolution in sculpture, she was ceaselessly exploring other media, modeling resilience, and teaching us how to be good citizens.

When I first learned about Asawa's life, I had no idea her work was on the threshold of the global renaissance we see today. It was 2014, and her story of creative genius in the face of brutality and bias had captivated me. It was the story of a survivor overcoming poverty and racism to make great art—independent of worldwide acclaim or material reward.

Born in rural poverty, sent to a World War II prison camp, and denied her college degree on the basis of her race, Ruth made her way to the magical Black Mountain College, where fellow artists embraced her unique creativity, modest charm, and stupendous work ethic. Who wouldn't love the story of a woman who transformed barbed wire into transcendent sculpture?

Sadly, Asawa's status as a hero for our time is made even more relevant amid the ongoing scourge of anti-Asian hate crime. Her experiences speak to millions.

To tell the truth, I would have fallen in love with Ruth Asawa's journey, and written her life story, even if she had never sold another sculpture or had another major exhibition. But I was gratified to find out that at the end of her life, the New York curator Jonathan Laib discovered her and set out to relaunch her career by auctioning a single sculpture at Christie's that fetched an astonishing $1.4 million. It was a supreme irony for this most unmaterialistic of artists, who once rented out sculptures for a song or simply gave them away.

But even after the Christie's triumph, so few in the art and publishing worlds see what Jonathan and I clearly both saw. I was furious when arbiters of literary worth replied to my book proposal that Asawa was by their lights a minor cultural figure, lesser-known, lacking name recognition. But I was determined to write Asawa's biography whether or not it would be a blockbuster, and I would find the agent and the publisher with the vision and appetite for risk to embrace Asawa with me. After running the mandatory gauntlet of rejections, I found my ideal agent in Carrie Hannigan of HG Literary in New York, who embraced my pitch. "I would buy this book and I would read this book," she said. My book found its home with Chronicle Books and editor Mirabelle Korn, whose experience in publishing gorgeous art books was perfectly matched to Asawa's exquisite singularity.

Still, when I sat down to write the book, I felt I should begin my prologue with the Christie's auction and the vindication that came with that $1.4 million hammer price. In doing this, I faced questions from an astute early reader who asked why I chose to launch the story in the materialistic world of auction sales, when the artist cared so little for the marketplace. Asawa knew what her art was worth. To paraphrase her mentor Josef Albers—who told his Black Mountain students "art knows nothing of graduation"—art knows nothing of hammer prices.

Today, I watch with wonder the growing list of Asawa's one-woman and group exhibitions mounted in galleries and museums worldwide since I undertook this project: New York, St. Louis, England, Stavangar (Norway), Paris, Barcelona, Stanford, Houston, San Francisco, and more. I also see with a sense of mingled irony and gratification those mounting auction prices. Like her floating wire sculptures woven from a single wire, Asawa's appeal defies gravity.

Marilyn Chase
San Francisco, 2024

AUCTION, 2013

When the auctioneer's hammer came down, the winning bid topped $1.4 million for an 11-foot-long sculpture of wire mesh so light its shadow and substance seemed to merge. The delicacy was deceptive. Years of weaving such wire into gossamer globes had scarred the artist's small hands.

Christie's May 2013 show, *Ruth Asawa: Objects and Apparitions*, was the sculptor's first solo exhibition in New York City in over fifty years. The evening auction at Rockefeller Plaza fetched four to five times the sculpture's estimated value of $250,000 to $350,000. Some people in the San Francisco gallery world had worried about putting Ruth's piece on the block, where it could disappear into private hands, out of public view. She belonged in galleries and museums that would display and not disperse her work, they said. But on the New York art market, it was a triumph. The record auction price for an Asawa vaulted the artist into the stratosphere. Christie's senior specialist of postwar and contemporary art, Jonathan Laib, was elated and convinced that Ruth's resurgence was under way.

Ruth's children, raised to put creativity over commerce, were stunned. This was Mom's work, one of many pieces she wove in her home studio where her children also saw her cooking dinners and mopping floors. For as long as they could remember, her sculptures had hung from the rafters, sheltering their lives, casting moving shadows. Watching the act of making sculpture

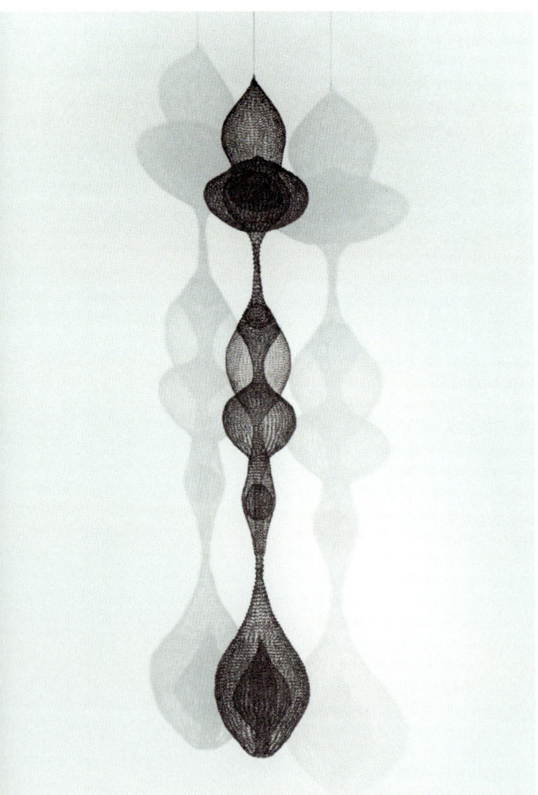

Untitled (S.108), *ca. 1970*

had expanded their world beyond the brown-shingled house where they grew up in San Francisco into limitless realms of art.

Far from the frenzied bidding at Rockefeller Center, the artist kept a lookout over her garden, a profusion of green she tended for most of her eighty-seven years. She watched the windows for the emerald flash of hummingbirds that sipped nectar and wove nests in her honeysuckle. She had survived the Great Depression and World War II, slighted for her gender and interned for her race. She had toiled in the fields, the studio, and the classroom, elevating work to a form of Zen practice, her hands never still. Now arthritis had stiffened her once-agile fingers. Fragile from strokes, she had spoken little in the six years since losing her life partner, the architect Albert Lanier. Together they had lived without a blueprint and loved across color lines. They raised six children and fought for the education of thousands more. They mastered the art of shaping space—Ruth in sculpture and Albert in architecture. As their health failed, the couple had lived in hospital beds in the sunny room that had once been her studio. Her children knew best how to deliver the big news from the auction—and how to read her response.

Innocent of the previous night's bidding, Ruth looked bemused as her daughters Aiko and Addie drew close. When Addie whispered the sales figure in her mother's ear, Aiko watched her mother's eyes and mouth widen in wonder as if to say, *Really?*

"Mama," Addie said, "you're playing with the big boys now!"

But it had not always been so.

CHAPTER 1

WAR

On December 7, 1941, faraway bombs broke the peace of a working Sunday.

The Asawa family was working in the fields of their Norwalk, California, truck farm. The family would soon fill sacks with farm vegetables as a holiday gift for the school bus driver. The simple offering embarrassed their middle child, fifteen-year-old Ruth. As she worked, she reflected on the coming Christmas break, which would bring not parties and presents, but the season for planting green onions, passing seedlings hand to hand, pushing them into the earth, and pressing the furrows closed in endless rows.

Around noon, the rhythms of that life exploded in chaos. Shouts reached their ears in the field: Japan had attacked Pearl Harbor. The Asawas dropped everything and ran back to the farmhouse. Gathering around the radio, they listened to reports about the unfamiliar place now in flames, learning for the first time that it was a military base in Hawaii. As the chaos cleared and the attack came into sharper focus, Ruth's confusion turned to dread.

Terror struck all of us. We wondered how our classmates would react. On Monday the 8th our high school principal Mr. Ralph Burnright called an emergency assembly to make the announcement that the United States and Japan were at war, but assured the student body the Japanese students at Excelsior Union High School were not responsible for it.

On the school bus, Ruth met hard stares. Withdrawing into a shell, she sought comfort from fellow Nisei—second-generation Japanese Americans who, like her, were born in the United States. A girl in choir class was bereft because her boyfriend wanted to enlist. But after Pearl Harbor, the army rejected Nisei volunteers.

The principal's speech briefly soothed Ruth's nerves. But her father, Umakichi, was uneasy. Born in Japan sixty years earlier, he feared being seen as an enemy despite devoting four decades to tilling American soil. After the bombing, his family took down the emperor's picture. Once as common in prewar Japanese American households as pictures of the king or queen in British homes, now it had to go. Any memento of his old country might seem suspicious. He resolved to purge his home of souvenirs like the kendo equipment Ruth and her older sister Lois used to practice Japanese fencing: a bamboo sword, body shield, gloves, and *hakama*, or culottes.

Ruth watched him build a bonfire and feed pieces of his past life to the flames:

To rid the house of any Japanese artifacts, he dug a big hole to bury the kendo gear and burned the hakama, *beautiful Japanese books on flower arrangement—tea ceremony, Japanese dolls, Japanese badminton paddles. I still see Lois weeping and pleading with him not to burn them. He was afraid of being implicated.*

Days after Pearl Harbor, Los Angeles began blackouts. Reports of unidentified planes over the city drew antiaircraft fire that awakened Norwalk residents from midnight to two in the morning as spotlights blanched the night sky. Enemy aircraft were never confirmed, but fear of an attack stirred anxiety from California to the East Coast.

War inflicted differing levels of sacrifice on the home front. Families said goodbye to their sons. People adjusted to shortages and ration coupons for sugar and gasoline. The wartime hit parade spun platters like "Rosie the Riveter" and "Don't Sit Under the Apple Tree (With Anyone Else but Me)." Japanese Americans faced a different reality: slurs and menacing gangs that beat up anyone who, to their eyes, looked anything like the enemy. Some Asian Americans wore buttons to distinguish their origins: "I am Chinese." Guides appeared on "how to spot a Jap," promoting vicious racial stereotypes of yellow skin, buckteeth, squinty eyes, and shifty demeanor.

More than 2,600 miles away, in Washington, D.C., President Franklin D. Roosevelt's administration feared that spies in the Japanese American community were aiding Japan in an imminent invasion of the West. Hysteria drowned out any opposition—even from the nation's top cop, FBI Director J. Edgar Hoover, who insisted there was no evidence of sabotage. Few listened.

Politicians on the home front employed a chilling new term. Even before Pearl Harbor, in October 1940, Navy Secretary Frank Knox had handed Roosevelt a fifteen-point program to get ready for a possible war with Japan. The twelfth point: "Prepare plans for concentration camps." President Roosevelt himself used the term. The world hadn't yet come to equate concentration camps with the death camps of Nazi Germany that exterminated millions of Jews. But a clear-eyed view of history must recognize that what Washington originally planned to hold Japanese Americans—aliens and citizens—weren't evacuation centers for their safety, but concentration camps.

Newspaper editorials calling for a roundup of Japanese Americans grew venomous. "Speaking as an American . . . I am for immediate removal of every Japanese on the West Coast to a point deep in the interior," declared Henry McLemore in a column published in the *Los Angeles Times* and the *San Francisco Examiner*. "I don't mean a nice part of the interior either . . . Personally, I hate the Japanese. And that goes for all of them . . . Let 'em be pinched, hurt, hungry and dead up against it."

Cartoonists stoked hatred with caricatures of slant-eyed spies. In "Waiting for the Signal from Home . . . ," artist Theodor S. Geisel pictured hordes of smiling saboteurs lining up for cakes of TNT to blow up the whole West Coast. The cartoon bore the pen name Mr. Geisel would later use on scores of his popular children's books: Dr. Seuss.

Congress chimed in. "All Japanese, whether citizens or not, must be placed in inland concentration camps," opined U.S. Representative Leland Ford, a Republican from California. Ford urged loyal Nisei, who were American citizens from birth, to join in and enter the camps voluntarily to safeguard the military security of their home country, the United States of America.

Supporters of the roundup and incarceration of Japanese Americans included California governor Culbert Olson and California attorney general Earl Warren. Warren—the future governor, Supreme Court Chief Justice, and progressive hero of the 1950s who helped strike down school segregation—called for putting people into camps by showing a map illustrating "Japs in vicinity" of strategic sites like airports, railroads, and dams. Conspiracy theorists held that Japanese American farmers could lay out crop rows like signposts, pointing the way for invading bombers to hit key targets. (While a vigorous supporter of the Japanese exclusion during the war, retired U.S. Chief Justice Warren would later voice remorse in his memoirs for the imprisonment of children.)

Roosevelt's cabinet backed the roundup with little dissent. Attorney General Francis Biddle opposed the action but, as a newcomer, he carried little weight. First Lady Eleanor Roosevelt, a civil rights champion, appealed to her husband. The president listened coldly and told her never to bring it up again.

On February 19, 1942, Roosevelt signed Executive Order 9066, authorizing the removal of people of Japanese blood from a broad swath of the western United States that was seen as a sensitive military zone. The area included coastal California, Washington, and Oregon, plus southern Arizona. The program would uproot between 110,000 and 120,000 people, order them into assembly centers, and transport them to the camps. For many, their homes and property would be hastily sold at a fraction of their value, stored and later looted, or simply abandoned and lost. The American Civil Liberties Union would call the action "the worst single wholesale violation of civil rights of American citizens in our history."

Umakichi Asawa had come to the United States in 1902 at age nineteen to avoid being drafted in an earlier conflict, the Russo-Japanese war. His life on American soil began with a desire to avoid fighting. He belonged to a farmer's association, sent his children to Japanese-language school on Saturday, and took his family to a Quaker church on Sunday. He found bloodshed so distasteful that he tasked his wife, Haru, with butchering the family's weekly chicken. Neighbors couldn't believe that this lean, weathered farmer with the large, hardworking family could be a secret saboteur in their midst.

The first wave of arrests began quickly and quietly, just after Pearl Harbor. The Asawa family noticed community leaders disappearing. The children's Japanese teacher, their sensei, was among the first to go. A new wave hit in February 1942 with the arrests of religious and business leaders—including local farmers.

Two lawmen descended on the Asawa farm one day that February, flashing their badges as Umakichi knelt over his strawberries. The scene was seared in Ruth's memory:

> *Without warning . . . two FBI agents appeared looking for Father. They went out to the field to get him. It was around 11:30 in the morning. They allowed him to eat lunch. My sister Chiyo had baked a meringue pie. We ironed him a white shirt, pressed his black suit, and away they went.*

Ruth wouldn't see him again until after the war.

Umakichi was raised in a very poor family in Fukushima province. As a young boy, he peddled natto, or fermented soybeans, from a cart in the street before sunrise, crying "Natto! Natto!" But beneath his humble roots lay a powerful origin myth for the Asawa family, a name that is all but unheard-of in Japan. The story goes that Umakichi's family was descended from the samurai class, and "Asawa" was originally "Asano." Lord Asano was a famous eighteenth-century retainer to the Shogun whose ritual suicide in a bloody court feud left his forty-seven samurai followers (or ronin) leaderless. The samurai from

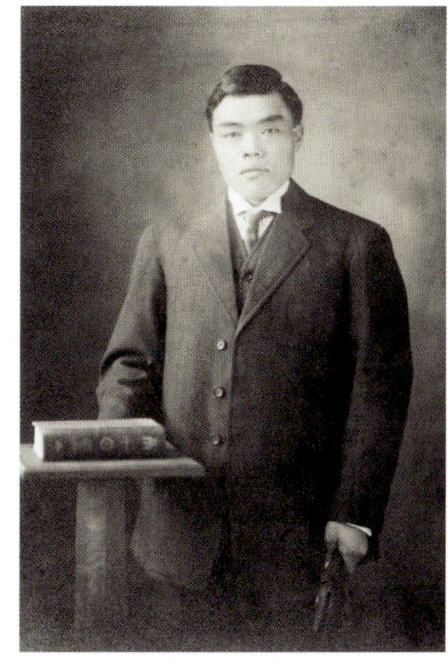

Ruth's father, Umakichi Asawa, as a young man in the early twentieth century

whom Umakichi descended sought revenge, which meant he also had to commit ritual suicide. But before taking his life, he sent his family into the mountains, told them to become farmers, and changed their name from Asano to Asawa. Ruth regarded this as "a tale," savored in the oral tradition, passed down with a dash of skepticism.

Umakichi fled Japan with his brother in 1902 to avoid being drafted into the coming Russo-Japanese war. After crossing the Pacific, they toiled in Hawaii's sugarcane fields and then crossed into the mainland via Mexico, eventually working in Utah's sugar beet industry, saving their money. In Southern California, they leased fields just off of Rosecrans Boulevard and built their own farmsteads.

Like many a lonely immigrant bachelor, Umakichi wanted a wife. Families arranged long-distance engagements through the exchange of formal portraits with young women from home, known as "picture brides." These betrothal pictures, the century-old predecessor of selfies on dating sites, were carefully composed to show prospective mates at their most elegant and eligible. A fiancée, looking sober and demure, might be flanked by her mother and sister, garbed in a fine kimono, her hair piled up in a glossy pompadour. This was Umakichi's first view of Haru Yasuda, the youngest daughter of a family that raised silkworms and wove silk for kimonos. (She was actually the second candidate, an older sister first having backed out of his proposal.) In 1919, Haru crossed the Pacific Ocean and landed in San Francisco. She met her fiancé, a seasoned laborer who was more than a decade older than her, and together they boarded a southbound train to share a life of companionship bound up in toil. Seasons were marked by onions, broccoli, and cauliflower in winter, strawberries in spring, and tomatoes and melons in summer. Haru was following in the footsteps of many a picture bride, and more would come. Her older sister would soon arrive to wed Umakichi's brother Zenzaburo.

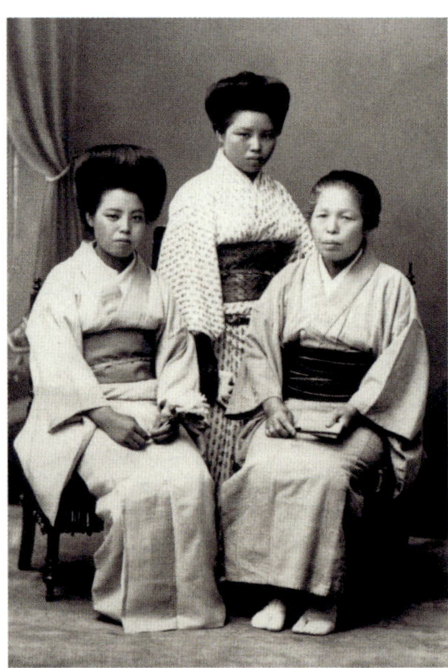

Ruth's mother, Haru Asawa (center), with her sister Ura (left) and her mother in Japan

Home was a simple farmhouse in the small rural town of Norwalk, later incorporated into sprawling Los Angeles County. Umakichi built the board-and-batten house with its paper ceiling and tin roof. He built the barn and the garage. The spare shelter was graced with an encyclopedia and a player piano. There was little money for luxuries.

Norwalk saw biplanes buzz its cornfields in the early twentieth century. With a population of four thousand, its economy comprised farms, a blacksmith shop, a tire factory, and the Dr. Ross Dog and Cat Food factory, which turned old horses into pet food and Silver Tone soap. A three-bedroom house rented for $12.50 a month. A merchant's lunch cost forty cents. As city fathers wooed commerce, Hollywood discovered the town's railroad station as a set for a movie starring Lana Turner, *The Postman Always Rings Twice*. But it wasn't Hollywood glamour that sustained Norwalk through the Depression. It was the sweat of farmers like Umakichi Asawa that kept the town going. Despite alien land laws that barred them from owning the fields they tilled, Japanese farmers produced bumper crops: 40 percent of California's fruits and vegetables coaxed from 1 percent of its farmland.

Umakichi and Haru were prolific partners in the fields and in the nursery. Their family grew to include Lois, George, Chiyo, Ruth, Bill, Kimiko, and Janet. Public displays of affection were rare, but their devotion was palpable. Haru gave birth at home and nursed each baby for two years—or until the next child came along. She carried her youngest on her back in the fields as she worked. Umakichi fashioned toy tractors from empty spools and rubber bands. The children were expected to be silent at meals—youngsters asking questions were considered nosy and rude—but they were allowed to crawl into bed to hear their parents' stories.

A jet-haired newborn, Ruth wailed her way into the world on the winter afternoon of January 24, 1926, protesting expulsion from her mother's warmth into the chill. That's how she would remember it in wartime, as the world got even colder:

> *I, being a winter baby, had an excuse to squirm and yell when I first made my debut. As an infant, I had my way or else!! I rarely had my way.*

Making her way was an act of will. As the middle child of seven on a small truck farm, she stuck up for herself but pitched in with the rest to help grow, pick, and transport produce to the Los Angeles farmers market. Ruth worked in the field and the packing shed after school—planting, harvesting, sorting, and crating vegetables from four until eight, when she turned to her homework until midnight under the watchful eye of her older sister Lois.

Perched on the back of her father's horse-drawn leveler was when she let her daydreams out to play. Dangling her bare feet in the dirt, toeing in and out, she traced hourglass designs in the soil. No one watching the girl could guess that in those furrows, Ruth Aiko Asawa was planting the seeds of her future in art.

The life of the Asawa family was forged in a frugality that put calluses on Ruth's hands but never coarsened her dream of art. True to her astrological sign—an earth ox—she followed the Zen path of "chop wood, carry water." Her American name, Ruth, recalled the biblical figure of family loyalty. Her Japanese name, Aiko, means "love child." Her black bob framed a moon face that often was pensive, but her apple cheeks popped out when she smiled. She drew constantly.

For her parents, tilling 80 acres and rearing seven children took grit. Haru rose at three each morning to start the day's rice cooking in an outdoor pot. Umakichi was up at four to check his gopher traps and returned for breakfast at six. Then it was back into the fields for workdays so relentless that visitors wanting a word with him had to catch up with him in the fields. For the children, walking a half mile to the bus and attending school was a respite from chores.

For all their labors, the first-generation Issei (Japanese immigrants) couldn't yet become citizens or purchase property. (Their children, known as Nisei, who were the first generation born in the United States, were classified as American citizens from birth.) Amid California's history of white protectionism and anti-Asian bias, the state had passed the Alien Land Law of 1913, which barred Umakichi from owning the very land he tilled. Norwalk landlords who observed Umakichi's productivity agreed to lease land to him. And he made good by endlessly working, skimping, and strategizing. He enhanced his yields by saving his very best tomato, not to eat but to pluck out superior seeds to grow next season's crop better than the last. Saving the best for next season became a habit.

The Asawa sons and daughters joined their parents working in the fields every day but Saturday—which was devoted to Japanese-language school. Ruth's other chief chore was to chop wood and stoke the fire under the family's traditional wooden bathtub, or *ofuro*, where they would line up their *geta* (platform sandals) to soak their weary bodies after the workday. After everyone had bathed in the *ofuro*, Haru used the warm broth of field dust washed off their bodies to sprout bags of seeds before planting. Along with working the crops and heating the *ofuro* bath, Ruth repaired the thin wooden crates used to hold vegetables. She planted beans and trained the vines up trellises. All were solitary tasks that her parents assigned to their headstrong middle child to avoid sibling spats. The habit of incessant toil stuck with her for life.

Nothing was wasted on the Asawa farm. Umakichi saved old nails and straightened them out for reuse. The family lived on vegetables and fruits they grew, one quart of milk a day for cereal, plus their one chicken a week. If a ripe melon cracked, the family ate it. On hot days, when Ruth sought shade under a water tower with Mexican farmhands, she got to share their tortillas, warmed over a wood fire.

Umakichi was a truck farmer, who drove his harvests weekly to the Los Angeles farmers market. In the Depression, truck farmers scraped by, getting a nickel for a box of tomatoes, fifty cents for six dozen radishes, thirty-five cents for a crate of cabbage, and ten cents for a box of two dozen melons. Sometimes shippers would trick suppliers, contracting for all of the farm's celery and tomatoes, and then packing it up and declaring bankruptcy. Growers rarely got ahead. Umakichi exhausted his savings in paying medical bills when his brother fell mortally ill, so the family's hand-to-mouth existence later included his brother's widow and children. For working the whole summer, Ruth, like all her siblings, got ten dollars to buy school wear—maybe a pair of shoes for $1.95, underwear, and a couple of dresses.

Umakichi was proud and independent. Ruth remembered sitting around the table, hearing her father read an article about a farmer who couldn't afford to provide for his five children. He took a shotgun to each of them rather than accept charity. Umakichi told his wife he would do the same thing before he took a handout. The Asawa children, raised not to talk at meals, eyed each other in shocked silence. But for all their father's fierce pride, his children were never spanked.

The Asawas attended the local Zen Buddhist temple for funerals and memorials. On Sunday, the family went to the Quaker church because it was one of the few Christian houses of worship that welcomed Japanese Americans. Ruth liked it until, one day, the churchyard pond looked too inviting. Leaning over the water, she lost her balance and fell in with a splash, drenching her clothes. Offered a change of clothes from the minister's son, she spent the service chafing in boy's garb and then avoided church until she was fifteen.

Later, when war broke out, the Quakers would remain among the few groups to stand by the Japanese Americans. "They were fearless people," Ruth would say.

As the girl in the middle, Ruth fought for her place. With three siblings above her and three below, she stood her ground, saying: "I was bossed, and I was boss."

Ruth's earliest memory was of fever. At three years old, she crossed paths with someone who sneezed or coughed. But it was no ordinary germ. Her throat grew sore and coated with a tough gray membrane that made it hard to swallow or breathe. It was diphtheria, a contagious bacterial disease known as "the strangler." Before routine vaccination, it was a major killer, especially of young children.

Sounds of discord reached her bed: her parents in rare heated argument. Her father was fighting to take Ruth to the hospital while her mother pleaded to keep her at home.

"If you don't let her go, she will die," she heard her father say.

Umakichi prevailed. Ruth was admitted. The family was placed under quarantine.

As a toddler on a hospital ward, the lonely, frightened three-year-old wept for her father's visits. He promised to bring her home when her fever broke, but the recovery was slow. After two weeks—and a cloying hospital diet of stewed prunes—Ruth was finally strong enough to leave. The ordeal impressed upon her that life is short and time too precious to waste, she would say. In a school essay, she later crafted a happy ending to the terrifying episode:

Fortunately, Father drove me home from the hospital in our very best Model T in time for Christmas. All I could remember was a beautiful doll and a tree that touched the ceiling.

For most of her life, Ruth remained sturdy and robust, and the shadow of life-threatening disease passed over her, not to return for more than half a century.

In March of 1933, when Ruth was seven years old, Los Angeles was jolted by a violent earthquake that rocked the farmhouse, making its timbers lurch and groan. Ruth clung to the wooden beams for a long half minute until the shaking subsided. Haru regaled the family with stories of epic earthquakes in Japan, when yawning crevices opened and swallowed people whole.

Farm life held all manner of dangers for all children in the pre-war years—not just illness or natural disaster, but also poverty, farm equipment, and open fires. Ruth once saw her older sister Lois scalded by boiling water. After drifting in and out of consciousness, Lois told her little sister that she dreamed a friendly man with a long white beard in a horse-drawn chariot came for her, but she refused to go because she heard her mother calling. Lois recovered from her burns, but that vision lived in Ruth's memory. When Lois died later in old age, Ruth wrote to her sister's son, saying Lois's sense of adventure gave her strength and dispelled her fear of death. "Maybe," she wrote, "the bearded charioteer had returned for Lois at last."

Home canning by thrifty farm families also held hazards. From a bumper crop of tomatoes, the Asawas once cooked up jars of homemade ketchup that went bad, swelling under pressure. The jars exploded, shattering glass and a shower of red sauce. But the family didn't quit canning. They learned from the misadventure, sweeping up the shards and splatter, and cooking up another batch.

"Crying doesn't help," Ruth would tell her friends.

Ruth worked to live and lived to draw. When she wasn't in the fields or bent over her homework, she delighted in sketching the cartoon characters Blondie, Flash Gordon, Little Orphan Annie, and the Katzenjammer Kids. She discovered Norman Rockwell and drew 1930s child stars like the blond Shirley Temple and brunette Deanna Durbin. Encouraged by her art teachers, Gwendolyn Cowan and Edith Loewe, she drew polar bears lit by the aurora borealis. In the eighth grade, Ruth won a prize for her design of a patriotic poster of the Statue of Liberty against a red background. Her reception of the award was the only occasion Ruth remembered that her shy and hardworking parents visited the school.

Teachers were free with discipline and parsimonious with praise. Miss Cowan rapped unruly boys with a ruler so hard that it broke—provoking howls of laughter from the class that reduced the teacher to tears of frustration. Ruth was impressed that Miss Cowan cared so much about her craft. Miss Loewe tartly remarked that Ruth's bold originality in abstract studies was marred by a certain lack of neatness. This theme would later be picked up by the most revered teacher of her life. But Ruth was undaunted. By age ten, she was sure: She wanted to be an artist.

Ruth kept an indelible memory of those farm wagon rides, dragging her feet and carving traceries in the dirt with her toes, weaving a trail of curved lines in the wake of dust between wheel tracks. Those shapes would resurface in the undulating forms of her wire sculptures.

Crafting beauty from cast-off materials—a byproduct of scarcity—was another lifelong habit. As a little girl, Ruth would unwind the fine wires used to bundle vegetables and refashion them into bracelets and rings, studding them with a red bead she imagined as a ruby. She reveled in found objects, scrounging supplies and recycling trash into treasures.

Despite the austerity of their lives in America, the Asawas preserved the culture they had left behind. The family spoke Japanese at home. Umakichi learned enough English to conduct his business, but Haru never did. Ruth Aiko learned English when she entered grammar school, where teachers insisted she assimilate and be called simply Ruth. On Saturday the Asawas sent their children to study at the *gakuen*, or Japanese school. The Saturday ritual began with Lois honking the horn of the family's old gray Plymouth sedan, calling all the children to pile in for the drive to lessons. Language was taught by a stern sensei. If Ruth drifted off, he brought down a stick on the table with a sharp smack. The children were caught between linguistic tradition and pressure to speak English in school. The part of Saturday school Ruth loved best was calligraphy, learning to create Japanese characters and designs. It took exquisite arm control to sweep the brush from one stroke to the next, balancing the lines and—equally important—the spaces in between the lines.

The Asawa children also got a chance to spend time in Japan studying with relatives. But when Ruth's turn came, her host uncle fell ill, so her journey was postponed. By the next opportunity, she had outgrown the kimonos sewn especially to wear on her trip. It was then 1939, and she was looking forward to high school. So her younger sister Kimiko went to Japan in her place, accompanied by older sister Lois. From such trips, the children brought back art and dolls, *ikebana* flower-arranging books, and treasures that preserved a touch of tradition in their farmhouse.

They didn't yet know that keeping up their culture carried a cost; that respecting their heritage would mark them as alien enemies; or that children educated abroad, known as *kibei*, would face special scrutiny. They didn't know that rising tensions in autumn 1941 would find Lois boarding the last boat home before Pearl Harbor. They didn't know that Kimiko's widowed aunt would keep her in Japan, helping fulfill civilian duties like smoothing the runways for a nearby *kamikaze* base. There was no question of what *she* wanted. Her longing for home was simply lost in the fog of war. As she later reflected: "People do not understand what it was like."

Compared to farm chores, school seemed like playtime. No one wanted to get sick, because sick days didn't spare you from housework. Ruth was studious—good in English, art, modern dance, and chorus, though less keen in social studies. She played shortstop on her school baseball team even though she said she couldn't catch. She saved stacks of her school memorabilia: artwork from class, and programs from Christmas concerts and a school operetta in which she was cast as a dancing gypsy.

She packed away issues of the *National School Newspaper*, a student tabloid that briefed students about Washington politics. More and more, it featured stories about rising tensions between the still-neutral U.S. government and rising militants in

Germany and Italy. An ominous headline
read: "President Warns Against Dictators."
She penciled "Ruth Asawa" in cursive
at the top of each front page, and saved
sheets that grew crisp and yellow—a time
capsule of her early life.

Through middle school, Ruth vowed a
hatred of boys "as strong as ten thousand
octopus suckers." She softened after reading Longfellow's poem "The Courtship of
Miles Standish," in which the outspoken
Puritan girl Priscilla invites John Alden,
her suitor's spokesman, to express his own
affections with the famous line: "Why
don't you speak for yourself, John?" That,
she liked. She soon experienced her first
crush, on a handsome blond boy, discovering romance across color lines.

Ruth was blossoming into adolescence
with a strong will and a sure hand with a

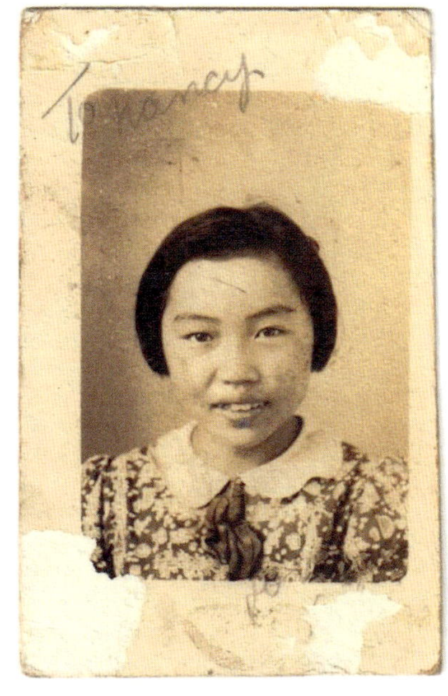

Ruth, age 13, 1939

paintbrush. She helped look after her younger sisters and brother, and obeyed Lois's
stern directives at kendo practice, Japanese school, and homework time. The hardscrabble life afforded no frills. But growing up surrounded by six siblings set a view
of family life and a vision for her future. However poor they might be, she would one
day tell her future fiancé, she wanted six children of her own.

On her way to Excelsior Unified High School, Ruth walked her half mile and
boarded the bus each day in her well-worn cotton dresses, waiting for the sensei's
daughter Alice Imamoto to take the seat beside her. Together they rode to high school
as they had done since elementary school. The demure Alice was a piano prodigy,
groomed by her scholarly parents to attend a music conservatory. She was 4 feet
8 inches tall with tiny fingers that would master Mozart, but she lacked the hand span
to play Rachmaninoff. She sat beside Ruth in art, admiring her friend's deft hand with
drawing. Ruth was sturdier at 4 feet 11 inches. With her farm-bred work ethic and
cartooning skill, Ruth's dream was to attend an art school.

The heady hopes of two Japanese American schoolgirls would soon be put on hold
by World War II, politics, and the hatred unleashed on them by their fellow citizens.

After February 1942, when the FBI arrested their father in his fields, the Asawa children interpreted wartime directives for their fifty-year-old mother. Not knowing Umakichi's whereabouts, the family struggled to keep calm, go to school, and run the farm. Just as her mother's family had woven traditional silk kimonos from cocoons, Haru wove ancient cultural values into the fabric of Ruth's daily life. Ruth would say these traits were drilled into her:

Gaman—Endurance

Nintai—Patience

Enryo—Restraint

Shikata ga nai—It can't be helped. What can we do? What's done is done.

Feisty by nature, Ruth strove to comport herself by these rules for life, whether in war or in peacetime, at home or at school, in the studio or out in society.

Soon, the Asawa children stopped attending school to help with the farm. Then, in mid-April 1942, came the orders for all West Coast Japanese Americans to prepare to vacate their homes. Officials didn't spare orphans, including mixed-race infants with any Japanese blood, who were sent to the "children's village," an orphanage at the camp in Manzanar, California.

Notices of an impending roundup—which the government called an "evacuation"—appeared on walls and light posts around town. Under orders from the Western Defense Command and the Army's Wartime Civil Control Administration, all Japanese Americans were to pack bedding, toiletries, clothing, and dishes, "limited to that which can be carried by the individual or family group." Families forced to sell their property got ten cents on the dollar. Others stored belongings at neighbors' homes or churches, but such property often fell prey to looters.

The Asawas left behind the farm with four workhorses, chickens, equipment, and trucks. They bid farewell to their mongrel dog, Butch, and abandoned the spring strawberries ripening in the field. Because of the Japanese farmers' bountiful harvests, historians note, agriculture lobbying groups admitted they weren't sorry to see their rivals go. Along with the government orders, homemade signs sprouted up, reviling neighbors now labeled "Japs."

No one needed to come and arrest the Asawas. Like many families who obeyed orders, they formed a car caravan with their cousins from Norwalk and drove themselves to the designated assembly center, Santa Anita Racetrack. This was one of the regional holding areas set up while permanent detention camps were under construction across the country. Ruth recalled the scramble to leave, and the degrees of shock at what was in store:

*April 14 was the last day in Norwalk, my home town. Before that day I shopped
madly all over town to find boots, stockings and heavy clothing, for I was prepared
to go to Manzanar. Then our notice came to leave on April 14 for Santa Anita, the
greatest racetrack in the world.*

*With tear-drenched eyes, I said goodbye to my friends. When we entered the
Baldwin Gate at Santa Anita I was happy to see white barracks thinking I would
live in one. We passed those finding that they were for the Army. Then I saw black
barracks. This time I was surely happy, confident of making this my new home. And
what do you think I landed in? A horse stable. . . .*

The palm tree–lined racetrack, once the turf for thoroughbreds like Seabiscuit and
Man o' War, sheltered nearly half of its eighteen thousand inmates in barracks in the
infield and parking lot. Less fortunate families like the Asawas were assigned to horse
stables, converted for human habitation with a quick coat of whitewash and a linoleum
patch over the stalls' dirt floors—a slapdash remodeling that failed to block the stench:

*Hairs from the horse['s] mane & tail were stuck between cracks of the walls. The
heat of summer accentuated the odor of recent tenants.*

To say accommodations were austere would be an understatement. Families had to
stuff their mattress ticking with straw for their beds. The Asawas were issued cursory
health checks, assigned numbers, and given color-coded buttons assigning them
to the Red Mess Hall beneath the grandstands. Toilets were about a block and a
half away. Until July 1942, only 150 showers were available for the 18,000 internees.
Later, six more shower buildings, with seventy-five showerheads each, improved the
ratio to one shower for every thirty inmates—still below the camp average. A central
laundry was outdoors under a canopy, where rows of tubs with metal washboards
thrummed into the night as thousands tried to scrub away the animal odor.

Mess halls assaulted body and soul. The mass feeding stations fractured families.
Menu staples included S.O.S.: generic meat and gravy on bread, which soldiers called
"shit on a shingle." Worse was the mess hall habit of transforming today's starch into
tomorrow's dessert, an affront to Japanese palates that left Ruth with a lifelong aversion.

*Two of the worst things that happened to us [were] the erosion of the family,
noticed especially at mealtime. Young teenagers would go off to eat with new friends
they had made. Parents lost control. The other terrible thing was serving us rice*

Official visitors came to inspect the center, including director of the War Relocation Authority Milton Eisenhower, the brother of future president General Dwight D. Eisenhower. On those days, Ruth saw administrators and their guests tuck into steak, french fries, and ice cream.

"The eyes of the nation are upon us," reported the *Santa Anita Pacemaker* newsletter. Written by inmates but controlled by the authorities, the paper likened the life of inmates to that of hardy pioneers in a frontier boomtown. It mingled upbeat notices for classes and recreation with draconian rules for inmate conduct. Collecting another person's mail, for example, was punishable with jail time or fines. Contraband items included knives, cameras, and even radios.

Putting a good face on prison conditions was the newsletter's agenda. Inmates could play twilight softball games at the "Anita Chiquita" field or dance to an Asian band named "Japanita Jive." Film fare included *The Gang's All Here*, and *Oswald Rabbit* for children. Talent shows and Maypole dances were offered to divert and pacify.

The Asawa family left their double horse stall during the day to breathe as much fresh air as possible, returning to sleep. Ruth attended class and occasionally took in a talent show. Her friend Alice was so fearful of getting lost, she didn't venture from her family's stall.

Freedom of religion, guaranteed by the Wartime Civil Control Administration, encouraged displays of piety rarely seen at a racetrack. Six worship services a week included Seventh Day Adventists, Catholics, the Friends Church of Norwalk, two Protestant congregations, and one Buddhist group. White and Asian clergy presided.

"You will have time to rethink the foundation of your faith in Christendom," the *Pacemaker* reported Dr. E. C. Farnum of the Los Angeles Church Federation lecturing to young Japanese. He called Santa Anita "a good laboratory in which experiments may be made in the study of sociology and psychology." The goal of such an experiment wasn't disclosed.

The U.S. Army put inmates to work at rates of $8, $12, and $16 a month for unskilled, skilled, and professional labor, respectively. The mess hall, maintenance division, and medical division also employed workers. What Santa Anita wasn't prepared for was the proper schooling of youth among the 18,719 people confined at the racetrack. College students like Lois volunteered in the classrooms to teach younger children, who could choose between going to school or work. Meanwhile Ruth climbed to the highest row of seats in the Santa Anita grandstand, where her class met. There, she took in a sweeping view of the racetrack settlement, including a group of inmates who chose a work detail weaving camouflage nets to assist the war effort in the Pacific.

One day the squalor of the stables was briefly eclipsed by a stroke of movie magic. Three Japanese American artists from Disney Studios arrived as internees at Santa Anita. The artists were veterans of animated features like *Snow White* and *Pinocchio*. Tom Okamoto, Chris Ishii, and James Tanaka offered to teach drawing and perspective to students held at the racetrack. Ruth jumped at the chance. She regarded Okamoto in particular as an early mentor.

How lucky could a 16-year-old be, to study, for the first time, with professional artists; they were generous with their time and supplied us with paper, charcoal, pencils & ink.

The artists also penned a cartoon strip mascot in the *Pacemaker* called L'il Neebo, short for little Nisei boy. The character was a rascal who made wisecracks about camp life as a safety valve for the indignities of incarceration. Neebo got transferred with his creator, Chris Ishii, to a permanent facility at Camp Granada (also known as Amache), Colorado. When federal officials saw Ishii's talent, they recruited him to make propaganda posters and sent him to Shanghai. By then, Neebo was so popular in Colorado, other inmates carried on the cartoon strip. Yet for Ishii, Santa Anita was a way station en route to camp, and art class came to an end.

Resentment mounted at Santa Anita over oppressive living conditions: herd-like feeding, remote toilets, and intrusive searches for contraband. Police, suspecting the presence of contraband articles, rummaged through inmates' meager belongings. Their rough searches provoked charges of jewelry theft. Suspecting the raids were sparked by tips from Asian American spies in their midst, inmates became furious. In August 1942, a riot erupted that ended in the severe beating of a suspected informant.

Jeeps roared up to the Santa Anita gates to quell the disturbance. A curfew came down, and people were confined to their stalls without dinner. Three days of martial law cooled the rebellion. Ruth, like many, suspected officials enlisted Japanese Americans or other Asian Americans who understood the Japanese language to inform on them:

We all knew that, imagined or not, each block had a paid spy, "Inu," dog.

In September 1942, after half a year in the horse stalls, the Asawas and other Japanese American families got word they were to be moved inland. They would board trains to one of ten permanent "relocation centers": Manzanar and Tule Lake, California; Gila River and Poston, Arizona; Minidoka, Idaho; Topaz, Utah; Heart Mountain, Wyoming; Granada/Amache, Colorado; and Jerome and Rohwer, Arkansas. They were the concentration camps Washington had foreseen even before Pearl Harbor, set on remote wastelands far from coastal military zones.

It must have been near September 15 when our notice for [the] relocation center came. We started packing everything as before, only on a smaller scale. Our last Caucasian friends came to visit us. I couldn't imagine how far we were going from there or for how long.

Photographs of mass transport show Japanese American families crowding the train platform dressed in their best. Men wore suits or what would be called "Eisenhower jackets" with snap brim hats. Women wore modish print dresses and heels, their hair curled under hats, turbans, or snoods. In one hand, they gripped hatboxes, suitcases, and bundles, while the other clasped children in sailor suits or Superman T-shirts, clutching a toy or doll. From their smart attire, they might have been setting off for a holiday or a family reunion. But despite a mask of composure, their faces looked ashen and strained.

Ruth's excitement about taking her first train ride vanished when she saw the dilapidated railcars. All available modern rolling stock had been requisitioned for the war effort, leaving only antique trains with gaslights and wooden bench seats. As the train left Los Angeles, Ruth saw Norwalk receding in the distance.

Dim, hot, and crowded, the cars teemed with passengers jostling in the aisles. Rocking on the rails left Ruth's mother nauseated from motion sickness. People slept in their clothes, sitting up or lying on the floor, hoping not to be trampled. They lined up at the tiny washrooms to brush their teeth and wash their faces. With windows shut to keep out the soot, the close heat left bodies sticky. Shades were drawn shut, which had several effects: It observed the blackout, hid the identity of the passengers from curious locals at the stations they passed, obscured the landscape, and concealed their route. Cutting off the view also kept riders from seeing the horizon line, disorienting their senses and provoking motion sickness among many in the lurching cars.

A young public health physician riding the trains, Dr. Harold B. Alexander, befriended the Asawas. The quiet, industrious Japanese teenager he saw bustling about, helping car monitors watch children and feed babies, impressed the young ophthalmologist.

He remembered the name Ruth Asawa, following her future fortunes and corresponding with her for decades.

After working with the monitors, Ruth felt relief as she went to the dining cars, where she found the black porters to be friendly. She heard fellow passengers passing the time by singing folk songs. After sundown, she ventured a glance out the windows of the moving train, making mental sketches of the changing landscape that flashed by as she sped toward her unknown destination:

> *. . . It was near nightfall when I saw the first glimpse of California desert. Needles, Arizona, was our first stop after California. . . . a few minutes out of Needles, with the moon above, the Colorado River wound its way around and under us.*
>
> *Passing through New Mexico, with its Indians, I first noticed the sharp distinction of the colored and white. Houston, Texas, was the largest city in which we stopped and conversed with a carload of Army men. We sang "Pearl Harbor" with them.*
>
> *The Louisiana swamps were just as I imagined them to be . . . enchanting, beautiful and weird.*

After four days, the vintage engine slowed near McGehee, Arkansas, a small country town with dirt and gravel roads near the state's southeastern border with Louisiana. The cars creaked to a stop at a raw outpost, which evacuees learned was their new home. Ruth saw an old barn and fields surrounded on three sides by trees.

"Rohwer! Get ready to leave!" a soldier barked, moving through the train.

They had arrived at Rohwer Relocation Center, about 110 miles from Little Rock. Along with the neighboring site in Jerome, where Ruth's friend Alice was headed, the two Arkansas outposts were set in the Jim Crow South—the farthest camps from home.

Gathering up their children and bundles, a few older Issei picked up garbage on their way out and deposited it in the trash bins. Old courtesies died hard, even when going to prison. Passengers boarded trucks for the 12-mile ride to the camp. Audible groans arose when they saw the tar-paper–clad barracks of their new home with its barbed-wire perimeter. "Flanked by cotton fields and woods, the settlement at least wasn't a desert," one optimist observed.

Outside the barbed wire, Ruth saw the haunting shapes of cypress hung with moss. As she set foot onto the ochre yellow soil, a gust of wind kicked up dust. Inhaling the humid bayou heat of September 1942, she began her year of wartime exile in its "dismal, spooky air."

CHAPTER 2

THE CAMP

Weary families with children and battered suitcases piled out of the trucks onto the dry, weedy ground. The gates to the Rohwer camp were grimmer than the palm-lined entrance to Santa Anita, but at least the shelters didn't reek of horses.

Inside the 10,000-acre site were 500 acres, or almost 1 square mile, of barracks, divided into blocks. They were built over old cornfields and wetlands under supervision of the Army Corps of Engineers at a cost of $4.8 million. The barbed wire fence was studded with eight towers, each manned by armed guards.

The arrival of the Japanese Americans turned the Rohwer Relocation Center into Arkansas's sixth-largest city. Its capacity was nearly nine thousand inmates, and almost twelve thousand would pass through its gates between 1942 and 1945. Arkansas governor Homer Adkins, a onetime member of the Ku Klux Klan, resisted the placement of Japanese Americans in his state, but agreed when told the inmates would be held by armed white guards.

The camp's entrance was flanked by the military police headquarters, warehouses, motor pool, and administrators' apartments. On the northern side of camp were a cannery and hospital. In the central core were schools, a water tank and fire station, an auditorium and library, and an athletic field. Still raw and unfurnished, the camp took months to install equipment such as school chairs.

Looming towers raked the night sky with spotlights. Ruth, like other people, saw through the cover story that the guards were there to protect the Japanese Americans. If so, then why did guards point their guns inward toward the inmates?

Outside the barbed wire perimeter, the bayous were thick with overhanging cypress trees. Swamps and creeks were alive with poisonous cottonmouth snakes and razor-toothed gator fish, making escape a dangerous dream. Two youths wandered away one night but were apprehended on the interstate and held overnight in jail before being returned to camp with their heads shaven.

Prisoners could leave camp only with permission or when their work detail required it. Even then, the unaccustomed sight of a Japanese American outside the fence could ignite unpredictable reactions. One day a local man from the backwoods was out hunting wild turkey when he spied a group of prisoners surveying land. Thinking them escapees, the hunter yelled "Jap!" and fired his shotgun, emptying a load of pellets into the backside of a fleeing prisoner. "It hurt like hell, but I wasn't about to stop. I kept running," said the victim, who had the pellets extracted at the camp hospital.

Tropical weather and critters were a misery. Rains liquefied the Arkansas soil into soupy gumbo mud that sucked at shoes. Humid heat bred swarms of mosquitoes, and there was a shortage of quinine for treatment. Chiggers flourished in the camp too, burrowing into the skin, causing intense itching. Sufferers would light matches and get burned while trying to draw the insects out. Some folks, it was believed, took up smoking just to rout the bugs.

Fall brought sandstorms; winter, icicles. Transplanted Californians, unprepared for harsh winter snows, were issued black wool Navy peacoats, size large. Trundling over the frost-whitened ground in their stiff black garb, one inmate said, they looked like a colony of penguins.

Upon arrival at Rohwer, trucks took Ruth's family to their assigned quarters at their new address: Block 13-11-A. It was one block away from the barbed wire fence and within view of two guard towers. With Umakichi detained separately and Kimiko living under surveillance as a U.S. citizen in Japan, the family now numbered seven.

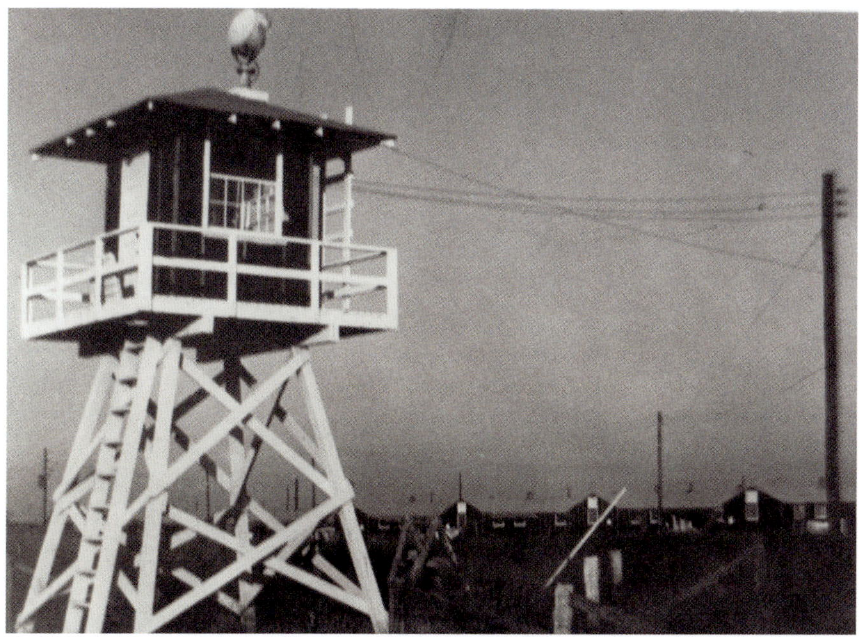

Guard tower at Rohwer War Relocation Center. Photo courtesy of the National Japanese American Historical Society.

They needed two adjoining rooms in the tar-paper barracks. Even such barren quarters, Ruth decided, were "100 percent better" than the manure-saturated stalls of Santa Anita.

The living quarters had bare metal bedframes, a single light bulb in each room, a pot-bellied stove, a bar for clothes, and apartment partitions that stopped short of the ceiling, so that the neighbors could hear each other's most private business. The green-timbered units were thrown together in such haste that the wood shrank as it dried, opening gaps to the dust or wind, rain or snow. Families had to stuff the cracks with scraps of paper or whatever they could find. Still, it didn't reek of horse.

Ruth and her siblings started school while Haru took a job serving in the mess hall. The family felt the absence of their father. Ruth's mother and youngest sister, seven-year-old Janet, suffered most acutely. Nerves frayed, Haru needed her husband to help guide the family in this forbidding swamp settlement. Janet, as the youngest, was her father's constant companion and couldn't grasp his separation from the family.

Meanwhile, though Umakichi's whereabouts were still unknown to the family, FBI documents tracked him from his seizure on the farm to an L.A. County jail, and then to Santa Fe, New Mexico, for a hearing as an "alien enemy." From there, officials ordered him to an alien enemy camp in Lordsburg, New Mexico. At the time of his arrest, the sixty-year-old truck farmer was just 5 feet, 5 inches tall and 137 pounds. Since immigrating in 1902, he'd done nothing but agricultural labor in Hawaii, Utah, and California. But to spy-hunters, his cultural roots were suspect, and his fields were too close to the Los Angeles airport.

Despite Asawa's life spent avoiding fighting, FBI interrogators bore down relentlessly on the subject of his children's fencing—a sport with martial overtones. Hadn't he paid for kendo classes? No, he said, his wife had paid for the lessons. When pressed, he later acknowledged that he had given his wife the money. Seizing on this shift, and making no allowance for his limited English, interrogators labeled him "decidedly evasive" and "potentially dangerous."

The Justice Department and FBI were fixated on links between his children's kendo club and a group known as the *Hokubei Botuko Kai,* or the Military Virtue Society of North America, which they alleged listed Umakichi as a member, and which counted among its overseas members some Japanese officials, including a member of the ultranationalist Black Dragon Society. Thus did investigators strive to connect the dots linking an aging truck farmer who couldn't kill a chicken to militants in Japan who posed a risk to U.S. wartime security.

The Asawa family apartments in Block 13, on the south-central side of camp, bordered on an H-shaped sanitary building that housed open rows of toilets, showers, and laundry tubs. Wood-planked paths ran between blocks to let people walk above the gumbo mud when it rained. Each block had a concrete-floored mess hall equipped with long, wooden outdoor-style tables and bench seating that forced family groups to face strangers. When the dinner bell rang, people got into line and held out their plates to receive a scoop of slop. As at Santa Anita, Nisei girls and boys ran off to eat with their peers, escaping parental control and fragmenting families. Parents and grandparents sat in clusters.

When Ruth, her mother, her sisters Lois, Chiyo, and Janet, and her brothers George and Bill surveyed their quarters, they saw a barren rectangle, sorely lacking comforts. (Quarters ranged from 20 feet by 16 feet to 20 feet by 24 feet.) Many residents improvised their own furniture and shelves, using tools forged from melted shards of waste metal. Vanities, chests of drawers, hutches, and wardrobe closets— some quite elaborate— took shape from scrap wood. Fantastic sculptures were hewn and polished from knotty burls of cypress wood, called *kobu.* Curtains were sewn for privacy.

Around their front doors, families dug gardens, some with tiny ponds. They built bean trellises to grow vegetables and lend blank facades individual, homey touches. Ruth posed for a photo, her hair covered by a bandanna, beside her family's beanstalks.

"Perhaps our most prized commodity, SEEDS" were squirreled away by Haru in her suitcase, which contained the makings of a little kitchen farm: "daikon, spinach, onions, carrots, and beets." Japanese eggplant flourished in the seemingly good-for-nothing soil. Gourds and melons grew fat and

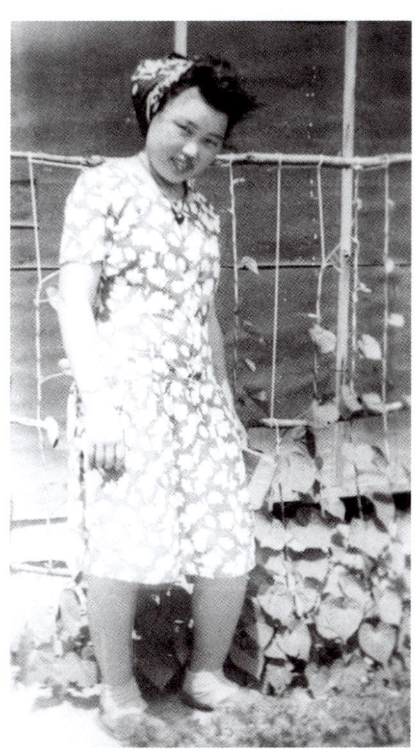

Ruth with trellised beans at Rohwer War Relocation Center, 1943

tempting. Even a flowering vine from Hawaii called *poka* bearing green fruit dotted with black seeds was coaxed from the dusty ground. The Japanese American prison version of victory gardens flourished.

Rohwer rations were portioned out for thirty-seven cents a day—well below the forty-five cents a day that it cost to feed G.I.s—to squelch rumors that the internees were being coddled. People rarely complained, due to what one inmate called the "Hey, at least they fed you people" syndrome. But Japanese gardens yielded fresh tomatoes, corn, and melons to supplement the Spartan camp fare. Abundant harvests drew envious locals to steal watermelons from the "Jap camp." Surplus camp vegetables were shipped to the military at nearby Camp Robinson and the state veterans hospital in Little Rock.

Mess halls were eventually taken over by Japanese cooks who prepared *okazu*, a side dish of meat, vegetables, or tofu to accompany rice. Ruth's mother helped serve. Men pounded soft glutinous rice to make rice balls known as *mochi*, eaten on special occasions. These were cooked in steamers that the inmates built from scrap wood and metal scavenged around camp. For a special taste of home, rumor had it that some of the older men either imported or built a sake still to make bootleg liquor.

Privacy was nonexistent in camp bathrooms, with their rows of open toilets—a daily humiliation. Some women took their chances in the bushes or devised other creative measures. An elderly woman in one camp improvised a stall by folding an Oxydol detergent crate around her and offered to share her screen with others. And the sulfurous shower water left bathers with a greasy residue that never let Ruth feel she was rinsed clean of soap.

Most stifled their complaints, but one who didn't was the sassy hero of "L'il Dan'l," a comic strip created by inmate George Akimoto and published in the camp's newspaper, the *Rohwer Outpost*. Sporting a Daniel Boone coonskin cap, L'il Dan'l griped about cold showers, foul rations, slithering snakes, stifling summers, and icy boardwalks in winter. As the first year in camp came to a close, Akimoto sketched a camp Christmas party in the mess hall, with a scrawny fir tree in one corner and a Japanese American Santa Claus passing out non rationed goods as presents. For the New Year, Akimoto painted a sensory portrait of camp:

> [T]he mess gong clanging in the distance—the clacking of geta *on the wooden walk leading to the shower room—fish odor from the mess hall—the crowded Canteen— lumberjacks—hospital smokestack in the distance—olive drab trucks thundering by— bawling babies—a morning glory beaming from the rooftop—this is Rohwer.*

Amid the squalor came a strange experience, new to Ruth's mother, Haru: free time. Even with her job in the mess hall, her work was light compared to the relentless toil of farm life. To fill empty hours, there were classes in crafts, carving, and sewing, as well as a hair salon. Haru got her first permanent wave. Looking back decades later, Ruth would drily observe that the camp experience was "the first vacation they had really ever taken."

Families attempted to preserve everyday Americana by packing Boy Scout uniforms and baseball gloves. The camp boasted thirty-two softball teams, whose games attracted thousands. Young girls used their $3.50-a-month clothing allowance for fashions from the Sears Roebuck catalog: bobby socks, plaid skirts, and cardigans. There were dances and teen beauty pageants.

Youth struggling to maintain their dignity as citizens ran into Jim Crow. When 125 Girl Scouts at Rohwer camp volunteered their time to help support the war effort, they were assigned to a private plantation—to pick cotton.

High schoolers had low tolerance for faux normalcy. After the last line of the Pledge of Allegiance, "with liberty and justice for all," a rebel voice would pipe up, "Except me!" Recalling social studies teacher Pearl Johnston, Ruth said, "She'd get so mad." But stories of the classroom protests flourished in the camps.

Ruth did her best to keep her spirits up, joining a social club called the Teensters and attending a classical music listening group. She wrote camp authorities asking for more records of vocal music she loved. She experimented with curling her thick black hair and applying crimson lipstick.

That fall in Rohwer, Ruth began her senior year of high school. She pursued a semblance of normal high school life, acting as art editor of the school newspaper and yearbook. She joined the Sketch Club and was a member of the National Honor Society chapter of McGehee, Arkansas, which was set up inside the Rohwer camp, where 98 percent of students earned A averages.

Relieved of endless farm chores, Ruth found time for her art and mentors who encouraged her. Among her Caucasian teachers, Mabel Rose Jamison in art and Louise Beasley in English did the most to nurture Ruth's fierce focus on sketching and painting—and her college aspirations.

Jamie, as Miss Jamison was known, had to make do without real art supplies. She repurposed all manner of random scraps and scrounged materials for crafts projects. She recycled mess hall cans to make hammered metal sculptures. She gathered rocks to paint and buttons to craft jewelry with. Surplus army twill and bolts of denim cloth became canvases. She lobbied authorities for real art supplies, finally receiving paper

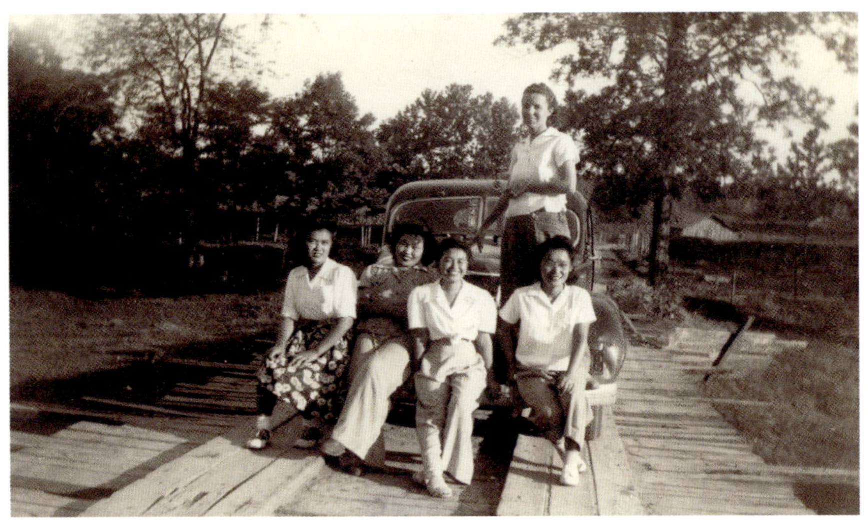

Ruth (second from left) and her teacher Mrs. Beasley (standing), with other students at Rohwer War Relocation Center, Rohwer, Arkansas, 1943. Photograph by Mabel Rose Jamison.

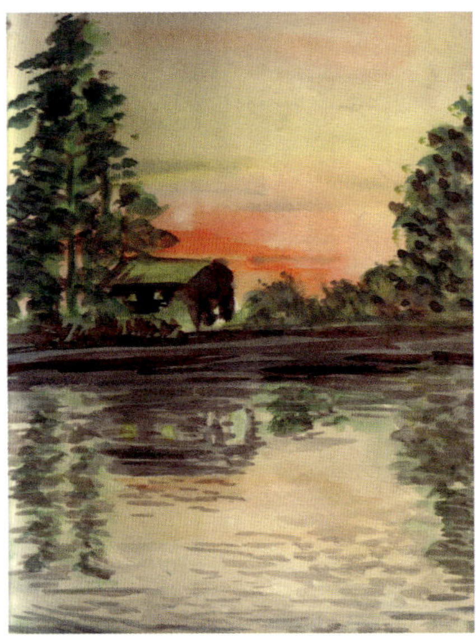

On the Bayou, *1943*
Watercolor on paper 12 x 9 in. (30.5 x 22.9 cm)

and poster paints for her students. Creative reuse of castoff goods was a habit Ruth remembered from her father's farm. It now became the rule in wartime.

In a rare treat, Jamie got permission from camp officials to take Ruth and other students on sketching trips outside the barbed wire fence in Mrs. Beasley's car. Jamie captured a snapshot of one outing showing Ruth and her classmates, grinning on the hood of the car, relishing the brief liberty of a field trip.

Ruth painted a watercolor study of the bayous in moody moss greens, with the tree-shadowed barracks reflected in the swamp water. She also painted a scene of sumo wrestling, a sanctioned camp sport, with crowds of spectators holding parasols to shield themselves from the fierce Arkansas sun.

Because cameras were still considered contraband, Ruth was appointed to draw Rohwer's high school graduates for their yearbook. One member of the first graduating class in winter 1942, Sachi Fujikawa, would write to Ruth:

> *I can still see you in my mind's eye sitting in my econ class at Rohwer High School quietly sketching the members of my class. I was half a grade ahead of you . . . and since we were not allowed to have cameras at that time, our yearbook consisted of sketches that you drew of each of us students. I have treasured that mimeographed publication.*

The habit of drawing students was one she'd keep for decades—a tradition extending into the classrooms of her future children and grandchildren.

But in wartime, haunted by her father's distant confinement, Ruth did more than draw in her free time. She would not passively accept her father's isolation. While still in Santa Anita in the summer of 1942, she launched a letter-writing campaign to every U.S. official in the Department of Justice and the U.S. Attorney's Office she could identify as being involved in her father's arrest, hearing, transport, and imprisonment. If she couldn't get herself out of camp, she could at least try to reunite her father with his family. Lordsburg, where Umakichi was held, was a special internment camp for Japanese Americans considered alien enemies, as well as Italian and German prisoners. It earned its tough reputation after two elderly Issei inmates were shot and killed during an alleged escape attempt, although the facts of the case were disputed. In a court martial, the responsible officer was exonerated despite testimony that age and disability had rendered the men unable to keep up with an order to walk 2 miles to camp, much less to run away.

Ruth found a typewriter to wage her campaign of letters seeking her father's release. Summoning a voice of authority beyond her sixteen years, she posted a letter that landed on July 8 on the desk of U.S. Attorney William Fleet Palmer in Los Angeles:

Dear Mr. Palmer,

    At this time I should like to ask a favor of you concerning the regulations of release. My father, Umakichi Asawa, is detained at Santa Fe, New Mexico, Immigration and Naturalization Station. We are having so much trouble with our business affairs and I feel that the responsibility is too heavy on my brother, so I wish to know what procedure to take for his release. . . . My mother seems very much worried. . . .

I have a younger sister who had been his very close companion, and without him she seems tremendously disappointed. I feel that she needs her father here. If you can, please help us in some way, I would appreciate it very much. We are now residing in the Santa Anita Assembly Center.

With hopes of a prompt reply
I remain,
Most sincerely yours,
Ruth Asawa

By coincidence, Roosevelt's attorney general sealed her father's fate that same day:

In the Matter of Umakichi Asawa,
ALIEN ENEMY. D.J. FILE NO. 146-13-2-12-2860
ORDER
WHEREAS, Umakichi Asawa of Norwalk, California, now being detailed at Santa Fe, New Mexico, a subject of Japan, over the age of fourteen years, is within the United States and not a naturalized citizen thereof and has heretofore been apprehended as being potentially dangerous to the public peace and safety of the United States, and,

WHEREAS the Alien Enemy Hearing Board has recommended said alien enemy be interned; now therefore, upon consideration of the evidence before me, it is ordered that said alien be interned.

(Signed) Francis Biddle
ATTORNEY GENERAL
July 8, 1942

Ruth sent another letter (see page 40 for a scan of the original letter) to U.S. Attorney Palmer, this time citing her father's civic responsibility, his paternal guidance, and the strain of his absence:

Dear Sir:

Having received notice of my father's transfer to Camp Lordsburg, New Mexico, I immediately thought of writing to you to ask a favor and advice for another trial for release. My father, Umakichi Asawa, was interned on April 2, 1942. From Tujunga Detention Station, he was sent to the Detention Camp in New Mexico and then later transferred to Camp Lordsburg on July 19.

If a release may be made possible, I would like you to help, if you can. Probably you have helped many others. . . .

The reason I write is that I think my father . . . is worthy of being with us. With his influence and ambition we have tried to learn many things. You see, he came to this country to start and help the community of Norwalk grow, being here when our community was still a bare portion of the West. For this community he has contributed and donated for various charities. We are educating ourselves to be good American citizens, and that is one of Father's great hopes. This favor of his release is not for me alone. . . . This war was really the very first separation since Father and Mother met, and Mother has taken it very hard. She worries very much for Janet's sake. You see, Janet cannot understand. So if you can, please assist me, my mother and the rest to release Father. Thank you very much for listening. I hope you can help.

Most sincerely yours,
Ruth Asawa

Ruth's siblings soon joined in the campaign. Her thirteen-year-old brother, Bill, who was in ninth grade, wrote the U.S. Attorney's Office in Los Angeles citing evidence found in his father's old papers dating back a decade before his birth. While Umakichi wasn't a fighter, Bill's handwritten letter landed on the attorney's desk on July 31, 1942, asserting his father had registered for the Army during World War I and helped the country doing what he did best: growing produce.

Dear Sirs . . .

I must first tell you that my father is loyal to the United States of America. We have proof of his loyalty. Among his numerous proofs is his registration card for the United States Army in World War I. Beside this, he also has a bill of sale for an order of his sugar beets crop which my father raised during World War I.

Bill closed by asking for his father's release from Lordsburg to lighten his mother's "burdens of worry." It must have pricked the conscience of an official, who would later cite Bill's plea in a key document, although it would take over a year for Umakichi to be allowed to rejoin his family.

Blist III, Bar. 1, Ave 1, U.17
Camp Santa Anita
Arcadia, Calif.

Hon. Wm Fleet Palmer
U. S. District Attorney of Southern Calif. District
Federal Building
Los. Angeles, California

Dear Sir:

    Having received notice of my father's transfer to Camp Lordsburg, New Mexico, I immediately thought of writing to you to ask an favor and advice for another trial for release. My father, Umakichi Asawas, was interned on April 2, 1942. From Tujunga Detention Station, he was sent to the Detention Camp in New Mexico and then later transfered to Camp Lordsburg on July 19.

    If a release may be made possible, I would like you to help, if you can. Probably you have helped many others, so I think I have confidence in you.

The reason I write is because I think my father, Umakichi Asawa, is worthy of being with us. With his influence and ambition, we have tried to learn many things. You see, he came to this country to start & help the community of Norwalk grow, being here when our community was still a bare portion of the West. For this community he has contributed and donated for various charities. We are educating ourselves to be good American citizens, And that is one of father's great hopes.

This favor for his release is not for me alone, but for mother and the youngest, Janet.

[...] the very first [...] father and mother. [...] has taken it [...] worries very much [...] You see, Janet cannot understand. So if you can, please assist me, my mother and the rest to release Father.

Thank you very much for listening. I hope you can help.

Most sincerely yours,
Ruth Asawa.

The Asawa siblings' campaign paused during the train ride to Arkansas and resumed once they were settled at Rohwer. On October 9, 1942, Ruth dispatched a poised letter to the Alien Hearing Board of Immigration and Naturalization Office in Washington, D.C.:

> *Gentlemen:*
>
> *My father, Umakichi Asawa, is at present interned in Lordsburg, New Mexico, and since our family is now relocated in Rohwer Relocation Center, Rohwer, Arkansas, I would like to know if he could be reunited with his family.*
>
> *Some time ago, I received a message stating that after the family is relocated, it would be possible for him to join his family.*
>
> *Your full consideration will be greatly appreciated.*
>
> *Most sincerely yours,*
>
> *(Signed) Ruth Asawa*
>
> *My new address –*
>
> *Block 13-11-A*
>
> *W.R.A. Rohwer*
>
> *McGehee, Arkansas*

From late 1942 through early 1943, Ruth rounded up character references for her father from among the family's Norwalk neighbors, landlords, business associates, farmers, and clergy. C. J. Hargett, scion of one of Norwalk's founding ranch families, declared:

> *I have known U. Asawa since 1904 when he first came to my grandfather's ranch to work and have been in touch with him ever since. He is of good moral character and in all business dealings of which I have been a party he has always been fair and just. He has a large family and to the best of my knowledge they are all conscientious workers. I have never heard criticism of him or his family's conduct from any member of the community.*

As it did with many wartime documents, the government marked the letter CENSORED without further elaboration.

Mrs. Edythe Byars of Norwalk filed an affidavit vowing Umakichi Asawa was "a peaceable, law abiding farmer, well liked by his neighbors," and ended with a pointed sermon for the justice officials:

During her letter blitz, Ruth and her mother began writing to Edward Ennis, a Justice Department lawyer who directed the Alien Enemy Control Unit. Ennis told Ruth that reconsideration of her father's case would depend on her supplying new evidence on his behalf.

As Ennis instructed, Ruth wrote to the new U.S. Attorney for Los Angeles, Leo V. Silverstein, pointing out she'd already filed a dozen affidavits of support from witnesses who swore they never heard Umakichi Asawa utter a pro-Japanese or anti-American sentiment.

Haru, who didn't speak English, now joined the letter campaign and got help in translating her grief into English. She wrote of the "inexpressible heartaches and loneliness" inflicted by the forced separation from her husband, and prayed officials would reach a "righteous decision," releasing him to rejoin his family.

Spunky and rational Ruth, whose letters were usually precocious and businesslike, now despaired as she thought of her father's health in New Mexico. She closed her February 1943 letter to Ennis with a plea:

For our sake, could you help us in having my father come to Rohwer? We are all praying that the Lord will help us in this time of great need.

Wartime bureaucrats would ultimately grant Umakichi a rehearing to consider the new evidence. If he prevailed, he might finally rejoin his family. But the bureaucracy's glacial pace would move too slowly for Ruth, who was now a high school senior nearing graduation. Graduates could become eligible for prewar release from camp if they got a sponsor and attended college in the interior. The price of early release was that she wouldn't see her father until after the war.

Before Ruth and her classmates could be released from camp to go to college, they, like all evacuees aged seventeen and older, faced a loyalty questionnaire. Two key questions probed their fidelity to the United States. and searched for hints of sympathy for the enemy:

> *Question 27: Are you willing to serve in the armed forces of the United States on combat duty, wherever ordered?*
>
> *Question 28: Will you swear unqualified allegiance to the United States and faithfully defend the United States from any or all attack by foreign or domestic forces, and forswear any form of allegiance or obedience to the Japanese emperor, or any other foreign government, power, or organization?*

Debates split families. Were these trick questions? If they answered "Yes" to Question 27, did it mean immediate military duty? If they replied "Yes" to Question 28, swearing U.S. allegiance and renouncing loyalty to Japan, did that equal an admission of prior fealty to Emperor Hirohito? Some were confused; others, defiant. For the older generation of Issei, who were still barred from U.S. citizenship, renouncing their roots was painful. For the younger generation of Nisei, born U.S. citizens, renouncing an emperor they'd never served seemed absurd.

Inmates replying "No" to both questions were deemed disloyal. About 808 people, just under 10 percent of Rohwer's population, were transferred to Tule Lake, California, in the fall of 1943. More were relocated later, raising their number to 1,430. The maximum security center on the state's northeastern border with Oregon was girded with a double-thick, 8-foot-high, "man-proof" fence and one thousand military police in armored cars and tanks. Among the people sent to Tule Lake was a small boy named George Takei, who would later become an actor, starring as Mr. Sulu in the television series *Star Trek*.

The majority of people incarcerated at Rohwer swore their loyalty to the government by replying "Yes" and "Yes." Among them were the Asawas. Ruth even stated willingness to join the Women's Army Auxiliary Corps, or WAAC. Her brother George would later serve in the military.

When Ruth's graduating class of 1943 got copies of their yearbook, called the *Delta Roundup*, friends inscribed pages of teenaged farewells in forties lingo: "Dearest Ruth, Aw gee! It sho' was supa dupa to have met such a swell chum . . . Love, Bonnie Masuda."

For the Who's Who section, Ruth drew caricatures of classmates chosen as most "brainy," "studious," "popular," and "neat." Ruth, named most "artistic," portrayed

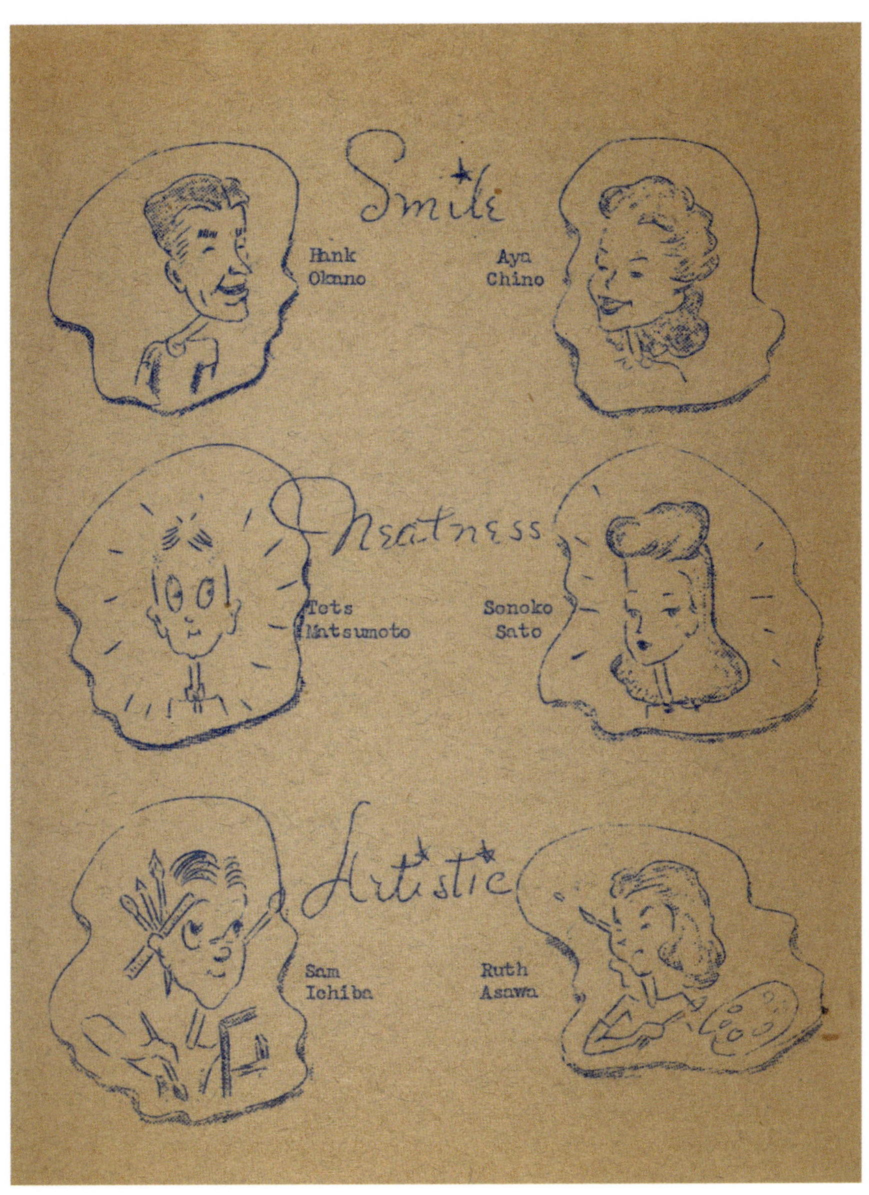

Student poll page from Ruth's 1943 Rohwer Center High School annual, Delta Round-Up

herself frowning in concentration, grasping a palette and a paintbrush, with a second brush stuck behind her ear.

Her counterpart, Rohwer's most "artistic" boy, signed Ruth's yearbook: "To a little lady with lots of talent and a big heart . . . Remember a bum named Sam Ichiba."

The son of a California gardener, Sam Ichiba was anything but a bum. Soon after the war began, youth like Ichiba were classified as 4F (physically, mentally, or morally unfit to serve) and later 4C (ineligible due to nationality or ancestry). As soon as the U.S. military realized it needed Japanese men in the war effort, Ichiba was eager to enlist. He initially met opposition from his father amid rumors that enlistees would be deported to Japan and shot. But Sam persisted. His father had a change of heart, saying it was his son's duty to fight and adding, "Don't bring shame to your name."

Sam Ichiba ended up joining the 442nd Regimental Combat Team, the Nisei fighting force that became the most highly decorated military unit for its size and length of service in American military history. Known by the jaunty motto "Go for Broke," the 442nd fought key battles in France and Italy. Ichiba and his weary ragtag unit forced the surrender of an elite SS unit dug into an Italian mountainside bristling with machine guns. Ichiba would go on to earn the Bronze Star, three Battle Stars, and the Presidential Unit Citation. "I thought I was in Dante's Inferno," he would say. "They used us as battering rams, but I did it for my country and to get my parents out of that camp."

As for Ruth, she narrowed her college ambitions to Midwestern schools that were far from California, as prescribed to avoid military zones, and cheap enough for her to afford. While weighing her options, she considered Mrs. Beasley's advice that "we must try not to be bitter because this would pass and we must think of our future." Trying to envision a future beyond barbed wire, Ruth figured her most viable option for combining her love of art with a practical career was to train as an art teacher:

> *She gave us college catalogs to look through. She gave me the Chicago Art Institute catalog. I had never heard of an art institute. The classes sounded exciting, but the tuition was beyond my reach. I chose Milwaukee State Teachers College because they had the lowest tuition of any school, $25.00 a semester. Mrs. Beasley arranged for me to live with a family as a student helper to help with meals and cleaning.*

Ruth's salary was to be ten dollars a week while working full-time as a domestic and babysitter before classes started, and one dollar a week for part-time housekeeping once school began. Her new employer, Mrs. John O'Brien, wrote that she would meet

Ruth at the Milwaukee train station, wearing a powder blue suit and accompanied by her young daughter, Mary, who wore blonde Shirley Temple curls. Ruth replied they could recognize her by her black bob and bangs.

Ruth's older siblings, Lois, George, and Chiyo, left to attend William Penn College, a Quaker school in Iowa. Ruth got a Quaker scholarship through the American Friends Service Committee. She prepared herself for the move to Wisconsin, leaving behind her mother and younger siblings, Bill and Janet, in high school and elementary school.

While she took to heart Mrs. Beasley's advice to buck up, Ruth would later look back on the whole of her Arkansas experience with a sense of incredulity:

Imagine telling a 16-year-old not to be bitter after an experience of separation, cold barracks, and dirty dusty roads to walk to school, no heat except in the corner of the classroom and tar paper flapping outside and wind whistling thru the cracks of the ripped black tar paper, walking thru bitter cold winds to get to school, and finding a hysterical student freezing.

On July 30, 1943, Ruth graduated from camp high school in a commencement ceremony that included her brother George. The high school chorus sang an anthem, "America, Thou Blessed Land," by Geoffrey O'Hara. What emotions were stirred by a patriotic song in a prison graduation can only be imagined. But Ruth saved the mimeographed program, brittle and faded, among her souvenirs for life.

Despite her tireless letter-writing campaign, the new graduate had to leave camp without seeing her father. Umakichi's parole process from Lordsburg Alien Enemy Camp began, at least on paper, with the letters and affidavits sent in the spring of 1943. But Ruth's window to leave camp for college opened while her father was still in New Mexico. The father-daughter reunion would have to wait for peacetime.

Ruth's new photo ID showed her unsmiling, looking older than her years, gazing out from a green-bordered card that read, United States War Relocation Authority, Citizen's Indefinite Leave, certifying that Ruth Aiko Asawa was allowed to depart Rohwer camp on August 16, 1943. Rather like an internal visa, it specified the cardholder's first destination was Milwaukee, Wisconsin. With the war still on and her father far away, Ruth bid a reverent goodbye to Haru.

I departed bowing to Mama, wondering what she was thinking.

Finally came a wrenching farewell to her English teacher. With candor rare for her time and place, Mrs. Beasley acknowledged that the camps imposed "a terrible

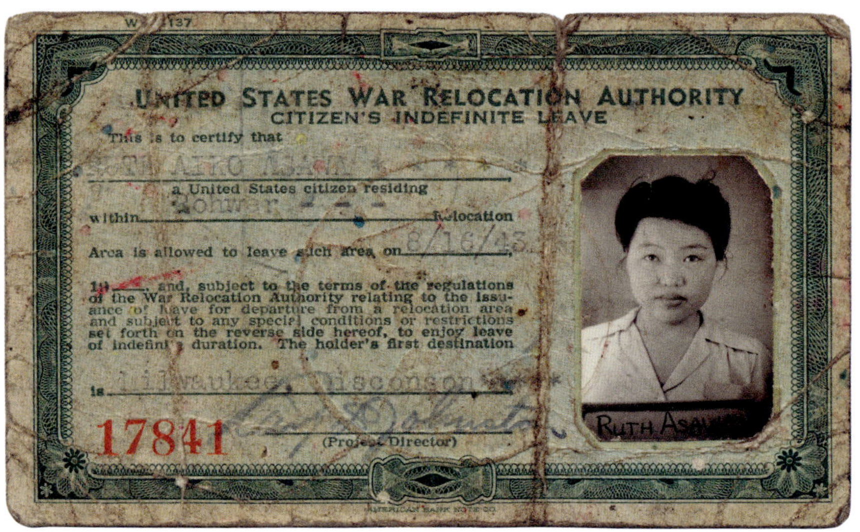

Ruth's War Relocation Authority identification card, 1943

injustice" on Ruth and her people. Still, she insisted that Ruth put it behind her and seize her future as a citizen. Driving Ruth to the McGehee train station, the teacher delivered a parting pep talk before sweeping up her student in an embrace:

> *Mrs. Beasley took me to the train station, a desolate swampland landscape. We stood on the platform. As the train arrived, she got on her knees and looked at me straight in the eyes and said, "Now Ruth, remember, always the future, not the past."*
> *I couldn't speak but nodded in the affirmative.*
> *She hugged me for a long time. That was the first time I had ever been hugged. We waved & I was off on a lonely journey into the future. I waved until the train turned.*
> *Her hug protected me.*

CHAPTER 3

GETTING UP IN THE WORLD

Ruth was alone now. On the train ride, she sat on duffel bags among soldiers heading to war, an unaccompanied seventeen-year-old leaving for college with excitement and trepidation about the world that awaited her beyond camp. She was headed to Milwaukee, 700 miles north—a city known for building motors, brewing beer, and tanning leather, but where she knew no one except the name of her new employers. It was light-years from the barbed wire and gun towers of camp.

But her release—like those of Lois, Chiyo, and George—was conditional, good only as long as she stayed away from the West Coast. Milwaukee itself was on the shores of Lake Michigan, which was used as a training area for military exercises by aircraft carrier pilots. Japanese Americans were forbidden to stroll the waterfront. Yet Ruth's curiosity drew her too close to the lake, breaking the rules. She got picked up and warned several times.

Meanwhile, freedom was incomplete with half the family still confined: Haru, Bill, and Janet in Arkansas; Umakichi in New Mexico; and Kimiko in Japan. But at least Ruth had gotten out of camp.

Once again, Ruth saw wrenching evidence of her father's exile in a brown paper parcel postmarked in New Mexico. Umakichi had sent his middle daughter a box carved from local scrap wood. The box top had a hand-tooled scene of a room with a chair, in the style of a Van Gogh interior, and on the underside he inscribed: "For Ruth" underlined with a red bow, and signed "Daddy."

As a housekeeper for the O'Brien family, Ruth was a bargain. Her description of the situation is starkly matter-of-fact:

> *Mrs. Beasely arranged for me to live with a family as a student helper to prepare breakfast, make lunches, help with dinner & dishes & cleaning on the weekends for room & board + $1 a week. . . . I ate my meals in the kitchen.*

That is all the young woman, reared never to criticize her elders, would write of her first experience of independent living. No carefree co-ed, she was a maid, and would face more hardscrabble years before her future could truly begin. For Ruth, it was now simply a matter of shelter and survival; there would be time later for finding friends and support.

Milwaukee State Teachers College was affordable at twenty-five dollars a semester. Ruth got a scholarship, arranged through the American Friends Service Committee, a Quaker group that supported peace and racial justice through two world wars. Her benefactor was a Philadelphia grandmother of eight named Ethel R. Potts. Mrs. Potts had traveled to Japan and loved its art. Imagine Ruth's surprise at receiving not just money but words of solidarity from an elderly white stranger:

> *Your Japanese inheritance, no doubt, gives you your interest and ability in art . . .*
> *How sad that nations cannot live together in peace and brotherhood as God surely*
> *intended them to do.*

Mrs. Potts signed her letter, "Your friend." Ruth held on to that letter her whole life.

Artistically, Ruth found the Milwaukee State Teachers College faculty to be "a ball of fire," alive with talent. The course of study for prospective art teachers at Milwaukee State was a smorgasbord of arts and crafts, allowing Ruth to sample painting, drawing, jewelry making, and weaving. A semester of each would let a future teacher build a portfolio of diverse skills for the classroom. She studied with Robert von Neumann, a German-born painter who was injured in World War I. His wooden leg was a visible reminder of other wars and other sacrifices.

Ruth threw herself into courses and worked for the college annual, *The Ivy*, penning faculty caricatures, much as she'd done for the camp's high school yearbook. Photos of the collegiate Ruth show her wearing lipstick, her hair permed into a cloud of black curls, an Asian woman in a sea of Caucasian faces.

Overcoming her reserve with strangers, Ruth seized the chance to make friends. With her classmate Mabel Galian, she read a new children's book,

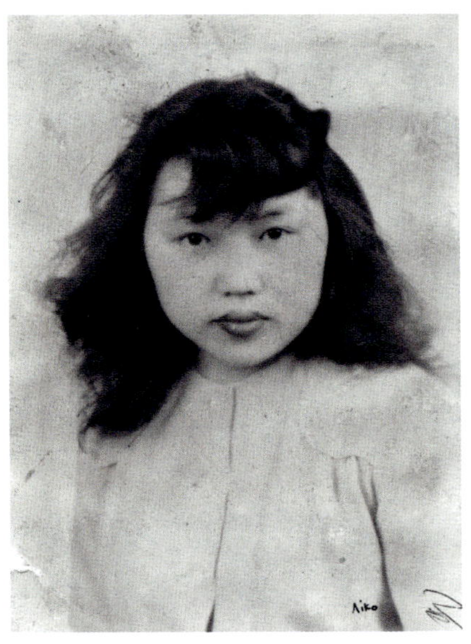

Ruth at Milwaukee State Teachers College, 1943

Make Way for Ducklings, published in 1941. The Caldecott Award–winning story featured a duck family waddling through downtown Boston, looking for a spot to build their nest and lay their eggs. After reading out the names of eight ducklings—Jack, Kack, Lack, Mack, Nack, Ouack, Pack, and Quack—Ruth and Mabel nicknamed each other Twick and Twack. Their friendship would last long after college.

Ruth's best friend in Milwaukee was Elaine Schmitt, daughter of a family of stained-glass makers. They were complementary colors on the personality palette: Elaine was as bubbly as Ruth was reserved. She brought Ruth to her family's home in Wauwatosa to meet her two brothers and a sister—all destined for art school. A gifted painter, Elaine had already attended the Ox-Bow summer session of Chicago Art Institute. There she had met a baby-faced, crew-cut nineteen-year-old from Detroit named Ray Johnson, who would become a major figure in American Pop Art. The two Midwestern teens befriended Ruth, and let her in on their plans.

Elaine wanted to follow her older sister Elizabeth, a dancer, to an experimental art school in North Carolina: Black Mountain College. Ray did, too. Both urged Ruth to join them for the summer there. The liberal arts curriculum was centered around art, and the school was radically democratic. School issues, from war and peace to the length of students' shorts, got thrashed out in raucous town hall–style meetings where everyone—students and teachers alike—had a vote. They all lived and ate together, performing in concerts, plays, and dance recitals. Everyone worked to build, feed, and maintain their tiny utopian community.

The school was financially insecure and austere even by wartime standards. So the work requirement wasn't just an intellectual conceit—it was a necessity. Teachers and pupils might find themselves mixing mortar and laying stones for a wall, hauling coal for the furnaces, or milking cows or growing vegetables for the dining hall. Students even trucked garbage to the dump.

Black Mountain College awarded no degrees, but it offered students an idyllic studio art experience where they could study color and design with working artists like Josef and Anni Albers, a Bauhaus painter and a weaver, respectively. Faculty and resident artists were creating and experimenting. The college would be the site of a revolution in the performing arts by composer John Cage and dancer Merce Cunningham. Painter Robert Motherwell and poet Robert Creeley taught there. And the student body sparkled with a constellation of mid-century stars, including Robert Rauschenberg, Cy Twombly, and Kenneth Noland.

Ruth began to send tentative queries to the school, though she was still pursuing a practical career plan to work as an art *teacher*, not an artist. The timing was also wrong. Her older sister Lois, now studying languages at the University of Wisconsin, was coming to Milwaukee that summer of 1945 to pick up Ruth for a trip south of the border. Ruth needed to save her funds for the journey.

"I was all hot to go to Mexico," she would say. Mexico drew Lois as an opportunity to put into practice her study of languages. For Ruth, its colors, ceramics, decorative arts, and painting were a magnet. The sisters, although poor, were eager to experience all they could of culture abroad. Mexico offered the most affordable international study trip accessible by bus during wartime. Its allure was irresistible.

After working as a domestic, Ruth left the O'Briens' house to live with fellow student Elizabeth Christel and found a job as a checker in the shipping department of the Albert Trostel Tannery for sixty-six cents an hour. Processing animal skins (a byproduct of Midwestern slaughterhouses) into leather was a major industry in Milwaukee. No stranger to hard labor, Ruth signed on for the morning shift, five thirty to eleven. She also was no stranger to the earthy odors of farm life, but she found the fumes of hides soaking in lye and salt to be overpowering. After steeping in the "incredible, unbelievable" smell, she went to class until five in the evening—her ability to log twelve-hour days backed by her experience on the truck farm.

Compared to housekeeping, though, Ruth's tannery wages felt substantial, enough to salt away in a bank account. The savings would help fund her summer adventure with Lois in Mexico City.

"I was getting up in the world," she reflected.

By the summer of 1945, the Nazis had surrendered in Europe, and fighting in the Pacific was hurtling toward an end. With their indefinite leave cards from camp, Ruth and her sister booked seats on a Greyhound bus from Milwaukee, traveling south through Joplin, Missouri, and Laredo, Texas, toward the border.

On the road south, Ruth saw Jim Crow laws in action. Signs for "white" and "colored" water fountains and bathrooms enforced racial segregation. But the two young Asian American sisters weren't sure where they belonged. Locals asked Ruth if she was a Cherokee Indian. With white people guessing at their ethnicity, Ruth and her sister pondered their roots.

Lois and I didn't know what to do about the toilets. We looked at ourselves and decided we'd be better off using the Colored toilets and continued to do so through Texas.

Once they crossed the border, the focus on the colors of race dissolved into the brilliant palette of local artists. While Lois worked on her Spanish, Ruth studied with a Cuban-born furniture designer, Clara Porset, at the University of Mexico. Coincidentally Porset had been to Black Mountain College in the 1930s and spent time with Josef Albers. Ruth also studied painting and sculpture at the Escuela Esmeralda de Pintura y Escultura. She learned how to prime a wet "green" plaster with a trowel for fresco painting. She watched muralists perched on a scaffold applying swathes of color to a large social mural. The spectacle of artists at work fired her curiosity about a creative life.

As the Asawa sisters explored Mexico, American warplanes in the Pacific were roaring toward a cataclysm. On the morning of August 6, 1945, an American pilot loaded a nine-thousand-pound bomb into a B-29 plane called *Enola Gay*, after his mother. Its payload, a product of secret government atomic weapons research, was code-named "Little Boy." The bomb exploded some 2,000 feet above the industrial city of Hiroshima, killing seventy to eighty thousand people outright, injuring an equal number, and inflicting survivors with radiation sickness and cancer. Three days later, on August 9, another B-29 crew dropped a second atomic bomb code-named "Fat Man" on Nagasaki, killing more than thirty-five thousand people and injuring more. Japan's Emperor Hirohito yielded within the week and signed formal terms of surrender the next month. World War II ended with the birth of the nuclear age, which brought the war's toll to an estimated fifty million deaths worldwide.

For families in camps, peace produced warring emotions: relief that the camps would be closing, mingled with fear of an uncertain future. Many were concerned for the welfare of far-flung relatives, including those across the Pacific. Ruth's younger sister Kimiko was still in Koriyama, Japan, a city where townspeople practiced self-defense with bamboo sticks and held air-raid drills by plunging into a river. But such worries would be kept private, in keeping with the quiet code of *gaman*—endurance with dignity. Reflecting on that apocalyptic summer of 1945 in a later journal, Ruth compressed all the angst of an era into a laconic note:

While in Mexico, the Japanese surrendered.

There was no jubilation for the Asawas as long as Haru, Umakichi, Bill, and Janet were still detained. Umakichi had been allowed to rejoin his wife in late 1943. Kimiko would remain in Japan until her cousin Charles, a member of the U.S. occupational forces, could get her out on a military transport ship in 1946.

Upon their release from internment, Japanese Americans would get twenty-five dollars and a bus or train ticket home. But where to go? Where *was* home? Even for those who longed to return to California, the closure of the camps after three years was destabilizing. Houses and jobs were gone, and neighbors dispersed. Reports of lingering hostility and vandalism in California reached the camps. The War Relocation Authority, for its part, encouraged Japanese Americans not to return to their old enclaves, but rather to disperse and assimilate in new communities elsewhere.

Just so, many families resettled across the country in a postwar diaspora. Ruth's old school friend Alice Imamoto, the sensei's daughter, who was held at the neighboring camp in Jerome, Arkansas, made her way to Ohio, Pennsylvania, and Maryland. With their once-thriving truck farm long gone, Umakichi and Haru—who were nearing retirement age at sixty-three and fifty-one, respectively—faced starting over from scratch.

In camp, tiny home gardens around family barracks would soon be abandoned. For the second time in four years, inmates would be literally uprooted. Preparing to leave Rohwer camp, one woman composed a haiku:

Pulled out
Morning glory vines
As day of departure nears

The imprisoned poet, Kikuha Okamoto, was spared a bittersweet parting after all. Months before camp closed, she died of a heart attack, leaving behind a fifty-seven-year-old husband. (A study would later suggest that camp survivors experienced more than double the rate of heart disease and premature death of people who were not interned.)

As released prisoners boarded trains to leave camps, some observed a farewell ritual. Passengers held one end of a strand of crepe paper at the window, while well-wishers on the platform held the other end. As the cars departed, the paper strips stretched and snapped. Each friend was left holding half of a torn strand, ripped in two like their lives before and after war.

At the camp newspaper, the *Rohwer Outpost*, journalist Bean Takeda reported feelings of conflict about returning to an uncertain reception on the West Coast. "But I'm returning to California soon," he concluded, "and when I do, I shall expect to be treated roughly at first and perhaps even shot at."

Where could anyone go to start over with twenty-five dollars? It turned out that growers in Arizona needed farm laborers. The Asawas decided they could work doing what they knew and save money for their eventual return to Southern California.

Ruth returned from Mexico, her head ablaze with colors, to an uneasy peacetime in Milwaukee. She was starting her third year of coursework at the teachers college, prior to the final year devoted to student teaching. She resumed domestic work as a means of supporting herself, this time in the home of the Rices, a Jewish family who lived a block from school. There, she earned five dollars a week babysitting while experiencing another culture's comfort food: chicken soup with matzo balls.

But as she prepared for the year of practice teaching, as required for her degree and credential, she got a shock:

In the third year the college told me they would not assign me to a teaching position for my safety.

Wisconsin schools weren't ready for a student teacher of Japanese heritage. Framing the action as necessary for Ruth's protection didn't lessen the blow of the school's decision. Ruth was unable to complete her degree or earn her credential without the required practicum. While she had enjoyed classes and made friends, she would be unable to support herself as a teacher. She was out three years of her time, her scholarship and wages, and her hard-earned room and board.

With her career plans foiled, the campaign by Ruth's friends Elaine Schmitt and Ray Johnson to join them at Black Mountain College began to look more realistic to her. Other Milwaukee friends—Elaine's sister, Elizabeth Schmitt, and photographer Hazel-Frieda Larsen—were also committed to Black Mountain. The allure of the art college was growing more tempting. The roadblock to becoming a credentialed teacher, in effect, opened another pathway to pursue her childhood dream of becoming an artist.

Ruth was developing a knack for turning insult into opportunity. In Santa Anita Racetrack, she lived in a horse stall but found drawing tutors in the grandstand. Despite War Relocation Authority orders to stay in the Midwest, she had found sponsors, teachers, and friends in college. Now Wisconsin's rejection opened the door to North Carolina:

I decided to go to Black Mountain College.

Ruth sent in her application. Space was tight for the academic year, the school replied, but the 1946 Summer Institute was open. Her old roommate Elizabeth Christel, now director of a Milwaukee nursery school, wrote to the school in April 1946, recommending Ruth. Christel stressed that Ruth was an honors student who had her oil and water-color painting and pencil drawing displayed in the 33rd Exhibition of the Wisconsin Sculptors and Painters. She appealed to the art school's sense of social responsibility as well as aesthetic standards:

She bears hardships courageously and minimizes them. . . . For two years this girl has been glowing with the ardent desire to study at Black Mountain. I sincerely hope that some arrangement can be made for her attendance . . . I wholeheartedly recommend this modest, serious, and promising young Nisei.

Among the Milwaukeeans who supported Ruth's application to art school were Helmut and Cecelie Sieverts, a German couple who had fled Frankfurt with two sons aged three and four to avoid Nazi persecution. Cecelie, a secular Jewish musician who was committed to Quaker social action, learned in 1937 that her little boys faced expulsion from preschool due to her background. The family left Germany and resettled in Milwaukee, again gravitating to the Quaker meetings in local homes, where they met the young Ruth. Their shared history of wartime trauma, displacement, and love of classical music drew them together within that circle of yearning souls. Cecelie, a violinist who played chamber music, wrote to Black Mountain in May 1946 with this assessment of Ruth's character:

I regard Ruth Asawa as an unusually fine person. She has one of the most amiable personalities I have had the privilege to meet. She seems very quiet at first, but the better one knows her the more one realizes that she has a keen, highly sensitive mind, that she has a good sense of humor, an excellent measure of tact and is one of the true liberals who walk the ground. She is not free from prejudice because or on account of personal experience which she grew above, but because she is so in a very integrated manner. Hers is an innate tolerance and understanding. Her creative abilities are way above average. She has good ideas and her work—both poetry and art—has originality and quality.

One flaw emerged in her portrait of the twenty-year-old applicant:

Her only obvious fault is her sloppiness. However, I do think, that in a likeminded group, this may not bother anybody, and in a group which values appearances along with content, she may profit a great deal.

She is very active and perseverant. Among the activities she pursues is Modern Dance, and social work as far as time permits. She has better understanding of music than the average student (who is no music major) shows. When at our house, where a large record library is at her disposal, she would select works by Bach, Mozart, Hindemith, Prokofieff, and her remarks prove an amazingly sure instinct, though she is entirely untrained.

Money still posed a daunting roadblock. Black Mountain's tuition and fees were rising from a sliding scale of $450 to $1,200 in 1943 toward a flat fee of $1,600 in 1948, putting the program far beyond the reach of Ruth's meager earnings without some form of scholarship assistance.

Just as she was leaving Milwaukee State, a notice on a bulletin board caught her eye. A flyer from Church of the Crossroads in Hawaii, a pioneering Protestant congregation, was offering student aid. She applied and got a $200 loan that, combined with her savings, gave her just enough to attend summer session at Black Mountain. Surely a summer there would ease the sting of Milwaukee's rejection.

Elaine Schmitt, who had traveled ahead to Black Mountain, wrote to Ruth, prodding her to get ready for the summer session, tempting her with rhapsodic descriptions of the drifting petals of dogwood in bloom and the brilliant arts faculty:

I hope you have all your things packed and ready to leave for N. Carolina . . . Really, dear Ruth, I'd rather die than know you missed out the chance of having Albers.

So Ruth packed her trunk for six weeks at Black Mountain, where she hoped to study weaving with Anni Albers. She thought she might be good at this craft since she was so nimble at stringing up beans on the farm. Mending her unraveled career at Albers's loom seemed like the best course.

But once again, her plans would go awry.

CHAPTER 4

CLIMBING BLACK MOUNTAIN

This time, Ruth's journey took her from a life in black and white to a world of saturated color, with friends waiting for her on the other side.

Unlike the drab trains of the war years, the Southern Railway sported green cars with red and silver wheels. Its windows framed a verdant Southern countryside flying past. After winding through the Great Smoky Mountains, the train stopped near Asheville, at the village of Black Mountain, North Carolina. There, it deposited bags, parcels, and travelers, including the twenty-year-old novice from California by way of Arkansas and Milwaukee. Roiled by waves of excitement and insecurity, Ruth felt like a country bumpkin entering this fabled artists' colony.

At the station, she spotted a familiar face, Elizabeth Schmitt, who drove her to campus past forests lush with fern and tulip magnolia, flanked by blue mountains. Just as Elaine's letter had described, nature offered an open-air annex to the classroom and studio, where Ruth would gather leaves and flowers, twigs and bark for art projects. Approaching the Lake Eden campus, she saw spare buildings, grounds, and roads tended by work crews of faculty and students. The man clearing brush might deliver tomorrow's lecture; the young woman driving trash to the dump might be a Paris-schooled painter. Framing the entrance were spare white boards arranged by Josef Albers himself.

Ruth had arrived in utopia. Black Mountain College was a new species of higher education: a liberal arts college that integrated the arts into every discipline. It encouraged experimentation over standard measures of success like regular exams, accreditation, and degree programs. Above all, students learned from working artists—a principle that would shape Ruth's practice and life.

Black Mountain was founded in 1933 by two charismatic academic rebels: classics professor John Andrew Rice and physics instructor Theodore Dreier. The big bang that led to Black Mountain's formation was Rice's dismissal from Rollins College in Florida due to a series of faculty disputes over everything from the length of the academic day to the ethics of modern love and obscenity in art. The aftermath sparked the resignation of Dreier, an idealist from a wealthy family. Together with a handful of like-minded innovators, they found their site: the old, white-columned Blue Ridge Assembly of the Protestant Church near Black Mountain.

The school welcomed free-thinking artists and intellectuals, many fleeing Fascist Europe and drawn by an offer of artistic freedom, room and board, plus modest spending cash. The founders and faculty worked to make art the central core—and not a peripheral frill—of a liberal arts education.

Black Mountain burned brightest in the years just following World War II. Chronically poor and consumed by chaos, it would flame out by 1957. But in the autumn of 1946, the college was just reaching its halcyon moment of creative exploration and egalitarianism. The goal was to prepare students for a life devoted to art and communal responsibility, not producing a commodity or making a fortune.

Black Mountain was unaccredited. Faculty gave no regular tests and assigned letter grades only to establish transfer credits. Among Josef Albers's many aphorisms and oracular sayings was "Art knows nothing of graduation." Also missing from campus culture was football, although an annual students versus faculty scrimmage took place, mainly to poke fun at college gridiron madness elsewhere.

Students were given breathtaking freedom to experiment and create in their studios, and to make their voices heard on school issues and policy. There was no artificial separation between faculty and students in their lives outside class. They worked together, dined together, and held Saturday evening dances and concerts in each other's company. They shared their ideas endlessly, sometimes exhaustingly. Airing their opinions, they asked Ruth's opinions too. No one had ever done that before. Freedom reigned and raged. "The magnet of Black Mountain was not luxurious living, but luxurious minds," one student put it. Everyone was assigned chores and shared sleeping quarters, but all had their own private study, an 8-by-8-foot cubicle in which to work. Ruth had never experienced such dizzying liberty, and she attacked her studio work and her farm chores with equal fervor.

That summer of 1946, when Ruth put down her suitcase in a long, narrow dormitory with beds for eight young women, she saw the student body included students of color. One of her first roommates was a Spelman College graduate named Mary Parks. This stunning Georgian, who resembled the actress Dorothy Dandridge, took to Ruth right away. Reared gently never to wear slacks, Parks had just bought her first pair of "dungarees" after learning that jeans and sandals were art school staples. At Saturday soirées, Ruth soon saw that young women danced in floor-length frocks, sewn from dyed flour sacks. Perhaps a farm girl could feel at ease here after all.

Then came a letdown: Ruth's meeting with weaver Anni Albers didn't go as expected. When Ruth tried to enroll in her class, the earnest, soulful-eyed Albers said she couldn't possibly teach her to weave in just six weeks. Ruth would have to rethink her summer. At the weaver's urging, she signed up for Color and Design with Albers's husband, the painter Josef Albers. Amid Nazi pressure closing the Bauhaus and their mounting persecution of Jews, Albers fled Germany with Anni, who was of Jewish descent. He arrived in 1933, speaking little English, delivering his lectures in a distinctive Deutsch-flavored dialect, and punctuating sentences with "Ja?" His mission, he said, was "to open the eyes."

Josef Albers's first impression of Ruth during the Summer Institute was decidedly mixed. In a note to the Registrar's Office on August 16, 1946, he wrote: "A very good soul. Talented but very unorderly. Told me that she decided to help her father on his farm he rented recently."

Ruth didn't make a fetish of tidiness. But Albers, whose studio was likened by some to "a monk's cell in austerity," refused to make his usual site visit to her studio until she got it organized. In her notebook, she would pencil notes in block capitals—"CLEAN IMMEDIATELY"—and then, as directed, send a messenger to Albers as soon as the studio was spruced up and ready for his inspection.

Once Albers's order was established in Ruth's studio, their creative chemistry grew warmer. Albers brought Bauhaus values of functionality and beauty to Black Mountain. He exhibited humility toward materials and never threw anything away. In Germany, he had crafted stunning stained glass windows from green bottle shards and scrap metal, achieving an alchemy of craft and economy of means that Ruth admired.

Albers didn't worship free expression. His constant refrain was that his students should pursue free expression on their own time; in his class, they were still students, not artists. Students who had trained in Paris or mounted shows of their art were crestfallen. Resentment simmered over his stern rule, especially among the budding abstract expressionists. But his core values—learning to see things anew, developing technique through eye-hand coordination, working with everyday objects—all resonated with Ruth.

Impatient with trends, Albers also mocked cults of personality in art as: "Picasso-itis," "Klee-tomania," and "Matisse-somnia." He would scorn the coming wave of abstract expressionism as self-indulgent.

Albers's classes didn't feature conventional lectures. Rather, he presented a design problem for students to solve back in their studios. The next day they would bring their projects to class, spread them on the floor, and receive Albers's comments along with those of their fellow students. In that way, they got a range of views, from their peers as well as their professor.

Design problems posed by Albers included balancing figure and background, giving equal attention to the form in positive space and the empty or negative space that

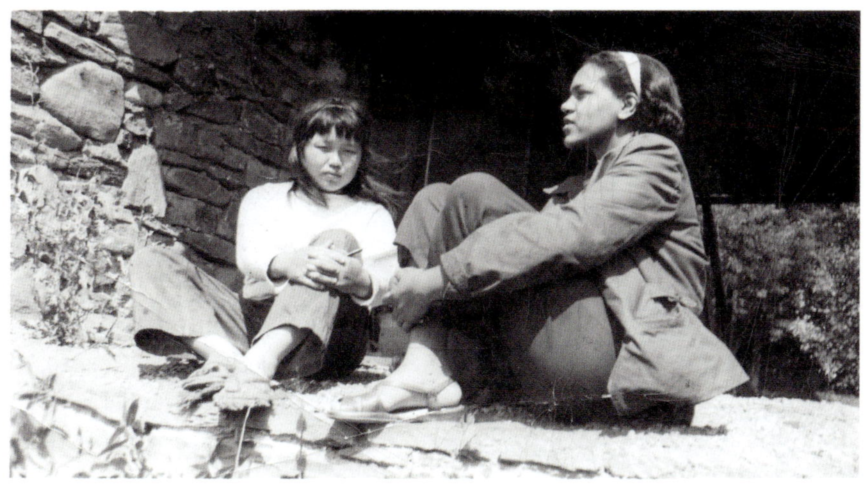

Ruth and fellow student Ora Williams at Black Mountain College, summer 1946. Photograph by Mary Parks Washington.

surrounds and defines it. He also would assign drawings of curved planes or intersecting lines, asking the students to show which one is on top and "indicate the air between by making air, not by touching." Writing one's name backward in the air was assigned to sharpen the coordination of eye, hand, and brain. Exercises in mirror writing and mirror drawing flowed from that. Students also were challenged to draw a Coca-Cola or cigarette logo from memory. While some bristled, Ruth was entranced:

> *I signed up for Josef Albers Basic Design and color classes and another world opened up for me. I also studied drawing and painting. Our subject matter varied. On rainy days, we painted umbrellas and rain boots. When the first daffodils popped open, Albers came in with a huge bouquet of yellow daffodils, when a later student drove up in his jeep, we would have a lesson in concave, convex ellipses using the hub caps and wheels. His most frequent statement in class was, "Draw what you see, not what you know." We drew a terracotta flower pot over and over again as a basic form. There were no advanced courses at BMC.*

Albers's mission to open the eyes included explorations of materials ranging from leaves to trash in exercises called "matière studies." One of Albers's signature lessons, matière studies asked students to focus on the visual qualities of a material that could look like something else—a trompe l'oeil to trick or, as he said in his accented English, "schwindle" the eye.

Paper could be pricked with a needle to look like terry cloth or crinkled to resemble leather. A layer of green mold could masquerade as velvet. Students raided the barnyard and butcher shop for materials.

Ruth observed that the texture of sun-dried cow manure resembled Ry-Krisp. Elaine Schmitt gamely fetched a glistening pile of cow intestines for her study. Mary Parks beat soapsuds into a white froth identical to egg whites. Albers, making rounds in class with his ruler in hand, stung her by saying that she didn't look at it correctly. Schmitt wrote home that friends celebrated her birthday with a faux feast in which a stone posed as meat loaf, and crowned her as the class's "matière momma." But not all were so enthralled. Dissident students once turned Albers's lesson on its head, submitting, as mock cow dung, the real thing. Very good, Albers said, until he got close and sniffed it, discovering he was the one who got "schwindled."

Ruth liked Albers's approach to drawing, especially his appreciation for positive and negative space. It invoked the principle of yin and yang from Taoist philosophy, which respects the balance of equal and opposite forces: male and female, light and shadow, day and night, life and death—each containing the seed of the other. Where others chafed, Ruth diligently absorbed lessons and performed exercises refining the coordination of brain, eye, and hand—recalling the discipline of her childhood calligraphy classes in Japanese school. She approached Albers's classes with her eyes open, her brain awake, and her hands nimble. She filled pages with wavy lines called "meanders," practiced lettering, and folded and unfolded paper, feeling the texture of the page to find the pulse of paper. Albers's habit of never throwing anything away deeply satisfied her sense of the frugal. His sayings resonated in her mind for life:

"Let the material express itself."

"Don't bring your ego with you."

"Heartbeat of paper."

Albers's views on the relativity and interaction of colors were fresh and daring—he argued that colors changed when placed side by side, like people who change in relation to each other. He respected the eloquence of a line and how it defines itself and the negative space around it. His focus on figure-ground relationships recognized the principle that the empty space in a design is as important a design element as the form or figure that is drawn or painted. His teachings recalled the precision of

Ruth's old sensei, who assigned endless practice in picking up and putting down the brush. In life drawing class, students drew a nude model without looking at the paper, directed to feel the flesh with their pencil. Albers's devotion to developing motor memory made sense to Ruth.

Albers engaged Ruth with his ideas about the relativity of color, and the importance of both positive and negative space in a design. As Ruth would later recollect in an interview:

> *He was primarily interested in color and relativity of color . . . to show color is not fixed; its relative to what's next to it. A color will change with its neighbor. And he always talked about the same thing—that people change, depending on who their neighbors are . . .*
>
> *The other thing was that he related Taoism and the oriental philosophy very much with black and white, white and black. And showing that even black will change . . .*
>
> *One of the problems that he gave in school, was never to see anything in isolation; that you can define space and you can define an object by defining the space around it.*

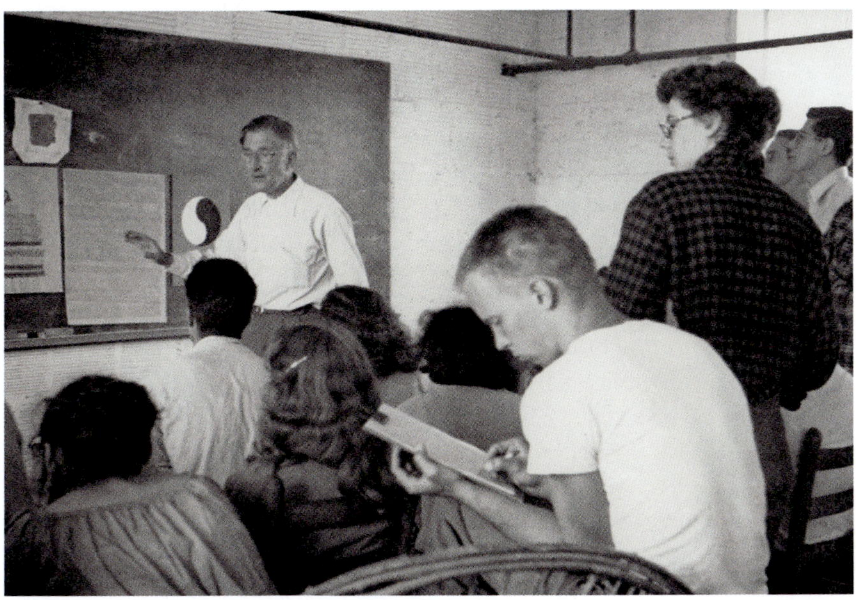

Josef Albers teaching. Photograph by Hazel Larsen Archer.

She welcomed Albers's discipline. Airing her feelings was alien to her upbringing and culture, so, she said, "I was a very obedient student."

Not so with all Black Mountaineers. Some students, who came to develop their style, didn't want to repeat basic color and design exercises. One who resisted Albers's Teutonic rule was the young Robert Rauschenberg. A Navy veteran who had studied at Paris's Académie Julian, Rauschenberg accompanied his friend Susan Weil to Black Mountain on the G.I. Bill. Frustrated by the rigors of design class, Rauschenberg found Albers a "beautiful teacher" and "an impossible person." He would discover a more congenial milieu in the New York School, an informal group of abstract artists, poets, dancers, and musicians working in mid-century Manhattan.

"Discipline!" Albers would say. "Who likes not discipline, let him leave soddenly!" His critiques could be withering: "Don't be proud of your work of 12 hours; I wait for your work of 12 weeks." Ruth wrote it all down in her notebook, along with other Albers aphorisms:

> *Art is never wrong.*
> *The purpose of art is to surprize!*

His rare words of praise—delivered in German—included a murmur of "*Schön, schön*" (beautiful) or an exclamation of "*Donnerwetter!*" (thunderstorm), an idiomatic expression of surprise.

Albers taught three-hour classes, from nine to noon, twice a week. All students brought their solutions to design problems, submitting to his appraisal. It was a case of "show me what you've got, or else." Those without work to show shouldn't come to class. Assignments carried consequences; no one could hide or bluff. Students spread their work on the floor. With quickening pulse, they awaited the element of theater that attended Albers's arrival in class, immaculate in his white jacket, a cigarette jutting from his lip, a lock of steely hair over his blue eyes. They braced for his critique with mingled reverence and intimidation.

In life drawing class, Albers extolled the roundness of the female form, and the ripe curve of the hip or folds of the belly of a prone model, explaining the anatomical perspective that he wanted his students to see and feel through their pencils. Ruth, in an interview decades later, recalled his public grasping of models:

> *When he taught drawing, he wanted you to look at the figure. He didn't care*
> *whether you did long, willowy figures. You know, he wanted you to see that one form*

was in front of the other if the model was lying. He'd want you to see the foreshortening. He would always talk about the grapefruit. He'd grab a breast or buttock of a student and say, "Mggrmh" or "ripe grapefruit," and he wiggled it a little bit. Today, he would never get away with it, I don't think. [LAUGHTER] But he made you think that your pencil was on the skin, on the flesh of the student, of the model. He'd say, "Now you're going to go over that flesh" and you'd try to feel that. But I didn't feel it because I was too young to understand what he was talking about.

In that interview given to historian Mary Emma Harris in the 1970s, Ruth made light of her professor's conduct in an era when students' reactions were circumscribed by prevailing attitudes of the 1940s. It was more than half a century before the #MeToo movement emboldened young women to call out male authority figures for unwanted physical contact at school or work.

Ruth's debut into Black Mountain society was reserved and even, in her own words, "antisocial." She worked constantly, and was at ease in the company of other workers. As a young woman who had toiled as a domestic and saw herself as a person of color in the South, Ruth at least initially avoided the dining room and chose to eat in the kitchen with the cooks. Heady conversations over dinner could be intimidating. Mary Parks said it was the only time she ever wished she smoked. The gesture of lighting a cigarette could fill the awkward pauses.

Known equally on campus for her art and her elbow grease, Ruth had little time for dalliance amid the schedule of her work details. Her chores included milking cows and trucking milk from the dairy to the college in a converted weapons carrier. She was one of only a handful who knew how to drive the farm tractor. She churned milk to make sweet butter and buttermilk, luxuries that the European faculty craved. She made the bed for painters Willem and Elaine de Kooning. She also swept floors and worked in the college laundry. Her labor infused her art with new ideas: Ruth turned the BMC laundry stamp into a graphic design for a class project that later became a textile print for mattress ticking. She volunteered as the school barber, using skills she picked up from her parents' homemade haircuts on the farm. Her service was free, though she asked for a ten-cent donation toward school fundraising, with discounts for needy cases.

Another student philanthropy effort she aided was Mush Day, when, once a week, students ate meals of gruel and potato soup to save money for donation to European postwar relief. Ruth was known for making piquant sweet and sour sauce to spice up the plain fare.

Up and out by dawn, Ruth kept farmer's hours and maintained a Zen-like focus on her work. "She would get out there and break the ground for a garden . . . the heavy work," Mary Parks recalled. "My job was making peanut butter and jelly sandwiches and punch." Her early rising prompted Albers to request that she knock on his door at first light. He wanted to go outside in time to photograph the morning mist that veiled the mountains in progressively lighter shades of blue.

Heavy duties were nothing new to the farm girl from Norwalk. On the Asawa farm, her work included planting, harvesting, crating vegetables for market, housework, cooking, and stoking the wood fire to heat water in the *ofuro*. At Black Mountain, she found equally hard work—sometimes involving staying up all night to fix a furnace until the handyman arrived. It could also be dangerous. One day Ruth and others climbed a ladder to explore the inside of a silo just as stores of corn were being poured in. They narrowly escaped burial by an avalanche of corn.

It is a wonder she had energy for art. Ruth began a habit of napping after dinner and then pulling all-night creative sessions in her studio.

Albers would judge one secret of Black Mountain's success to be its work program. Toiling side by side put men and women on a more equal footing and gave them a sense of self-sufficiency for life, he said. Years later, after leaving North Carolina to head Yale's design program, Albers explained the virtues of the Black Mountain system in his own special idiom: "So the girls and the boys, they knew each other sweating. And not like here, when you come Saturday evenings together with new makeup only. Ja?"

With nascent gender equality came a tentative embrace of minority students and artists. As a progressive college in the South, where segregation was the rule, Black Mountain began early steps to integrate in the spring of 1944, admitting a single female black student to its summer music institute. The move split in half a faculty that sought the higher ground, but feared flouting the customs of the community. (Precedents for integration were rare and chilling: An Alabama seminary that had previously added black faculty had burned to the ground.)

But Black Mountain students pushed for more inclusion, voting two-to-one in favor of expanding black admissions to the regular 1944 fall term. By the time Ruth arrived in the summer of 1946, she saw both African and Asian Americans on campus, including fellow Japanese American student Isaac Nakata, a native of Hawaii, and sculptor Leo Amino, who was born in Japan. Black painter Jacob Lawrence came as a guest artist with his wife, Gwendolyn Knight. African American students like Mary Parks were safe within the island of campus. But the atmosphere changed when they ventured into town, where they still witnessed reminders of the segregated South in white and colored water fountains. That didn't stop Ruth, after she turned twenty-one, from riding into town in a friend's rumble seat to have a beer at Peek's Tavern.

On campus, students and faculty of different ethnicities lived together more or less peaceably. However, Parks recalled that one father, on learning his daughter shared a dorm with a black student, summoned her home. "She was the sweetest girl," sighed Parks.

Black students brought their histories of discrimination; Japanese American students, their experience of exclusion and incarceration. Parks remembered a Japanese American classmate sitting by the lake and telling her about the camps. It was the first she'd heard of them.

Ruth's first six weeks at Black Mountain flew by. When autumn came and her scholarship money was gone, the administration searched for ways to keep the committed young artist at school. They found funds and awarded her a scholarship from an anonymous benefactor. She wondered about the identity of her sponsors. One was later revealed to be her classmate Lorna Blaine Halper, who had received money after her brother was killed in World War II. His sacrifice and her gift helped keep Ruth in art school.

Ruth was quietly gaining a reputation among faculty and fellow students as a camp survivor, a serious artist, and an Albers protégé. Painter Susan Weil, fresh from the Académie Julian in Paris, recalled:

> *Ruth was a beautiful, quiet person. The rest of us were students, but she was an artist. The school was small so you knew everyone. Two of my friends were Americans of Japanese descent who were put in camp . . . You can't believe it. She certainly told us. But we didn't talk about it. We were into the moment. She didn't seem bitter. . . . She had Albers's approval and that was unique. He didn't think anybody was very good except for Ruth. He'd say, don't take yourself seriously—you're not artists. (But) I think he was respectful of her.*

Weil's opinion counted. After studying with Albers—and chafing under his tutelage—she left Black Mountain with Rauschenberg, heading north for the New York School, where they married and had a son. She was still painting and exhibiting well into her ninth decade. Weil spotted Ruth early as a powerful artist with a unique creative vocabulary.

The autumn of 1946 brought a change for Ruth when Josef and Anni Albers left for a sabbatical in New Mexico and Mexico, which were hubs of creative energy for artists from Georgia O'Keeffe to Diego Rivera. In their absence, Ruth studied drawing with Ilya Bolotowsky, Josef Albers's successor, whose classes were more tolerant of self-expression, if less rigorous and challenging in Ruth's eyes.

By the summer of 1947, Ruth herself was longing to return to Mexico for a fresh infusion of color and inspiration. Mexico was a hotbed of painting, ceramics, weaving, decorative arts, and indigenous culture. This time, though, her trip would be coupled with a chance to give back to her Quaker benefactors through public service. She saw a notice from the American Friends Service Committee posted on the bulletin board; they were asking for volunteers to teach art and English to rural and small town families as part of a public health program in Mexico. Ruth had never forgotten the Quakers' support for Japanese Americans during the war, nor their generosity in arranging scholarship funds for her to attend Milwaukee State Teachers College. "I thought this would be my opportunity to repay these good people," she reflected.

Ruth journeyed by Greyhound bus, this time with another older sister, Chiyo, who helped to pay for their travel. They met up with Josef and Anni Albers. Together, the older couple and the Asawa sisters drove to the city of Chapingo, where Diego Rivera's paintings adorned the university chapel. Ruth agreed with her teacher, "The murals are truly beautiful."

The bold saturated colors of Mexico were like nowhere else for Ruth. She remembered how Albers would stop her and point at the vivid hues of a wall and say, "See, see, color is the most relative medium."

At lunch, Ruth remembered, Anni was constantly wiping her hands with alcohol, while Josef savored the local mangoes. Ruth wrote, "He went into ecstasy while eating a whole one."

Ruth and Chiyo visited the Mexico City neighborhood Coyoacán, site of the famous Casa Azul. This brilliant royal-blue house, with its accents of red and green, was where painters Frida Kahlo and Diego Rivera lived during part of their turbulent marriage. The sisters watched Rivera at work and conversed with him. Years later, Chiyo revealed that Rivera had complimented Ruth as having "a very interesting face." In her self-effacing way, Ruth dismissed Rivera's gambit: "Well, it's just nonsense . . ."

The journey offered artistic epiphanies for both Josef Albers and Ruth. Albers gathered inspiration from vibrantly colored adobe houses for his *Casa* series, seen as a precursor of the signature color studies he called *Homage to the Square*.

Ruth's discovery came during her service project in the small town of Toluca. She joined a team of girls from the United States who taught art classes. She made a friend, Janet Barber, who teased Ruth at siesta time, covering her with a serape and calling her Sleepito. A photo of the two girls shows them seated before a sunny adobe wall enveloped in their serapes.

The excited children were so eager for crafts instruction, and their schoolteacher was so grateful to the volunteers that, in exchange, he taught them a local method of weaving baskets used by locals for carrying eggs and produce to market. Intrigued, Ruth learned their technique for looping the wire—like knitting without needles or crocheting without a hook. The resulting mesh could be shaped into rounded vessels. Later, she would push this basic technique further and turn it from making utilitarian baskets to creating free-form abstract art constructs—wire mesh spheres, ovals, and teardrops—linking them into long garlands woven from a single wire. Mexico's gift to

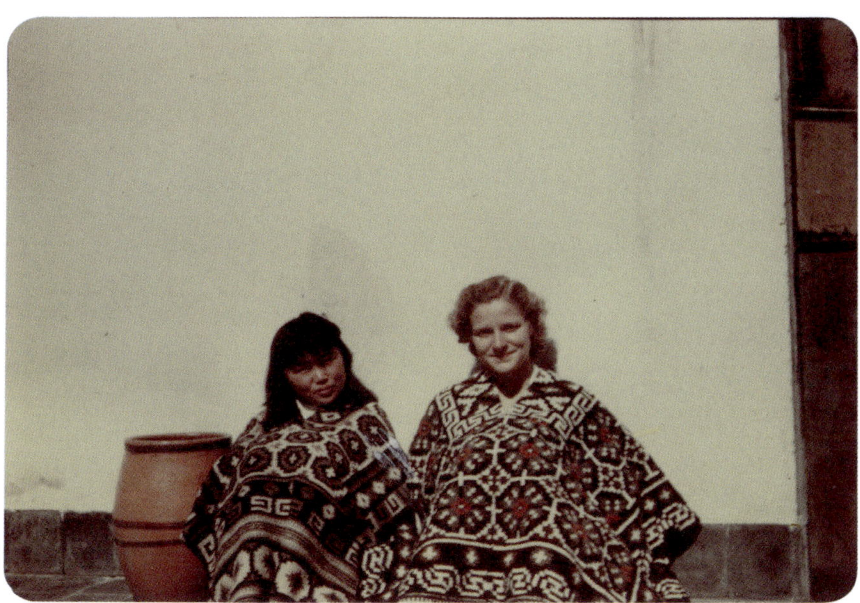

Ruth and Janet Barber in Toluca, Mexico, where she would learn how to loop wire baskets, 1947

Ruth was this exposure to basket weaving, which enabled her to use wire to draw in three-dimensional space. Her alchemy was to take this material, which also had been used by the military to build camp fences, and transform it into art.

Whether Ruth consciously intended a philosophical statement in her sculpture is hard to say. While she would become a feisty advocate for arts education, she avoided explicitly political speeches most of her life. But the swords-to-plowshares metamorphosis of wire turned into art can't be ignored. Wire studded with barbs surrounded her teenage years. Later she would discover wire could be simple and useful, or flared and voluptuous, reflecting light or casting shadows, hanging in stillness or turning on a breeze. As a twenty-one-year-old in Toluca, she was still exploring the nature of material, pushing its limits as Albers taught her to do.

"Wire can play," she wrote in her Black Mountain notebook.

With this new technique, Ruth returned to Black Mountain in the fall of 1947. She now began dividing her time between her painting and her new focus on sculpting with wire. Even her drawing instructor, Ilya Bolotowsky, who previously praised Ruth's elegance of line and excellent draftsmanship, noticed the change in her focus. On her course card, he noted she seemed interested less in drawing than in working with wire. As for Ruth, the summer of Mexican art infused her art school practice with fresh energy, as she would later write:

> *I returned filled with ideas and excitement because Albers would be back and we would begin working on color. The colors of Mexico were floating in my head, the strange combinations & mixes that I had never experienced . . . Here we have to imagine it.*

Armed with the memory of Mexico's palette and her new wire technique, Ruth was primed to explore. She began experimenting with looping wire, shaping it into small vessels, and even mounted a small exhibition of her baskets at Black Mountain College in 1948. While she continued her study of painting, it was wire that was to become her most original medium—and the one that would alter the course of her creative life.

Another, equally life-changing encounter awaited her. She was about to meet someone who would offer a most unlikely partnership. For while she was exploring Mexico, a trio of new architecture students was leaving Georgia Tech to continue their studies at Black Mountain College.

William Albert Lanier was the son of lawyer and district attorney Weylud Hudson Lanier and his wife, Bernice Bird Lanier, of Metter, Georgia. The family sprang from Southern gentry that traced their ancestry back to French Huguenots and English court musicians. After reaching America in 1670, the family served with patriots: Albert's third great-grandfather, Louis Lanier, fought in the Revolutionary War and received a sword from George Washington. By the Civil War, the Laniers had migrated to the South. Albert's paternal grandmother recalled salvaging kernels of corn that shook

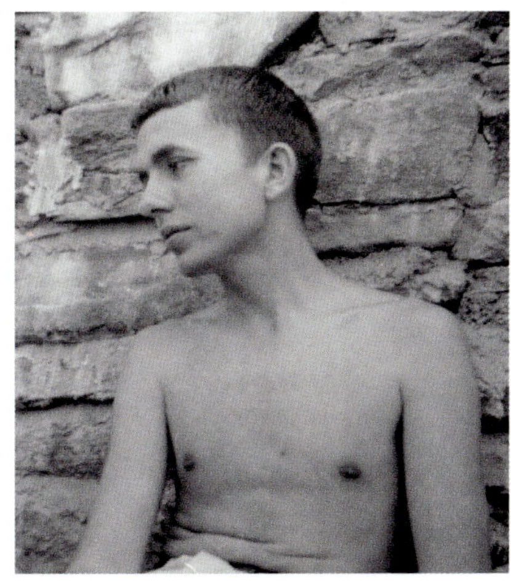

Albert Lanier at Black Mountain College, ca. 1948

from the wagons of Union General Sherman's troops as they ransacked supplies on their march through Georgia. The poet Sidney Lanier was a cousin of Albert's. They were proud of their blood and origins.

Precocious and restless, Albert entered Georgia Tech at age sixteen and left college to enlist in the Navy at eighteen. Upon his discharge in 1946, he returned to the rigorous Georgia Tech architecture department, open twenty-four hours a day, where he often worked straight through the weekends. But his postwar college experience at Georgia Tech lacked the excitement and hands-on creative opportunity he craved.

"It didn't work nearly as well for me as it had worked before going into the Navy," he said. "I spent another year there but discovered in the architectural library a catalog of Black Mountain College." Albert and several friends took a weekend to visit "and decided on the spot we were all going to leave Georgia Tech and go to Black Mountain College . . . I did do that in the fall of '47."

After the regimentation of the Navy and the rigor of Georgia Tech, Black Mountain offered a modern, experimental approach to architecture, with exposure to cutting-edge art and ideas. It suited Albert's straightforward ambition "to build beautiful buildings."

At Black Mountain, he and his fellow students, undaunted by a then-sparse faculty, invented their own program: to design and build a spare, 400-square-foot house fabricated from native wood and stone, along with industrial materials like surplus corrugated metal. This was long before it was fashionable to blend natural and industrial materials in residential construction. They christened their compact creation "Minimum House." Albert would hew to his aesthetic of the simple and functional over the contrived and ornamental for his entire career.

Slender and blue-eyed, Albert was a year younger than Ruth but crackling with confidence and wry humor. He was unattached and romantically inexperienced. Studious Ruth, meanwhile, worked in her studio and, during rare hours off, indulged her passion for the outdoors by hiking with math professor Max Dehn to pick blueberries and gather leaves for Albers's design class studies.

On the Black Mountain campus, wooded pathways carpeted with ferns and moss, ablaze with azaleas and rhododendrons, and fragrant with pink mountain laurel, invited exploration of all kinds. A pair of voluptuous mountain peaks near the campus were nicknamed Mae West. The campus, set on Lake Eden, had its own Garden of Eden, a lush spot that students and teachers could reach by a hiking trail. The area's rural beauty offered a natural extension of the classroom, a break from studies for hiking and romantic encounters. And on one walk in the Garden of Eden, Ruth ran into the new architectural student.

Neither Ruth nor Albert had been, in his words, "much of a dater." He was instantly taken with this quiet young woman on the path before him. The outdoor work, hikes, and lean living of Black Mountain had bronzed and slimmed her, exposing high cheekbones beneath her obsidian fringe of bangs.

"I thought I'd never seen anything as exotic looking as this girl," he later admitted.

It wasn't long before Albert, in a letter from college dated April 22, 1947, put his parents on notice that a new person had entered his life. Beneath two paragraphs of routine news, including thanks for a birthday gift of ten dollars, he buried his big revelation:

> *Sunday, Ruth Asawa, a Japanese girl who knows wild flowers here as well as you know those in your garden, Mother, took me to the water falls. It is a magnificent two hour climb and the flowers were simply unbelievable. The slope was purple with rank delphinium and there were trilliums, white and magenta, jacks-in-the-pulpit, purple and giant white violets, and solid areas of lavender iris under rock ledges near the water. It was the most fabulous place I ever saw. . . .*

The language of wildflowers sent a subliminal message to the elder Laniers that the young woman would become more than a hiking companion.

For Ruth, their chemistry had a practical side. However handsome, the fair-skinned Georgia boy would also help her with her math homework. In turn, she would offer aesthetic advice on his architecture projects.

After working on her own art in the studio, Ruth would visit the Minimum House building site in the late afternoons. She helped Albert finish the oak for the structure and cast a critical eye over his stonework. If a rock seemed out of place, she would quietly say that it looked wrong. Then she would insist he take the wall apart and rebuild it. Her fierce beauty, gravitas, and work ethic intensified his attraction to her.

The two became inseparable. Ruth took mealtime refuge with the cooks in the kitchen less and less often. She was photographed eating with Albert in the dining room. Friends watched their story unfold.

"He thought she was the most beautiful thing. He said, 'Mama, I met a girl!'" recalled Mary Parks. "He was bossy, but she didn't pay any attention."

Albert could be acerbic. Warren "Pete" Jennerjahn, Elizabeth Schmitt's future husband, found him abrasive. Once smitten, Albert grew a little jealous of Ruth's friends, lobbing sarcastic comments at Jennerjahn. Ruth laughed quietly at his antics and admired his spare design style. Her quiet focus fascinated him; his Southern yarns tickled her. Somehow, it worked.

Ruth sampled other courses from the curriculum. She took Geometry for Artists with mathematician Max Dehn. He also taught philosophy and, like Albers, invoked Lao Tzu—the ancient Chinese philosopher and founder of Taoism, or "teaching of the way," based upon compassion, frugality, and humility. She threw herself into modern dance classes with Merce Cunningham, her movements captured in a series of photographs by Elaine Schmitt's sister Elizabeth. She spent time with music teacher Johanna Jalowetz, a beloved figure on campus known as "Mrs. Jalo," and the widow of the Viennese conductor Heinrich Jalowetz. Ruth adored singing choral music by Johann Sebastian Bach at Black Mountain but dodged Mrs. Jalo's demure Saturday teas, which included listening to the Metropolitan Opera on the radio.

Cross-fertilization of the arts let painters dance, sculptors sing, and poets make pottery. Ruth and Rauschenberg performed in an uninhibited student production of Stravinsky's *The Rite of Spring*, which called for them to run down a hill in primitive costumes bearing torches. Seeing Rauschenberg dance in a loincloth, Ruth relished the playful side of her fellow artists.

Ruth's strength and confidence grew as she observed models of independent female artists at work: weaver Anni Albers, poet Mary Caroline Richards, musician Charlotte Schlesinger, and more. She had seen the powerful example of her mother, who worked tirelessly and sacrificed much to help her husband, harvest crops, and rear her children. Here were independent women who lived in the pursuit of a creative life.

The summer of 1948 was a golden season for Black Mountain students, and especially for Ruth and Albert. The futurist engineer Buckminster Fuller cut a curious figure, making his entrance on campus in a yellow Studebaker towing a silver aluminum trailer. Inside was a magician's toolkit of odd materials, including vast quantities of colored Venetian blinds and bolts, with which he planned to build a 44-foot-wide hemisphere. He forecast that the dome, when precisely bolted to his specifications, would rise on its own.

Fuller beguiled students, conjuring a vision for the future where less is more, energy is independent of fossil fuels, home design is "synergetic," and all humanity can live happily on "Spaceship Earth." Expecting the stocky, crew-cut Fuller to be "stuffy," painter Elaine de Kooning was ready to dismiss him until her husband, the painter Willem, urged that she wait to hear him speak. Then she found herself falling under his spell:

> *Bucky then whirled off into his talk, using bobby pins, clothes pins, all sorts of units from the five-and-ten-cent store to make geometric, mobile constructions, collapsing an ingeniously fashioned icosahedron by twisting it and doubling and tripling the modules down to a tetrahedron . . . dazzling us with his complex theories of ecology, engineering, and technology. Then he began making diagrams on a blackboard. He drew a square, connecting two corners with a diagonal line. "Ah," he said affectionately, "here's our old friend the hypotenuse." That did it for me. . . .*
>
> *The shimmering pale blue expanse of Bucky's eyes—immensely magnified behind his thick glasses—had us all mesmerized. They were, to us, the eyes of a visionary, a saint, all-comprehending, all-forgiving. We loved him and we hung on his every word. In turn, Bucky was wonderfully responsive, free with his praise, totally absorbed in each of us as he directed his fabulous gaze from face to face.*

Albert, bare-chested and wearing shorts in the humid heat, joined Fuller's crew for the promised raising of the dome. A crowd huddled expectantly under umbrellas in a warm summer rain. But the dome refused to rise. The aluminum strips lay as limp as noodles on the ground—inspiring the moniker "the Supine Dome." Chipper in the face of failure, Fuller predicted the dome's next iteration would stand. "You succeed only when you stop failing," he said. Indeed, the early experiment led to his signature invention: the geodesic dome.

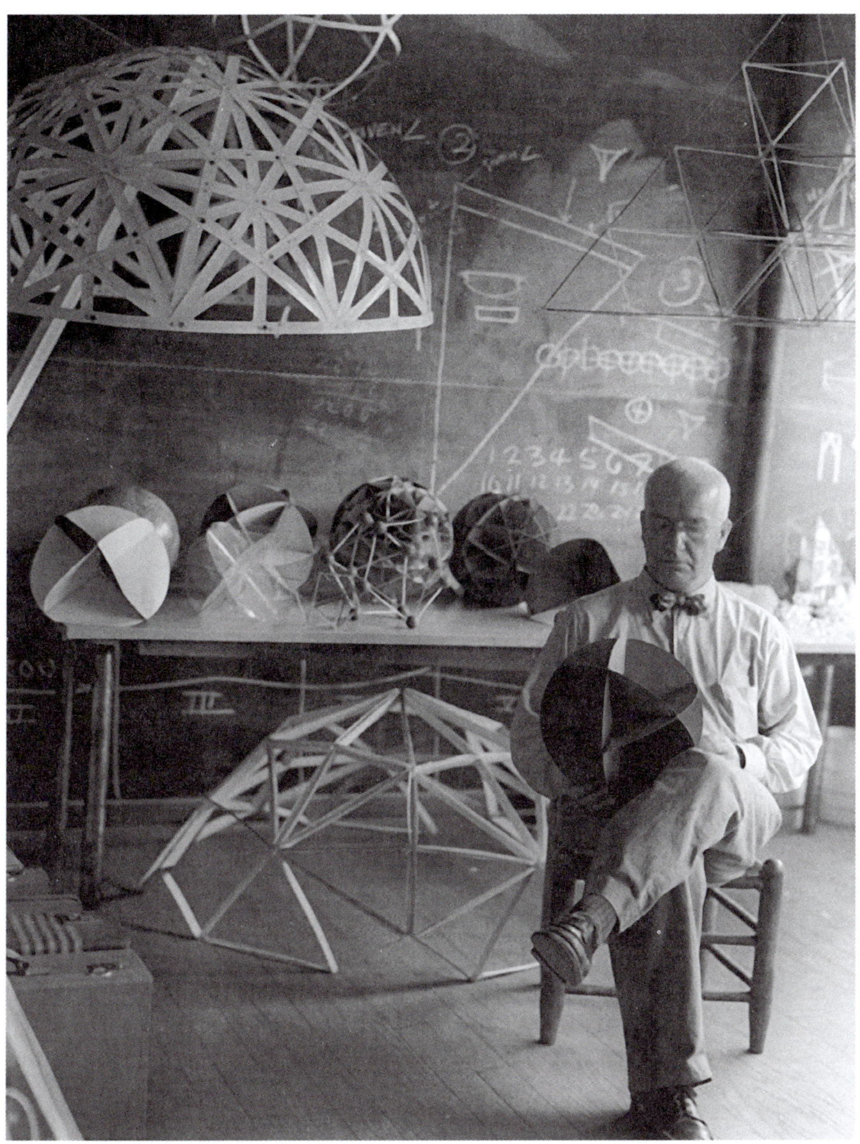

*Buckminster Fuller in the classroom, 1948. Photograph
by Hazel Larsen Archer.*

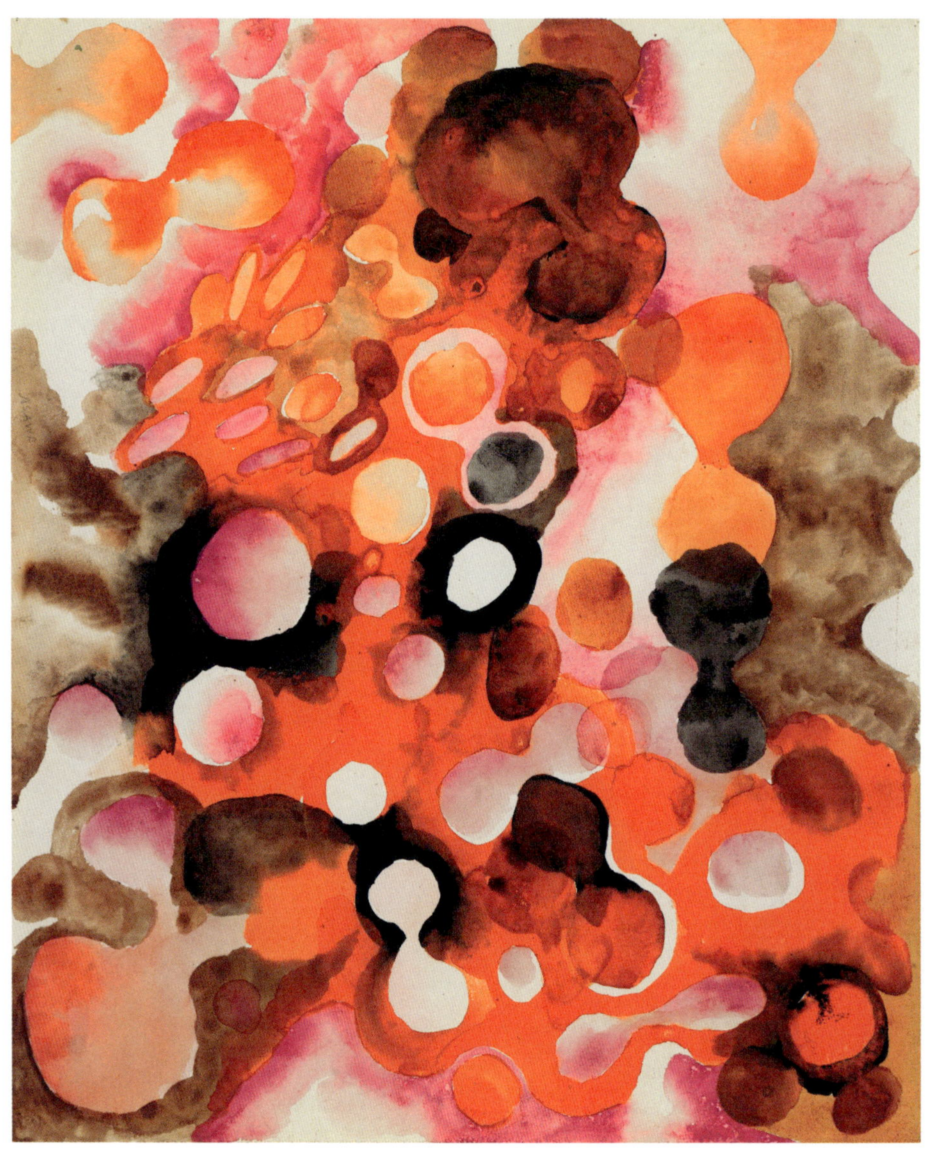

Untitled (BMC.107, Dancers), *ca. 1948–1949*
Watercolor on paper
19.75 x 16 in. (50.2 x 40.6 cm)

As school barber, Ruth gained a new client in Fuller, who showed her with his thumb and forefinger how he wanted his silver crew cut pared to one-quarter of an inch. She executed the trim to perfection. Fuller was so pleased, he made her a barber pole from red and yellow Venetian blind strips. Placed on the porch, Fuller's barber pole attracted more clients—and more dimes for the school's building fund.

Looking back at Fuller's lessons of the 1940s from a twenty-first century perspective, it's striking how many of his ideas we now take for granted: doing more with less, creating energy sources that lessen our dependence on fossil fuels, honoring the innate creativity of children. Ruth and her classmates inhabited a postwar world still raw from the violence and racial hatred of World War II. They lived in an economy of scarcity and were locked in a rigid class system. To the twenty-year-olds at Black Mountain College, Fuller looked stodgy and square with his silver thatch and bow tie. Yet he'd survived expulsion from Harvard, the death of his firstborn, recovery from alcoholism, and suicidal despair to offer ideas that were hopeful, radical, and bracing as a blast of oxygen.

When he pulled up to Black Mountain in the summer of 1948, he was greeted as a combination of a prophet and the Wizard of Oz. He put forth the audacious idea that Spaceship Earth held enough resources to nourish and support those who were its careful stewards. He believed houses should make maximum use of minimal materials—like the dome—and be planned from the inside out: function over form. He advocated holistic thinking and an educational system that produced broad-minded generalists, able to grasp the big picture of humanity's niche in the universe.

His elliptical flights of ideas—a blend of science, soul, and speculation—occasionally veered into the realms of the fanciful and unscientific, not to mention the politically incorrect. He would later suggest that female nudity kills the mystery that feeds male desire, and that homosexuality might be a humankind's biological response to overpopulation.

Ruth, of course, was free to pick and choose from Fuller's menu of ideas. Even if she didn't follow his leaps from physics to cosmology, or from Einstein to God, she loved his thoughts on preserving the planet and building an educational system that respects the innate genius in every child. She agreed with his belief that children learn best through direct experience, through the comprehensive integration of sensory stimuli. It was a principle she would put to work in later years, giving hands-on art workshops. He advocated creating an ambience where learning freely takes place and playfully advised her to give every kindergartener a PhD.

At Black Mountain, Fuller gamely joined students and faculty for an all-school production of Erik Satie's play, *The Ruse of Medusa,* in the role of the addled Baron Medusa. Surprisingly, the dazzling intellectual showman suffered paralyzing attacks of stage fright. Fuller overcame his fear through a series of goofy warm-up exercises that had players running around the stage. The student director in charge was one Arthur Penn, who would make his name directing *The Miracle Worker* and *Bonnie and Clyde.* Willem de Kooning designed the sets. John Cage provided piano accompaniment. Merce Cunningham danced. Ruth and Albert built props, including the baron's chair, which they fabricated from Venetian blinds coiled into curly-cues. Just as Satie had performed the original music on a "prepared piano" with paper between strings, Cage put pennies on strings to create new sounds like chimes, percussion, or an eerie music box.

Given the freedom to experiment, produce, and create, Ruth began to come into her own as an artist. In August 1948, the Addison Gallery in Andover, Massachusetts, mounted a show of student work from twenty-five of the country's top art schools, including Black Mountain. The Black Mountain work in the exhibition included a small oil on blotter paper painted by the twenty-two-year old Ruth, using a technique Albers had taught her to achieve a matte finish. Ruth's piece caught the eye of a reviewer from *Time*, who ranked her the most impressive of the "budding moderns": "An abstraction that looked like a diagram of ballet positions for a dancing telephone, by Black Mountain's Ruth Asawa, was the exhibit's high point in originality."

After that golden summer of 1948, Albert was torn between his desire to stay at Black Mountain to study with Fuller, and his hunger to get hands-on experience working in the building trades to prepare for his future practice of architecture. Impatient to launch his career, he decided to leave school and strike out on his own. He had customized a convertible 1929 Model A, with a top cobbled together from pipe and plastic clothes wire, and a radiator ornament made by sculptor Richard Lippold. He planned to drive west with friends to San Francisco in search of work. They had little money and no guarantee the jalopy would even make it to the West Coast.

But Albert Lanier left North Carolina with one certainty: He was in love with Ruth Asawa. As he drove, putting physical distance between them, their visions of the future began to merge around a shared understanding that, with or without the world's approval, they would follow the precepts of Albers and Fuller and make their lives in art—together.

CHAPTER 5

LOVE LETTERS

Albert's Model A jalopy was holding up and getting good gas mileage.

"It's the strangest looking car ever," he wrote to his parents in Georgia. "Children run out and wave and flock around us wherever we stop."

To avoid the heat, the young men slept during the day and drove at night. When they ran low on funds near the end of the trip, Albert resorted to selling his blood in Las Vegas. Tired from the procedure, he slept and awoke to find his traveling companions fresh from a gambling spree and sporting new shirts bought with his "blood money." They had barely enough for the bridge toll across San Francisco Bay. He'd laugh about it later.

By September, Albert moved in with his Black Mountain friends "Rags" Watkins and Peggy Tolk-Watkins. Peggy had drawn Albert to the City by the Bay with tales of a bohemian good life, where young artists could dine on a four-course Italian dinner with red wine for seventy-five cents. Reality didn't quite live up to the romance. Albert took work as a carpenter's apprentice for union wages.

Torn between staying at Black Mountain and helping her family resettle, Ruth took a short leave from art school in September and October of 1948 to lend a hand on their new farm near Los Angeles. The Asawas found temporary living space at the *gakuen*, the Japanese schoolhouse where Ruth had studied calligraphy in a long-ago childhood before the war. They occupied one room, partitioned with makeshift cardboard walls from a dozen other families who also resettled in the school after camp. Now twenty-two, Ruth pitched in to help her parents grow their new cash crop of asters and chrysanthemums, along with the staple produce of tomatoes, melons, beans, and cucumbers. How she longed to return to Black Mountain and her art. But as a daughter, she wrote Albert, her sense of filial duty left her "bound to the future plans of our home & farm. I cannot leave now."

Absence sharpened her feelings for him, but as she wrote to him on September 17, their pathway forward was still unclear:

> *I love you Albert, and wish I could say more definitely what I will do. . . . Will you come and visit us? . . . 6 of us sleep in a room . . . Father, Mother, brother, 3 daughters. . . .*
>
> *You have given me a great deal of courage and never will I forget it. . . .*

If I could promise you something it's that I'm all yours & part of all my thoughts is you, but when & where? I can't say yet.

Mother is quite shy about the house. She says we can't let you sleep in a sleeping bag, but if you care when you come, to hear 6 people snoring, you're welcome to our kitchen floor.

During their separation, Ruth and Albert would live through letters. Planning and dreaming, they pondered what it would mean to make a life devoted to art and each other. Agonizing over how to ease parental anguish over their interracial union, they wrote out their own long-distance love story. Each thought the other would destroy such an intimate dialogue. In the end, neither had the heart to do so. Their children would later make a convincing case to save their letters for history.

Laboring eighteen-hour days at farming, pickling, and canning, Ruth also tutored her sister Kimiko in English, to help her regain the fluency she had lost during the war, when she was in Japan. In a letter dated September 28, 1948, Ruth began introducing Albert to the family values he would encounter:

It is again so good to be with people who work thrice as hard as I do. . . .

Mama and I speak of marriage. She is gentle but firm in her beliefs . . . She wants me near but she will not hold me; She said today to "please study so that you won't have to be just a farm hand as I've been all my life;" and not to think of marriage too soon. I shall go as I've always gone, my own way, though it seems like the dutiful way, it is the way I prefer. . . .

We are crowded, but you have seen greater crowds than this; the family may not respond, but understand it is in their nature. They are not friendly, but kind-souled people. Do not worry. Hope you can eat our food. It's very different. We all eat with chopsticks and much rice.

Forgive me, I'm tired tonight, and hope for a sound sleep.

You've made me very happy and I celebrate by proxy this happiness with you.

The first weekend in October 1948, Albert appeared at the road to the Asawas' schoolhouse home, dressed formally in a dark suit. The reunion scene unfolded as if in a movie: Ruth running down the path to meet him, grasping his hands, and leading him up the wooden porch past the rickety player piano, which had somehow survived the war, and into the house for introductions.

"This is Albert."

Umakichi summoned enough English to make small talk, while Haru smiled.

Ruth made a lunch of soup, rice, and abalone, a shellfish prized in Japanese cuisine for its texture and tang of the sea. Kimiko and Janet watched him work on a mouthful of the muscular mollusk. He gulped it down in two minutes. Ruth swiftly cleared the table. Then, diverting attention from his struggle with the shellfish, Albert beamed his charm at Ruth's mother.

"Mrs. Asawa," he said, "you are so beautiful!"

Understanding little, Haru replied, smiling, "Yes."

Albert's introduction to the challenging dish was over, to everyone's relief. Ruth would later learn to make Southern fare like fried chicken and gravy, catering to Albert's palate—and thickening his narrow waistline.

Albert's brief overnight visit brought no easy storybook blessing of their union. But the Asawas, despite their reservations, had now met the young man vying for Ruth's hand. Albert, for his part, had a chance to witness the struggles of his beloved's family. This gave him an understanding of Ruth's deep sense of filial duty, which was crucial to loving and being loved by her. Bill, Kimiko, and Janet had a chance to meet the young Southerner who had won their sister's heart. Albert's deference and easygoing charm began to thaw her parents' reserve and kindle a nascent friendship with her siblings.

Once she had helped the Asawas resume planting, Ruth could heed the call of her mentors and her art, and make plans to complete her third year at Black Mountain. Money was as tight as ever. Albers didn't spare the superlatives in a September 18 letter recommending her for a Louis Comfort Tiffany Foundation scholarship:

> *Ruth Asawa is of an unusual artistic talent in painting as well as in design and in drawing. . . . You might have heard about the exhibition of art students' work at the Addison Gallery of Andover, Mass. I have seen three reports on that Exhibition in* Time *magazine, the* New York Times *and* Art News. *In all these comments Ruth Asawa's painting there is considered among the most outstanding . . .*

Tiffany turned her down. Albers assured her other funding could be arranged on her return. But Black Mountain still offered no degrees. So it would be a continued gamble.

Before returning to school, Ruth met with the editor of the Los Angeles–based magazine *Arts & Architecture*. Rather than promoting her own art, she talked up Albert's Minimum House at Black Mountain, sparking editor John Entenza's interest in a

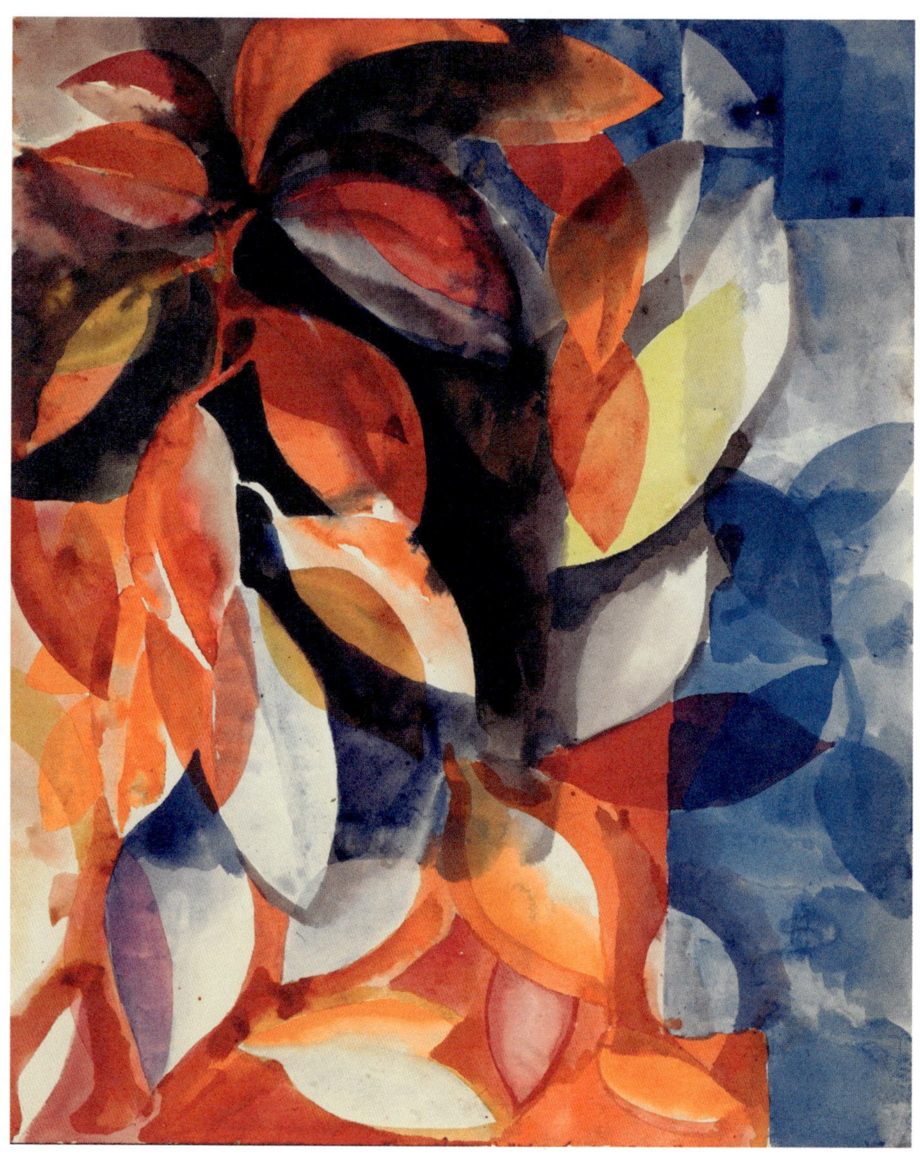

Untitled (BMC.68, Stem with Leaves), *ca. 1948–1949*
Watercolor on paper
19 3/4 x 16 in. (50.2 x 40.6 cm)

pictorial feature on the project. She arranged new photos of the house by her friend, photographer Hazel-Frieda Larsen. One of the Milwaukee group that preceded Ruth to Black Mountain, Larsen took soulful portraits, despite suffering from polio, their generation's most-feared epidemic, which had paralyzed the late president Roosevelt and left Larsen similarly encased in metal leg braces.

In mid-October, Ruth headed back across the country to Black Mountain, stopping on her way at two places that were dear to her mentors Albers and Fuller. In Taos, New Mexico, she took in the colors that had inspired Albers's palette—an ochre adobe, indigo sky, and pink Indian blanket.

"I passed as an Indian boy," Ruth wrote Albert in a card postmarked on October 18. The Indians asked her which tribe she belonged to: Apache, Navajo, or Cherokee? "They greeted me and it was thrilling."

Next, she stopped in Wichita to view Fuller's futuristic Dymaxion house, a 1,000-square-foot aluminum structure with moving walls and a profile like a spaceship that had touched down in a Kansas wheat field.

"It was like spreading the wings of a dragonfly to see what made it move," Ruth wrote to Albert upon her arrival back at the college on October 23. "I didn't understand it but such beauty unfolded."

On her first day back at Black Mountain, Ruth sought solitude in the places where she and Albert had fallen in love. Once back in her study, she put a pair of cacti on her windowsill, one lean and one rounded. It was, she wrote:

> *. . . like a portrait of us, looking towards the lake . . .*
> *Thinking of you really keeps me going. There's nothing like you ethereal and real. Being apart will maybe help us understand more. A lot we don't know together.*
> *I love the quiet so far. I must start painting to counteract all the brownness of the paintings around here.*
> *Memories are beautiful & controlled things. I haven't yet gone to your study.*
> *Moon is beautiful over the lake tonight. Part of it is already hidden modestly.*

Albert didn't hide from his parents his visit to the Asawa family. He frankly declared his admiration for their courage and industry in rebuilding their postwar lives, and his desire to design them a new home. He wasn't ready to tell his parents about his intentions toward Ruth—though they must have had a clue that this was a singular friendship. He shared his news first with his sister Laurie, who lived in Georgia with her husband, a prominent peach grower, and their two small girls.

Laurie wrote to her brother on November 1 that she was moved to tears by his confidence in her, but shaken by his plans. She praised Ruth as talented and sincere. But she warned him their parents would oppose a mixed marriage:

> *I was surprised beyond words when I realized that you are in love with Ruth. I had truthfully never thought of such a thing . . .*
>
> *When they disapprove of a marriage to Ruth it won't be hate as you put it. Neither will it be a lack of love. It will only be disapproval of your marrying into another race. Her people will probably feel the same—your folks won't be able to imagine grandchildren of Japanese descent, neither will hers look forward to blonde, blue-eyed ones.*

Facing a wall of parental skepticism, it seemed Albert and Ruth had work to do.

That same day, Albert heard from Ruth, who had resumed modern dance classes with Elizabeth Schmitt. Her joy in movement was tempered by witnessing struggles of her friend Larsen, now in physical therapy to reanimate her limbs after suffering from polio:

> *Dearest Albert, Hazel will walk again. It is more to see Hazel exercise than dancing students.*

Later in November, Albert sent Ruth a mysterious present in a nest of boxes. In the smallest, Ruth wrote, she'd been afraid she would find an engagement ring, which she didn't want due to her ambivalence about marriage, her distaste for showy baubles, her innate frugality—or all three. Instead, she was delighted by the surprise of an old watch on a chain that she could fit in her palm or open to watch its movement ticking away. She sketched it in her letter, marking the hours with words of love.

Gingerly, Ruth had started to share news of their relationship with a few select friends, like the émigré musician Charlotte Schlesinger, known by her nickname, Bimbus. In her thank-you letter for the watch, she reported:

> *I have begun to think more and more in terms of US.*
>
> *Bimbus is glad for us; but says that we must become independent of our friends and must work out our lives with work as our problem, not ourselves.*

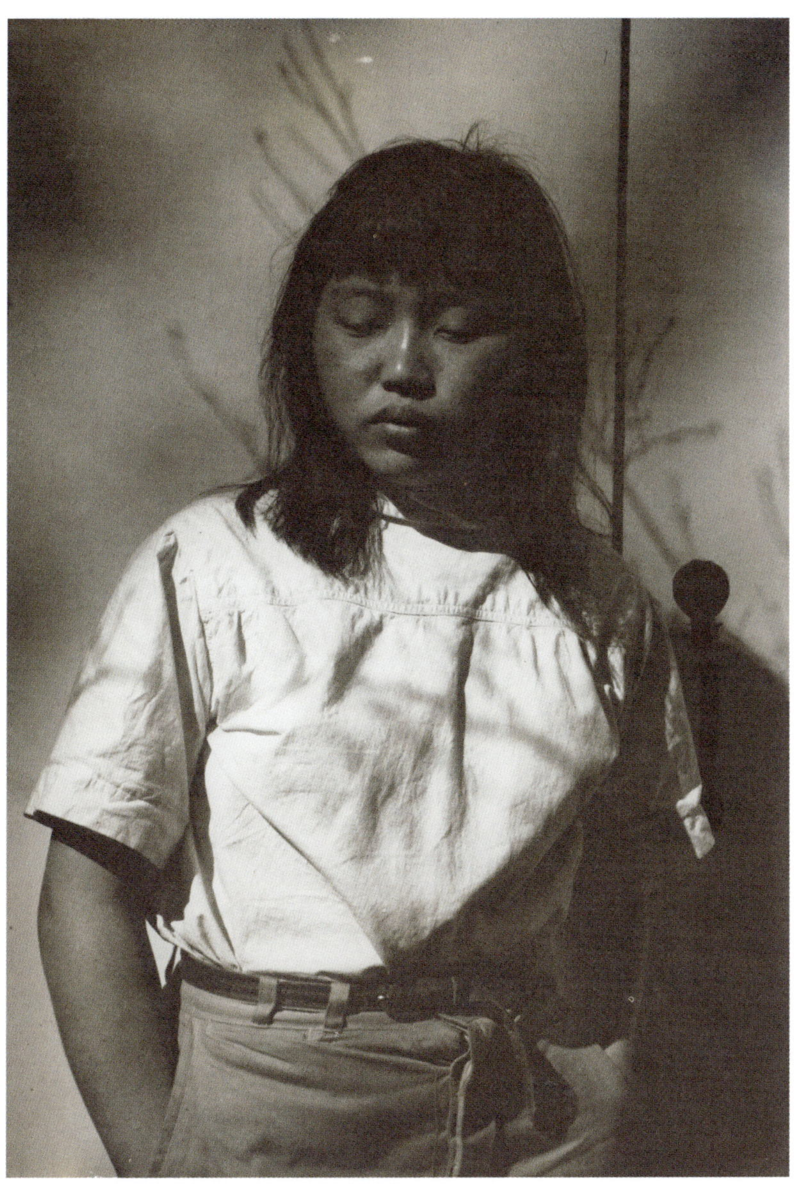

Ruth at Black Mountain College, 1946–1949.
Photograph by Hazel Larsen Archer.

As Ruth wrestled with problems of balancing work and life, Albert worked feverishly to allay her fears, using every tool at his disposal: reason, poetry, humor. One corny joke misfired and triggered a lover's tiff. Albert had written about having "dishonorable intentions"—perhaps code for his longing to be with her. Ruth didn't understand, wasn't amused, and even wondered if there were another woman in the picture.

In a letter written during a "stupid carpentry class" on November 22, Albert shot back that his joke was facetious and all his intentions were honorable and "all reserved for you." In this letter, he not only clarified the misunderstanding, but went on to state his case for marriage from a variety of angles.

Work in his tiny, sunless room had left Albert longing for space and light to clear his head. He reassured Ruth he was equally devoted to his vocation as she was to hers, adding that Fuller and Ruth were the lodestars guiding his great life decisions:

Albert's letter went on to address his own fears of family rejection; he hoped the Laniers would take "a sensible attitude." At the same time, he tried to quell Ruth's jitters on many fronts: matrimonial, artistic, family, and lifestyle. He wooed her with a description of their future life in art together as "nomads going from one job to the next in a Model 'A' or Jeep with the kids strapped in." Integrity to art and each other would guide them.

Boldly pressing his case for marriage, Albert suggested that they ask Fuller to design them a wedding ring. He didn't like ostentatious engagement rings any more than she did. He wanted to honor Ruth with a unique piece of art by their beloved mentor, a wedding ring whose worth would flow from Fuller's designing of it, and from Ruth's wearing of it. This time, she didn't object.

Albert braced for the lonely holiday season ahead:

Next Christmas we must be together—our first—and this our last apart.

By now, he told her, the flavors of everyday life were all infused with Ruth.

I just can't drink hot chocolate. That's our drink—We had hot chocolate after listening to "Pastorale" . . .

He closed the November 22 missive by begging Ruth not to exhaust herself or to overreact to his flippant jokes by imagining a rival:

My love, love, and no more letters too late at night or when you're too tired.

Around Thanksgiving, Ruth's qualms began to ease, and she wrote to Albert on November 30 that her older sister Lois now supported them:

Lois . . . hopes for a glorious beautiful journey for you and me. She is very good. She said, "Love him, not for his race, but as an individual." You certainly are an individual. She will come to L.A. in June so they will be at our wedding. Bimbus wants to play Mozart for us. I haven't planned anything. It almost frightens me to be thinking in terms of matrimony.

The week before Christmas, Ruth was madly rehearsing dances and hymns for Black Mountain's holiday recitals before school closed for the winter break. She helped deck the tree with metal spirals they had made the year before, lighting them with candles. She filled her December 16 letter to Albert with holiday news and sensual allusions to Black Mountain landscapes where they had spent intimate moments:

We dance tomorrow, scared; rehearse tonight. Tonight is Christmas for us, we sing Bach's "Praise our God" and O Jesu so sweet, a beautiful chorale. Then a haunted peace here, and a greater alertness to light & darkness. Too much moonlight tonight to suppress memories of beautiful nights with you. Mae West, moon, water; the night is filled with sensations.

Ruth would spend Christmas Eve with Josef and Anni Albers, and then, craving solitude, leave to build a fire by herself. She'd confessed to Albert in a letter postmarked December 23 that her head and heart were sometimes at odds:

When I say that I want children, one says "your work is more important." "One cannot do both." Then I begin to wonder about what is possible or impossible. Do I see the future clearly in believing that we can have a family, but still maintain our own work . . .

Do we know how to give & take. Yes of our service, but of the real gift? Do we know how to fight, not to destroy but to survive. Martyrdom now seems to be the survival for, not the dying for. . . .

I paint more often now, throw many away and start over each time.

Rubbing the now & here into the clay, I have a clean slate to think of tomorrow with you which seems too wonderful to imagine.

A hyacinth Albert had planted outside Ruth's window the previous spring put out a glorious purple bloom. She opened a holiday card from Fuller, postmarked on December 24, and found his promise of a ring, which he described in his arcane wizard's formula:

Much love to you! A wedding ring for you and Albert is in process of design—It is Dymaxion—i.e. Unity is at minimum twofold. UNITY = Minima2 Maxima Universe. (Signed) Buckminster Fuller

Ruth was puzzled by his cosmic equation, but delighted at the prospect of the ring. By now, Albert had a new job as an architectural draftsman for Bay Area architect Mario Corbett. But Ruth still held out hope he could somehow continue studies with Fuller, writing on December 28:

I am sure Fuller is the one, because he is so vast yet so intimate.

Seeking clues about her future, she had the poet Charles Olson read her fortune in the cards, which foretold that she would cross a body of water. "I hope it is only the S.F. Bay," she added.

Ruth told Albert that her siblings—"less sens[ible] and less rational" than family skeptics—supported their match. Her older brother, George, had liked Albert on first meeting him in L.A., and in any event would support his sister's choice. "Your trademark," George told his sister, "is made by either people living your life or living your own."

She told Albert her family's acceptance of him as a future son-in-law had been forged in suffering. For herself, from then on, she declared on December 29 that she would suffer only for art:

> *They dare to be tolerant, for we have all suffered intolerance innocently.*
> *I no longer want to nurse such wounds; I want to wrap fingers cut by aluminum*
> *shavings, and hands scratched by wire; only these things produce tolerable*
> *pains.*
> *You will have to look at me on streetcars or bus when you hear someone shout*
> *"dirty Jap." I hope we never have to experience it, but expect it, but do not fear it.*
> *I've overcome most of the fear. I've reached a point where I can no longer nurse*
> *such stupidity. This attitude has forced me to become a citizen of the universe*
> *by which I become infinitely smaller, than if I belonged to a family, or province,*
> *or race. Then I can allow myself to pass and not to be hurt as mortally by ugly*
> *remarks, because I no longer identify myself as Japanese or American . . .*

Racial differences weren't made by God but by man, Ruth reasoned. She embraced Albers's theory about the relativity and interaction of colors that vibrate and change in relation to the colors next to them, as people change and interact with each other. She wanted to resist social pressures to conform; she wanted to innovate like Fuller.

> *You painted me brown, and I painted you white. From our limited experience*
> *with color, we know red and green work together, there is activity, violence, but*
> *not red poisoning green. Together they can produce yellow without losing any of*
> *their strength. It is hard to look at, but exciting. If we suffocate under society's*
> *pressure, we will, I'm sure, realize our capacity and limitations; and we will be*
> *unable to follow Fuller. I know we will always be following him as children*
> *followed the Pied Piper . . .*

Giving herself up wholly to love required Ruth to be sure she and her lover could also remain true to their respective arts. So she repeatedly sought that reassurance from Albert. She closed her December 29 letter urging him to love his vocation as much as he loved her:

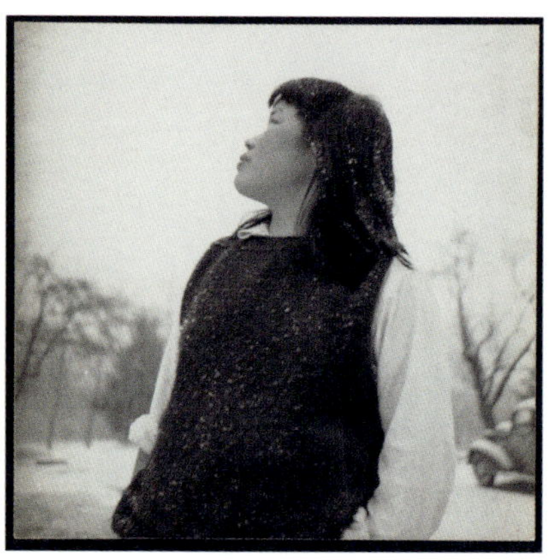

*Ruth in snow, Black Mountain College, ca. 1946–1949.
Photograph by Hazel Larsen Archer.*

*I will take no more love from you
until you have given your own work the
love it deserves. And put all of my love
into it. There is such an abundance of
it. Please use some of it at night. The
nights are so starved.*

All that agonizing about their future
began to fray Albert's nerves. On January 11, he tried to ease his fiancée's mind
and made his case for trust:

*The increasing frequency with
which you write about love versus
work . . . disturbs me. . . . I know I
have far to go—perhaps far before you will have me—but please do not think that it
will never be—only two must believe but one losing belief is fatal. . . .
Ruth, love me as you are tender to plants, as you love coils of beautiful wire, as you
love loneliness—knowing that time will wear rough edges smooth—that distance is
surmountable—that wire is stronger than stone—that God is good and God is love.*

But the new year, 1949, brought a new concern beyond matters of the heart.
Black Mountain's academic politics exploded into open conflict and mass resignations. Financial pressure, factions, and intellectual clashes between big egos
had weakened the school's fabric. The list of issues was long: money, faculty hiring,
course offerings, a need for leadership, and questions about whether faculty could
also administer the college and resolve disputes while they were teaching. The very
democracy and free expression that many had loved now ran amok. Albers, who
doubted the practicality of giving young students the same voting power as senior
faculty, now temporarily presided over the fracas as rector. Much of the animus
focused on Black Mountain's charismatic cofounder and physics professor Ted Dreier,
who'd put sixteen years and his fortune into the college. Now some questioned his
ability to lead.

With pressure mounting for Dreier's ouster, loyal artists and instructors quit
in protest, including both Josef and Anni Albers, Charlotte "Bimbus" Schlesinger,

Johanna Jalowetz, and almost the entire arts faculty. The resignations would be effective after the spring semester, in August 1949. Harvard architect Walter Gropius resigned from the Advisory Council, citing "the fatal blunder" of ousting Dreier, a man who had been the college's "heart and soul."

Ruth dashed off the news to Albert in an undated letter:

> *Resignation of all definite. We must have new faculty, to continue the College. No one is indispensible, we will survive, and continue to exist as a college, working for things & ideas bigger than personal feelings & fears. [Max] Dehn returns. We have the possibility of improvement or degeneration. Spirit is set forward to build & reconstruct but not renew old ulcers. . . . Albers leaves a gap.*

Although sad about her mentor's coming departure, Ruth took a quiet, measured approach to the transition, her maturity winning respect among her peers. Never politically ambitious, she soon got a surprise, as Albert's friend Si Sillman wrote him at the end of January: "There was a battle & an election . . . & in the heat of the student meeting . . . Ruth was made/elected Student Moderator. A complete dark horse."

The post of student moderator was like that of a student body president, and it brought her faculty status plus a seat on the Board of Fellows, which met in New York. Along with her credibility as an artist, Ruth's resolve to stay neutral and float above the fray added to her stature. Despite her heavy new role, and longing for Albert, Ruth ventured out, gamely trying a new dance. But ultimately she found the party scene dreary, as she wrote him:

> *. . . Our Valentine party ended gay-drunk. I was sober & bored by it. But I learned to jitterbug—the lindy; and all night I jitterbugged. Hazel was high. None of the charm of the Satie night . . .*

But it was impossible to heal the rifts and restore Black Mountain's original magic, just when so many faculty were heading out the door.

New leadership was recruited from Swarthmore to head a reorganization, with the understanding that faculty would no longer take part in administrative policy decisions. Amid continued struggle, Ruth poured out her frustration to Albert in letters. They loved the artistic autonomy of Black Mountain, but not its factions or infighting. There was little to hold them after June—only the hope of Fuller's return. Meanwhile, Albert was adjusting to the demands of his profession. They had a whole life to plan, their skeptical families to manage, and legal obstacles to surmount.

At the time, marriages between whites and members of other ethnic groups were rare and even illegal under many states' anti-miscegenation laws. But Albert was determined to wed, even if it meant he and his bride-to-be would have to hitch a ride to Reno, as he believed Nevada to be the nearest state that would allow their marriage.

They weren't alone among young couples seeking to break barriers. The previous year, in Los Angeles, a Mexican American woman, Andrea Perez, and her African American fiancé, Sylvester Davis, had paved the way for racial equality in marriage. When they originally applied for a license, L.A. County Clerk W. G. Sharp refused, citing California Civil Codes Sections 60 and 69, which declared illegal the intermarriage or issuance of licenses for a Caucasian to marry a "Negro," or for that matter, a "mulatto," "Mongolian," or "Malay" (archaic statutory language used to designate people with African or Asian heritage).

Perez and Davis sued. The California State Supreme Court agreed to review their complaint. In October 1948, in the case of *Perez v. Sharp*, the court decided in their favor. Chief Justice Roger Traynor ruled that the ban violated the equal protection of the laws clause of the Fourteenth Amendment of the U.S. Constitution. California's high court declared that marriage is a fundamental right that can't be denied on the basis of race, freeing couples to wed across color lines in the Golden State. The victory came nearly a decade before the landmark U.S. Supreme Court case of *Loving v. Virginia* extended that right across the nation.

So Albert and Ruth could get hitched without hitchhiking to Reno.

Still, there were two sets of parents on opposite sides of the country to convince. There would be tears in Georgia and stoic silence in California. Ruth later confided in a private memoir: "Albert's mother cried. She had hoped Albert would marry a sweet blue-eyed girl from Metter and live nearby and attend the Methodist Church on Sundays." Mr. Asawa would quietly keep his own counsel, but as Ruth wrote in the memoir, "That is how many Japanese express 'no.'"

The young couple waged some shuttle diplomacy. Albert courted the Asawas by drawing up a floor plan for their dream house. Ruth visited Albert's sister Laurie Pearson in Georgia. She chatted easily with her prospective sister-in-law, poring over Albert's baby pictures. She showed Laurie's girls how to eat with chopsticks. Posing for snapshots with Laurie in her garden, Ruth was all smiles in a demure shirtwaist dress. She began to win over Albert's sister as Laurie surmounted her fears for the young couple and became their ally for family acceptance.

With Laurie coming over to his side, Albert announced his plans to his parents in an Easter letter, voicing hope his news would give their holiday an extra reason to celebrate. He sketched a beguiling portrait of the young woman they'd never met:

> *She is very beautiful, quiet, energetic, and unaffected and believes almost religiously in work. She is five-feet, two-inches tall and has very black hair. Besides her painting and design work she likes to grow things and cultivates mad little gardens at school and had rather dance than eat. Last year we worked on several projects together and we work beautifully together. She finished all the oak in the minimum house and still insists that all the stonework should be done over because one stone is wrong. Besides cooking food that would fatten anyone but me, she gives haircuts that are second to no one's. During the year, she has contributed over $800 to the college's milk house fund since she doesn't charge for haircuts, the boys and faculty can contribute to the fund instead.*

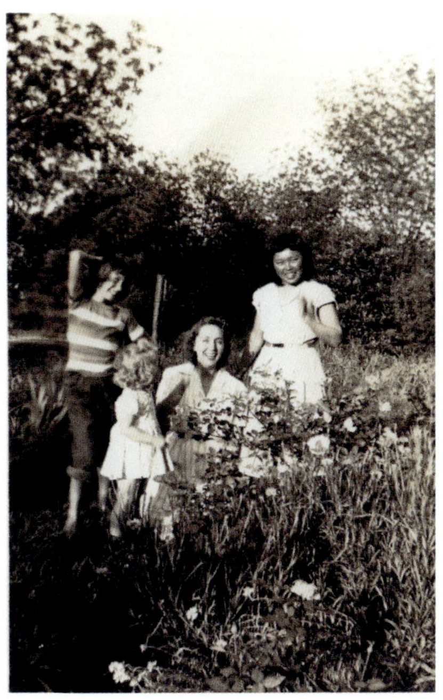

Ruth with her future sister-in-law Laurie Lanier Pearson (center) and Laurie's daughters Peggy and Ann in Georgia, spring 1949

Mrs. Lanier took Albert's letter into her bedroom and shut the door. Laurie heard weeping from within, but she wrote Albert that no "hard-ugly things" were said.

With the Laniers reeling in shock, Ruth summoned the strength and poise on May 6 to send them this introduction:

> *I am Ruth Asawa, the girl whom Albert will marry. Not knowing my background nor the acquaintance of similar people, I realize that it is almost impossible to imagine*

your son to consider marriage with me . . . It is as much an offence against my family as you perhaps feel it is to marry out of one's race. I have talked to them about it, and though it is a sadness to them, they do not say "no," nor do they exclude me from the family for what we are about to do.

Ruth wrote that she hoped they would reply to her, but added she would understand if they didn't want to meet her.

Soon enough, though, Albert's mother found her voice to let Ruth know just how she felt in a frank May 10 reply:

You and Albert! How I've worried about the situation. I still believe that such a marriage is not right for you or for him. However, there is not anything I can do about it—He told us about the marriage—he didn't ask. . . .

You must be a very attractive, versatile and, in fact just a fine person. I don't want to say things to hurt you but it is just the differences in race, background and in general just the ways and ideas of the world that it is going to be hard to get adjusted . . .

I've written to Albert that if and when you're married to bring you home when he comes and we'll do our best to treat you as we would [his sisters] Laurie, Jewel Bird or Helen. . . .

Albert broached the issue of social stigma with diplomacy:

Daddy, "such marriages" are not common here but legal. Thanks to the advantages we have both had, and to the talents we both hope we have, our friends and associates will be rather uncommon and people who know us quite free from our nationalities.

Denied a blessing by both sets of parents, Albert and Ruth had made their best case for simple consent. Next they began debating where to live. Reuniting at Black Mountain had one great virtue: It would let him continue to study with Fuller. On the other hand, opening a new chapter in San Francisco would let both of them launch their professional lives as an architect and artist.

Albert wrote to Ruth that he was warming to San Francisco, suggesting a tilt toward the West Coast:

I love our city so much it will be wonderful to be here together days and nights and to have time for love—

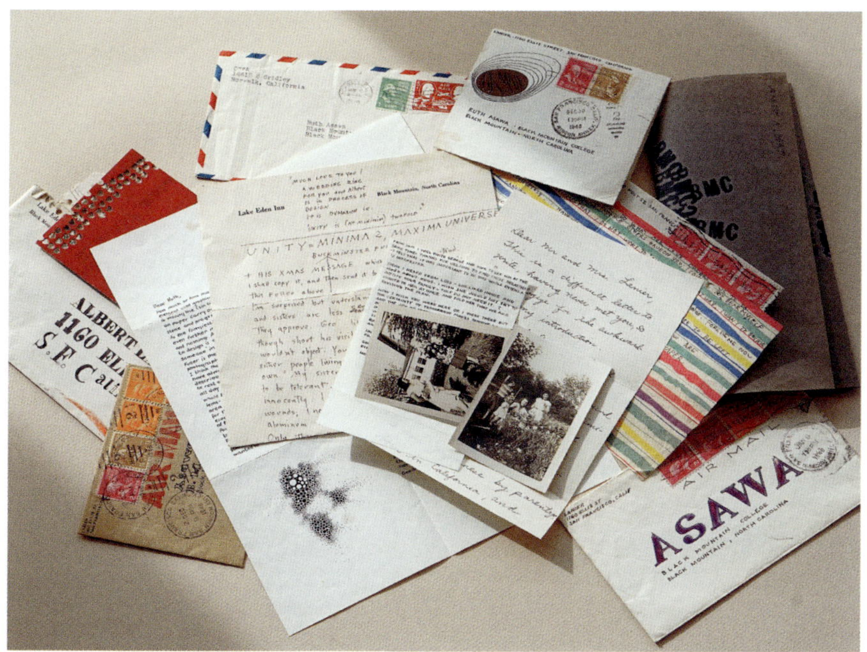

Love letters between Ruth and Albert, making plans for their life in San Francisco, 1948–1949.
Photograph by Laurence Cuneo.

> *Last night and today I have been in love with everything—torn billboards, brick walls, my little room and most of all you. . . .*
>
> *Another thing you must promise—do not make your working an absolute necessity—I want you to work if you want to but if a fair job is not available immediately—wait—you are an artist and my lover—this is a full occupation.*

Although she still had no degree, Ruth was now completing her sixth year of college. She was fed up with school politics, and eager to make art and live with Albert. Their debate over where to live turned more favorably toward the West Coast:

> *San Francisco will make all of us happy, including Mama, Papa . . . The idea of San Francisco excites me and with all little notes for paintings and wire, I will be content in working by myself and having love with you, and looking at your face and hands and body. I can hardly wait. . . .*

Please don't let anything come between us. I fear that—not the marriage. I want one clean room with windows for people to see whom I love. I do not know my energy to love, it is very strong. . . .

. . . Oh I remember the pains of it and the frightfully beautiful love marks on the sensitive nerves. . . .

I dance all of the time, and love all of the movements which are possible. Albers calls me "biological" in color class. The peepers are crying, singing; I am awaking at 5:45 a.m. to catch the morning sun at the farm. Everything I do, I love; (except moderate). The way I feel about becoming that is as Truman must have felt when he won over Dewey. It will be the death of me yet, but we are having a relatively peaceful productive semester. Albert, it is soon that I shall hold you again.

They finally agreed that they would make their home in San Francisco, but the next challenge was finding affordable housing with space for Ruth's art in the Bay Area. After joking they could live in a chicken coop in Marin County, Albert finally found their first home.

Number 135 Jackson Street was a cavernous loft above a seed company and onion warehouse overlooking San Francisco's clamorous produce district. It was big and bare, measuring 25 by 60 feet, with scant amenities but plenty of space to work and watch the city go by. Some Black Mountain friends conveniently stored a piano, a double bed, an icebox, and a record player there, giving them a few amenities. Albert wrote Ruth on May 10 that the loft was perfect for them, although no conventional honeymoon cottage or starter home with two bedrooms and a bath, known in the trade as a "junior five":

I begin to feel the loft is home. I must warn you that it is in a very disreputable neighborhood and not at all a "junior five." All that I can promise is that it will be clean and relatively isolated and big. I love it and cannot wait to be there with you . . .
I only pray that I can keep you as sweet and beautiful as I find you.

That month, Ruth's faculty friends at Black Mountain began preparing their student to be a bride, in their unconventional fashion. Anni designed and made Ruth a wedding hat, and acquired a length of black fabric, which offered a sophisticated art-school twist on the traditional wedding gown. Mrs. Jalo and the school's Dutch dietician Pietronella Swierstra began sewing the bespoke creation. It was two-piece and floor length, sober like the bride who would wear it. Ruth confided to Albert it was "a beautiful dress, and it frightens me to see it, but in an exciting way."

Albert agreed he would make one last trip east to visit his parents in Georgia and reunite with Ruth at Black Mountain. He would also help her hang the art for her final student exhibition. Albert assured his parents it was the right move:

What I really want to do now is work and Ruth has been there too long, had become too much the servant, too indispensable to the place and the people.

The month of June gave the couple a chance to seek the blessing of their college mentors before embarking on their new life. Albert approached Fuller about their plan to blend art and architecture with family life. Fuller was exuberant:

The world is your oyster. You become the pearl. You rub and you rub and make a big pearl.

Ruth shyly sought out Albers for her final conference. In the past, when she stood up to him, saying she preferred painting flowers over abstract designs, he had responded: "Fine, just make sure they are Asawa flowers."

Now, unable to meet his steely blue gaze, she lowered her eyes.

"Come in, Asawa; what do you want to ask me?"

"I want to have a family but also I want to become an artist. Do you think it is possible?"

"How many children do you want?"

"Six."

Albers grabbed her chin and gave it a little shake. He inhaled, tightening his lips.

"Ya, ya, you make babies, that is your art. Be sure to make them Asawas."

When Albert went to talk to Albers, the painter told him, "Don't ever let her stop doing her work."

CHAPTER 6

A LOFT FOR A NEW LIFE

On July 3, 1949, Ruth stood beside Albert in their loft before a small circle of family and friends. After mapping their life so carefully in letters, they were wed in a free-wheeling service that brought as much laughter as tears.

Gathered in the loft over the onion warehouse were Ruth's sister Chiyo, and Black Mountain College friends including musician Charlotte "Bimbus" Schlesinger and artist Peggy Tolk-Watkins, with her baby, Ragland Jr.

It was just ninth months since the California Supreme Court legalized intermarriage; Ruth and Albert had gotten a marriage license at San Francisco City Hall. They avoided wedding conventions. "Albert did not like diamonds because the ladies in his home town always showed off their diamonds . . . bragging about having the best," Ruth would recall. They waited eagerly for Fuller's ring, which wouldn't arrive until after the wedding.

Ruth's somber attire was the antithesis of the white gown and billowing veil adopted by brides since Queen Victoria's day. But she was right in step with postwar brides, who'd lived through shortages and often were married in simple suits and hats rather than gowns. Every stitch in Ruth's ensemble was a personal part of her Black Mountain College story. Although a sophisticated art school creation, the dress was practical, too, because she could shorten it later to wear on the street.

Officiating at the ceremony was an African American minister Albert had met at work on a construction site. The Rev. Talbert Whitfield said he'd be delighted to conduct the ceremony. He said nuptials should "spring from the heart" and decided to skip practicing the vows. The spontaneous service hit a few snags, as Albert would tell it:

Talbert probably prayed a little and then commenced marrying us. It was true that we really didn't need a rehearsal for the ceremony but we should have rehearsed him on the pronunciation of Ruth's name because he began,

"Do you Ruth Ansawa . . ." and there was a lot of laughter when I had to correct him and he started over again.

"Do you, Ruth Ass-a-wah . . ." and I had to correct him again.

And finally we went on with that and the ceremony was really quite long. . . . When it was over, I turned to Bimbus, who was a great pianist, and said, "For God's sake, let's sing Bimbus. Play some music."

Ruth, for her part, would recall:

> *They all laughed and we cried and we laughed and we got through it. The baby, Ragland was crawling on the floor and it was a riot. It was like a three ring circus.*

The bride and groom then piled into Albert's Model A and led a small caravan of guests over the Golden Gate Bridge, through Sausalito, and up to Wolfback Ridge, a high road with sweeping views of San Francisco Bay. Albert's boss, the architect Mario Corbett, lent his house there to the newlyweds for a week while he was away. The Corbetts provided the couple with a roast chicken, Champagne, and a fully stocked refrigerator. After all the toasts, the guests drifted away and, Albert said, "Our honeymoon commenced."

Buckminster Fuller's custom wedding ring for Ruth was ready in September. The three-stranded silver band clasped a smooth black river stone set in a silver web that formed three interlocking As—as in Asawa. Black Mountain architecture student and jeweler Mary Jo Slick Godfrey fabricated Fuller's design. In portraits of Ruth, the bold piece adorns hands that that were often bound with masking tape to prevent or cover wire cuts.

The newlyweds settled into their loft in the produce market. For all its spaciousness and romance, they sacrificed certain conventions—like walls and a kitchen. Set between Chinatown and the waterfront, their block offered an immersive view of street life surging about them twenty-four hours a day. Their rent was sixty-five dollars a month. It was the "one clean room" of Ruth's dreams, a loft in which to paint and sculpt and celebrate love with Albert, like a happier version of Mimi and Rodolfo in *La Bohème*.

Albert and Ruth celebrated moving into the loft in Chinatown and brought back Champagne to dedicate their new home. The newlyweds had no Champagne glasses, but the loft was equipped with glass tumblers that once held cheese spread, so they charged their cheese jars with bubbly and

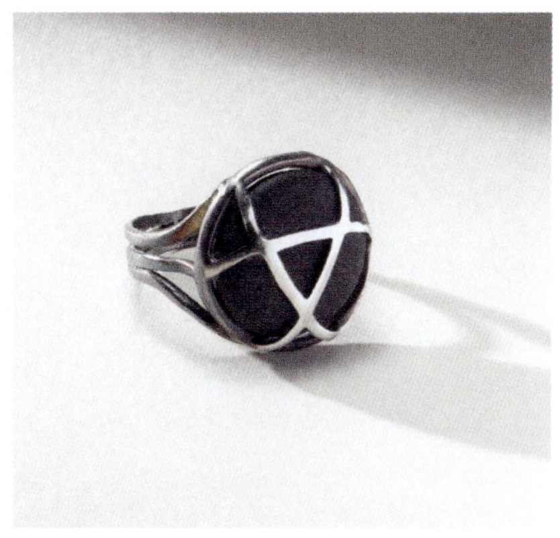

Ruth's wedding ring, designed by Buckminster Fuller and made by Mary Jo Slick Godfrey in 1949. Photograph by Laurence Cuneo.

clinked, toasting to their new life. As Ruth recalled, "The Champagne tasted just as good."

Ruth worked days in contented solitude in the loft, sculpting or drawing, sometimes using as her model a bouquet Albert had picked up at Union Square. A secondhand radio played music while she worked. At five in the evening she would improvise dinner, making rice on one burner of the hot plate. She sliced meat and chopped vegetables to fry when Albert returned at six thirty. Humming a song, she reflected on her husband's promise he would "never ever let her work as a secretary," even if it meant eating macaroni until payday.

Albert gave joy rides in the jalopy to footloose street kids who were often out late playing on their scooters. The newlyweds saw a production of *A Streetcar Named Desire* at the Geary Theater. They took in the sights, including Joe DiMaggio's restaurant on Fisherman's Wharf, with one of Ruth's sisters who was visiting. It was a disappointment, with "too many nosey tourists buzzing about," Ruth wrote to the Laniers. "We were probably as bad as the rest of them."

In the still of evening, they strolled around their neighborhood and saw scavengers rummaging in garbage bins. One played a shepherd's pipe until he found a morsel. Ruth also shared the gritty side of their urban life in letters to her parents-in-law.

She didn't yet understand the contemporary art scene in San Francisco, she said; perhaps its transient air arose from the sense that the Pacific Ocean offered escape to other places. Still, Ruth found San Francisco "a warm, enchanting city and I love it because I no longer have to dream or long for such a place." With architecture jobs mounting, she explained Albert's workload was to blame for gaps between his letters home:

Understand that Albert's silence is not neglect, please. I shall try to help with the work so that he will have a little more time.

The produce market lurched to life at two in the morning, with a rumble of trucks and shouts as men unloaded crates of fruit and vegetables bound for groceries and restaurants. Once acclimated to the pulse of the district, Ruth and Albert could sleep through almost any din—except when fights broke out, drawing night watchmen and police. During one brawl, Albert's curiosity tempted him downstairs, but Ruth called out to wait until the street was cleared. At a quarter to five, they descended in safety and watched the lines of ravenous produce men ordering giant breakfasts of half a dozen eggs with toast, orange juice, and coffee. Ruth and Albert shared a coffee and doughnut for seventy-five cents, counting their change until payday. The newlyweds' breakfast wasn't enough for two canaries, some workers commented. Ascending to the loft, Albert shaved and Ruth made him the tuna sandwich he couldn't afford to buy.

San Francisco in 1949 was a small town with a big cosmopolitan attitude. The 7-by-7-square-mile city had long had an international flavor, being the portal to the Pacific Rim. With its roots in an Indian settlement, Spanish mission, and gold miners' camp, it had a diverse populace. But that didn't guarantee an enlightened welcome for all. Racist animus toward Asian people had festered in the city since the late nineteenth-century exclusion laws barring immigration, the twentieth-century Alien Land Laws barring property ownership, the events of Pearl Harbor, and World War II. The founding conference of the United Nations had been held there in 1945. Yet Japanese Americans, driven from their homes and emerging from confinement in the camps, were cautious about resettling in California. Ruth and Albert relished the anonymity that urban life gave them, but old biases died hard.

One evening, as Albert took Ruth and a female friend from college for a drive, they drew unwanted attention. To local cops, the mixed trio suggested some shady commerce was under way, as Albert recalled:

Police would stop me because they thought I was suspicious driving that car around the produce district at night. They were generally satisfied I wasn't handling dope or anything.

. . . I told them we lived at 135 Jackson and we were just going home. Why didn't they drop in and see that there was nothing sinister going on. They let us go. We got home and we got ready for bed and the doorbell rang and I went downstairs and the cop said: "Say, Lanier, which one of those women is your wife?" They thought I was running a house of prostitution, I think.

Although Albert's wry yarn makes it sound like a scene from a screwball comedy, there was nothing funny about the implicit bias of the day, and there was more to come. Later, when Ruth and Albert took road trips in their Model A, onlookers saw the young couple as actors in an old racial narrative. Some asked if Ruth was a war bride, assuming the Asian wife of a Caucasian man must be the victor's prize. They tried setting people straight, but stereotypes proved hard to correct. So after a time they just said yes, and found people were nicer. Some folks even gave them pies.

As the 1950s approached, San Francisco was on the cusp of change, brought by a new breed of artists and poets who were challenging the old social order. Nearby North

Beach would become a magnet for beat literary figures like Jack Kerouac. San Francisco and Berkeley were settings where Allen Ginsberg would write *Howl*, to be published by City Lights Bookstore on Columbus Street, a short walk from the loft on Jackson.

On the edge of the bohemian scene, Ruth and Albert's friend Peggy Tolk-Watkins was opening nightclubs. The Tin Angel, which had two locations in Sausalito and the city's Embarcadero waterfront, drew an eclectic mix of artists, suits, and gays to hear jazz, folk songs by Odetta, and ballads by Johnny Mathis. For her second club, the Fallen Angel, Tolk-Watkins wanted a spectacle. She booked the stripper Tempest Storm to perform in a milk bath. But utility problems chilled the act: The club's hot water was turned off, so Storm froze in a slurry of powdered milk.

Albert continued to work in Mario Corbett's firm for about a year, trying to convince clients to give up clutter for a spare and open mid-century-modern style that would become his trademark. Ruth was painting, sculpting, and even designing wallpaper. Although she avoided secretarial jobs, she did work a stint as a restaurant hostess to make ends meet.

In an olive branch to the young couple, the elder Laniers asked Ruth and Albert to choose a silver pattern. Albert wrote to his parents that they were inundated with working and with outfitting the loft with shelves to function better as an apartment. He delegated to his bride the silver issue, which Ruth handled in a postscript:

> *We have selected "Old Maryland" by Kirk and Sons of Baltimore. . . . I hope it is no trouble to find this pattern, also that no one will feel compelled to send us gifts. Love, Ruth.*

Even with silverware, the loft was more a workshop than dream house. And they loved it. Albert wrote to the Laniers:

> *With wallpaper spread on the floor—paintings all over—my drafting board—in addition to a big sign we are making for Ruth's parents, it is impossible to see how we could have lived in anything less than a loft.*

He and Ruth were putting Albers's color theory to practice to help the Asawas sell their vegetables from a roadside stand. On an 8-by-2-foot sign, they painted TOMATOES in bright red letters against a vivid green background. Putting contrasting colors of the same intensity side by side creates a vibration—making viewers blink. Ruth offered to make one for Mrs. Lanier's garden.

During her last year at Black Mountain, while she was contemplating her future, some of Ruth's abstract paintings of dancers had featured concentric ovals and nested pear shapes. Although clearly titled to suggest choreography, the ovoid forms could also be seen as fertility motifs. Indeed, by October, just three months after their wedding, Ruth herself was swelling with new life. Their baby was due in June.

Ruth wrote contentedly to her mother-in-law about her gardening plans and her gift of sculpture to raise funds for a Buckminster Fuller project. She described the city skyline at night, rhapsodizing about Coit Tower, the bridges, and the moon on the bay. But she didn't yet share her big news.

The truth was, as much as Ruth desired a large family, her early pregnancy was far from blissful. Over the next few months she suffered such intense morning sickness that she lost weight. By February, her stomach was settled enough for her to write to Bernice Lanier—now addressed as "Dear Mother."

> *. . . Everything is fine now. Any advice you have on babies, I would like to have you tell me . . .*

Despite waves of nausea, Ruth never stopped dreaming of her ideal half dozen. She'd grown up surrounded by six siblings. She now viewed herself again surrounded by six of her own.

Then an opportunity arose to jump-start the process while helping others. Through a friend, Ruth learned of a pregnant woman who couldn't keep her child. Ruth suggested to Albert it would be nice for their baby to have a playmate. He initially thought the plan would entail too much work. But after growing up on a farm and attending school while working in the fields and caring for younger siblings, Ruth was determined and confident that she could make it work. They discussed it and agreed that this child, who was of mixed racial heritage like their baby-to-be, could thrive in the love and tolerance of their blended family.

On Albert's twenty-third birthday, Ruth wrote to share their plan with the Laniers:

> *We have more news for you. Besides our baby which will arrive in June, we are adopting one which will be born around . . . 6 weeks before ours. We are making plans for the two. . . . We are just hoping now that both the first mother and I don't have twins on top of it all. It is very exciting, and I think we both realize the work involved in it.*

With two babies now imminent, the couple realized the limits of their romantic aerie loft. Albert located a three-room apartment with a kitchen at 9 McCormick Place. With a single window over the sink, it was dim and clad in dark green paint. The couple worked all day and night, Ruth scrubbing away layers of grease in the kitchen, and Albert giving it several coats of white paint to obliterate the gloomy undercoat that kept seeping through. They finished just in time to welcome home the adopted baby that beat the stork.

On May 2, 1950, Francis Xavier Lanier, a gray-eyed boy weighing 6 pounds, 7 ounces, was born at the University of California San Francisco hospital. Named after a poet friend of Albert's from Georgia, he would grow up to be a builder and craftsman. As Ruth's pregnancy advanced, her younger sister Kimiko moved up from Los Angeles to live with them. She would help Ruth with childcare, attend San Francisco State College, and continue refining her English fluency.

On June 26, Ruth delivered a brown-haired, brown-eyed girl weighing 8 pounds, 4 ounces, at the old Stanford Hospital. After trying out a number of longer names, they decided to call her Aiko, "Love Child," after Ruth's Japanese name. In contrast to the ebullient baby boy at home, who laughed and cooed, Ruth described her infant daughter as quiet and serene. She would inherit her mother's calm creativity and a round-the-clock work ethic that left little time for sleep. Ruth bottle fed Xavier until Aiko was born. When her own milk came in, she nursed them both. As Mrs. Lanier fulfilled her grandmother's prerogative of sending newborn clothes, Albert advised his mother to choose yellows and orange-pinks to match Aiko's peachy complexion, and blues to set off Xavier's milky tone.

A portrait of the period shows the young couple as new parents, each balancing a baby on their knees. Ruth, twenty-four, wears a glossy pageboy; Albert, twenty-three, looks formal and proud. Having taken the plunge to complement their biological family with adoption, they were too young and in love with life to consider themselves poor.

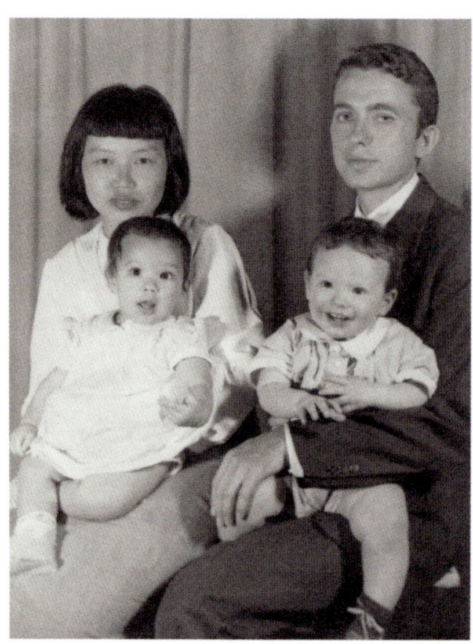

Ruth and Albert holding Aiko and Xavier, 1951

Blending adopted and biological children by design was an act of radical generosity—uncommon in 1950, a good half century before it would become a social trend. But to the practical Ruth, two babies were as easy to diaper and feed as one. She proved a natural. She wanted six children, and Albert agreed they should start their family while they were young. As in their marriage, they were pioneers, with a baby blueprint that quietly helped change the definition of what it meant to be a family.

Just after Thanksgiving of 1950, Ruth wrote to the Laniers that Albert's Model A jalopy had been stolen, but their two babies were thriving:

> *Aiko and Xavier are doing well; their colds are gone, and X is just about ready to stand by himself. It is a little early for him so I'm not encouraging him, strong as an ox. . . .*
> *Aiko is singing to herself in the kitchen, she is really so cute.*

One shadow marred their happiness. Just a day before Aiko's birth, North Korea's invasion of South Korea had ignited the Korean War and placed a question mark over Albert's civilian life. After World War II, he'd remained in the Naval Reserve, and he might be called to serve. Ruth wrote:

> *We are beginning to wonder about Albert's Naval status, news seems to be more critical, and nothing is definite about whether he will be called or not. We can't wonder about it too much or else we'll be nervous wrecks.*

Happily, Albert did not have to serve in another war. To celebrate their first Christmas as a family of four, Ruth and Albert stamped their infants' footprints in red and green ink on a homemade Christmas card with a verse for their grandparents:

> *Aiko's Red*
> *Xavier's Green*
> *Xmas Feet*

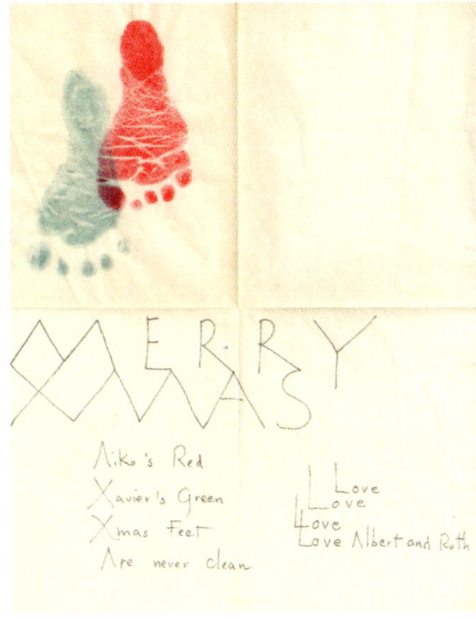

Christmas card from Ruth and Albert to his parents, December 1950

Generous and charismatic, Ruth and Albert made friends easily. And a singular friendship was soon to enter their lives through the viewfinder of an old-fashioned box camera.

One day, Albert attended a photo shoot at a building site and struck up a conversation with the photographer Rondal Partridge, who invited Albert to come meet his mother, also a photographer. Visiting a small house on Russian Hill, Albert saw a tiny, birdlike woman with a tart tongue and wayward wisps of white hair. Rondal's mother turned out to be the art photographer Imogen Cunningham, known for her black-and-white botanical studies, enigmatic portraits, and nudes.

In introducing Albert, Partridge mentioned he was married to a Japanese American woman. When Cunningham asked why, her son quipped, "Because he wants to _____ with her." (The redaction was Ruth and Albert's in their retelling.) Imogen poked Albert in the ribs and said her boys just talked like that. The salty introduction launched a lifelong friendship that Cunningham sealed with a jar of her homemade satsuma plum jam.

Cunningham and Albert shared an April 12 birthday, which they marked at joint celebrations in Golden Gate Park with epic picnics and music. When Cunningham met Ruth, the two discovered a shared love of gardens and country outings to glean fruit for making preserves. Cunningham would travel miles for free stone fruit but didn't drive, so the Laniers chauffeured her. Ruth grew to admire Cunningham's way of turning her lean lifestyle into a kind of elegant frugality. And Cunningham saw in the sculptor and her art a source of arresting images for her lens.

Positioning her bulky box camera in Ruth's studio, with a cloth over her head, Cunningham began taking eloquent black-and-white portraits of Ruth in the 1950s. Click: Ruth at work, fierce and focused on her sculpture, with the light illuminating her cheekbones. Click: Ruth surrounded by her children at play. Click: the Laniers on a windy beach, or gathered around the table with their growing family.

Cunningham—who freely gave unsolicited advice—told Ruth to stop signing her work with her married name and instead sign her work as Ruth Asawa. Ruth took this advice to heart, and "Asawa" quickly became an indelible artistic signature. Cunningham, who had three sons of her own, also told the young sculptor to stop having so many "brats"—advice Ruth cheerfully ignored.

Rearing two one-year olds didn't slow Ruth down. In 1951, she got in touch with her old mentor Josef Albers, now chair of the department of design at Yale. Albers wrote to San Francisco State College, recommending Ruth be granted senior standing toward a Bachelor of Fine Arts degree. "I consider her as a most gifted art student and one of the most talented I have ever had," he wrote. Accepted at San Francisco State, Ruth studied silk screening, adding another medium to her portfolio. But at age twenty-five, caught between studio and nursery, she didn't complete the units needed to graduate.

Instead, Ruth continued looping wire. As she developed the technique she had learned in Mexico in 1947, she filtered it through Albers's lessons at Black Mountain, exploring the nature of wire and pushing the material to its limits. It was like drawing in three-dimensional space.

Ruth's work with wire at Black Mountain consisted mostly of baskets, but in San Francisco the shapes lengthened and evolved into long hangings. She knitted without needles and wove without a loom, coiling wire around a dowel into a chain of *e*'s, then linking those coils into a mesh that was pliant and transparent. She shaped spheres, ovals, and teardrops, with smaller spheres nested within them, into long garlands of transparent lobes—often all crafted from a single filament. She turned surfaces around like a Möbius strip, in which the outside turned in, and the inside out. She linked the lobes of copper, iron, or bronze mesh into long chains. Unlike conventional sculpture, which is anchored to earth on a pedestal, Asawa's wires were suspended from the ceiling, turning subtly on the breeze and casting moving shadows.

Making the delicate-looking traceries took equal parts vision, manual dexterity, and sheer strength. Coiling wire on a dowel and shaping mesh took a chronic toll on her hands, cutting her fingers, which she covered with masking tape much of the time. Ruth worked nonstop, sculpting at night after her family was asleep, or rising before dawn to complete a piece. "Insomnia," she once wrote to Albert from Black Mountain, "is nothing more than a fear of losing time."

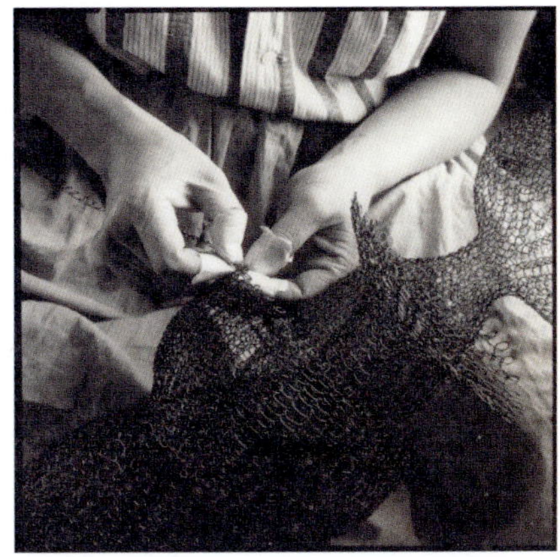

Close-up of Ruth's hands looping a wire sculpture, 1954. Photograph by Nat Farbman.

Ruth certainly lost no time once she began her studio practice in San Francisco. In 1951, she had a painting shown in the *Texas Wildcat* exhibition at the Fort Worth Art Museum alongside artists like Richard Diebenkorn.

In 1953, Ruth was chosen to appear among forty-three painters and sculptors at the San Francisco Museum of Art (now called the San Francisco Museum of Modern Art). Reviewers noted the striking silhouettes and interpenetrating shapes of her hangings. Design Research in Cambridge, Massachusetts, mounted an exhibition of her sculptures—one of her first professional one-woman shows. Each new venue put her name and art before a new piece of the American public.

She didn't shun the unconventional venues. In June 1953, her friend Peggy Tolk-Watkins mounted a show of Ruth's art at the Tin Angel, alongside work by the Greek-French artist Jean Varda. Varda had been an artist in residence at Black Mountain, where he had lectured on labyrinths, made a Trojan horse, staged happenings, and thrown parties. He had a shock of white hair and a hot-pink convertible. Like other Black Mountaineers, he had migrated to the West Coast, where he now lived on a houseboat in the Marin County waterfront village of Sausalito. The tiny show in a cabaret made an imperceptible splash in the wider world of art, but it introduced Ruth's work to Tolk-Watkins's circle of sophisticated club-goers. It included the heir to the Matson shipping line, William Matson Roth, who fancied Ruth's style and paved the way for her debut in public art commissions in the next decade.

Meanwhile, Albert was designing the San Francisco showroom of the prominent New York–based interior design firm Laverne Originals, known for its sleek, translucent mid-century-modern glass and plastic furniture. Erwine Laverne liked the look of Ruth's sculpture and wanted to display her sheer wire pieces to complement the company's line. In Ruth's first documented sale of a sculpture, Laverne Originals bought an Asawa mobile for the sum of seventy-five dollars and placed it in its East Side showroom, where her work was then visible to discerning Manhattan collectors.

Ruth and Laverne's association was a strategically brilliant, if odd, fit. Laverne proposed that Ruth mass-produce her pieces as functional and decorative accessories to coordinate with their interior design pieces, in much the same way that Knoll was marketing Harry Bertoia sculptures and chairs. Laverne even wanted to know if Ruth could make wastebaskets. To boost production, the company offered to hire Ruth a housekeeper and nanny, which would free her from domestic duties so she could focus on her output.

But that was not her vision. Ruth declined the offer, resisting the pull of a commercial contract that came with strings attached. Fearing disruption to her young

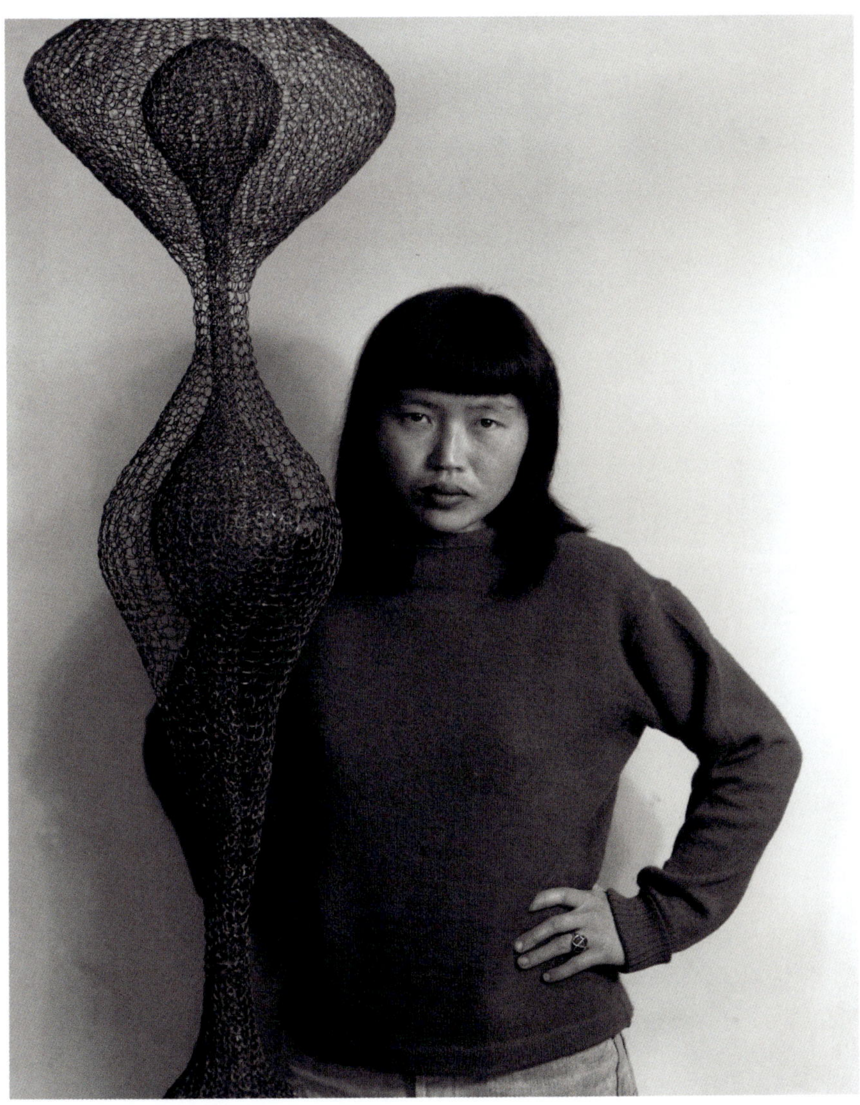

Ruth, arms akimbo, stands behind a form-within-a-form sculpture, 1951. Photograph by Imogen Cunningham.

household, she didn't want to delegate childcare to a stranger. Rather, she wanted the pleasure of raising her own children and working in her home studio, amid all the warmth and chaos of a young family. As a sculptor, she also worried that the commercial design and corporate art world would use her up and leave her burned out by age thirty-five or forty, her work discarded for a newer novelty. After designing wallpaper for a time, Ruth did create a three-dimensional wall covering, resembling an enlarged origami paper-fold, in plastic. She also enlarged her BMC laundry stamp design, which was adopted by textile designers in printed fabric for mattress covers. But in the end, these projects and the Laverne showroom arrangement were finite ventures. Ruth and Albert hadn't gone to Black Mountain and gambled their future on art just to mass-produce corporate commodities.

In early 1952, Albert's parents traveled from Georgia to visit their son and his young family in San Francisco. Albert, Ruth, and the two babies had quit the dark apartment on McCormick Place for more space and light. For a time, they dreamed of building a house in Sausalito, acquired the land, and initiated plans. But the dream ended when the local government took their land under eminent domain. Instead, they bought a flat in a Victorian house with Albert's new architecture partner, and together put in tons of sweat equity, cleaning, refinishing stairs, and hauling rocks for the garden. The house at 47 Alpine Terrace was on a steep, breezy hill just above the city's Haight-Ashbury district, near Buena Vista Park. Kimiko lived with them while attending college and helping with childcare. She took breaks in the park to take in commanding views of San Francisco Bay.

When his parents flew out, Albert drove to the airport to meet them, but amid mixed signals, he missed them. Meanwhile Hudson and Bernice Lanier—who were known in Southern style as Daddy Hud and Mama B—hailed a cab and arrived at the front door. There, they found Ruth's younger sister tending the infants. The shy Kimiko—who, now residing back in the United States, sometimes used her American name, Nancy—was intimidated by the formidable couple.

"Is Ruth like you?" the Laniers asked. Kimiko didn't know how to respond. She brewed tea for the in-laws. Hudson Lanier quizzed her on American jurisprudence. "Nancy, do you know what *habeas corpus* is?" he asked. Again unsure of how to reply, Kimiko pivoted and introduced the couple to their grandchildren. When the Laniers met baby Xavier and Aiko, their lingering resistance to the match began to thaw.

They ended up staying a week, their tolerance growing. Ruth earned points as a daughter-in-law by starting to add to her culinary repertoire some savory Southern dishes like fried chicken, grits, and gravy. She catered to Albert's taste, and during her marriage rarely prepared Japanese dishes, sticking to hearty American staples. She collected recipes that dotted her journals and daybooks. Her stove bubbled with abundance.

After the visit, Albert wrote his parents, "We all hated to see you leave so bad . . . The babies acted strangely and Nancy said it was so lonesome without you." Albert wrote as often as he could now, sharing stories of their two twenty-month-olds learning to talk, saying "Please," and making art:

> *Aiko got into the paint Sunday night and painted her first picture. All day she was kissing it and then Xavier was kissing it and tonight it was so dirty and tattered it had to be burned. Maybe I can teach Xavier to do erasing.*

For all her indifference to trends and publicity, Ruth's national profile began to rise. And in 1952, her wire hanging sculptures began appearing in magazine spreads in *Vogue* as a sinuous modern backdrop for a fashion layout featuring trendy suits and hats.

In what would have been a breakthrough for any twenty-six-year-old artist, the June 1952 cover of *Art & Architecture* featured Asawa wire sculptures as photographed by Imogen Cunningham. (The magazine credited the artist as Ruth Lanier, Imogen's sermons to Ruth on using her maiden name not yet having taken full effect.) The international design press took notice. In its July-August 1952 issue, the Italian architecture magazine *Domus* praised her work's "*leggerezza aerea*" (airy lightness)—along with her "*tre bambini*" (three babies). Ruth's looping technique, the magazine said, required "*una pazienza antichissima estremo orientale*" (a very ancient, far-Eastern patience). Fifties journalists and critics were quick to exoticize an artist who never billed her work as "Oriental," nor yet even visited Japan.

All this ink might have turned the heads of other artists. Ruth was busy with life. On June 26, 1952, the day of Aiko's second birthday, she was in the hospital, giving birth to a second son, Hudson Dehn Lanier. The baby, who would follow his father into the study of architecture and building, was named after his paternal grandfather and a favorite college professor, Black Mountain mathematician Max Dehn. Dehn was brilliant enough to have solved Hilbert's famous math problem, and kind enough to forgive an exhausted Ruth for falling asleep once in class. It was Dehn who led the hikes in the lush North Carolina woods, during which Ruth collected botanical specimens for her art. The day after his namesake was born, Dehn was out preserving dogwoods from the woodcutter at Black Mountain and collapsed from an embolism. He is buried beneath the rhododendron flowers near the college.

Five Laniers, needing ever more room, moved to 21 Saturn Street, on the sunny side of Twin Peaks. It was a neighborhood Ruth liked because it reminded her of the bohemian village air of the city's North Beach, only less frenetic and commercial. Near their house lived families of other young artists, including the jeweler Merry Renk and her husband, potter Earle Curtis. Ruth would show her work with Renk in museum shows, and the two couples would strike up a friendship that lasted five decades.

It was on Saturn Street that Ruth's children began to make their earliest memories. Xavier's first recollection was of an Easter when he woke to find sponge-painted bunny footprints hopping across the floor and disappearing into a heater. Ruth worked in her studio, located in a playroom. Xavier remembered not being told, "Don't do this; don't do that." Rather he would be advised, "Try it."

Albert was traveling for work projects more and more, to Chicago, Seattle, and New York. At home, the couple invested more sweat equity into their new house, often working past midnight on fireplaces or flooring.

"[Ruth's] baskets are selling fairly well," Albert wrote to his parents in September 1952. She was focused on finishing entries in an arts festival and installing them.

Then, just before Christmas 1953, Ruth's sculpture in the showrooms of Laverne Originals on East 57th Street caught the eye of a well-regarded gallery owner, who wrote Ruth to inquire about organizing a show of her work. Louis Pollack's Peridot Gallery on Madison Avenue drew art lovers with prominent names, discerning taste, and deep pockets. Ruth pulled together a portfolio of photos and began to ship Pollack her wire hangings in copper, brass, and black iron.

The Peridot Gallery was interested in mounting a solo exhibition of Ruth's sculpture but set strict limits: Sculptures couldn't be more than 7½ feet long due to the gallery's 8-foot-high ceilings. The gallery also outlined expectations of the artist's role in the relationship: She would pay for photos, advertising, and shipping, plus a one-third commission to the gallery on any sales of her work.

Like other artists, Ruth paid for the chance to expose her art to an elite buying public, and shared risks with the gallery. In turn, Pollack introduced Ruth's pieces to an influential New York audience. The first Mrs. Nelson Rockefeller purchased an Asawa, as did the architect Phillip Johnson. At twenty-eight, Ruth went east for her 1954 opening, feted by friends from Black Mountain College who came to see her new works: Ray Johnson, John Urbain, and Bobbie Dreier, the wife of the college founder Ted Dreier. Dressed in a straight skirt and black-framed glasses, with her jet hair swept into a ponytail with thick bangs, she projected an air of gravitas and austere chic at the opening cocktail reception.

The Peridot platform put Ruth's art in good company. The gallery's forte was American art, including abstract paintings by Philip Guston and sculpture by the French-born Louise Bourgeois (who became a naturalized U.S. citizen). The gallery also showed work by European luminaries Paul Cezanne, Constantin Brancusi, Henri Matisse, and Henry Moore. The affiliation sparked four years of intense productivity in her home studio. As museums follow gallery trends, Ruth was invited to submit a piece for a show at the Whitney Museum of American Art, and another for the rental gallery at New York's Museum of Modern Art (MOMA). Ruth fed Pollack's appetite for her works, and in turn Peridot fed the interest of collectors and museum curators.

The Manhattan art scene was a critical arena for the young sculptor, but it was far from Ruth's natural habitat. She wasn't brought up to tout her successes or indulge in celebrations. She would later reflect she was "grateful" for all the good things and the important sales that flowed from this exposure. *Gratitude* is a word that appears with increasing frequency in her letters and speeches as she aged. But the young Ruth, taking on the fraught New York art market, kept a low-key profile and humble tone about it all. It was almost as if she reverted to her truck farm work ethic. She got back to her studio work. In her correspondence with Peridot, she focused on determining the gallery's appetite for sculpture of a certain metal, finish, or dimension, and the nuts and bolts of whether it could be shipped safely, had arrived intact, or got damaged and needed restoration. Her work was arduous and unrelenting—especially since she was often nauseated from morning sickness, nursing an infant, or tending toddlers at her feet.

In 1954, the San Francisco Museum of Art in Civic Center—precursor of the city's Museum of Modern Art—mounted an exhibition titled *Four Artist Craftsmen*. The show in fact featured four *female* artists' work: sculptures by Ruth Asawa; jewelry by Merry Renk; weavings by Ida Dean Grae; and pottery by Marguerite Wildenhain, another émigré from the Bauhaus. The show was something of a family affair: Albert designed the exhibition and installed it with Ida's husband, Dan Grae. It drew good reviews, yet the label "craftsman" stuck to Ruth's early work, however devoid it was of the utilitarian features that mark pure craft. Although Albers's Bauhaus ethic dissolved walls between art and craft, Ruth was aiming for recognition in the fine arts.

San Francisco Chronicle art critic Alfred Frankenstein wrote of her looped wire creations, "Miss Asawa's sculpture is perhaps the most remarkable of these four expressions . . . fluent and beautifully rounded. . . . [T]his method, introduced in tentative fashion some years ago, has decidedly come of age."

Growing artistic prominence didn't guarantee easing of financial pressures on the young couple. They didn't waste money and were happy to accept friends' offers of hand-me-down children's clothing. But there was little to spare. When a friend wrote to Ruth and Albert from Mexico in 1954 seeking a loan of $200, they acknowledged, "We have no money." Hudson had just begun to walk. They were all just trying to stay on their feet.

If a single review signaled Ruth had arrived, it was the piece that appeared just after New Year's Day 1955. *Time* magazine, in its January 10 issue, ran a double review, titled "Eastern Yeast," reporting on two separate exhibitions by the revered sculptor Isamu Noguchi and the young Ruth Asawa. With European art in "the doldrums," the piece said, Americans were turning to the art of Asia:

> *Noguchi, 50, has long been recognized as a leading U.S. sculptor . . .*
>
> *Ruth Asawa, 28, is a San Francisco housewife and mother of three. She was born and raised in California, studied under Abstract Painter Josef Albers at Black Mountain College. Her show consists of big, wholly abstract sculptures, made of woven wire and suspended from the ceiling. If Noguchi's ceramics demonstrate a certain grinning bounciness in the Japanese heritage, Asawa's wire constructions show the opposite side: austerity and calm. In their openness, delicacy and symmetry they somewhat resemble blossoms, odorless, colorless, outsize, yet refreshing to contemplate.*
>
> *Noguchi and Asawa share one quality of Oriental art that Western artists often lack: economy of means. Their Japanese ancestors devoted vast efforts to making a single brush stroke look easy. By confining themselves to simple shapes made of patted mud and woven wire respectively, Noguchi and Asawa also achieved a pleasing quality of ease and oneness with their work. Judged by one standard test of art, i.e. the proportion of visible effort to effect, their sculptures stand high.*

The review was an extraordinary validation of so young an artist. It put her on the map before the broadest possible swathe of the American public. Yet, it was a mixed blessing. While *Time* recognized Asawa by reviewing her with Noguchi, it also

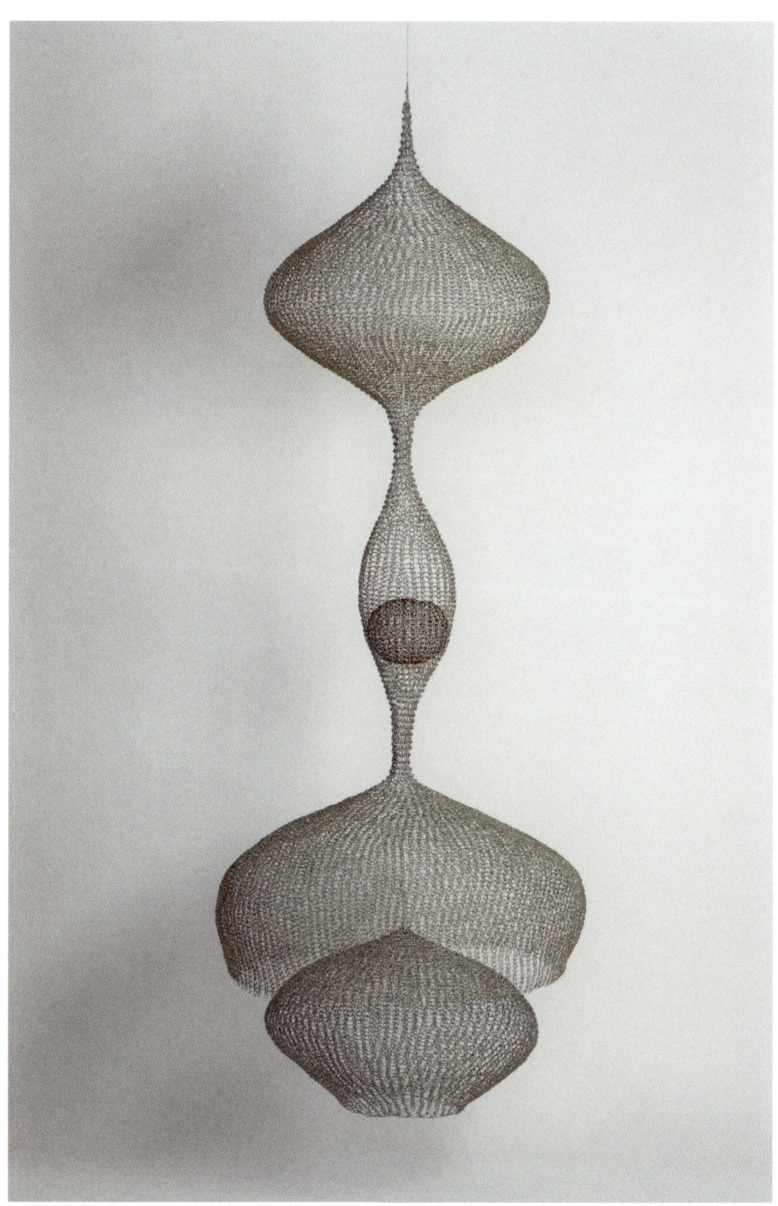

Untitled (S.042), 1954
Aluminum and brass wire
90 x 36 x 36 in. (2.3 m x 91.4 cm x 91.4 cm)
Photograph by Laurence Cuneo

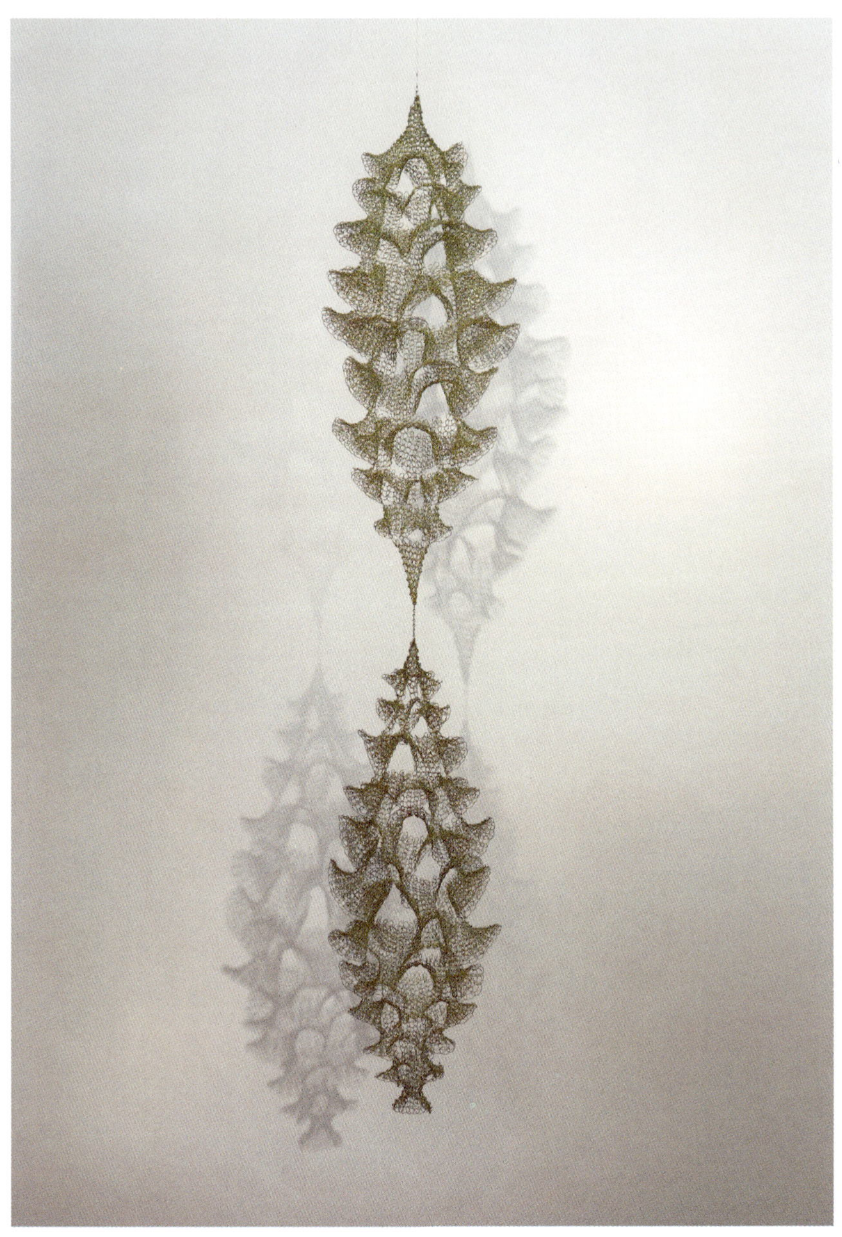

Untitled (S.302), *ca. 1954*
Brass wire
68 x 15 x 15 in. (1.7 m x 38.1 cm x 38.1 cm)
Photograph by Laurence Cuneo

described the Black Mountain–trained fine artist as a "housewife and mother." Twin impulses to domesticate her and to exoticize her as "Oriental" were both reductive. This attitude also ignored her true origin story as a Southern California farm girl, interned for Japanese parentage, who transcended a wartime imprisonment to make wire into art of surpassing beauty. Ruth's American story would take decades for the public to appreciate—and almost as long for Ruth herself to acknowledge explicitly.

Such biases seem less bizarre considering the cultural context of 1955 America, as reflected throughout that issue of *Time*. At home, the magazine noted, Americans tuned into television shows starring dogs, Rin Tin Tin and Lassie. In theaters, the top-grossing film was *White Christmas*. On the eve of his State of the Union address, President Eisenhower played a round of golf at the segregated Augusta National Golf Club, where his press secretary handed reporters buttons saying "Relax." Fifties pop culture was in full cry. For their part, Ruth and Albert refused to get a television for many years, fearing it would stunt their children's imaginations.

Even so, Asawa's sculpture steadily drew recognition at home and abroad. The Whitney Museum of American Art 1955 and 1956 Annual Exhibitions included wire hangings by Asawa. Her sculpture traveled to Brazil for the North American Exposition of the third Biennial de Sao Paulo in October and November of 1955.

Ahead of the Seventy-Fifth Annual Painting and Sculpture Exhibition of the San Francisco Art Association in spring 1956, critics and juries still wrestled with whether Asawa's sculpture was art or craft—and even whether it was sculpture at all. This was because it was suspended rather than being anchored to earth like, say, a Henry Moore; and unlike Calder's mobiles, her sculptures turned on a single axis. Bolstered by Albert's advocacy, she made the case for her work belonging to the world of art and sculpture, but the struggle to secure her place in fine art would continue.

Despite her steadily rising public profile, Ruth was reserved with people she didn't know, and protective of her time and privacy. When a prospective purchaser in Indiana wrote asking if his students could visit Ruth's studio, she dodged the request:

> *Please do me a favor and not pass my address around to your students. I am quite anti-social and self-conscious and would feel like a monkey at the zoo.*

She also kept busy filling up her nursery. In June 1956, Ruth wrote to Louis Pollack of the Peridot Gallery:

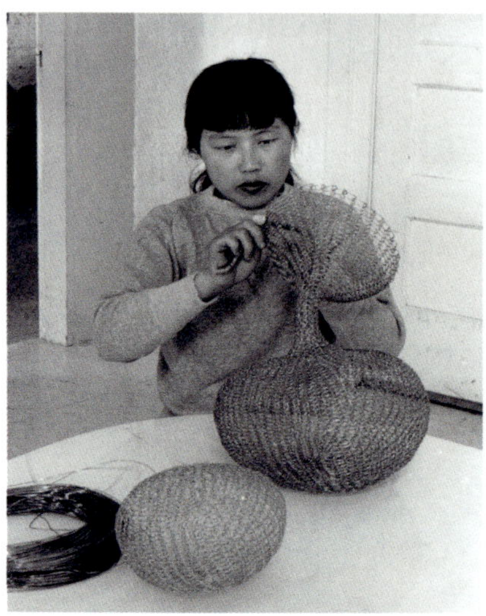

Ruth, looping a transparent sculpture from a coil of wire at left, 1956. Photograph by Imogen Cunningham.

. . . [N]ews of another baby. We are adopting him; he is now 10 days old. All of us are very happy.

Nesting happily that summer, Ruth wrote Pollack that she planned to stick close to home with their new baby boy, Adam, their three other children, and a plastic pool in the backyard. Her new arrival, the child of a Japanese mother and Caucasian father, was quietly adopted out of their continuing conviction that his Asian American background would let him blend imperceptibly and thrive in the Lanier family. Ruth happily shared her news with a couple of collectors who were purchasing a sculpture in August:

He is 7 weeks old and a joy, incidentally he is howling his lungs out this minute.

Asawa didn't luxuriate in domesticity for long. She longed to return to her roots in Japanese calligraphy, this time studying with Zen master Hodo Tobase in San Francisco. He resuscitated her love of the exquisite simplicity and discipline of the brush defining a line in space. She applied herself to her brushwork, and even wrote letters to the Peridot Gallery to suggest they mount a show of Tobase's work. The gallery declined her effort to promote the master's art.

Friends began sending—and Ruth began saving—clippings of reviews. In the *New York Times*, a critic mistook her sculptures' beauty as merely decorative:

Ruth Asawa's sculptures form an unusual exhibition at the Peridot Gallery, 820 Madison Avenue. Miss Asawa, who works on the West Coast, has invented a technique related to the old system of weaving chain mail. Her globular forms are created with a single silver, brass or gold wire, patiently woven in a uniform, delicate pattern. Airy and buoyant, these sculptures hang bobbing cheerfully, and turning slowly so that light weaves gossamer patterns on their surfaces. At times the shapes are like extended gourds, at times like straw hats atop one another. At times they are conical or columnar. Miss Asawa achieves graceful effects by suspending smaller forms within the larger and animating the whole. They are beautiful if primarily only decorative objects in space.

But the *San Francisco Chronicle*'s veteran critic Alfred Frankenstein continued to stress her importance in his reviews:

Ruth Asawa's huge abstractions in knitted wire mesh, with transparent black and gold forms, interpenetrating in subtle rhythms, remain among the most important contributions to sculpture to emerge from California.

With juries and critics debating art versus craft, sculpture versus decoration, Ruth was caught between their insatiable appetite for the new and their lack of vision or critical vocabulary to comprehend or describe it.

Yet she continued to delight the eye. In April 1956, the journal *Arts* reviewed her Peridot show:

The eye is actually dazzled when, as in some pieces, the wire is intricately interwoven, the innermost shape barely discernable through its several-layered shell. Like shaped weavings of various sizes are hung together; there is a conglomeration of various-colored wire balloons. It is a beautifully fanciful notion to pursue so thoroughly; the delight in it is at once as evanescent as the shadows the works cast, and as penetrable as their surfaces.

Louis Pollack wrote on April 17 to praise the critical success of Ruth's latest show, if not for its commercial yield:

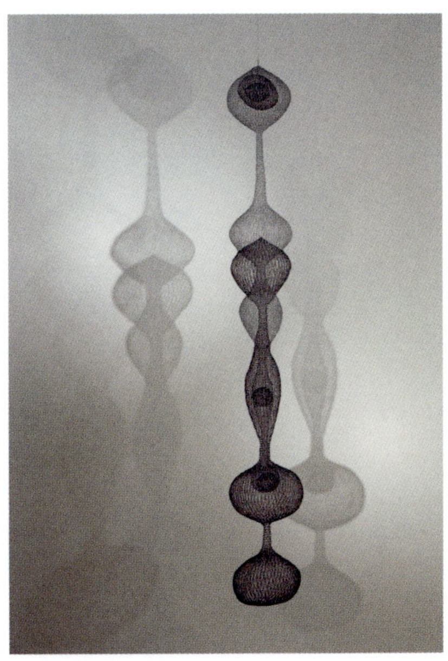

Untitled (S.250), *ca. 1955*
Iron and galvanized steel wire
121.5 x 16 x 16 in. (308.6 x 40.6 x 40.6 cm)
Photograph by Laurence Cuneo

. . . I've been meaning to tell you for some time now how beautiful your show was. It made a marvelous exhibition and drew a very good attendance all the time that it was hanging. The reviews were good (I'm enclosing copies—another is in the current issue of Art News*) and helped some. Sales I'm sorry to say were not stupendous but we did sell the big black and gold piece (which is now in the current Whitney Museum annual) and the other day we sold the small round gold sculpture for $200 to Philip Johnson. We haven't been paid for either piece yet but as soon as the checks arrive I'll send you a check for the amount due you. And there are other possibilities coming up.*

A few days ago we loaned the tear-shaped trio of sculptures to Black, Star and Gorham for display in their 5th Ave. window. It has already brought several people into the gallery to see more of your work. And yesterday we finally sent 9 of your older pieces up to Design Research in Cambridge. . . .

Quite a few people were interested in the piece that Philip Johnson bought last year and I'm sure that if we had anything like it we could have sold a few more. . . .

And that's about the news of the moment. Or haven't I told you that I became the father of a girl a couple of months ago. Our first. Her name is Claude. So this has kept me busy. Write soon. All best regards. Lou

Ruth allowed herself a moment to absorb his news, and wrote on May 3 that Kimiko had attended the show.

. . . How nice to hear about Claude! Send me a photo, before she gets too big.

Thank you for the letter with reviews, and good news of the show. Hope sale paid rent at least for you. We'll never get rich on sculpture will we? Glad to hear that Philip Johnson is still interested. I asked a friend about Black, Star and Gorham. She said !! "The Duke and Duchess of Windsor shop there!"

We've been working on a plastic sculptured wall covering, a geometric patterned thing which is beautiful, durable and white. The St. Francis Hotel ordered some for their Orchid Room . . . We don't expect to make millions on it, but it is very exciting to work in plastics. The field is wide open for new expression.

My sister visited your gallery. Do you remember seeing her. She is soft spoken, and has a beautiful face, and long black hair. Knowing her she probably did not bother to introduce herself. She wrote me saying the show was wonderful . . .

Sculptures in gold, silver, and monel wire were now selling at Peridot for as much as $500. If that seems substantial for the time, it was balanced against the risks artists took in shipping works across the country for shows. Ruth had to pack her delicate pieces and handle repairs and losses if the fragile lobes were mishandled and smashed in transit.

A financial statement from her spring 1956 exhibitions at Peridot shows how the artist's share of overhead cut into her sales revenue:

Expenses at Peridot, March 1956:
Advertising (N.Y. Times, Herald Tribune, Arts, Art News), *Envelopes, Postage*
and Photo Reprint.   Total $127.68.
Sales—Philip Johnson (gold wire, $200)
Howard Lipman (black & gold, $540)
Total due to artist from sales—$493.33
Exhibition expenses—$127.68
Balance due to Asawa—$365.65
5/7/56—Pd. Asawa for Lipman sale $360.00
less exhibition expenses—$232.32
Balance due—$133.33.

In early 1958, Ruth continued winding wire to fill brisk demand, while managing business correspondence with Pollack. It took strength of will to stay focused. Not only was she pregnant again, but also fighting her usual extended bouts of nausea. She wrote:

I apologize for the slow reply. I've been sick for the last four months from my new baby due in June. This will be our 5th, but I'm one of those who remains sick thruout the pregnancy, but I am working and will have enough ready for the March show. I want to also exhibit drawings this time and am working on that too. I will be submitting photographs to the Museum of Modern Art Sculpture show due the 24th of this month, so would like to know which pieces are available at your gallery to submit them.

In June, Ruth and Albert welcomed their fifth child and second daughter, Addie Laurie, named in honor of Albert's sister, who had been the first in the Lanier family to befriend Ruth. Addie would be an avid dancer as a child and later become a teacher. Now, at thirty-two, Ruth was a mother of five.

Pollack's partner, John Hohnsbeen, dispatched businesslike notes urging Ruth to keep sending new ideas because he said he lacked enough first-class pieces to anchor a new show. Ruth replied somewhat dejectedly to Pollack that she feared he was getting bored with her work.

Even on the edge of working poverty, Ruth was too proud to take any purely commercial commission that came her way. In October she wrote to Erwine Laverne relating a recent request for a sculpture to adorn a building she thought was called Bolero. It turned out to be Bowlero, a fifty-six-lane bowling alley where her sculpture would look woefully out of place and "superfluous" amid the rolling balls and crashing pins. Ruth asked Laverne to be discerning and avoid sending such incongruous commissions her way. Still, she closed on a cheerfully defiant note, declaring that, with the arrival of Addie, they were "too busy to consider whether we are happy or not."

Peridot was ready to send a bright brass hanging 66 inches long to New York's Museum of Modern Art, but a couple of clients "fell in love" and bought it for $750, yielding $500 to the artist. The gallery sent MOMA a red and black wire piece instead. On November 26, 1958, Ruth wrote Pollack:

Dear Lou, The $500 is certainly encouraging. Hope there are more sales.

Since she was now in her fourth year of an exclusive relationship with the Peridot Gallery, which even controlled her ability to show and sell elsewhere, she inquired about a contract, which might offer her some security. The gallery turned her down, saying it never struck such deals with artists.

Then sales slumped around the New Year of 1959, with the gallery blaming "holidays and inertia . . . a terrible combination." But Hohnsbeen added on a cheerier note: "Your sculpture is importantly hanging in the Whitney display window on the street level. HAPPY NEW YEAR."

It was in fact a mixed new year. In April, Ruth was diagnosed with a minor heart murmur, which the doctors dismissed as medically insignificant. She'd been pushing hard on as many fronts as she could. In addition to the recently concluded *1958 Annual Exhibition: Paintings, Sculptures, Watercolors, Drawings* at the Whitney, her sculpture appeared in *Recent Sculptures USA*, organized by MOMA in 1959.

At home in San Francisco, she had two sculptures in the city's art association annual, a national juried show. However, she'd not yet had a one-woman show in San Francisco, and her last major museum exhibition was as one of the *Four Artist Craftsmen* in 1954. "I feel finally that I must show something," she wrote.

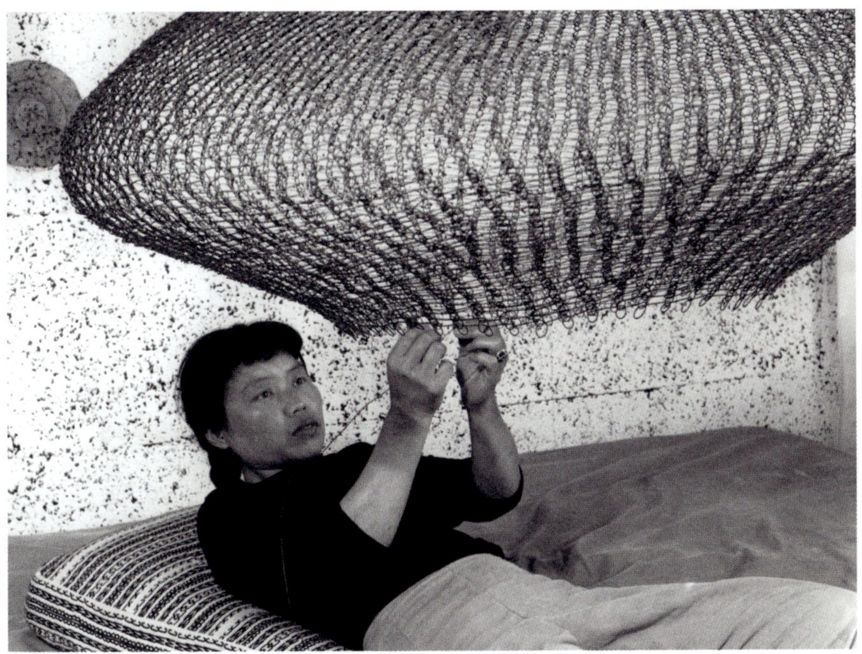

Ruth, forming a loop-wire sculpture, 1957. Photograph by Imogen Cunningham.

Worried about the great expense of mounting such a show, she hoped to combine it with a New York exhibition to reduce the expense. Having discussed the idea of a fall 1959 show with the curator of painting and sculpture at the M. H. de Young Memorial Museum, she hoped it could then be shipped to Peridot and shown there.

Is that possible . . . Would it be possible sometime to have a show of drawings? I have been drawing a lot and eventually hope to paint too and leave wire alone for awhile . . .

But Peridot, while willing to mount a show of mixed media, adding some drawings to a sculpture exhibition, said no to a show based entirely on Ruth's drawings. Added to that disappointment were logistical complications: Ruth's new wire hangings were growing too long to hang comfortably in Peridot's low-ceilinged space. Asawa's now five-year collaboration with the gallery seemed to be hitting a plateau.

Meanwhile, a writer for the *Christian Science Monitor* wrote Ruth requesting background for a feature profile to be published on its Women's Page. Ruth agreed to correspond and let her in on the secret of juggling sculpture and family: "I'm used to noise and confusion and hard work." Then, in her usual fashion, she tried to share the spotlight and deflect the reporter's attention onto her friend:

> *You should do an article on my photographer and friend, Imogen Cunningham. She has been photographing since 1901, and still takes pictures now . . . An amazing and most wonderful person who would and has given much courage to face old age. She is past 70 and still more active than us. . . .*
>
> *Miss Cunningham has been photographing my work for years. She has been paid practically nothing for photographs reproduced with articles. If the* Monitor *pays a fee, I would appreciate her being paid, since her livelihood depends on it . . . She is tops.*

In spite of market doldrums, she and Albert were again planning for an expansion. Her ideal family circle was finally coming into sight, amid a resurgence of that now-familiar queasiness. She announced her news matter-of-factly in a letter to the Peridot gallery:

> *. . . I'm pregnant again and feeling low. This is #6 for us.*

Paul Asawa Lanier, born in 1959, completed the circle of six children that Ruth had pictured since her school days. Her youngest son had his mother's jet-black hair, and his artistic drive focused on the design of ceramics.

Albert, meanwhile, had long dreamed of founding his own architectural firm. After working with a string of San Francisco architects—Mario Corbett, Roy Maru, and John Funk—he found a partner in Paul Sherrill. Together, in 1960 they launched Albert's most lasting venture, Lanier & Sherrill (later Lanier, Sherrill, Morrison). Locating an office on Mission Street in a building of brick and old wood, Albert suspended airy Asawa sculptures from the ceiling over each of the firm's seven desks. The atmosphere was low-key and companionable, with classical music on the radio. During breaks, Albert would smoke and listen to opera, offering dry commentary. When a soprano sang a plaintive aria, he would drawl in mock dismay, "Pore thang!" When a romantic tenor hit the climactic high note, Albert would say, "He's gonna get 'er!"

Lanier & Sherrill's early projects included converting the century-old Southern Pacific Hospital on Fell Street into the Mercy Terrace senior apartments, and design-ing the Casa de Vida, an apartment designed for the disabled. Albert fought for preservation of old buildings over their demolition. His signature design elements were space and light, according to a longtime colleague. In his residential designs, he prized simplicity and function over grandeur and gadgetry.

But now he had to turn his attention to securing shelter for his own family. With eight people under one roof, the Asawa-Lanier household was bursting the seams of Saturn Street. Once again, Ruth and Albert scanned the city for new living quarters. For Ruth, the 1960s would be a decade of transitions and shifting relationships: a new home, a new one-woman show, and new directions for her restless energy.

CHAPTER 7

A WORKSHOP IN NOE VALLEY

The quest for space to live and work drove the Laniers and their tribe of six from the crowded Saturn Street house to a neighborhood in the city's Outer Mission district, now known as Noe Valley, south of Market Street.

The sunny hollow, sheltered from fog coming off the ocean, boasted the best weather in the city. The land had been part of a nineteenth-century rancho owned by the city's last Mexican mayor, José de Jesus Noé. Through the mid-twentieth century, it was a neighborhood of working-class houses. Gentrification would make it a magnet for tech tycoons like Facebook founder Mark Zuckerberg in the twenty-first century. But back in 1960, the intersection of the Outer Mission and Noe Valley had a funky, family-friendly air.

A tip from a friend drew them to a humble cedar-shingled house dating back to just after the 1906 earthquake, when the city experienced a building boom. Designed in a rustic style pioneered by Bernard Maybeck, it had originated as a two-bedroom honeymoon cottage for a newlywed couple. The house had some quirky features, like an organ loft. It needed a massive overhaul when the Laniers bought it in 1960.

But it had a sunny garden and room to expand up and down. Though the house was modest and unassuming from the outside, its Douglas fir living room had high-beamed ceilings for Ruth to hang her sculptures from, and space to add a workshop-studio and sleeping quarters for their children, now aged one to ten. One museum director would say it was like entering "a rustic cabin . . . a gold miner's cabin," and finding a cathedral of art within: "high ceilings, wood interior, with sculptures . . . it's magic."

Getting it into shape for a family of eight took time. So Ruth spent the summer up on the Russian River with her half-dozen kids. Albert had bought a simple barn north of the city, in the town of Guerneville. He chose the spot because it was close to their Black Mountain friend and fellow artist Marguerite Wildenhain's pottery workshop, Pond Farm, where their son Paul would later study for three summers. The Laniers' rural retreat was a primitive structure with a smoky firepit but plenty of space to unroll sleeping bags for visiting friends and guests. As Albert and Ruth's sons grew, they would later remodel the property.

Turning a summer adventure into a work experience, Asawa used the time to introduce her older children to the physical labor she had known as a farm child. A grower paid the Lanier children $3.75 per half-ton bin to pick windfall Gravenstein apples off the ground, for use in pressing cider and making vinegar. They were too young to climb ladders for picking eating fruit off the trees, a more dangerous job that paid a higher rate. They worked alongside migrant laborers in the searing Sonoma summer and were often joined by friends' families. On a good day, working from eight to five, the groups with their mothers could pick nine bins; a poor day's yield was five. Said Xavier of the time:

> *The idea was to show us what work was. We were kids and couldn't climb trees, so we'd pick them up off the ground for juice or vinegar. My mom would give us peanut butter sandwiches. That's how we spent the days, picking apples and going to the river after. I got fifty dollars for the summer for school clothes.*

Ruth sweated alongside all the children—all except Addie and Paul, who were excused from apple picking because they were toddlers. Sometimes in the heat of long workdays, mischief erupted. One day the Satterfields, an African American family with eight kids, joined the picking. The kids and their mothers all piled into

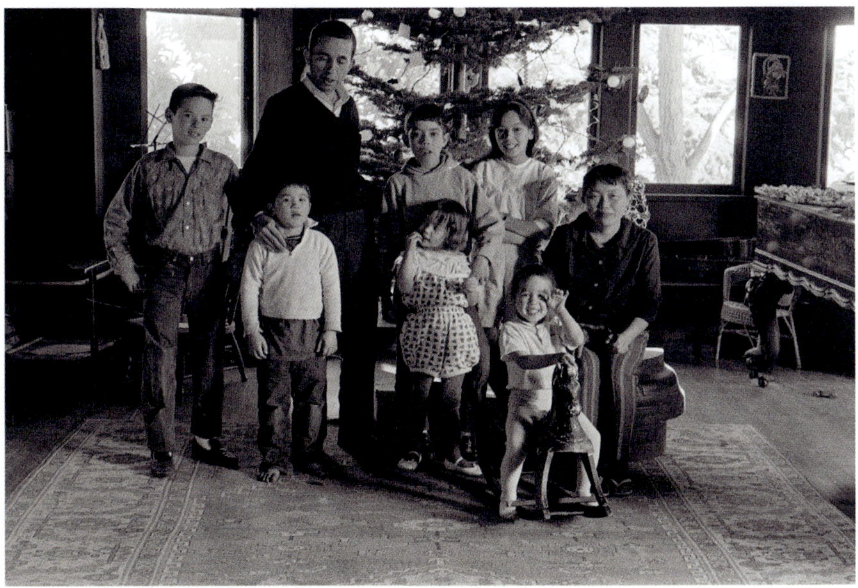

Asawa–Lanier family, Christmas 1962. Photograph by Paul Hassel.

a Volkswagen van (in the days before seatbelts were the law). After a long grueling week, the two families were on the way to pick up their paycheck. A nearby pigpen owned by the orchard owners had in the past become a tempting target for the kids. Occasionally, somebody started hurling apples at the pigs, and Ruth wanted to avoid barnyard mayhem. She hastily herded her kids into the van with a lecture.

"OK, we're not going to throw apples at the pigs," she said. "Are we, Xavier?" "No." "Hudson? "No." "Aiko?" "No." The roll call continued until she got to Adam.

"Adam? Adam? ADAM??" There was no answer from five-year-old Adam, only an alarming silence.

He wasn't in the van. Just as all of the other kids and two moms were boarding the van to leave, Adam had ducked behind an apple bin to relieve himself, and in the crowd, they had driven off without him. His absence discovered, Ruth pulled a fast U-turn back toward the apple orchard.

About a half mile from the field, they spotted a dusty, tearful straggler. There was Adam, barreling down the center of the country road from the orchard to catch up, determined to find his way back home.

Once soothed, Adam came to love Guerneville for its campouts under the stars. It was a summer destination for family and friends like Imogen Cunningham, who seized every chance to go out with Ruth and glean plums destined for her jams, compotes, and *Kuchen*. Ruth and Albert's July 3 wedding anniversary often fell during their stay. They would celebrate with a waltz to "The Beautiful Blue Danube."

Meanwhile, Albert renovated the Noe Valley house with thrift and gumption. He used recycled and repurposed materials. His work team included friends, schoolboys, odd jobbers, a few union workers, and alcoholics who stashed empties around the site. "We kept finding them for years after," Albert said. He paid Hudson and Xavier $1.25 a weekend for helping with the house, with an extra quarter on Sundays, which they spent at the local Bud's Ice Cream store.

The motley crew transformed the house into a five-bedroom home, enlarging the living space up and down without losing any precious garden space. It now had a large kitchen, an attic bedroom for the girls, and dormitory-like sleeping quarters for the boys suspended between Ruth's studio and the backyard. It had a brick terrace in front, and a deep backyard for growing things.

Albert and Ruth planted a sentimental garden, fragrant with roses, wisteria, bleeding heart, rosemary, columbine, and iris. A teenaged Xavier would craft spherical white lamps according to a geodesic dome design licensed from Buckminster Fuller. Anticipating the future "high-low" style of design, there would be art by Asawa and Albers mixed with furniture from secondhand shops Albert called "junk stores."

Over time, Albert would use savings to buy adjacent houses and take down the fences that divided their backyards, making a family compound and opening up a communal garden. Albert and Ruth's fruit trees, vegetables, and herbs would feed their family and fill gift baskets for their friends, continuing the Asawa truck farm tradition of shared harvests.

Albert built Ruth a large butcher-block table with space to set extra plates for visiting neighbors, friends, and artists who stopped by. She'd share duties like making salad dressing, and teach friends how to whisk up a batch of gravy, then quietly set them a place.

"Ruth is a feeder," Albert would say. That table saw many years of epic family potlucks on American holidays like Thanksgiving and Christmas, as well as celebrations of the New Year in Japanese style, when 125 guests would come to eat sushi, sashimi, and home-cooked mochi—pounded rice cakes that bring good fortune to the festive table.

The master plan of the home, studio, and garden fulfilled Ruth's dream of merging a family home and a working artist's studio with an urban garden. The house became the hub of activity that satisfied her needs—now increasingly inseparable—to make art and to rear her children under one roof, with Albert as chief engineer and architect.

"Albert had incredible space sensibilities," said architect Bill Bondy, who would become a draftsman for Albert's firm. "He would organize around space and light." Albert's designs were a blend of form and function, spare of ornament, producing airy, open dwellings out of modest space and materials.

Lessons learned from building the Minimum House at Black Mountain stuck with Albert. He wanted a dwelling open to the outdoors, bringing in the light. He used practical materials like pegboard, stainless steel, and butcher block in the kitchen before they became hallmarks of industrial chic. He incorporated artisanal touches like handmade tiles. His credo of maximum effect with minimum effort was a legacy of Buckminster Fuller's engineering and Josef Albers's aesthetics.

Albert defended his aesthetics with an acid tongue that could be comical or cutting, depending on which side of the debate you found yourself. He slammed a local library for being so vulgar and encrusted with kitsch that it needed only a lighted jukebox and neon cocktail glass with a girl on the rim to complete the effect. Albert's design sense would get him invited to serve on the city's landmarks board; his "abrasive" style would get him fired from it.

After the tight quarters of their Alpine and Saturn Street homes, Ruth reveled in the space in Noe Valley. "We are moving to a bigger house so that we could get all of our 6 children in. The house will have a big workshop for all of us," she wrote to Lou Pollock at the Peridot Gallery.

The studio workshop accommodated Ruth's artistic output. And the house inspired and invited her to pursue two additional art forms: hand-carved wooden doors and life masks, which adorned the exterior. For the entrance, Ruth began carving massive redwood double doors with an abstract design of interlocking waves and whorls, a pattern reminiscent of Albers's design class exercises known as "meanders." She let each of her children work at carving curls, so they contributed their hands to part of the whole.

Not all of the kids immediately appreciated living with artist parents in a handcrafted house.

"Please, Mom, can't we have a normal American door?" asked Hudson as he approached his tenth birthday. "This house is freaky enough as it is." Eventually, as Ruth told a friend, he became resigned and made a model of the family's living room for a school project. But he still protested having to lay stones in the garden while his friends were out playing. "Look, you and Dad can work all the time if you want to," he said, "but I'm going to play some and work some."

"As a child, I wanted to be called Linda or Kathy, rather than Aiko," Ruth's oldest daughter said. "I wanted my mom to dress like June Cleaver, not in holey jeans,

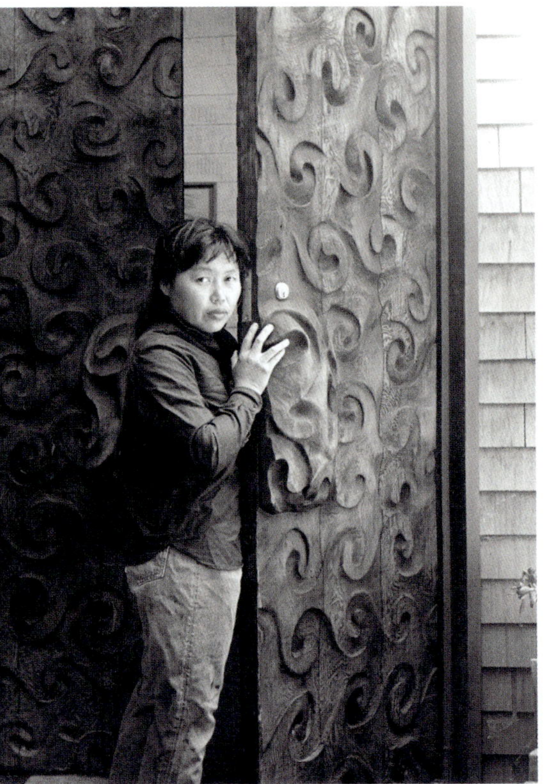

Ruth, poised before the redwood doors she carved by hand with her children for their home in San Francisco's Noe Valley, 1963. Photograph by Imogen Cunningham.

holey sweatshirt, holey sneakers." As an adult, Aiko abandoned the *Leave It to Beaver* sitcom standard of motherhood. "Now as an artist, I appreciate it," she said. She saved the holey jeans and sweatshirt.

The house's shingled exterior was a perfect space to hang the life masks Asawa was casting of her family and friends. Mounted there by the dozens, the masks formed growing clusters of three-dimensional portraits. Life-casting sessions became a regular feature of the Laniers' social gatherings. Guests would lie down while Ruth framed their faces with cardboard and coated their skin with Vaseline. Then, inserting straws in their nostrils as breathing tubes, she would slather their faces with quick-setting plaster. It was fun for the adventurous and a challenge for the claustrophobic. When dry, the cast became a mold for the masks. Guests emerged shining with a slick petroleum jelly on their faces to await the final creation in buff or terra-cotta clay. Over time, the faces populated the outside of the house, like a band of benign spirits.

Into her years of marriage and parenthood, Ruth kept the spirit of Black Mountain alive. Unlike some students who discard their college notebooks like sepia souvenirs, Ruth preserved her class notes as a living link to her mentors. She nurtured friendships with Albers and Fuller reverently, with the same care with which she looped wire and tended gardens.

Fuller visited Ruth in San Francisco. She made a life mask of Bucky's face and cast his hands in bronze. As an artist and a young mother, she never forgot his lessons about living with less and creating a space where experiential learning could flourish. She would go on to honor his ideas about the inborn genius of children by "giving every kindergartener a PhD." And she would practice principles of his synergetic learning, with peer participation.

"Bucky used to visit us. She'd take him to the schools and they'd fold milk cartons," Hudson said. "We knew when Bucky came to town, we'd have steak for dinner. We didn't have steak a lot. Though the steak was nice, you'd have to pay the price, and she'd make us sit around. He was talking about the icosahedron. He'd get out the butcher paper and this thing would go on for days. I don't think any of us knew what he was talking about. I remember him talking and using his hands a lot."

Xavier recalled, "I thought the guy was really out there. And he was. We were young. When he was talking to the adults, he was so far over our head[s]. People would just go silent. I remember him saying there were enough minerals in earth we'd never have to take anything more out. That had to do with waste."

Albers, as austere as Bucky was exuberant, remained Ruth's artistic lodestar. When he left Black Mountain to lead the design department at Yale, he and Ruth kept up their student-teacher dialogue. For Ruth, Albers's lessons on opening eyes, respecting materials, and placing craft above ego stayed fresh. Where some of his other students, like Robert Rauschenberg, were glad to escape his stern rule for New York, Ruth remained a most faithful disciple in San Francisco.

She also coveted his art. In 1956 while attending an Albers show at the San Francisco Museum of Art, Ruth fell in love with Albers's painting *Pastures*. Thinking it was within reach at $300, she wrote to the Sidney Janis Gallery in New York about buying it—only to learn $300 was the insurance value, and the retail sale price was $750, which she couldn't afford. The gallery offered to sell it to her at a discount for $500. "I am touched by Mr. Albers's generous offer, but cannot accept it for I feel that he should be paid what his paintings are worth," she wrote.

Years later, a mysterious package arrived. Ruth opened the white wrapping paper to find a radiant green painting from Albers's *Homage to the Square* series. He had gone around his gallery to send it directly. It was accompanied by a mischievous note on the wrapper:

Dear Ruthie
This is just for revenge
And it is yours for the promise not to acknowledge receiving it.
Love, A

A small, undated yellow note from the giver went a step further:

Dear Ruthie,
Some time ~~I want~~ I hope to exchange a scultpure of yours with a painting of mine.
Love, A

The secret gift hung in the Lanier home, a testament to Albers's evergreen mentorship, its hues subtly evolving with the sun's rays. Ruth was ecstatic:

Dear Mr. & Mrs. Albers:
This painting is magical. It vibrates, merges, reappears, changes each hour of the
day. Only a magician could do it. You have given me more than my share of your
love. I cherish it, as I still cherish the memory of those years as your student.

Big hug
Love
Ruth

Albers's green painting from his *Homage to the Square* series gave her years of pleasure—and incidentally increased exponentially in value, until it became a literal lifeline.

Ruth, in turn, shared her latest wire sculptures with Albers and Fuller. While the Alberses were away from Yale, lecturing and touring museums in Europe, Ruth sent them a wire sculpture with the undulating inside outside surfaces replicating the turns of a Möbius strip—one of Josef Albers's favorite motifs. Anni Albers typed a delighted note on January 23, 1960:

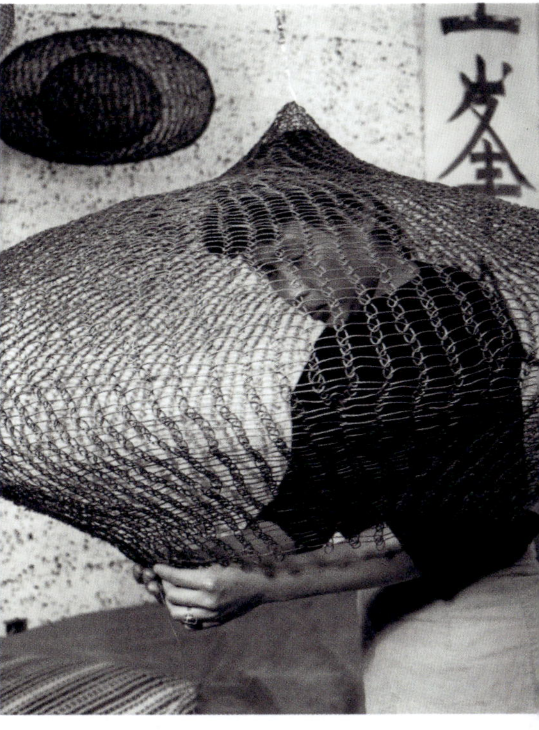

Ruth, working inside the lobe of a looped-wire sculpture, 1957. Photograph by Imogen Cunningham.

> *At our return from abroad, we found a big and mysterious box here and it was a marvelous surprise to find your fine sculpture! Thank you very much for sending it and for your great generosity . . . [I]t hangs at the time in our living room and we are still puzzled by its intricate movements, its Moebius tour. . . . We hope you and Albert are fine and also the many little ones . . .*

Josef Albers added a postscript in his tiny, elegant hand:

> *Dear Ruthie, I am so pleased that nowadays old Moebius is honored more and more. . . . Sometime you must come here and see all the reincarnations and all the other "structured" sculpture. Therefore, Auf Wiedersehn!*
> *Many many thanks and all our love.*
> *Yours, J.A.*

Ruth also shipped a wire sculpture to Buckminster and Anne Fuller. The couple installed it inside their dome house in Carbondale, Illinois, and telegraphed their thanks on October 15, 1961:

> RETURNED CARBONDALE LAST WEEK AND TODAY UNPACKED AND HUNG OUR MAGNIFICENT [ASAWA]. IT DIVIDES LIVING AND DINING AREAS AND DOMINATES DOME WITH ITS BEAUTY. SMALLER SPHERE HAS GONE TEMPORARILY TO NEW YORK . . . AND WILL RETURN TO LIGHT OUR LIVING AREA. WE LOVE YOU DEARLY [ARE] AMAZED THAT ANYONE CAN CREATE SUCH BEAUTY PUT SO MUCH OF HER LIFE IN TO SUCH WORK AND BESTOW IT OUT RIGHT UPON FRIENDS AND THANK YOU JOYOUSLY
> ANNE AND BUCKY FULLER.

Such mentors strengthened Ruth's confidence in her own independence as she wound down her relationship with the Peridot Gallery in New York, where she was literally outgrowing the space, as Louis Pollack wrote:

> [T]he fact remains, as you yourself point out, that some of your finest pieces are far too big for Peridot Gallery, since my ceiling is only eight feet high. [I]f you find that you are going to be working on larger pieces, it would be advisable for you to change galleries and you have my blessings. I have always enjoyed having your work around me and I regret very much that this step must be taken. I wish you the best of luck in finding another gallery and all the happiness to you and your family. Perhaps some day we will see each other again.

So Ruth and the Peridot Gallery ended a six-year working relationship of creating art, mounting shows, and selling her sculptures. In stepping back from the New York gallery scene to focus on family and her home studio after 1960, Ruth drew from lessons Albers had taught at Black Mountain. He had always placed artistic integrity over advancement. He encouraged her to think for herself after the challenges of war, imprisonment, and Milwaukee. Being asked her opinion and assigned to solve design problems gave her confidence in her own vision and voice, as she expressed it in a later interview with historian Mary Emma Harris, who founded the Black Mountain College Project:

> I think that's what Albers was saying. He wasn't interested in making artists out of us. He was interested in making us see, look. It's hard to define that. It's hard to say what

it was that he gave us, but I think it shaped me because, I had endured the internment and the discrimination before when Asians couldn't become citizens and they couldn't own property. I mean, all that happened before the war. Then during the war, we were interned, and we just went like sheep. You know, we followed. We were told to do this, so we did it. Then, suddenly, you come to a place like Black Mountain, and they say, "What are you thinking?" . . . Every moment they were asking. It was very hard. But I think the experience made me understand what to work on. . . . You can't work on how you were treated in camp and as a child in the Depression . . . You have to deal with what is unfair now. So, I had the choice of going to New York and building a career, making a name for myself, getting an exhibit, getting a gallery, getting all of that. Or I had to decide being a parent what I had to deal with what was at hand.

As Ruth prepared to work on her own, she tied up her unfinished business in New York with a grand gesture. Two big sculptures were left unsold at Peridot: a 6-foot nickel-plated copper-wire piece and a 6½-foot copper piece. She decided to make them gifts, one for Pollack and the other for Lorna Blaine Halper, her once-secret scholarship angel at Black Mountain.

"Overwhelmed" by Ruth's generosity, an abashed Pollack wrote to thank her, adding that he'd have bought one of her works if he'd ever had the spare cash.

In her New York apartment, Halper already owned one Asawa sculpture, whose silhouette filtered the morning sun. After visiting the Lanier family in San Francisco, she learned a second piece was awaiting her at Peridot. She eagerly collected her gift, and wrote to report that her new sculpture was mounted in her apartment, and "breathing elegantly."

Ruth's departure from Peridot—after three shows and several major purchases in 1954, 1956, and 1958—reduced her visibility as an artist on the New

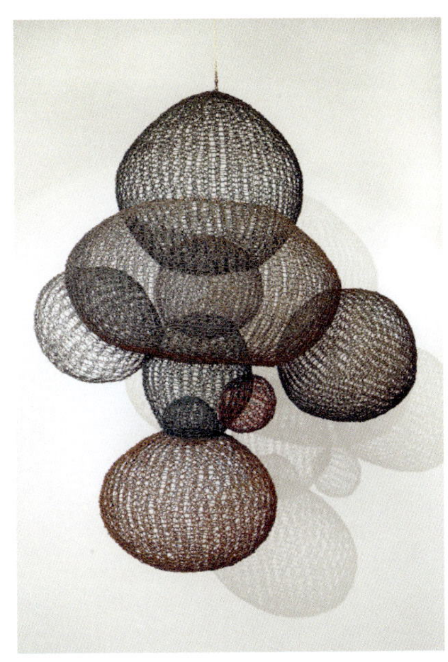

Untitled (S.055), ca. 1955
Galvanized steel, enameled copper, and brass wire
31.5 x 26.75 x 17.625 in. (80 x 67.9 x 44.8 cm)
Photograph by Laurence Cuneo

York art scene, where the influential curators, critics, and collectors were heavily concentrated. Maintaining a presence in New York had been lucrative, and introduced her to a world of tastemakers and connoisseurs with cash. But working with a Madison Avenue gallery was fraught with risk and expense for the artist. Arranging New York shows left her on the hook for shipping costs, and liable for potential damage to her wire sculptures if they were improperly packed or crushed in transit. These weren't trivial concerns for Ruth, with so many kids and so little cash. Creatively, too, she told an interviewer, Peridot had become too confining:

> *I decided that I wasn't interested in sending things to New York, although they sold my work, and many nice things happened out of that first show: Mrs. Nelson Rockefeller (the first one) came and bought a piece and Mrs. John D. III bought a piece out of that show. These were sculptures; it was only a sculpture show. And subsequently I wanted to do a show of drawings with my sculpture and the gallery felt that they had built up an image of me as a sculptor; they didn't want to cloud the issue. So they refused to show my drawings, which I thought was too bad.*

California was now the home and epicenter for her family and her art. She was on her own, no longer having to credit or pay Peridot as her representative when she sold a sculpture. Unlike some of her peers in art, Ruth seemed unconcerned with the prestige of her gallery representation or her own status. But her move left open the question of whether future art historians would honor her independence from the New York scene, or consign her to niche status as a regional craftswoman.

The first to show a solo Asawa exhibition in the post-Peridot era was the M. H. de Young Memorial Museum in Golden Gate Park. The de Young was born as a fine arts exhibit within the Midwinter International Exposition of 1894. The chair of the organizing committee was Michael H. de Young, founder of the *San Francisco Chronicle* and a collector of gems and curiosities.

Set in a green oasis in the heart of San Francisco, the de Young was vulnerable to earthquakes that regularly shook the city, so it required regular repairs and, much later, a total tear-down and rebuild in the new millennium. The museum would work hard to shake its image as a cabinet of curiosities and reinvent itself as one of the most-visited art museums and centers of art education in the West. In years to come, Asawa would serve the museum as artist, advocate, and trustee.

Happily, the de Young exhibition in 1960 didn't limit Asawa to a single medium, but included both sculptures and works on paper. To Ruth, the two media were inextricably linked: Her ink drawings grew from her calligraphy training as a child, and her sculpture embodied the calligraphic line in wire, following it through into three-dimensional space. The show would, in Albers's phrase, open the eyes of San Francisco museumgoers, including conservative socialites in heels, hats, and gloves, who were photographed wandering about the sculpture gallery like tourists visiting some silvery, space-age aquarium of the future.

Ruth was still confounding the conventional critics, who strained to describe her works. Miriam Dungan Cross, an art reviewer for the *Oakland Tribune*, wrote:

> *Ruth Asawa's webs of wonder, called "sculpture" for want of a better word, lace the upper reaches of the de Young Gallery.*

The webs of wonder didn't confuse *Chronicle* critic Frankenstein, who recognized a new form of sculpture without any need to put quotation marks around the word:

> *Miss Asawa possesses one of the most original and unprecedented styles of any sculptor in America.*

Ruth was drawing daily, while her children were napping or playing at the park, as well as overnight as the family slept. From a childhood spent rising before dawn on the farm, she established an adult working life that rarely included more than four hours of sleep. Her work of the period began to merge the abstract with the personal, including genre pieces that embedded references to her daily domestic life and family. In a 1960 ink-and-graphite drawing, *Addie*, a geometric study of stitches across a voluminous quilt dominates the field, while one corner holds a tiny, tender portrait of her sleeping two-year-old daughter.

Ruth's drawings and sculptures went downtown to the San Francisco Museum of Art, the precursor of the city's Museum of Modern Art, which was then housed in the city's Civic Center. Drawings of plane trees and redwoods, and botanical studies of persimmons and pumpkins were on sale—none of them for over $250. (*Addie* was marked "NFS," or not for sale.) The wire hanging sculptures in copper and galvanized steel mesh were offered at prices ranging from $300 to $650. At that time, sculptures shown by the museum's rental gallery cost a few tens of dollars a month. Art lovers could rent to buy an Asawa, much like purchasing a piano on time. However, artists had the unenviable job of sending letters to prompt tardy renters to pay up. The truth was, Ruth disliked selling her work—comparing it to selling her children. She often preferred to give away work or offer it on an extended loan with the condition she could recall it for a show. The critic Frankenstein praised her ink drawings of simple things, rendered with subtlety he labeled as being in the "Oriental" tradition.

The label "Oriental" was a term critics tossed around through the 1960s without inducing the cringes it would elicit today, as a word suggesting cultural condescension. Even then, the label failed to reflect the more complex reality that Ruth was, notwithstanding her bloodlines, an American-born and -educated artist.

Ruth was no fan of any labels—female, Asian, modern—preferring to stand on her own, as an individual "minority of one," making works as a pure exploration of the material itself.

By design, Ruth worked with her children nearby, pausing only to make a sandwich or prepare a bottle as needed. Xavier and Aiko helped look after their younger siblings, pitching in to wash laundry and change diapers. (Xavier recalled that his father, though a breadwinner and ardent supporter of his artist-wife, didn't change very many diapers.) In a black-and-white portrait, Imogen Cunningham captured the scene of Ruth at work with her children clustered around her, absorbed in their play or observing their mother at work, while a naked baby Adam drinks a bottle.

It was a lean lifestyle, and the Lanier children learned not to waste or whine. School clothes included hand-me-downs, Xavier remembered. Ruth shopped with her kids in tow at the farmers market, where vendors always slipped her a little extra, and at the discount grocery Xavier called "the dented can store." Ruth was a frugal but hearty home cook, he said, and, "We always ate well." Dining out might be limited to Chinese banquets a couple times a year. But they were rich in art, tools, and projects everywhere.

In 1962, Ruth received the present of a desert plant that sparked a whole new form of wire sculpture. Photographer Paul Hassel, who shot photos of many Asawa sculptures, took a desert trip and returned to San Francisco bearing a spiky bush whose shape he thought she might like to draw. The tumbleweed-like growth, bristling with branches, fascinated Ruth. But its structure was so complex, it eluded her pen. To tease out its structure from the tangle of branches, she decided to take a bundle of wires and tie off successively smaller bundles of branches from the center. She sculpted the plant's structure.

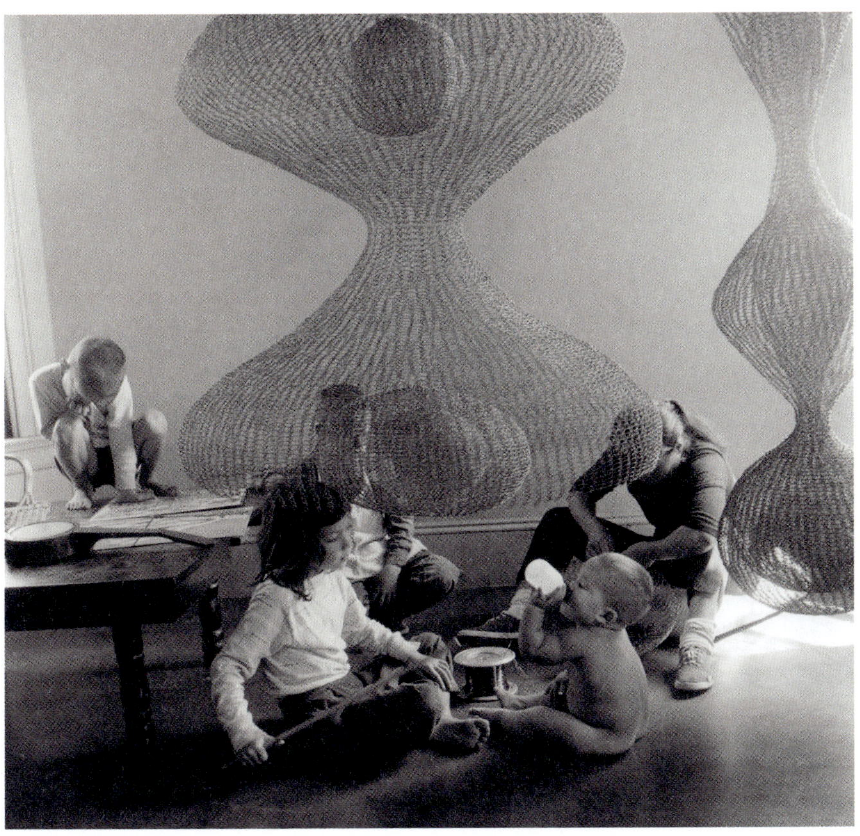

At work in her home studio, Ruth is surrounded by her children, 1957. Photograph by Imogen Cunningham.

Thus were born Asawa's "tied-wire" sculptures—sharp and edgy counterparts to the softly undulating wire hangings. When set on a pedestal, some resembled spherical dandelions on stems or topiary trees. Others were flat and two-dimensional, with branches radiating outward like a sunburst or star form, meant to be mounted on a wall. Inspired by dewdrops on evergreen tips, Ruth dipped the ends in a clear resin to create the effect of dew sparkling in the sun, as she later explained in an interview:

> *You know how, in the winter, how the water hangs loose on pine needles and branches? I've done that so that it looks like water . . . And then all these circles in the light reflects all the colors.*

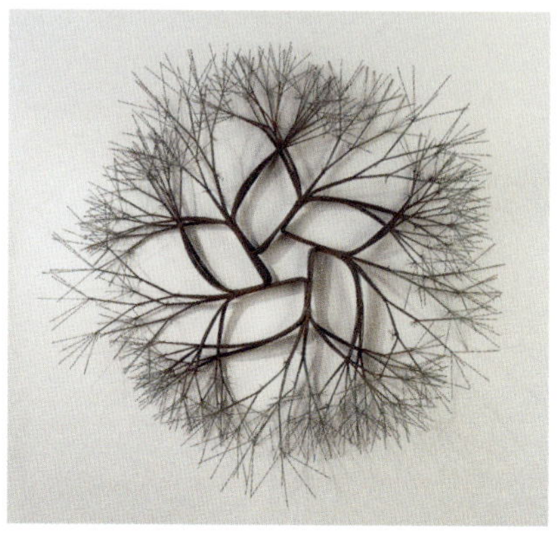

Untitled (S.238), *mid-to-late 1970s*
Bronze wire with natural verdigris
42 x 42 x 8 in. (1.1 m x 1.1 m x 20.3 cm)
Photograph by Laurence Cuneo

The next move, aided by Memphis-reared designer Geré Kavanaugh, was taking Ruth's sculptures from the rarified air of galleries and museums into the public marketplace. Kavanaugh had been one of the trailblazing female industrial artists known as "damsels of design" at General Motors in the 1950s. She worked with architect Victor Gruen, known as the father of the shopping mall, and also as a freelance designer sharing a studio with architect Frank Gehry near Los Angeles. She reimagined everything from square patio umbrellas to urban planning blocks. By 1960, she counted among her corporate clients San Francisco's trendy Joseph Magnin apparel store, owned by Cyril Magnin, who was known as Mr. San Francisco. Magnin's daughter and son-in-law, Walter and Ellen Magnin Newman, ran the stores and were also avid collectors of modern art. Kavanaugh pitched them the idea of using Asawa sculpture to give their stores a spare, modern aesthetic:

> *I made a presentation and was so enthralled with Ruth's work. I said, "We don't want to hang flashy glass chandeliers. Why not hang sculpture by Ruth Asawa?" Little did I know that one of the first things Walter and Ellen bought was a Ruth Asawa sculpture.*

Seven wire sculptures in black, brass, and copper wire were hung from the ceiling at Joseph Magnin, bringing Ruth $2,700 in 1960. The company also hung her sculptures in JM stores in the Southern California cities of Santa Barbara and Topanga Canyon. Working with architect Victor Gruen in Detroit, Kavanaugh also got Ruth a commission for an installation at the restaurant in Hudson's Department Store. The installation featured ten tied-wire sculptures, arrayed like a stand of trees with dew-spangled branches.

The department store commissions were lucrative and introduced Asawa to a wider public. They also provoked "backbiting" by other artists in San Francisco, Kavanaugh recalled. "They said, 'You've gone commercial.' . . . They were jealous."

With Ruth's increasing success came paperwork and legal obligations that artists don't learn about in art school. In 1962, she was audited and started paying a

4 percent sales tax on sales of her sculptures. She needed a seller's permit, a retailer's permit, and registration as an employer with the California State Board of Equalization for the grand sum of one dollar. She listed her occupation as "Sculpturess."

It wasn't all taxes and red tape, though. The JM store sculptures sparked a long friendship between artist and patron. The Magnins and Kavanaugh would visit Ruth's bountiful table in Noe Valley, talking about art over a dinner of her chicken with ginger.

Ruth also stayed in touch with Lou Pollack in New York, letting him know she'd moved on to other venues that were displaying her work in different media. She wrote to him:

> *I've been very busy with our new house. It is beautiful and has much space. I am working on a show for Los Angeles, where my parents live. They have no idea what their crazy daughter is doing. I will show our front doors (which I carved last summer and fall), and sculpture and drawings.*

Imogen Cunningham, ever on the lookout to defend Ruth's image, sent her a dismissive review in 1962 that termed her pieces small, bland, feminine, and decorative. But the Los Angeles show Ruth mentioned to Pollack—a one-woman exhibition at the Ankrum Gallery in Los Angeles—would start to change that stunted critical perception, although it won more critical plaudits than sales for the artist and the gallery.

Los Angeles Times critic Henry J. Seldis recognized that Ruth was not well known in Southern California:

> *Her gently turning shapes deservedly won her wide fame not only in her home town but in New York. This extraordinarily gifted sculptress is little known in this area. Her work deserves a wide and appreciative following here.*

And in *Art Forum*, Gerald Nordland praised her sense of space and movement, so central to the Constructivists, plus the austere elegance of mid-century international style. Among post–World War II sculpture, he wrote, Asawa's works were "surely among the most original and satisfying new sculpture to have arisen in the western United States."

Ruth apologized to gallery owner Joan Ankrum that the show was a commercial disappointment. But Ankrum wrote her that the show was a success because a committee of the Los Angeles County Museum of Art was "enchanted with your sculptures" and asked to borrow four for its rental gallery, opening the door to further exposure and sales. "Your doors have made a great hit," Ankrum wrote, adding that Harry Franklin of the Franklin Gallery of Primitive Art, a connoisseur of doors, declared Ruth's carved redwood portals "the most beautiful doors he has seen anywhere in the world."

The Ankrum show gave Ruth the chance at last to bring her parents, Haru and Umakichi, into a gallery to view her artwork. And the young Laniers got to visit their grandparents' farm, now relocated to the suburb of Anaheim. Xavier said:

We were always excited to go to the farm and ride the tractor. They had a huge stash of fireworks. I don't think we ever lit them. They were in Anaheim. We could see Disneyland. They lived on Beach Blvd. We could run across the street. Now it's eight lanes. Amazing. They had a gigantic avocado tree and would send us a big box. Our other grandparents in Georgia would send us pecans and peaches. . . .

The Japanese ones couldn't speak English. My grandfather had a pipe. We always remember the smell of his pipe. He smiled a lot. Without words.

Xavier, Aiko, and Hudson all studied Japanese for a time at a Zen Buddhist temple in San Francisco while their mother practiced calligraphy in an adjacent classroom. But Xavier was a bad student of the notoriously difficult language, he said. Aiko, who was more attentive, went on to study Japanese dance and learned to play the *samisen*, a square, three-stringed lute. Addie later took Japanese and learned enough to converse a bit with her grandmother.

Back in Noe Valley, Asawa quietly enforced the tough work ethic her parents had instilled, according to Xavier:

We did laundry, changed diapers. . . . Back in those days you didn't refuse. She was pretty stern, not mean, but she didn't have to nag us. If she asked us to do something, we did it.

Ruth and Albert didn't proselytize their kids about pursuing art as a career. The children's attraction to craft was more a matter of "monkey see, monkey do," Xavier said. But there were tools available, encouragement to learn by example, and chances to build, experiment, and get dirty. "She was teaching us all the time."

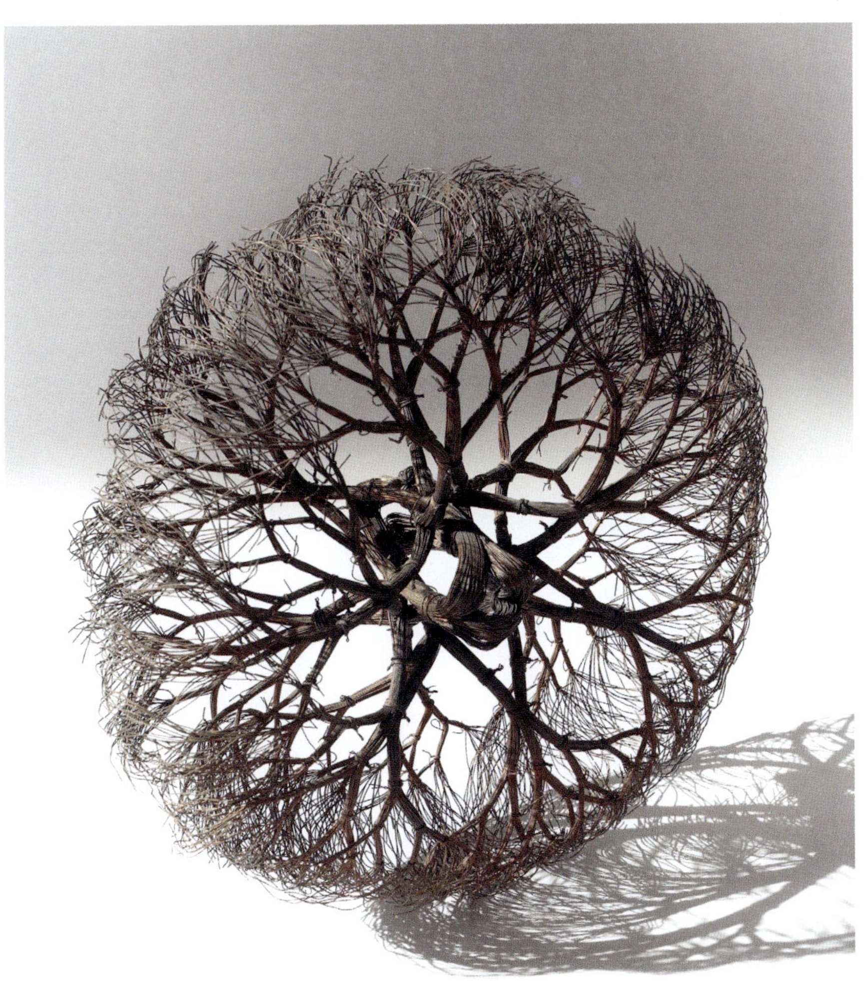

Untitled (S.229), 1964
Oxidized copper wire
20 x 20 x 7.5 in. (50.8 x 50.8 x 19.1 cm)
Photograph by Hudson Cuneo

Xavier also witnessed racial abuse hurled at his mother. "I remember people calling her Jap," he said. "She didn't react." No matter the provocation, Ruth didn't tolerate any racial bias in her children. In the 1960s, when the Black Power movement brought violent protests to his high school, Xavier recalled being hit from behind and knocked out. Hurt and angry when he came to, he remembers using a slur within his mother's earshot. "She said: 'Don't you *ever* say that!'" he recalled, "because of her stuff in the war."

"If we hurt someone's feelings, we'd get a forty-five-minute lecture. If we said, 'Oh, that's stupid,'" Aiko said. "If someone said 'Chinaman,' you saw her get mad."

Albert, for his part, made sure his children didn't become arrogant. Aiko remembered that "'the unimportance of being important' was one of my father's famous quotes."

Meanwhile, back in New York City, Ruth's work was far from forgotten. For the lobby of his new Chase Manhattan Bank building, David Rockefeller acquired an Asawa sculpture. Overseeing the deal was architect Edward Charles "Chuck" Bassett of the firm Skidmore, Owings & Merrill. Bassett purchased the piece on Rockefeller's behalf and sent Ruth a check for $800. The sale kindled an important new relationship for Ruth and her sculpture. Bassett stayed in touch, and his client connections would open doors to a major commission from the Pritzker family, owners of the Hyatt Hotel chain. For one of their hotels, she would fashion a bronze sculpture, cast from an original that was modeled from a child's craft material: baker's clay concocted from flour, salt, and water.

The sales were good for Ruth's finances and public profile. But the ongoing dialogue with her teachers sustained her artistically and spiritually, whether sales were robust or lean.

Josef and Anni Albers got holiday greetings and invitations to visit California, always with a note of gratitude for their teachings. In May 1962, the Alberses did visit Ruth and Albert, and meet their six children, while on a lecture trip in the West. Ruth shipped them a sculptured clay altarpiece for Christmas 1963, along with a wire sculpture and photographs of her with Albert and the children.

The correspondence between mentor and disciple endured for decades. On Ruth's part, letters were tender and reverent. On Albers's part, they were by turns warm and paternal, or cool and formal. Once, after receiving a family photo of the Laniers, Albers seemed to draw a line limiting their intimacy:

Dearest Asawa,

It was awfully kind of you to send me the excellent photos of you with your children, a most wonderful bundle.

But I think these pictures will be much better with your family than in our house with only two old ones.

So, I have returned them to you yesterday with many thanks. And added a few sample prints by me which your children may like.

But please do not write me about them, not having received them nor any thanks. Because I like best your silent acceptance.

With love and all all our best wishes for a very good summer to you all.

Yours

Anni and Josef.

Ruth did as he asked, tactfully reserving comment on his gift of prints. Still, she fed their friendship with art, letters, and requests for advice.

Like many artists living piece to piece, Ruth regularly applied for fellowships and grants to sustain her exploration of new media and designs. She asked Albers to recommend her for a Guggenheim Fellowship, the prestigious award for scholarship and art. He tried to temper her expectations:

Dear Ruthie,

Yes of course I should be glad to recommend you. But I must be asked for it by the foundation.

And right away I must warn you: Because in all my years in the U.S., I probably have recommended at the Guggenheim maybe 30 if not 40 candidates but not one of them has received the G—Fellowship as if there were a black star after my name.

So my consequent advice is: do not ask them to ask a recommendation from me.

Despite of this, I wish you good luck with very best wishes to all of you.

Albers's caveat was prophetic.

Asawa's quest for Guggenheim support was frustrated over five decades, from the 1950s to the 1990s. On its website, the foundation indicates it never discloses its reasons for rejection as a matter of applicant confidentiality. Aiko said such disappointment only made her mother work harder.

In 1965, eager to learn the art of printing from stone, she seized a chance to explore the medium of lithography. The Tamarind Workshop in Los Angeles offered Ruth a lithography fellowship in September and October. The prospect of a new medium and fresh tools was a tonic. Leaving the younger children in the care of Albert, teenage Aiko and Xavier, and neighborhood mothers, Ruth went south. She endeared herself to the program's head, June Wayne, by her aptitude for the craft, and to the staff of printers by cooking them dinner.

The break from homemaking and childcare gave Ruth a chance to focus her energy on art, and her family an opportunity to test their resources. Aiko and her brother Xavier took care of the younger children while their mother explored the new art form. The family's Noe Valley neighbors pitched in at dinnertime and sent notes reassuring Ruth that the family was fine.

"Dear Ruth, I sense the symptoms of long distance maternal concern," wrote her neighbor Sally Woodbridge, an architectural historian. Woodbridge's daughter Pamela was a playmate of Addie's. The young girls were sewing jumpers. Woodbridge was making a Styrofoam robot for Paul's sixth birthday and Halloween. Adam had gotten into an unspecified scrape at school that brought him detention, but Woodbridge assured Ruth it was "no problem at all."

"Dinner at your house was a model of taste and organization," she wrote. "The house was clean, the people were clean, etc. etc. and if anyone had any dirty thoughts, he kept them to himself!" Woodbridge urged Ruth not to worry, but rather to soak up the new art form.

"Having seen what you produce with 6 children etc. to distract you, I can only imagine the energy you are pouring into lithography," Woodbridge wrote. "To hell with results; I only hope you are having a ball!"

Ruth took advantage of being in L.A. to spend weekends visiting her aging parents. Umakichi, now eighty-five, was suffering the after-effects of a disabling stroke. Haru, seventy-two, was nursing him as best a 4-foot-10 woman could. Ruth called up Imogen Cunningham and asked her to fly down and take portraits of them. Cunningham, now eighty-two herself, caught an early plane and spent a day shooting film of the elder Asawas, seated outdoors in traditional kimonos.

Relieved of domestic duties, Ruth's output exploded. During the autumn fellowship, she designed fifty-four lithographs. She made bold botanical studies of poppies and chrysanthemums; family portraits, including a demure profile of Aiko in a headscarf; and images of her father and mother based on Cunningham's photographs. Umakichi's likeness shows him seated serenely, wearing a pendant honoring his mother. Haru's portrait, however, would remain something of a mystery, unseen by the public due to an accidental flaw.

Lithographs, when printed, show the image in reverse. Ruth pictured her mother's kimono wrapped left over right. But when printed, the image would show her kimono wrap in reverse, right over left—a style used only when dressing the dead. Such an image of a living person was believed to bring very bad luck.

Kimiko noticed the mistake and alerted her older sister:

To this day, I feel guilty. . . . She showed me Mama's print and the kimono . . . I said, "Oh, Ruth, when people are dead, they do that." . . . I feel guilty because I don't think she issued those (prints).

Haru would outlive her etching by a quarter century. Kimiko's distress over her sister's unmade prints would linger far longer.

The two months in Los Angeles were a creative windfall. Ruth gave gifts of

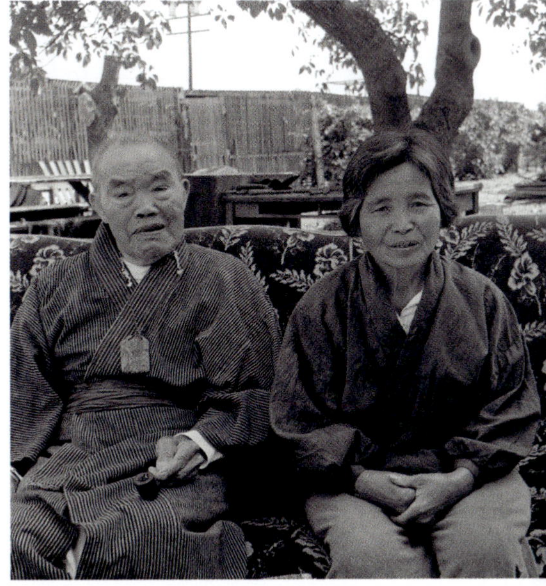

Ruth's parents, Umakichi and Haru Asawa, 1965. Photograph by Imogen Cunningham.

sculpture and prints to Tamarind's founder, June Wayne, who wrote her: "It was a joy to have you . . . [A] love affair between Tamarind and Asawa." Wayne would join the growing list of artists recommending Ruth for the elusive Guggenheim Fellowship.

In her letter to the foundation, Wayne explained that Ruth's gift was her power to transform, like an alchemist, the most humble of materials—from wire to flour and salt dough—into art of transcendent freshness and purity.

"Anything she touches" becomes art, Wayne wrote. "She could make art of a mud puddle if she wished to."

CHAPTER 8

GAMBLE WITH THE YOUNG

Ruth's calendars were a blur of art and family life: doctor appointments, ballet recitals, piano tuning, peace marches, sculpture shipments, and shows. Dance classes and tai chi kept her body fit and her mind clear. Dinners with Cunningham, Fuller, and other luminaries animated evenings at her big table at the house in Noe Valley.

Juggling art and kids was a marathon of multitasking: "Taught Adam to iron; Drew daffodils," she jotted in her datebook in March 1967.

And keeping it all under one roof wasn't easy. When New York executive Herbert Fischbach, a collector of Asawa sculpture, visited her studio, he arrived in the midst of a rowdy play date. Ruth wrote apologetically to his wife, Marilyn, to explain why his visit was so short:

> . . . [T]here was such confusion of children coming and going that I felt as though he fled in self defense. We didn't really sit down to talk at all. I had two extra children that afternoon. I have six of my own so it is lively all the time. I'm glad you are pleased with my work . . .

The Lanier children respected their mother's pursuits. Ruth set no walls between life and work; she wanted them to observe her making sculpture as naturally as making dinner. She strove to weave a seamless tapestry of sculpting and parenting, answering children's needs around the rhythms of her studio. She'd put down a sculpture to make a peanut butter sandwich, then resume looping wire. When she needed to talk to her mother, Aiko recalled, she would pick up a dowel and start winding wire to help her prepare it for sculpting—art and conversation going hand in hand.

At dinnertime, Asawa shifted her creative gears from the studio to the kitchen, turning out abundant meals. Her datebooks are dotted with menus for family and company dinners, with recipes for noodle soup with barbecued pork, double corn polenta, or rhubarb upside-down cake.

"Her chicken, her roast pork, her salad dressing, her gravy. She could have sold her gravy," Hudson said. "We just can't get that sticky teriyaki! We try to copy it, but it's not the same." The garden-to-table trend, Ruth's everyday MO, would be nothing new to them, he added. "Who's that chef, Alice Waters? Pfft! We were doing that in 1962!"

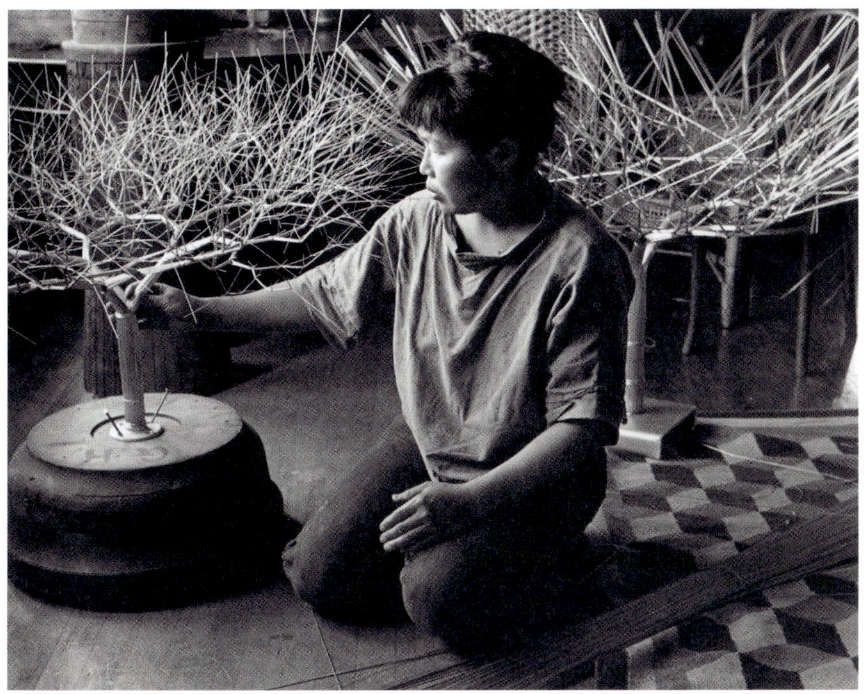

Ruth, kneeling amid tied-wire sculptures in her dining room, 1963. Photograph by Imogen Cunningham.

Sometimes art and life collided in the kitchen with less savory results. One weekend morning, Addie confused plaster of Paris for flour, as the two were stored side by side in the kitchen cupboard. Once heated, it congealed into a chalky crust in the waffle iron. Ruth's friend Sally Woodbridge summed up the atmosphere as "beneficial chaos."

As the young Laniers started school one by one, Ruth was dismayed to see them bring home mimeographed sheets with Thanksgiving turkeys or Easter bunnies to color in. Those handouts passing for art launched her second vocation: promoting art in public schools.

Even as a child in Depression-era Norwalk schools, Ruth had had the chance to sing, dance, paint, and draw. She was proud of her picture of a polar bear with the aurora borealis and her prize-winning poster of the Statue of Liberty. As a teenager confined to a Santa Anita horse stall, she'd studied drawing with Disney artists. Art redeemed the darkest days of the war. She wanted that experience for her children. Black Mountain had taught her that working artists could best guide young hands.

But during the height of the 1960s Space Race, when Soviet and American satellites competed to circle Earth and land on the moon by the decade's end, public school systems were under fierce pressure to focus scarce funds on math and science.

Re-creating the utopian vision of Black Mountain in fiscally starved public schools would be impractical, if not impossible. But what if Ruth could offer a school art workshop staffed by volunteers, using donated or discarded materials for art supplies?

From an informal babysitting collective that hung out in the park, her Noe Valley neighbors had grown into an active PTA that now was ready for the next challenge. Ruth and her art historian friend Sally Woodbridge enlisted their group in the new effort. Gathered around Ruth's kitchen table, they planned a push for art.

Ruth and her cohort proposed a summer art workshop at their local school, Alvarado Elementary. They raised fifty dollars to buy flour and salt, which they would mix up into batches of a baker's clay that children could use at home or school to model little sculptures. The baker's clay recipe was cheap, safe, and simple.

Ingredients:	*Directions: Mix dry ingredients before adding*
4 cups flour	*water. Knead until smooth. Shape figures. Bake in*
1 cup salt	*a low oven at 250 to 325°F until hard. When cool,*
1½ cups water	*paint and seal.*

One batch served six to eight children. The recipe would be repeated many thousands of times across the city in classrooms and studios—including Ruth's own.

The Alvarado parents also collected paper, wood, fabric, yarn, and egg and milk cartons. Kids from kindergarten through sixth grade were able to create crafts including papier-mâché, baker's clay modeling, weaving, stitchery, origami, and carving.

Alvarado's principal and the district okayed the shoestring venture. In the summer of 1968, the Alvarado Arts Workshop started as a summer school program, with workshops from 9:15 to 11:40 every morning. It was staffed by volunteers and included demonstrations by professional artist friends of Ruth.

"I remember Ruth saying she started the program because she had four children and two adopted, and loved teaching these little children," said music teacher Kathleen

LaRusso. "And Albert said, 'Well, there's a whole school down the street. Go down there and teach them, and stop having babies.' I thought that was cute."

Ruth rallied friends who could paint, sculpt, weave, write, act, dance, or throw pots. If they didn't have a skill, she suggested they learn one. She held kitchen table training sessions. She lobbied the school district to help her hold workshops. She cadged funds from donors, foundations, and government agencies to buy supplies. To honor their Noe Valley neighborhood, the group came to call themselves the Valley Girls.

Once she got an idea, Ruth was tenacious; she was not to be denied. When she assigned Valley Girl Judy Burns to learn and then teach the craft of macramé, it got done. "She was a quiet mover," said Burns. "Like water moving over a rock."

The Alvarado vision was born in 1968, at the height of community activism. It was a year after the Summer of Love in the Haight-Ashbury District. Idealists were sobered by the assassinations of Martin Luther King Jr. and Robert F. Kennedy. The Vietnam War gave rise to the peace candidacy of U.S. Senator Eugene McCarthy—whose media profiles Ruth clipped and saved. As minorities and women asserted equal rights, Ruth didn't rush to the barricades but quietly stood her ground as a citizen and an artist.

Ruth and Albert sent letters supporting a young conscientious objector, a friend of their son, in his bid to avoid the draft and perform alternate service. Ruth wrote that the CO was curious, responsible, and mature in neighborhood art workshops. "His alternative service will benefit many," she wrote. Albert, who had enlisted in WWII at 17, added, "I hope my country can accept his offer of alternative service . . . in lieu of his learning to march, take apart a rifle, to shoot the rifle on command, to not worry about whom or what he kills."

The Valley Girls' style of 1960s voluntarism predated the careerist 1970s and '80s, when more college-educated women worked outside the home. Ruth gave time to projects that benefited kids and peace, and recruited her friends to join her—but she stopped short of identity politics that put a label on her art or her ideas. She embraced her Zen Buddhist heritage without being confined by it. In her art as in her civic action, she called herself "a minority of one."

"Ruth had a lot of energy," said Andrea Jepson, a new mother who would be a model for one of Ruth's rare—and popular—figurative sculptures. "You couldn't say no to her."

At times, however, what was stimulating for kids and satisfying to the Valley Girls upset the established order of public school faculty and staff, who found their classrooms and playgrounds turned into ground zero for the band of exuberant but uncredentialed volunteers. On this, Jepson said:

Teachers have a lot to do, and we were, on some level, disruptive. We'd come into class and kids would get excited and we'd bring stuff in and make a mess. We'd clean up, but it's not their environment while we were there.

Some doubts yielded in the face of the students' enthusiasm. Judy Burns was shocked to see fourth-grade boys sacrifice their recess time to stay in and finish a crafts project. While some teachers initially resisted, others, like music teacher Kathleen LaRusso, joined the volunteers to put in time beyond her assigned classroom duties.

So did wealthy San Franciscans with family philanthropies, to whom Ruth appealed for grants; shipping heir William Matson Roth, paper executive Harold Zellerbach, and money manager Claude Rosenberg Jr. and his wife, Louise, all dug deep. The San Francisco Foundation, an incubator for community investment, got on board along with growing numbers of private philanthropists.

The Alvarado summer school workshops were such a success that programs continued into the fall on a voluntary basis and expanded to James Lick Junior High School.

Meanwhile, Ruth's profile in the city was rising. The artist—who groused that, for the price of a professional haircut, she could buy five trees for a schoolyard—now found herself a regular on the A-list for society events. They weren't her natural habitat. But, given a chance to mingle with the elite, she saw a strategic opening to pitch the Alvarado message and her sponsorship of art for kids.

In April 1969 Ruth was invited to a luncheon at the Top of the Mark, a restaurant at the Mark Hopkins Hotel on Nob Hill. Socialite Charlotte Maillard, who became the city's chief of protocol, wanted to mark the anniversary of the Great Earthquake of 1906 by gathering one hundred San Franciscans who could put the city back together after the next "Big One." Although more accustomed to eating at her kitchen table in clay-speckled sweats than lunching with couture-clad socialites, she seized the moment to lobby her hostess:

Dear Mrs. Maillard,

Thank you for inviting me to your quake party. I am not holding my breath for the big one, but am working in our elementary school trying to give more 1st hand experience to the children in doing things with their hands. Next month we will have an exhibit of what the mothers, teachers, and principals have done in a cooperative way at Alvarado School. I hope that all of your guests at the party will help so such a program can be city wide. I shall gamble with the young, since they will truly inherit all of the good and bad that we adults produce.

She gave Mrs. Maillard a whimsical sculpture of a sea creature to mark the occasion. Her hostess sent thanks on heavy, coral, monogrammed stationery:

My dear Mrs. Asawa,
What a very thrilling and delightful surprise to receive such a beautiful dough
sculpture. . . . I shall cherish my be-speckled delightful character of the sea . . .

Ruth's "gamble with the young" caught fire. She developed networking savvy, connecting people who had ideas and energy with people who had funds and social clout. She began turning up in the society columns, often presenting prominent hosts, socialites, tycoons, and museum patrons with a drawing, a sculpture, or an invitation to have their faces cast. The once-reserved young woman who called herself "antisocial" was reinventing herself in her early forties as a citizen-artist and social entrepreneur.

Support from affluent art aficionados began flowing in to help fund art education. Foundations, in turn, asked city schools to match their philanthropy with sustained support. The next hurdle would be to get the Alvarado School Art Workshop's funding written into the San Francisco school budget. Moving from receiving the soft money of grants and private donations to becoming a line item on the school budget required Ruth to escalate her campaign. She became a regular at school board meetings, where she sketched public figures while awaiting her turn to testify on behalf of arts in schools. Jepson recalled:

She drew all through the meetings, which were deadly dull. . . . She understood the
politics of showing up. She'd be there in her jeans and T-shirt . . . her hands behind
her back. She was very strategic about the people she'd pull into the project.

Ruth schooled the school board about the thousands of volunteer hours given, thousands of children served, mounds of yarn scraps and egg cartons donated from the community, and the explosion of arts and crafts now issuing from Alvarado, Edison Elementary, and James Lick Junior High. She didn't shrink from shaming the district for its anemic outlays for art supplies:

What has been accomplished is nothing short of a miracle, more so, since your allot-
ment for art is only 2½ cents per day per student in the junior high school and senior
high school and less than 2 cents per day in elementary schools. This skimpy budget
reveals a lack of awareness in the broader and more profound aspects of education.

The Alvarado program served all children, including the gifted and disabled, Ruth said. Dedicated teachers were spending their own money on materials. Making art exerted a civilizing effect on youth in schoolyards scarred by graffiti, broken windows, drugs, and violence, she argued.

Associate Superintendent for Instruction E. D. Goldman said requests for funds exceeded the available money. So Ruth went to the top, courting then-superintendent Thomas Shaheen by inviting him to visit Alvarado. Despite fiscal constraints, she won the superintendent's support for a cash grant of $2,000 in the 1970–71 school year.

Buoyed by a taste of success, the volunteer moms increased their lobbying efforts. Parents and children packed meetings, displaying Alvarado banners, giving testimonials, and showing slide presentations of their colorful handiwork.

It worked. For the 1972–73 school year, the district boosted its share of Alvarado's funding to $35,500. Alvarado Elementary's acting principal Jack Whisman marveled:

Dear Ruth, . . .
[T]hirty-five thou. WOW!

Ruth gained a young ally in her movement: graduate student Joan Abrahamson. The daughter of former city board of education president Lucille Abrahamson, her passion for art in public spaces matched Ruth's. A product of Yale, Stanford, Harvard, and Berkeley, she would later work with the National Endowment for the Arts (NEA) and as a lawyer for the White House. Lucille, a school activist and member of the board of education herself, told her daughter, "I met the most amazing person." Abrahamson wanted to meet Ruth too, and when she did, was captivated by her spirit and the Alvarado mission. Although of a different generation—she was the same age as Ruth's children—Abrahamson became friends and comrades-in-art with Ruth. She took the reins as acting director of the Alvarado summer program and translated Ruth's vision into crisp policy statements and polished grant applications. But first, she had to figure out Ruth's filing system. Abrahamson remembered:

She opened the door behind the kitchen and there were piles of everything. I was
shocked. Everything was in its place. There were all these papers. Ruth never had a
system. If she needed something for a grant, she'd paw around there and she'd find it.

A generation younger than Ruth's volunteers, Abrahamson became both a colleague and a surrogate family member, helping with dinner in Ruth's kitchen. She relished mealtime camaraderie, learned to make Albert's favorite gravy, and joined in after-dinner sketching sessions with children as models. She vowed to replicate the ambience of the Asawa-Lanier home when she had her own family.

"How do you deal with six kids?" she asked Ruth.

"It's not that complicated," Ruth replied. "It's just as easy to take care of two [as one]. You're making the same meals." She confided to Abrahamson that giving birth to four children and adopting two more gave her the ideal family of six she had always wanted. Seemingly without fuss or drama.

Among the sundry errands Abrahamson performed for Team Asawa was picking up visiting celebrities like Buckminster Fuller from the airport when he came to town. Like the Lanier kids, the Valley Girls got to experience the Bucky magic as he conjured geometric shapes out of milk cartons.

"Often those things didn't work," Jepson remembers. Staple gun crafts would often misfire. As with Fuller's first dome, the attitude was, "Oh well, do it again. . . . [Ruth] believed you could make mistakes and go on." But students weren't always awed by the presence of a living legend. When his demonstration went into overtime at a local high school, the bell rang and students just walked out—embarrassing Ruth.

After these demonstrations by Fuller, the team went out to eat at a Chinese restaurant to celebrate his visit. Jepson recalled, "He was hard of hearing so we were yelling at him."

Alvarado's art energy animated classrooms and overflowed outside to brighten drab concrete playgrounds. At the time, school walls were painted a drab noncolor that volunteers privately called "San Quentin gray-green." Soon bright murals materialized from donated paints and mosaic tiles. The children painted and cemented tiles under the watchful eyes of Ruth and her friend, the artist Nancy Thompson. (Some mosaic tiles used in schools came from Ruth's payment-in-kind as designer of the mural called *Growth*, a blue and coral tree of life installed inside the Bethany Center Senior Housing complex in the city's Mission District.)

Looking around contemporary San Francisco schoolyards, it is hard to imagine the time before Alvarado Arts, when school walls were unrelieved stretches of bland stucco. Now many city school grounds are vibrant with painted or mosaic murals teeming with wildlife, or cityscapes alive with children under smiling suns.

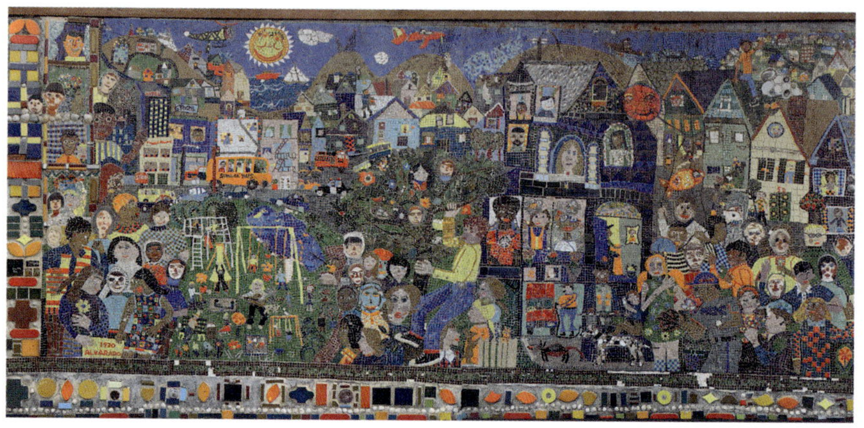

Alvarado Elementary School mosaic, 1970. Photograph by Aiko Cuneo.

In Ruth's vision, art went hand in hand with gardens as a tool for enriching the curriculum, beautifying the school, and teaching responsibility for tending a project—be it a sculpture or a flower. She argued that plants could be used to teach science, botany, poetry, and drawing. She marshaled teams to hammer donated redwood into planter boxes. She cadged every spare plot of dirt to plant with marigolds or Swiss chard. The colorful contagion would spread over the whole district.

But Alvarado activists couldn't just barge in and beautify. They needed approval from janitors and unions to garden, just as they did to paint the school walls or outline hopscotch squares in pink or red instead of regulation yellow. They needed permission from the school's buildings and grounds officials to cultivate weed-choked playgrounds. Alvarado activists chafed at the red tape but learned to work with, or around, the bureaucracy.

Ruth's drive to brighten schoolyards drew her into spaces where artists rarely ventured, like the Juvenile Court's Youth Justice Center. High on a hill in the fog-bound Inner Sunset district, the center housed youth in detention. She led them in the researching and painting of large history murals on the walls of the facility. The theme was Shakespeare's Seven Ages of Man, and she invited youth to paint themselves into the tableau. Judges sent thanks.

In Ruth's view, youth who didn't respond to conventional school might be reached with hands-on art, good food, and TLC. The Juvenile Justice Program had been proposed on the basis of Ruth's individual work with a youth named Jimmy. She fed him, encouraged him to pursue art and writing, and offered him tutoring and support in her home.

She nurtured and taught Jimmy art with her next-door neighbor Mae Lee, who had studied art but didn't maintain her own studio. Instead, Lee became a sort of silent partner in Ruth's studio, assisting in many art projects—whether winding wire around a dowel for hangings or preparing baker's clay models for sculptures—and assisting in art education programs.

Ruth also enlisted her son Adam, who reported Jimmy was making progress modeling with baker's clay and building frames. In a folder, she saved poems Jimmy had written while under her supervision:

> *. . . I got those sad old weary blues.*
> *I don't know where to turn.*
> *I don't know where to go*
> *Nobody cares about you*
> *When you sink so low.*

Ruth wasn't a remote leader; she showed up. On school work days, she appeared in jeans and a sweatshirt with a hoe or broom in hand. By plunging into the unglamorous work, she got others to volunteer as well. She asked for donations of coffee grounds to enrich the mulch and taught kids to make worm boxes to aerate soil. Ever the farm girl, she sculpted expert furrows to ensure abundant blooms.

With so many students and so little land to cultivate, giving each child the joy of planting a flower and watching it grow was a feat. Some artful reuse was needed. Jacques d'Amboise, former principal dancer of the American Ballet Theater, toured her school garden one day and marveled at how Ruth stretched the use of scant space. After dividing up a small garden patch into a grid, she then created a paper map of the same plot for each class and grade, over and over, marking each square with a child's name, as if it were exclusively theirs. It was not.

Teachers ushered out each class, handing each student a bulb to put into the ground. After each class went back inside, Ruth dug up the bulbs, smoothed the earth, and let the next class replant the bulbs as their own. And so it continued, until the whole school had a turn. "And as every class came out, they'd claim: 'There's mine!'" d'Amboise said, laughing at the memory of it. "She said I wish I could make every school a garden, but the principal only gave me a little square."

The Valley Girls' continued engagement was a testimony to Ruth's force of personality. "She listened . . . you felt acknowledged," said Kathleen LaRusso, the music teacher. To a volunteer lamenting that her artwork looked like a third grader's, Ruth replied: "That's it! If you can express your third-grade self, that's the trick."

For some, Alvarado's gardens were therapeutic. Volunteer Sharon Savage Litzky recalled that if someone was feeling depressed, Ruth gave the prescription: "Buy bulbs—flower bulbs—because when the flower comes up and blooms, it gives you its new life."

But the intimacy of the Alvarado project in neighborhood schools, with its circle of Valley Girls and Moms, collided with a new educational and legal imperative. In 1969, a black father named David Johnson sued to end racial imbalance in the city's public schools, where African American students topped 65 percent of the student body in twenty schools, and almost the total population in half of those. By 1971, a federal court ordered the city to bus students across town to distribute students more evenly by race.

Busing inevitably dispersed students from Alvarado and Edison Elementary schools all over town, from Chinatown in the north to the largely black Hunters Point community to the south. Parent volunteers brought stories of tensions back to Ruth's table, and volunteers fanned out with trays of art supplies and musicians to try to ease the adjustment with crafts and folk songs. What Alvarado lost in cohesion and neighborhood intimacy, it gained in awareness of culturally diverse art projects, from Chinese kites to Mexican piñatas.

With busing, Alvarado's volunteer-based vision also came up against the economic pressures on parents in poor and working-class neighborhoods. There, many parents needed to hold full-time or even multiple jobs for family survival, limiting the time they could devote to volunteer work. With the integration order and neighborhood arts programs at odds, Ruth's initial support for busing ebbed over the years. In a letter to the editor, she would later charge that busing failed to achieve meaningful integration, while eroding a sense of school community and opportunities for parent volunteers. It put the burden on children to accomplish social goals that their parents and government leaders couldn't achieve.

Alvarado teachers and volunteers strove to keep creativity stoked up. In the busing program, LaRusso was deployed from Alvarado to Sir Francis Drake in Hunters Point, a kindergarten through sixth-grade campus near public housing projects. She found receptive kids with willing voices:

> *Kids loved to sing. . . . We did Chinese things in Hunters Point and "zoop bop shang-a-lang" in Chinatown.*

Gardens followed bus routes too.

> *Somehow we got started planting flowers in this desolate place. Ruth gets involved and now we're going to plant two thousand daffodil bulbs around the playground. Then there's this ugly construction and demolition site across the street. She arranges someone with a big truck to come and clean up the whole square block of debris. I said I only wanted to plant flowers, not clean up Hunters Point. My back has never been the same.*
>
> *We planted two thousand daffodil bulbs. I remember saying, "Are they going to come back next year?" I remember it became the saying: A daffodil for one year is better than no daffodil at all.*

After court-ordered busing blew Alvarado Arts around the city like dandelion seeds, the program got a break from a new federal job-funding program that the artists could tap. In 1974, the federal Comprehensive Employment and Training Act (CETA) gave money to sponsoring agencies to create public service jobs for the unemployed. Although many jobs went to clerks, guards, and construction workers, artists were unemployed too. When the city art commission was named a sponsoring agency, Alvarado applied for sixty positions as its share, to be evenly divided among visual artists, performing artists, and gardeners.

Among the thousands applying for CETA jobs were poets, PhDs, puppeteers, and a young actor named Peter Coyote. Coyote, a student of Zen Buddhism, was mesmerized by Ruth's calm and focus at CETA meetings. He watched her hands in perpetual motion, sketching politicians and speakers in public hearings, and liked her quiet style. He became a partner with Ruth on many campaigns for the arts in education, helping artists apply for CETA grants. He credits his observation of Asawa in action for helping reignite his own acting career.

> *The first thing I noticed, she was never without a pad and pencil, always practicing her art. And the second was she was always looking for a place for public art. . . . She never intruded on the silence.*

Another CETA hire was sixty-eight-year-old Morris Diamond. Diamond had been a struggling actor and writer off-Broadway before he came west and reinvented himself as Tommy Roberts the Puppet Man. He lived in a Tenderloin hotel and proclaimed himself "the only sober man in the neighborhood." The CETA program hired him half-time in 1974, sending him to perform his shows in convalescent and mental health hospitals around the Bay Area. His 4-foot-8 figure and crusty patter became a staple not just in schools, but also in clinics and on street corners.

Ruth was a fan, and in 1976 sculpted a puppet in Tommy's image—right down to his craggy face and knit cap—which the puppeteer named Tomaso and used in his act. After an Asawa exhibition, he sent her a handwritten review in free verse:

> *Ruth Asawa—the little giant towers a million miles*
> *Above the pygmies and lice who enslaved her and her people—*
> *The power of her love and talent smashed walls—ripped out barbed wire—*
> *With her magic fingers she wove barbs of rusted wire into enduring works of*
> *art—Which will live on and shed light and promise for eons of time—*
> *Long after racists and bigots are*
> *Dust, forgotten and gone—*

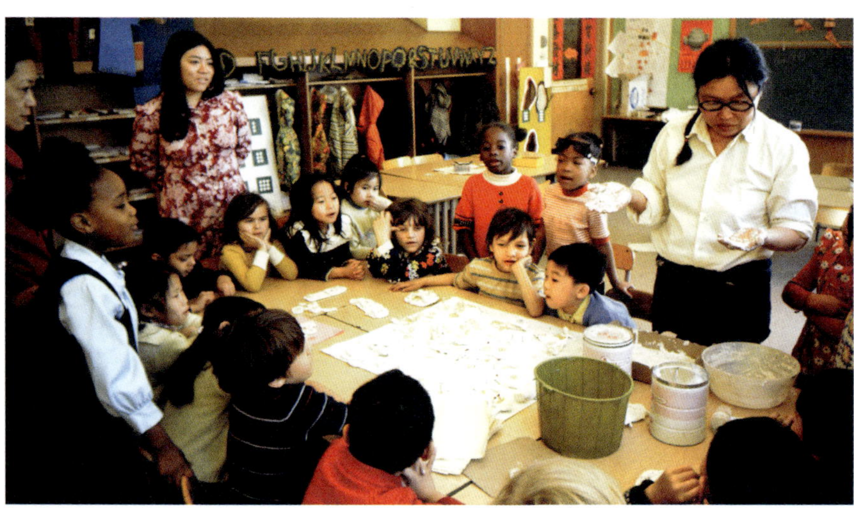

Ruth teaching a class about plaster casting, 1973. Photograph by Laurence Cuneo.

While CETA gave artists subsistence salaries of $135 per week, it didn't cover the costs of art supplies they needed to teach workshops in the schools. This need gave rise to another spinoff project. One day, while visiting San Francisco Art Commission member Harold Zellerbach, Ruth learned that his paper company, Crown Zellerbach, had leftover rolls of paper that were destined for the dump.

Don't dump them, her group asked Zellerbach. Beautiful surplus paper was welcomed by penniless artists who were used to dumpster-diving for material.

The city of San Francisco was starting a recycling program, but Ruth's team saw a more efficient and ingenious strategy in r*eusing* castoff material for crafts. They began collections for Alvarado art classes—and eventually expanded availability of the supplies for citywide classes. Anne-Marie Theilen, who had trained as an artist in France, took the lead with Ruth in gathering surplus materials from homes and businesses. Fabrics, leather, paper, paints, crayons, postcards, stickers, twine—any usable item once destined for the landfill or recycling center could be repurposed in art class.

"We had an orange truck called Maude," Theilen recalled. A crew from the Department of Public Works would also deliver truckloads of compost for community gardens.

They wanted to call their new agency the Center for Reusable Art Parts, but quickly realized the unfortunate acronym would be CRAP. So they added a word and christened it the Scroungers' Center for Reusable Art Parts, or SCRAP. Theilen, sporting a black beret, would run the massive art supplies depot and distribute tons of free or cheap material for four decades. She remained a commanding presence into her late eighties.

Ruth's ultimate vision of providing artists-in-residence within the schools was realized through CETA grants for people like ceramist Earle Curtis (husband of her friend Merry Renk). The NEA sponsored Nancy Thompson, who began as a parent volunteer, working at every grade level in the Alvarado program, and who became an artist-in-residence, redesigning the face of schoolyards by overseeing children's painted and tiled murals.

Thompson, who would later work in Ruth's studio on major sculpture projects, kept a journal for years, recording the small daily triumphs of working with kids:

Paul Revere School, Elementary School, May 15, 1974.

Nice day but extremely windy. Literally blew the paint right off the kids' brushes.

May 31, 1974.

The weather is awful! Foggy and cold with wind but the little first graders weren't about to go inside! They painted away bundled in their coats with paint smocks over, one hand in a pocket to keep warm, the other clutching a paint brush!

June 3, 1974.

About three more days to finish—the wind is severe and blows the kids off their feet! But we persevere—

That year, Alvarado volunteers marked Ruth's forty-eighth birthday with a multi-colored quilt, with each square embroidered or appliquéd to depict a different art or craft. Merry Renk Curtis depicted a heart and hand. Judy Burns made a square with the macramé Ruth had ordered her to learn and teach in the workshop. Ruth lay down and placed the blanket over her, playfully closing her eyes for a beat. In a photograph of the party, she looked tired.

By 1975, the scrappy summer program of 1968 was running year-round in forty schools. Its budget topped $158,000, with a mix of funds from the district, donors, foundations, CETA, and the National Endowment for the Arts.

Ruth was named a member of NEA's Artists-in-Schools Panel, jetting off to Washington, D.C., for meetings rather than tending to her own studio, garden, and morning tai chi. She felt the tug of her family and her art projects. As Alvarado approached its tenth anniversary and its budget neared $427,000, she would ponder stepping back from time to time.

The Congressional Record in November 1974 cited Ruth's leadership of "one of the most vital and successful programs" in the artists-in-schools movement. In 1975, the NEA's director of education, John Hoare Kerr, credited Ruth, Abrahamson, and their colleagues for proving the principle she learned at Black Mountain College: The arts can be a central pillar of a liberal arts education.

"San Francisco with the arts is building a city of gold. It has wide civic and national ramifications. It is an important act," Kerr wrote.

Ruth's advocacy for the arts caught the attention of President Jimmy Carter and First Lady Rosalynn Carter, who made mental health one of their signature issues. In 1977, when Carter formed the President's Commission on Mental Health, Ruth was appointed to its Task Force on the Arts in Mental Health. That autumn, she again shuttled back and forth to meetings in Washington, making her case that art promotes mental health and is therapeutic to intellectually and emotionally challenged youth. She made quick turnarounds to be home as soon as possible.

With public service commitments on top of their art and architecture, Ruth and Albert were cheerfully overscheduled. Albert, as an ardent preservationist, was fighting to save historic buildings on the city's Landmarks Board and working to promote youth hostels. He had his own round of meetings and campaigns.

At times, the couple would pass each other in the evenings, meeting briefly or missing each other at dinner entirely, leaving hasty notes on the phone stand as they sped off to a night meeting. One message to the family, perhaps dictated by Ruth on her way out the door and jotted by a household helper, shows her determination to feed her flock:

> *Ribs in the oven. Spaghetti on the stove. Eat hearty.*
> *Your concerned mother*

Albert, off to an appointment at seven in the evening, posted his reply:

> *Save me a rib and some spaghetti.*
> *Thanks,*
> *Dad*

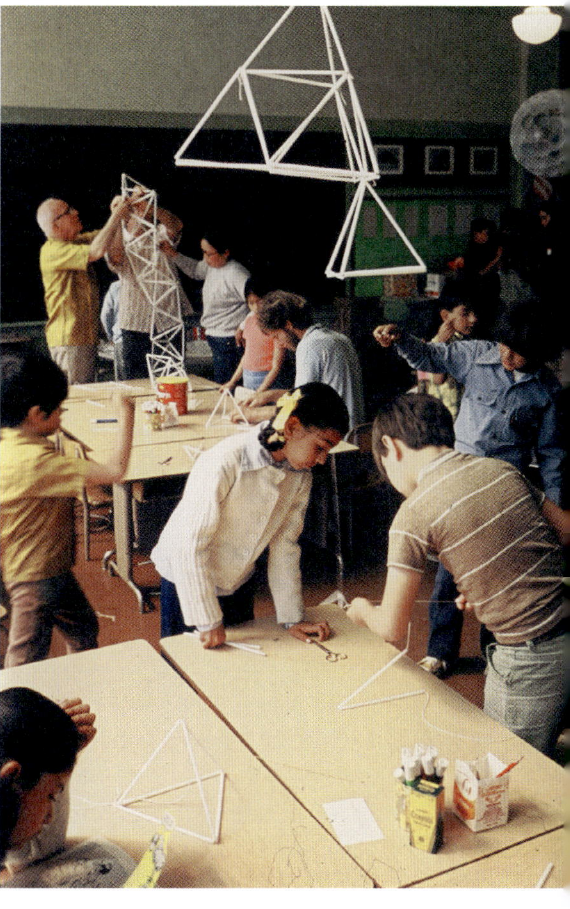

Buckminster Fuller and Ruth, background left and middle, at a San Francisco public school, ca. 1974. Photograph by Laurence Cuneo.

CHAPTER 9

THE FOUNTAIN LADY

Artists and patrons make marriages of vision and money. Sometimes these unions come about in unexpected places. Just as the early impressionists met buyers for their paintings in Paris cafés, Ruth's shift from private sculptor to the city's "fountain lady" began in a waterfront bar.

Shipping heir William Matson Roth occasionally visited the Tin Angel, the club run by Ruth and Albert's friend Peggy Tolk-Watkins on the Embarcadero. Tolk-Watkins asked Ruth to donate a piece of art to a school auction, and Roth bought it. He liked Ruth's style. Roth was an unusual tycoon, a progressive with a preservationist's spirit. (He also served on the Board of Regents of the University of California.) Back in 1962, he'd purchased a pile of red-brick Victorian buildings on the waterfront, site of the old Ghirardelli Chocolate factory, saving them from being leveled for condominiums. To design the plaza, Roth had picked a powerful landscape architect, Lawrence Halprin, who wanted a fountain. In 1965, Roth Properties inquired whether Ruth would design a sculpture for the fountain at the heart of the square.

In a simple story, one could say, the rest was history. But for Ruth, it wasn't simple. She had recently been designing abstract tied-wire sculptures for the lobby fountain in the city's Fox Plaza office tower. When Roth Properties invited her to create the sculpture for Ghirardelli Square, it opened a new chapter of figurative art in her career—and with it, a Pandora's box of public controversy.

Because the Ghirardelli Square site overlooked the bay, with its flotillas of little boats and flights of seagulls, Ruth imagined her sculpture as a fanciful seascape, mixing mythical and natural creatures. There would be nubile mermaids astride giant sea turtles, bathing in a circular pool bedecked with lily pads and frogs.

Early in the fountain's initial design phase, Ruth made undated sketches of slender, youthful mermaids seated on the turtles. She studied sea turtles at the California Academy of Sciences and made some sample castings. They revealed that willowy mermaids would be at the wrong scale—dwarfed by the great leathery reptiles.

Now an earthier mermaid, a mother with child, began to take shape in Ruth's imagination. She found inspiration in her neighbor Andrea Jepson, who sometimes modeled for her and was then expecting a son. Ruth proposed casting her pregnant belly. "I wasn't up for that," Jepson said. "But she wanted to make a statement about nursing mothers. So, when I had Matt in 1967, she did a body sculpture."

In the afternoons, while the infant slept nearby, Ruth came to sketch and cast Jepson's body, basting her with a slick of Vaseline and a coat of plaster. When her baby awoke and cried, the sculptor and her model took a break so Andrea could feed her baby. As a mother of six, Ruth was unfazed by the demands of a hungry infant. She simply removed the mold from Jepson's torso and breasts so Jepson could nurse. For Jepson, an unexpected perk of the sittings was being anointed with an emollient blend of petroleum jelly and breast milk.

The baby would cry, the milk lets down, and I would be covered by Vaseline and milk. I had the most gorgeous skin—like Marie Antoinette. I am here to tell you she had a reason to bathe in milk.

Ruth constructed Jepson the mermaid in pieces, with her torso, belly, and breasts cast separately from her head. Sometimes Ruth would assemble the headless sea siren in the front seat of her Volkswagen van and drive to Jepson's house.

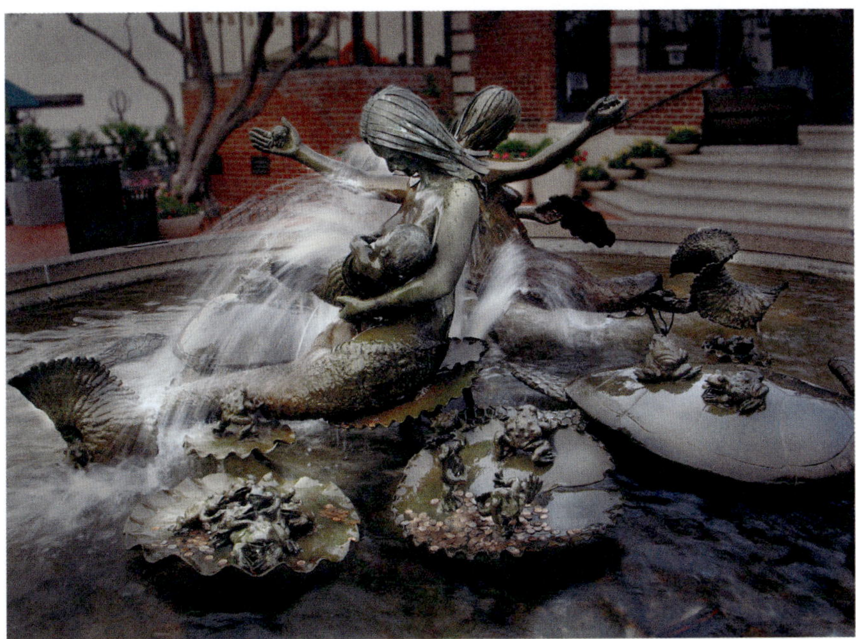

Andrea, *Ruth's first public commission, Ghirardelli Square, San Francisco, 1968. Photograph by Aiko Cuneo.*

"Ruth," Jepson would ask in mock alarm, "what are people saying when they see this body in the front seat of your VW van?"

For the face, Ruth planned a life mask. She liked that Jepson, who was Italian American, had a link to the ethnic heritage of the North Beach quarter, located near the square. During the sitting, Jepson looked serene, giving the mermaid the expression of a Renaissance Madonna.

Styling a mermaid's hair and tail presented design challenges. After trying out several methods of sculpting her tresses, Ruth rolled out wax into flat strands like fettuccine and draped them from a center part to the mermaid's shoulders. For the two mermaids' tails, she returned to her roots, looping wire as she had done for sculptures, and brushing wax over the mesh, producing a scaly, finny texture. Ruth's assistant on the project was again her neighbor Mae Lee, a quiet woman who preferred assisting Ruth in her Noe Valley studio to pursuing her own practice of art.

Ruth's decision to depict one of the mermaids nursing a baby at her breast raised some eyebrows. But the scene resonated with supporters of the nascent women's rights movement. The sculpture's seminude female form was ripe and sensual, but offered a wholesome counterpoint to the topless dancers grinding away nightly on Broadway in North Beach. The public jury was still out.

But the principal architect of the square had made up his mind: He hated it. Halprin had a starkly different vision of what the fountain should be. Halprin wanted a tall, abstract sculpture with towering jets of water descending from a grand height, in stark contrast with the red brick Victorian gingerbread structures surrounding it. He didn't merely dislike Ruth's design; he loathed it. Her sweet scene fueled a volcanic antipathy.

Halprin's outrage grew. In a letter to Roth in February 1967, he complained the design was too "cute and Disneyesque," an affront to the sleek abstract concept he wanted for his plaza centerpiece. He said the mermaids only made sense as an exercise in "camp," like a plastic deer on the front lawn of a modern house. While aware of their artistic differences, Ruth stood her ground. A once civil, even cordial professional relationship between the two grew tense and frosty. Meetings and a volley of letters between Halprin and the developers failed to achieve artistic peace.

Despite having his own worries over the scale and baroque style of the mermaids, Roth gave Ruth near-total design freedom to create her sculpture, which she named *Andrea*, after her model. He wrote Ruth in July 1967 telling her he'd instructed the property company to give her a green light:

> . . . *[Y]ou should go ahead and have the lady cast and if it didn't end up in the fountain, it might end up in my bathtub.*

Roth told Ruth to keep working. He didn't bar her from sculpting the frogs that, posed piggyback, appeared to be mating. Roth only drew a hard line against her notion of piping in sound effects. He wanted no croaking amphibians.

Ruth now assembled all of her mermaid's body parts in plaster before taking the sculpture to the foundry. And by mid-March 1968, the mermaids were cast in bronze, with their turtle and frog companions all burnished and ready for their debut. Few knew to what lengths Ruth and her family had gone to get the details of the frogs just perfect. Her children went to Chinatown to purchase one of the frogs sold in the district's traditional markets. On the way home in the car, the frog escaped and got stuck under the gas pedal. Somehow it avoided being squashed during acceleration, and miraculously survived to serve as a model.

To avoid a public scene when the sculpture was complete, its installation was scheduled late at night, with only a lone drifter on hand to witness the operation. Before the water jets were turned on, Asawa climbed to the rim of the basin in the darkness to uncork a bottle of Champagne with her team. The mood of celebration was short-lived.

On March 22, Halprin issued what became known as his Mermaid Manifesto, a two-page statement of aesthetic protest against the sculpture and its creator. Halprin charged that the design violated his vision of a much-needed balance between Victoriana and modernity, which he had envisioned as a spare metal shaft with a 15-foot geyser.

The seascape didn't simply offend his aesthetics. Ruth, he said, had also flouted his authority under the Renaissance "first man" principle, which holds that the main designer of a work (Halprin) sets the design, and a supporting designer (Asawa) must follow it. Her mermaids broke that rule. "We are violently opposed to it!" the statement read. ". . . Remove the mermaids, the turtles and the frogs!"

Halprin's statement of protest went out to Roth, the American Institute of Architects, assorted artists and designers, and the media. The press gleefully reported on the clash of artists, drawing public curiosity, debate, and—no doubt—more crowds to the square.

Ruth told the *San Francisco Examiner* that she meant her sculpture to be "something everybody can enjoy, not just the art-conscious." She said she didn't mind being criticized, but hated being in the center of a media maelstrom. "It's not that important. He's entitled to his opinion," she said. "I'm not upset by that. But I didn't want all this publicity."

Ruth also explained her pivot from abstraction to a representational scene:

For the old it would bring back the fantasy of their childhood, and for the young it would give them something to remember when they grow old. . . . I wanted to make something related to the sea . . . I thought of all the children, and maybe even some adults, who would stand by the seashore waiting for a turtle or a mermaid to appear. As you look at the sculpture, you include the Bay view which was saved for all of us and you wonder what lies below that surface.

The public took up their pens on either side of the controversy. Letters poured in to the principal players and the papers. A few partisans sided with Halprin.

"Ruth Asawa, you messed it, the Ghirardelli fountain," wrote W. Merle Weidman. "It's just too poorly proportioned and photo realistic resulting in poo."

Other visitors were beguiled. Some compared the sculpture to Copenhagen's *Little Mermaid*, a waterfront statue based on a story by Hans Christian Andersen.

"Hope you retain Ruth Asawa's charming fountain," wrote Mrs. D. Douglas to Roth. "There are more than enough abstractions in the world to confuse those of us who like to recognize what we see."

Still others hailed the fountain as a victorious battle in the gender wars.

"May I suggest that Mr. Halprin is offended more by the fact that a phallic symbol has been changed into a maternal one than by his logical objections to a mermaid piece in the Square?" a fan wrote. "After all, what is a 15-foot steel pylon, with water issuing, but a phallus?"

All the publicity ensured the Ghirardelli Square mermaids were now the most popular fountain in the city. Ruth was horrified by the thought that anyone might think she had engineered the controversy for PR purposes, to help boost her work's popularity. She wrote to Roth to dispel any notion that she was playing a part in a media stunt:

> *Dear Bill,*
>
> *This is to clear myself of any collaboration with Larry to seek the radio, newspaper, and T.V. coverage on the mermaids. I hope also that this is not used as a vehicle to get back at Larry. He is not too popular with his colleagues and now with the public.*
>
> *Women have called me asking how the "statues" could be saved. They have offered to organize a vigilante and appear before the Board of Supervisors. Most of them do not realize that it is a private affair, which I feel makes your intent to preserve Ghirardelli for the people of San Francisco a great success. Women were on the verge of tears. They threatened never to come back to the Square if it is removed, and promised to bring all of their friends if it remains. I now wish I had made a monument so that all of this fuss was worthwhile . . .*

Meanwhile, the mermaids attracted a powerful fan at City Hall. Mayor Joseph Alioto told reporters as he toured the embattled square:

> *I don't agree with Mr. Halprin. After all, this is just an old chocolate factory, and I find the sculptures of frogs and turtles and mermaids, particularly the mermaid with the baby, an arresting and imaginary [sic] concept. . . . I think Miss Asawa's work is in complete harmony with the whole décor, the whole motif of Ghirardelli Square. I want to publicly congratulate her.*

In the wake of the mermaid splash, Alioto went further and named Ruth to the San Francisco Art Commission. Among the commission's duties were sponsoring city art festivals, debating public art issues, and selecting artists for public art projects. Along with a higher public profile, Ruth's appointment ensured she'd face Halprin again in public debate, even as her art won popularity in the public sphere.

From the time Ruth critiqued Albert's stonework at the Minimum House at Black Mountain, she'd held firm views on design and art in public spaces. In the past, she expressed her views privately. Now, after her bruising initiation into the public arena over Ghirardelli Square, she found her voice and began speaking out on new designs planned for San Francisco's Civic Center and the Embarcadero Center.

When Halprin again advocated towering geysers of water, this time for the Civic Center Plaza, Ruth raised a practical objection. She pointed out that the stiff bay winds would blow the fountain sideways, soaking the plaza and dousing passersby. This time, others on the commission shared her views. But she wouldn't always have the majority on her side.

Her first major commission vote concerned art for the new Embarcadero Center, a column of retail and office towers arrayed along Sacramento Street from Battery to the Bay. The towers faced the stately Ferry Building at the foot of Market Street. But the waterfront view was obstructed by a concrete eyesore: the freeway. The Embarcadero Center's plaza would house a sculpture. The top contender for the commission was the French-Canadian sculptor Armand Vaillancourt, who designed a pile of rectangular concrete tubes 40 feet high, spewing cascades of water. Vaillancourt won Halprin's support. Ruth argued that the concrete freeway shouldn't be mirrored by more concrete slabs in the sculpture. She was outnumbered.

In November 1968, she cast the lone vote against the Vaillancourt fountain, which was built over her objections. In an ironic footnote, the freeway would be demolished after an earthquake shattered it two decades later. But its artistic reflection survives in the Vaillancourt fountain. Droughts periodically cause the water to be turned off, leaving a dry structure frequented by skateboarders and the homeless. Once, after the water was turned back on, a prankster decided the fountain needed cleaning and poured soap into it.

The summer of 1969 was to be a season of service. Ruth agreed to show her work and demonstrate sculpting techniques at the Los Angeles County Fair in Pomona. Just before the fair opened, her father died at age eighty-seven. The truck farmer who survived an enemy alien camp in New Mexico had been in declining health four years after a disabling stroke. But Umakichi's image, kneeling over his strawberries before his arrest by the FBI, was seared in Ruth's memory—and destined to find its way into her art.

Ruth went ahead with her commitment to the Los Angeles appearance. She enlisted her children to help her demonstrate the craft of modeling with baker's clay. Southern California sweltered in the late summer sun around Labor Day, but Ruth thought little of roughing it in a geodesic dome, and working at the fair would be good experience for the young Laniers.

In her years of fighting to fund arts in the schools, Ruth made her own art at night while her family slept. She often had her hands in baker's clay, her jeans and sweat-shirt flocked with the floury paste. Asawa told a reporter:

Friends said to me, "This is child's play. You should do serious, permanent things." So I began making bronzes by means of dough models instead of traditional clay. People agree that even an artist's sketchy drawings on flimsy paper can be permanent. So can dough.

Baker's clay was so cheap and versatile that Ruth wanted to try using the home-made dough to mold three-dimensional sketches for larger works. She found another backer who didn't dismiss the medium as child's play: San Francisco architect Edward C. "Chuck" Bassett. Bassett's portfolio would encompass sophisticated urban megaprojects ranging from San Francisco's Davies Symphony Hall to the U.S. Embassy in Moscow. But his taste was eclectic and democratic.

While visiting an exhibition of works by Ruth and the Alvarado art project students at the Redwood Association, Bassett saw the centerpiece: a 2-by-4-foot bas-relief in baker's clay depicting the school and its students. He loved the naive folk art texture and tactile quality that Ruth was achieving with baker's clay.

Bassett brainstormed with Ruth about enlarging the bas-relief concept into a giant cityscape of San Francisco. They envisioned a tableau of urban scenes wrapped around a cylindrical fountain, like a massive cookie or gingerbread scene. Dough would be the first step, used to mold the figures before casting them in bronze. Then they would wrap the bronze bas-relief panels around a cylindrical basin and top the fountain with dense plumes of water.

The fountain would adorn the steps up to the plaza of a new 35-story Hyatt Hotel that Bassett's firm was planning in Union Square. Bassett wanted Ruth to design that fountain. He started lobbying the president of the hotel corporation, Donald Pritzker. It wasn't an immediate hit; serving up a giant cookie on the corner left some cold. But to Ruth's delight, "Mr. Pritzker agreed to gamble on Chuck's crazy idea."

The commission for the Hyatt Union Square fountain was signed in 1970. To render the clay scenes into bronze, Ruth lined up the San Francisco Art Foundry. Next, she scouted San Francisco landmarks, historical figures, and scenes of everyday city

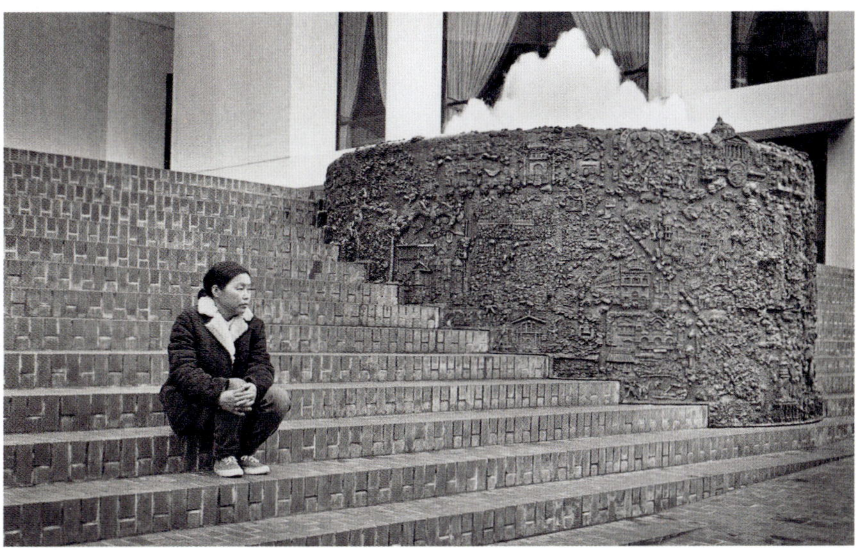

Ruth and her San Francisco Fountain at the Hyatt in Union Square, 1973. Photograph by Laurence Cuneo.

life. She wanted to include both real and imaginary figures in her cityscape. As a connoisseur of cartoons from childhood, she had a soft spot for the *Peanuts* strip created by Charles Shultz, who lived just north of San Francisco in Santa Rosa. So she asked to include the flop-eared dog Snoopy in her tableau.

Ruth and Bassett agreed upon a list of sixty-six San Francisco scenes that would stretch out over forty-one panels, encompassing city history from the Spanish priest Father Junipero Serra and the basilica of Mission Dolores to Haight-Ashbury hippies and peace marches. Ruth included tourist spots like the Powell Street cable car, Fisherman's Wharf, and the Golden Gate Bridge. A Chinese New Year parade and the Japantown pagodas would depict Asian traditions. A North Beach scene would capture Italian flavors, and a St. Patrick's Day parade would represent the city's Irish community. Cultural touchstones ranged from maestro Seiji Ozawa conducting the San Francisco Symphony to the rock band Jefferson Airplane. Ruth slipped in a love scene of a hippie couple smiling blissfully in bed.

Both sculptor and architect wanted the fountain to connect directly with street life, blending the light and sound of water with design elements that would engage people on the sidewalk and invite them not only to stop and look, but to touch as well.

Bassett estimated the more than two-year project would require about $80,000, of which $23,800 would go to the artist's fee and $29,800 to the labor-intensive process of bronze casting. The rest would go for the unseen working parts of a fountain: the plumbing, pumps, lighting, copper bowl, and concrete base. There was also insurance coverage, and the mechanics of installation with workers, cranes, and barricades.

The hotel executives wanted to hold the line at $75,000. As often happens in public projects, the artisanal bronze work took longer and cost more than sponsors anticipated. Bassett campaigned to close the gap between the estimated and real costs. A shortfall remained.

Ruth got to work. She enlisted her Alvarado colleague Sally Woodbridge, her neighbor Mae Lee, and her daughter Aiko as her main assistants. The constant stream of visitors to the house in Noe Valley, old and young, were drafted into working on the project too, and invited to grab a ball of dough and start modeling. Ruth wanted the fountain figures to differ in style and texture, to reflect the work of many hands.

Early in the project, art had to take a break for life as Ruth took on a new role as mother of the bride. Aiko, now studying art at the Pratt Institute in New York City, was engaged to marry her art school classmate, photographer Laurence Cuneo Jr., in 1971.

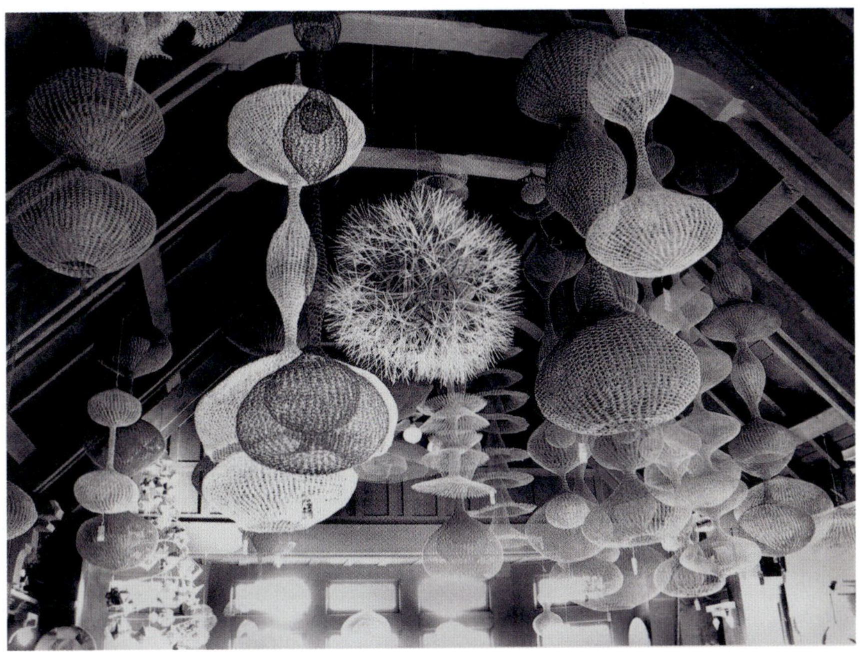

Living room of the Asawa-Lanier home, 1995. Photograph by Laurence Cuneo.

Aiko and Larry celebrated their wedding at the brown-shingled Noe Valley house on June 19. The home and studio, typically bursting with art projects in various stages of completion, underwent a transformation. White and yellow daisies turned the living room into a wedding bower for the ceremony, with Ruth's wire sculptures floating aloft from the beams. The radiant couple, Albert's daisy bouquets, and neighbors and friends catering dishes from sushi to the wedding cake comprised a wedding celebration fit "for the gods," one guest wrote.

Ruth included a scene of Aiko and Larry's wedding procession on the Hyatt fountain, right between Dolores Street and Twin Peaks. Her son-in-law would become one of the photographers—alongside Imogen Cunningham, Paul Hassel, and others—who documented Ruth's sculptures and museum installations.

As the fountain's work got back on schedule, Ruth invited more friends and neighbors to model clay figures, turning the project into a massive collaboration. Joining Ruth, Sally, Mae, and Aiko were about one hundred neighborhood volunteers aged three to eighty-eight, who would stop by the studio to make baker's clay figures and

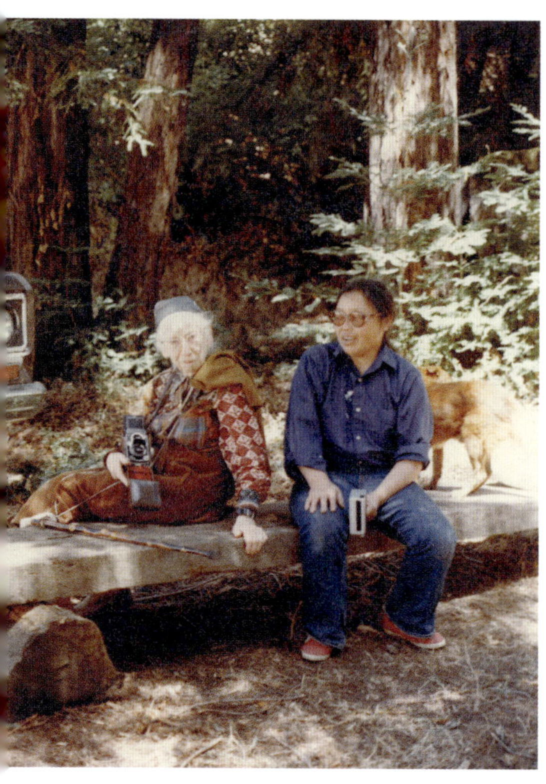

Imogen Cunningham and Ruth, 1975.
Photograph by Xavier Lanier.

scenes for the fountain. Ruth liked the collective artistry of large works, from murals to medieval cathedrals, in which many craftsmen would contribute and feel a sense of communal ownership.

The most senior artist-helper was Cunningham, who made palm trees. Ruth's mother, Haru, visiting from Los Angeles, specialized in the fine detail work of sculpting seagulls, trees, and tufts of grass—she achieved their soft, wavy texture by squeezing baker's clay through a garlic press. Aiko, who'd worked with baker's clay since middle school, created the serpentine form of a Chinatown dragon and the meandering path of the city's most crooked thoroughfare, Lombard Street. The scene around the studio table was relaxed, with Ruth providing more encouragement than direction to all willing amateur hands.

It was a logistical challenge to take a technique, originally designed for school crafts, and scale it up to produce forty-one curved panels arrayed around a cylindrical drum 7 feet in diameter and 10 feet high. The project consumed 1,400 pounds of flour and salt. The panels, too bulky to bake on a cookie sheet, had to be air-dried. In San Francisco's rainy season, the dough sucked moisture from the atmosphere and refused to dry, causing figures to melt rather than firm up. The figure of City Hall listed, and the Ferry Building cracked as if hit by an earthquake. Electric lamps and oven heat helped dry the clay figures. But some of the fractured features had to be rebuilt.

Albert, who gave technical support for many of Ruth's projects, helped by making working drawings for a full-scale wooden model of the fountain's inner drum, assembled and installed in their yard, to aid in fitting the panels to the fountain's curved surface.

Once all of the scenes and figures were formed and dried, the panels were trucked to the San Francisco Art Foundry on Bluxome Street to be cast into bronze. The foundry used the ancient "lost wax method," developed over millennia to make bronze sculpture from models. First the original sculpture—in this case, baker's clay models—gets sealed with shellac to create a nonporous surface. Then the models are used to make a negative mold of latex rubber. Next, wax is poured into the mold and cooled to create a positive replica of the clay model. After smoothing the wax model to create a perfect surface, workers encase it in a ceramic or plaster shell, fitted around its surface with little tubes called sprues or gates that become channels to pour in the molten bronze. The wax encased in the plaster shell is heated to burn it out, creating a cavity for the molten bronze to fill.

Crucibles of the fiery liquid metal are hoisted on poles by a team working in a choreographed synchrony by means of hand motions. Workers clad in fireproof silver suits and masks pour the red-hot bronze into the sprues, or channels, that lead into the ceramic mold. The molten bronze slowly fills the space. Once cooled, the bronze sculpture is released from the mold.

In the case of the Hyatt fountain, the bronze pieces were then welded together with other panels, polished, and finished with a patina. This process—"the dance of the pour"—mesmerized Ruth: the slow-motion teamwork of the foundry workers, the danger and beauty of the blazing liquid bronze, the heat waves felt by viewers standing yards away.

During more than two years of design and fabrication, Bassett had been the artist's advocate, championing her vision and writing notes to cheer her on. Sadly, another Ruth supporter, the head of the client corporation, Hyatt Hotels president Donald Pritzker, died suddenly of a heart attack at age thirty-nine before the project's completion. Ruth immortalized Pritzker as a figure on the fountain, shown seated at his desk, doing business in the shadow of his hotel.

Scenes of San Francisco took form on the cylinder, which resembled a stout toy version of Trajan's Column in Rome. The sculpture's formal dedication was set for February 14, 1973. The hotel declared the work a valentine to the city, in a bit of press agentry that—given Bassett and Asawa's feel for the popular taste—actually turned out to be true. The press and public turned out. Champagne flowed. Children from the Alvarado Art Project came out in force. Ruth appeared in news photos wearing a poncho over her dress, in a stark contrast to the hotel executives' wives in their chic suits. *San Francisco Chronicle* art critic Alfred Frankenstein likened the fountain to an ancient Hittite relief as reinvented by puppeteers from television's *Sesame Street*.

Ruth and Bassett shared a belief that the fountain should be touchable art, inviting the public to stroke its surfaces. Bassett pictured crowds like those in Florence, who touch the seventeenth-century bronze boar known as *Il Porcellino*. Rubbing the piglet's nose is said to ensure your return to the city.

"It has the shiniest snout in Italy . . . ," Ruth said in a statement for the opening. "We all want that to happen to the fountain."

In that spirit, the fountain over its lifetime would welcome visitors from the Rose Resnick Center for the Blind and Visually Impaired (now called the Lighthouse). The blind would slowly move their hands over the bronze panels, expressions of recognition lighting their faces as they found landmarks like the Golden Gate Bridge.

The fountain's story has a bittersweet postscript. Cost overruns—which are not uncommon in large art installations—put the foundry under financial pressure, and it closed. Afterward, Ruth ended up offering to pay several thousand dollars out of her own pocket to reimburse a portion of the shortfall to the foundry's operator, who had already left town. "The artist always pays for the privilege of doing it," Ruth later said of large projects. Aiko, in an interview, echoed the sentiment: "Mom always lost her shirt."

In 1974, the American Institute of Architects (AIA) awarded its Fine Arts Medal to Asawa for her fountains and sculptures enlivening public spaces in San Francisco. Almost as if in response to critics who preferred her abstract wires to the playful popular pieces, the award cited her Ghirardelli Square mermaids and the Hyatt Union Square cityscape.

That May, Ruth and Albert traveled to Washington, D.C., for the awards ceremony, held at the Daughters of the American Revolution Constitution Hall. To receive the medal, Ruth was at her most elegant, wearing a silky blue-gray dress and twisting up her hair in a chignon.

Ruth didn't rush to share the news of the AIA Fine Arts Medal with her mentor, Josef Albers. While it's impossible to know her reasons, it wasn't in her nature to boast. Especially since Albers had cautioned her about the fickleness of awards and hadn't received this particular prize himself. But that was about to change.

After Ruth named Albers in a survey as the most creative and extraordinary person she knew, he got wind of her tribute and wrote a note, asking mischievously how such a thing could possibly have happened. He also delivered the news that he had been chosen to receive the AIA Fine Arts Medal the year after her:

> *. . . [M]y best wishes to you all for the holidays. Also from Anni.*
> *I also learned that you received from the AIA last year's Fine Arts Medal. So belated my congratulations.*

The 1975 medal came to Albers very late. Three decades after Ruth had met him, and nearly a quarter century after he had moved to Yale, Albers's austere profile had softened and his steely forelock had gone white. The year after accepting the AIA Fine Arts Medal, he was admitted to Yale New Haven Hospital for treatment of a possible heart ailment. There he died in his sleep on March 25, 1976, at the age of eighty-eight.

An obituary in the next day's *New York Times* captured Albers's fervor in explaining, as he had at Black Mountain, his color theory as an act of procreation:

> *"Just putting colors together is the excitement of it," he once told an interviewer. "The way green submits to blue, for instance, or vice versa. What interests me is the way they marry, interpenetrate and produce the baby, the color and that is their product together."*

When an Albers commemorative stamp was later issued bearing an image of his red-orange, apricot, and melon painting entitled *Glow*, Ruth bought sheets of it. The image was so beautiful, she wrote Albers's widow, she couldn't bear to use the stamps.

Hard on the heels of Albers's death, the Lanier family lost another of its elders. After more than twenty-five years of her jams, spiky wit, and unsought advice, Imogen Cunningham died in June 1976 at the age of ninety-three. She had shared birthdays with Albert and her love of satsuma plums with Ruth. She had given them an incomparable series of black-and-white portraits of Ruth sculpting and with her family; they had given her family dinners and trips to their summer place in Guerneville. Asawa had come to revere Cunningham for knowing the Latin names of plants, and for her devotion to the six Lanier "brats," which no amount of scolding could hide. Asawa said:

> *. . . I remember Imogen most for being able to turn frugality and poverty into meaningful elegance. She taught me that poverty is a state of mind, that is you're poor only if you dwell on it. That in child rearing the artist can still create by observing what is around them, children, plants, and making images that can be savored when we are old.*
>
> *Our last real visit with Imogen was coming back from Guerneville. She nodded off to sleep in the front seat of the car. She turned to Albert and said, "I think I am getting old." Albert's reply: "Well, you're entitled to it."*

After her excursion into representative art and fountains depicting a playful sea-scape and cityscape, Asawa began to explore her ancestral culture in public art.

Like many in her Nisei generation who came of age during World War II, she emerged from internment to make a happy—and in her case, mixed—marriage. She created a big blended family and a decidedly assimilated lifestyle. She avoided labeling her art with identity politics, whether as an Asian American or a female artist. She shrugged off the mantle of victimhood.

But as time passed, Japanese themes beckoned to her sense of advocacy and her art. She fought for recognition of the gardeners who had nurtured Golden Gate Park's Japanese Tea Garden before the war, only to lose it during the internment. Ruth joined park activists to push for the restoration of the garden, and in 1974 she created a cast bronze plaque, formed over a large rock, honoring Makoto Hagiwara and his family, who had tended the tiny green oasis for a city that spurned them in war.

In cherry blossom season, Ruth wrote to City Supervisor Dianne Feinstein (later mayor and U.S. senator), asking her to rename the street for the gardeners. Hagiwara Tea Garden Drive, which fronts the garden and neighboring de Young Museum, became the city's first street named for a Japanese leader.

San Francisco's Nihonmachi, or Japantown, offered Ruth another challenge that tapped her Japanese roots. Architect and planner Rai Okamoto, who had studied at Yale with Albers and had admired Ruth's wire sculptures in the 1950s, asked Ruth to submit a design for a pedestrian Peace Plaza he was designing. For the central plaza ringed by restaurants, tea shops, galleries, and bookstores, Okamoto wanted a fountain as its focal point.

When she practiced origami, Ruth loved the paper's ability to assume a new form without being destroyed. It was another act of alchemy from Albers's matière class that joined her cultural tradition with the Black Mountain experience.

In her design proposal for the Japantown fountain, she reimagined the paper folds of an origami flower and rendered them in metal. Ruth created two flower forms, opening upward like lotuses or water lilies in a pond. The fountains were surrounded by meandering paths of river stones. She also joined Okamoto in adorning the wood benches he designed for the plaza, by leading children of nearby merchants in sculpt-ing dough figures from Japanese fairy tales, which were assembled into concrete bas-reliefs.

For the material of the fountain, Ruth initially chose steel that would oxidize to a velvety rust finish when left out in the elements. However, the original rusted steel deteriorated, requiring the fountains be recast in bronze. The fountains also endured cycles of water shortages that required that the water be turned off. Over the years of drought, as the bronze blossoms dried, old plumbing and high rehabilitation costs would complicate efforts to restore the flow. But the burnished origami flowers still stand in the plaza where neighborhood elders sit in the sun.

Working in steel and bronze prompted Ruth to reflect on how her time was spent. As the nation's bicentennial and her fiftieth birthday approached, time seemed a finite resource. So after eight years, Ruth decided to quit the San Francisco Art Commission. On December 2, 1975, she wrote to fellow commissioner and Alvarado Arts angel Harold Zellerbach to explain:

> *My reason for leaving is that I am self-employed, and need the time to study and research new methods and materials. I hope you will understand that eight years of administrative work, attending meetings, and appearing before the public, made it difficult for me to work in depth.*

To the incoming mayor, George Moscone, Ruth offered her congratulations and her resignation. She wished health and luck to the new mayor, who would soon enter City Hall—but wouldn't live to finish his term. In

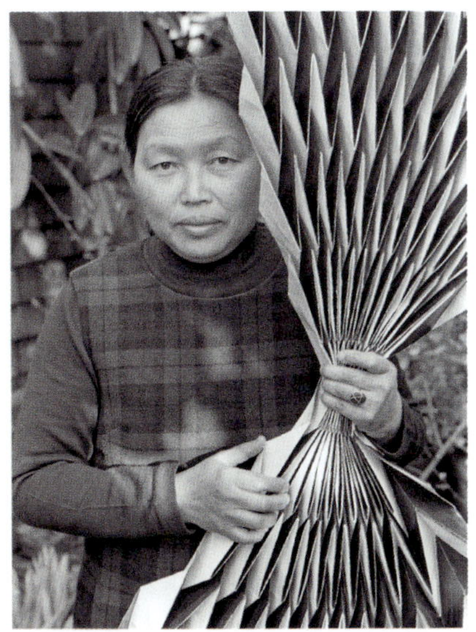

Ruth holding one of her paperfolds, ca. 1975. Photograph by Laurence Cuneo.

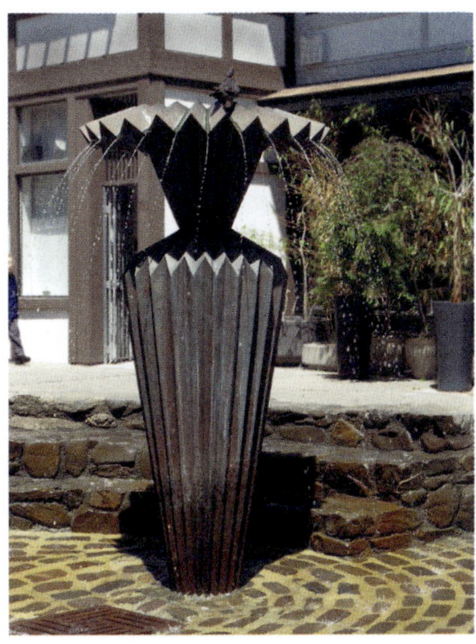

Origami Fountains, *Nihonmachi, San Francisco, 1976, 1999*
Corten steel, 1976, later cast in bronze, 1999
90 x 48 x 48 in. (2.3 x 1.2 x 1.2 m)
Photograph by Aiko Cuneo

November 1978, Moscone was assassinated by former city supervisor Dan White, who also shot and killed openly gay city supervisor Harvey Milk. Dianne Feinstein became the city's new mayor.

Despite Ruth's resignation from the city's art commission, she kept getting appointed by politicians to serve. And she found it hard to say no. California's Governor Jerry Brown recognized he had a charismatic arts advocate in Asawa. Brown, a former Jesuit seminarian with intellectual ambition, wanted to shake things up by abolishing the old state arts commission, heavy on money and patronage, and create a new California Arts Council led by working artists including Ruth, poet Gary Snyder, actor Peter Coyote, and playwright Luis Valdez.

The council gave Ruth a new platform for her campaign to put working artists in the public schools. It also introduced her to Snyder, a poet whose work spanned the beat movement, Zen Buddhism, and environmental themes. Ruth and Coyote trekked into the Sierra foothills to Snyder's Zen retreat, called Kitkitdizze, after the Indian word for a fragrant mountain shrub. Snyder hosted them for an evening of sharing ideas over an open fire and a rustic meal of freshly caught game. Decades later Snyder reminisced in a letter about his visit with the sculptor:

> *. . . I had her and Peter Coyote to my house in the foothills and we killed, dressed and cooked a rabbit. She was completely at home with that and also interested and curious about the details. We sat by an open fire in the center of the house—modeled after a North Japanese farmhouse, and she was entirely at home . . . with forest and farm, but also with the classy San Francisco art world. I found her easy to be with— as did my wife Carole—and a kind of model to follow.*

Ruth later drew the subject of Snyder's poem, "Axe Handles," in which the poet teaches his son how to throw an axe and muses about the passing of craft and culture from generation to generation. It was a theme dear to Ruth's heart at home and in school. Delighted, Snyder wrote her:

> *The Axe Handle pencil drawing you gave me is a treasure!*

But the new council got off to a rocky start, drawing conservative criticism for its new-age flavor and its push to more than double its own budget to $3 million by its second year. Ruth and her fellow council members, Coyote, Snyder, and Valdez, worked to extend state grants to underrepresented artists and make the grants reflective of the state's environmental diversity. Fiscal conservatives mocked council support for eco-themed projects; they ridiculed a dolphin preservation effort that used marine mammal sounds, calling it "playing music for whales."

In 1978, after two years and tax cuts that gutted state art funding, Ruth bowed out of the California Arts Council too. She would remain a citizen artist at heart. But her head was full of fresh ideas, and she was eager to get back to the studio. She also had a new education goal. Elevating the Alvarado Arts concept to the next level, she wanted to give her city a secondary school to equal New York's High School of the Performing Arts, which would be immortalized in the movie *Fame*.

Ruth sent letters to School Superintendent Robert Alioto and the San Francisco Foundation, proposing a magnet high school for the arts in San Francisco. The alternative arts high school would blend required academics with a diversified multiart curriculum, opening up opportunities for careers in the visual arts and performing arts—from voice and instrumental music to dance, theater, and theater tech. Ruth would incorporate lessons learned at Black Mountain and champion the use of working artists to teach.

Once more, Ruth plunged into lobbying and fundraising, attending school board meetings and appealing to friends in business, politics, and the arts for their support. She visited arts magnet high schools in other cities like Dallas. San Francisco had a rich tradition of symphony, opera, ballet, and museums. So why not tap those resources as learning hubs to give city youth a path to life in the arts?

In September 1982, the newly established San Francisco School of the Arts welcomed its first group of 150 students, sharing classroom and studio space on the existing campus of McAteer High School. High on a windy hill overlooking upper Market Street, McAteer was distant from downtown arts hubs, and therefore a far-from-ideal site.

Ruth's long-range vision for the school's location was focused on the grand ruin at 135 Van Ness, the old Commerce High School, built in 1926 in Spanish Colonial Revival style. It had become the administrative headquarters of the San Francisco Unified School District. Behind the ornate facade, adorned with figures of medieval scholars and tiles in peach and green, the interior had suffered from years of deferred maintenance, compounded by earthquake damage. But with a prime location near to the symphony, opera, and ballet, 135 Van Ness was Ruth's dream site.

Years of blueprints and battles lay ahead, and decades of shared and temporary school sites. Ruth's campaign—which helped win voter support for multimillion-dollar bond issues—would be outpaced by spiraling cost projections, seismic repair needs, competing capital demands, and bureaucratic inertia.

But meanwhile, the School of the Arts doubled its student body from 150 to 300 in its second year. The school became Ruth's seventh child—hungry, gifted, and ambitious—looking for home.

CHAPTER 10

THE WOLF AT THE DOOR

Ruth and Albert's thirty-fourth anniversary brought the couple's first trip to Europe. In the summer of 1983, they capped a monthlong movable feast of art, food, and friends with the opening of the Josef Albers Museum in Bottrop, Germany.

In France, Ruth visited the studio of Paul Cezanne in Aix-en-Provence, where—barred from taking photographs—she sketched the painter's smock and beret. She and Albert wandered through Claude Monet's gardens at Giverny, which were clad in summer hues of red geraniums, orange poppies, blue and gold iris, magenta rhododendrons, pink water lilies, and lavender wisteria. They toured Antoni Gaudí's Barcelona, and rode trains to Florence's and Venice's galleries, churches, and courtyards. Like a honeymooner, Ruth jotted notes on every experience of culture and cuisine, every museum and meal. After getting sunburned on the beach in Cannes, the couple swam in the Mediterranean and picnicked with their friends Merry Renk and Earle Curtis. As much as masterpieces, little things moved Ruth: a hotel manager's kindness in Paris, a train passenger's gift of local cherries, and a cemetery in Aix where headstones sprouted ceramic flowers.

Crossing from Switzerland into Germany, the couple attended the opening of the Josef Albers Museum, viewing almost one hundred of his paintings, prints, and experiments in sandblasted glass. Paying homage to her mentor and his widow, Anni, Ruth met Black Mountain College friends, heard string quartets, and sampled her teacher's favorite German dishes of salted herring, cabbage, cauliflower, and potatoes. Vice President George H. W. Bush happened to be visiting the country to honor German immigration to the United States. When he traveled with Chancellor Helmut Kohl by helicopter for the museum dedication, the two were met by leftist protesters opposing the planned deployment of U.S. anti-Soviet missiles in Western Europe. The demonstrators waved signs that read: "Yes to Albers, no to Bush." Ruth took home a poster as a souvenir.

Before flying home, Ruth visited Pietronella Swierstra, the Black Mountain College friend who had helped stitch her wedding gown, in Amsterdam.

"We arrived home on July 4th to San Francisco reality, which we were ready for," Ruth wrote. After being on the road for nearly a month, running for trains and climbing stairs to walk-up pensions, the fifty-seven-year-old sculptor, who normally subsisted on four hours of sleep, was weary. Her travel journal noted a dizzy spell in

Venice, perhaps caused by heat or jet lag. Even after shaking off fatigue, she was troubled by vague and mystifying symptoms for the next several months.

Ruth and her friends wondered if the sensations could be linked to a recent art project. The year before the European trip, she had completed a major commission that exposed her to toxic chemicals. In the "Faces of San Francisco," part of Macy's annual Easter flower show, she'd sculpted a dozen celebrities' heads. The 4-foot-tall caricatures of local personalities—from baseball legend Joe DiMaggio to singer-activist Joan Baez—used a synthetic fabrication technology.

Beginning with 1,500 pounds of clay, Ruth and her son Paul led a studio team that sculpted the heads in her front yard. Then the clay heads were swathed in plastic wrap and encased in a shell of celastic, a plastic-impregnated fabric treated with the solvent acetone. The process released fumes, requiring the artists to wear ventilator masks. When dried, the heads were painted to a high shine. As an artist, it wasn't Ruth's first encounter with chemicals—her tied-wire sculptures used resins to create the effect of dew-spangled branch tips—but this was her first major acetone exposure.

The "Faces of San Francisco" was an amusing and popular installation, which Macy's displayed in the storefront windows and feted with a dinner in Union Square. But the glossy, grinning heads had worried friends like Andrea Jepson, who wondered if they were all worth the risk to Ruth.

After her trip and through 1984, Asawa developed skin rashes, stomachaches, and odd pins-and-needles sensations in her extremities. Her symptoms multiplied during a season of high demand, when she was taking on a trio of big new commissions—along with her usual civic obligations and family activities.

A fountain was in the works for the forecourt of the Johnson & Johnson

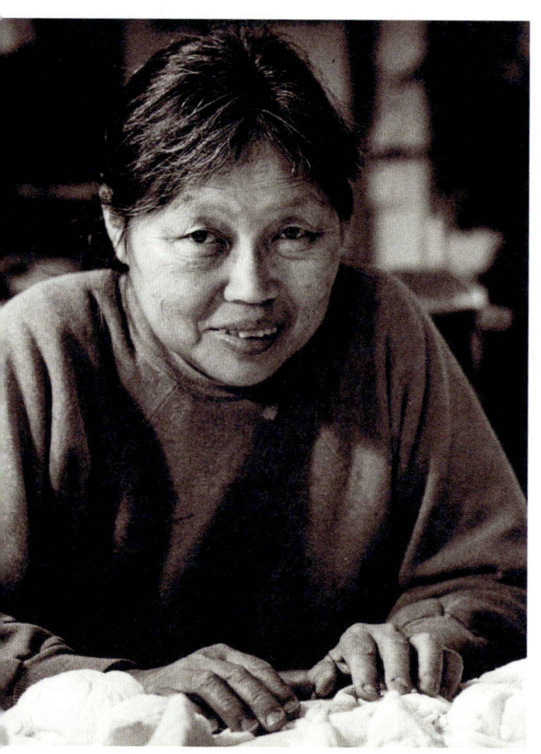

Ruth working with baker's clay, 1983. Photograph by Allen Nomura.

San Francisco office, which faced the waterfront and the Bay Bridge. Ruth adapted techniques of origami to design a mammoth sunburst in stainless steel, veiled in a flow of water. She would call it *Aurora*, for the Roman goddess of the dawn. Working with the landscape artist Mai Arbegast, Ruth envisioned surrounding the sculpture with greenery. Synergy between art and gardens always energized her, and *Aurora*'s site was perfect: framing the rising sun.

Amid her health issues, Ruth's second professional challenge beside the *Aurora* fountain came from Santa Rosa, 55 miles north of San Francisco. Out of a field of candidates, the city chose Ruth to design a fountain for the city's courthouse square. The project became contentious when the city selected her over a previous prizewinner. Ruth contemplated withdrawing if wrangling led to litigation and halted the project. After the Mermaid Manifesto, she wanted no more public spats.

But Santa Rosa confirmed its choice of Ruth and the city embraced her design: four walls of bas-relief depicting the history and natural beauty of Sonoma County. She hoped the city would cast the fountain sculpture in bronze. In that, she would be disappointed: Fiscal limits dictated the use of cast concrete, reinforced with fiberglass. However, Ruth didn't compromise on her collaborative vision: She wanted to involve the community's schoolchildren in sculpting one of the panels. Conceptually, her design—like the Union Square fountain—was made to showcase the work of many hands, especially little ones.

Ruth's third major commission of the period came from a downtown hotel, the Ramada Renaissance (now the Parc 55). It hired Ruth to create a 60-foot-wide, 6-ton concrete frieze to flank its entrance, depicting scenes of San Francisco from the 1906 Earthquake to the present day. Seeking synergy with her education programs, Asawa turned the sculpture process into a Master-Apprentice class for students from the new School of the Arts. At the frieze's dedication in 1984, the emcee declared: "She's better than Grandma Moses."

In fact, Ruth was now a grandmother in real life—six times over. Aiko and Larry had two boys, Ken and Hudson. Xavier and his wife, Gerri, had Chris and Xavier Jr. Hudson and his wife, Terry, had Max and Lilli. And Ruth was on her way to ten grandchildren. Eventually, Addie would marry Peter Weverka and have Sofia and Henry. Paul would wed Sandra Halladey and produce Emma and William. All would live within ten blocks of Ruth and Albert's home. She commemorated the new generation by casting the mothers' pregnant bellies, and the newborns' hands and feet.

Grandparenthood didn't slow Ruth's pace. Her projects required massive coordination and mobilization of her studio assistants and her corporate or government sponsors. Months, often years, of correspondence, bids, design development, site analysis, and materials selection had to take place before work could begin. Rounds of fee negotiations and signing of contracts preceded the creative process. The burdens on the artist to keep her vision intact, and her energies fresh and focused, would have depleted a less-determined spirit.

Ruth drove herself relentlessly. Since her childhood ordeals of diphtheria and internment, she'd vowed never to waste time—even at the expense of sleep. She traced her insomnia to a fear of losing the opportunity to create. So she put her hours of sleeplessness to good use, drawing and sculpting, all in an effort not to lose precious hours. Her hair, once a shiny jet bob, now was sprinkled a salt-and-pepper gray. Beneath large-framed glasses, her eyelids wore fine lines of fatigue.

Among the friends who had worried for some time about Ruth's health was Buckminster Fuller. As early as May 1982, Fuller urged her to slow down, citing a suspected "allergy." After she cast his face and hands, he wrote a letter discouraging her from making another sculpture of his famous head:

> *Darling Ruth:*
> *Am deeply concerned over your allergy. I don't want you to risk sculpting any-thing of anybody, let alone of me. There are already too many of me by others. Six in all. The Noguchi head is as yet very satisfactory.*
> *The masks you made of me and my "hands" are excellent. That's enough.*
> *All Anne's and my love to you.*
> *Faithfully,*
> *Bucky*

It was one of their last communications. Just over a year later, in July 1983, Fuller was in Los Angeles, keeping a bedside vigil for his wife, Anne, who was suffering from advanced gastrointestinal cancer and hospitalized in a near-coma. At one point, the eighty-seven-year-old inventor stood up, exclaiming, "I know she is squeezing my hand; she is squeezing my hand!" Moments later, he had a heart attack and died, followed by Anne thirty-six hours later.

In 1984, Asawa's constellation of odd symptoms intensified: Pins and needles pricked her feet, and her intestines rumbled. A rash reddened her neck. In November, she awoke with excruciating stomach pains. She consulted doctors at Kaiser Permanente Medical Center in San Francisco, who ordered months of tests to consider all the potential causes of her sensations.

On February 19, 1985, Ruth and Albert
went back to Kaiser for a 10:20 a.m.
meeting with internist Phillip Perloff
and rheumatologist Paul Feigenbaum.
Ruth's symptoms weren't caused by
cancer, germs, or chemicals, the doctors
had concluded. Instead, the cause was
likely a hyperactive immune system
attacking her own organs.

The field of medical diagnostics in
the mid-1980s was beginning to get a
grasp of the immune system, but tests
were still general and nonspecific.
Patients who presented with Ruth's
complaints typically underwent an
ANA, or antinuclear antibody test. The
purpose of the test was to detect certain defensive molecules that normally
help fight infection, but sometimes run
amok and attack the body's own cells, as
when soldiers' "friendly fire" hits their
own troops in combat.

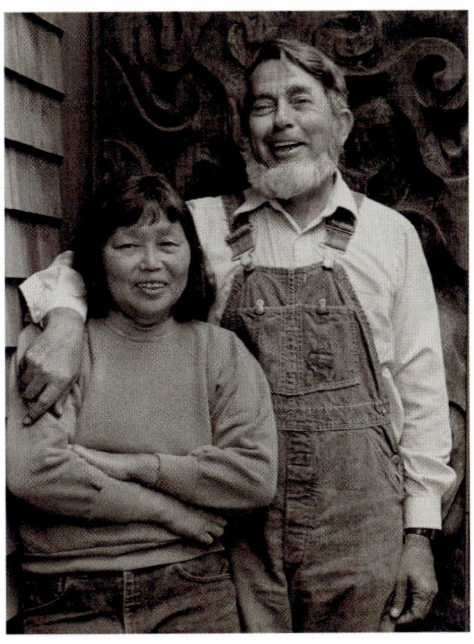

*Ruth and Albert at the front door of their home in San Francisco's
Noe Valley, 1984. Photograph by Phiz Mezey.*

Such tests aren't perfect; sometimes they give false positive results in healthy people. But they can indicate an immune system in overdrive, attacking itself in what is
known as an autoimmune reaction. This state of hyperactivity can be mild or severe,
and can trigger widespread inflammation of many organ systems, including the skin,
nerves, stomach, kidneys, lungs, and blood vessels.

Ruth's specific diagnosis was systemic lupus erythematosus (SLE), or lupus, which
means "wolf" in Latin. The disease was named in ancient times for its characteristic
mask-shaped rash, which resembles the muzzle of a wolf. The condition affects women
more than men, and people of color more than Caucasians. At greatest risk are women
of African, Latin, Native American, and Asian descent.

If the wolf's onset was stealthy, its cause was even more elusive. Although
researchers have cited environmental, genetic, and hormonal factors, a single
trigger remains unknown. Ruth had collected articles about the occupational
risks of artists' materials, so she was aware that acute acetone poisoning can

cause nausea, lethargy, and skin and eye irritation. But any speculated link to lupus was unproven.

Andrea Jepson reserved her doubts long after hearing Ruth's diagnosis:

> *Most of us were not surprised because there were all those big vats of chemicals in her house. She was putting patinas on things. People didn't know so much then, about how toxic things were. All those chemicals were in an enclosed space, almost a giant closet, in the basement of the house.*

Lupus follows a waxing-and-waning pattern, making it unpredictable. Treatment can induce a remission, only to be followed by a relapse. Mild cases may respond to simple anti-inflammatory drugs like ibuprofen and cortisone cream. Severe cases call for greater intervention.

Ruth was, in fact, seriously ill. Her doctors prescribed the strongest regimen then available. They started her on prednisone, an oral steroid, to calm the inflammation. But within weeks they would need to add a second medication, cyclophosphamide, or Cytoxan, a chemotherapy drug commonly used to treat cancer. One of the chemo's side effects, immune suppression, is a drawback in cancer but a benefit in lupus because it dampens the hyperactive immune system. This regimen would bring about an array of side effects: sleeplessness from the steroid; hair loss, mouth sores, and stomach upset from the chemo.

Ruth's tai chi practice and preference for natural remedies were at odds with such heavy pharmaceuticals. She raised questions about possible alternatives. In her case, the Kaiser doctors said, it would be unsafe to abandon traditional drugs. If left untreated, lupus inflammation can attack multiple organ systems, damaging the heart, kidneys, and vascular system, ultimately leading to organ failure and death. Alternative or traditional remedies could be a complement to, but not a substitute for, conventional treatment. The doctors would retest her blood and urine after a few weeks to see if it was safe to reduce the dosage.

There was so much to take in during the long February 19 meeting. While Ruth absorbed the news, Albert took careful notes in his slanted architect's printing on the pros and cons of more testing and treatments, and other possible organ involvement such as the blood vessels and kidneys.

The couple returned home around two in the afternoon. While bracing for their mother's diagnosis, the young Laniers had pitched in with housework and made plans for providing meals while Ruth was ill. Aiko had cleaned the whole house, with Hudson assisting in the kitchen.

As Ruth's diagnosis fell on the Lunar New Year, Mae Lee served her a Chinese banquet: a "monk's meal" of vegetables, tofu, and mushrooms. Then came an array of stuffed oysters, chicken, tied green onions, spinach, rice, nectarine, plum, ice cream, and cake. At 5-foot-2-inches and 120 pounds, Ruth partook of the feast and downed her first three prednisone pills.

Starting a lupus diary the next day, she contemplated a life after diagnosis:

2/20/85 Beautiful spring day. 1st pill 7:30 AM. Ate leftover monks food. Feel almost normal but a little weak. Mae visited. SLE may change my life. The prescription is to remove stress from my life. Eliminate unnecessary work, meetings, big projects. I may have to start painting watercolors, looking out my back windows, scrutinizing our flowers in our garden.

Hudson's wife, Terry, brought over her children, Max and Lilli. She helped her mother-in-law by vacuuming the office while Ruth played with and sketched the children and their teddy bear, Mischa, on the sun porch, giving them the drawings to color in. After lunch, Terry and the grandchildren left.

More friends rallied as word spread. At two in the afternoon, Merry Renk and Earle Curtis brought Ruth a book, *The Lost World of the Impressionists*, and volunteered to read her a chapter. During their summer travels, Ruth and Albert had visited Renk and Curtis in France. Now she imagined retreating to her own private Giverny with watercolors and brushes:

Their visit today is subconsciously gearing me up to a new life for painting and a quieter life . . .

Ruth's younger daughter Addie stopped by to join her parents for dinner. Taking her medicine, Ruth marveled at how well she felt after her sixth pill: hungry and energized enough to jump up and wash the dishes, as she hadn't in a long while. Mild euphoria can be a prelude to prednisone's harsher side effects.

Still, odd neurological sensations shot through her extremities. Ruth described them with an artist's eye:

Still not steady on my feet, I still feel my feet but they feel different, not tingling but a carpet of nerves.

On her second evening after the diagnosis, she drew the first buds of spring:

the flowering quince boughs friends had brought her for the Lunar New Year. She stayed up to watch about six late-night television shows, and then wrote about her experience until nearly two thirty in the morning. Still wide-eyed, she plunged into the next chapter of the impressionists book and read until four thirty.

By February 21, Ruth was bone-weary, but sleep wouldn't come. Fueled by the prednisone, she felt hyper. Through another wakeful night, Ruth recorded in her notebook a feeling of numbness spreading over the fingers of her left hand. Only her pinky retained normal sensation. Her arms ached. Her sensitive feet and skin rash persisted. The next day, Xavier's wife, Gerri, took Ruth to Kaiser for an appointment with her doctors to monitor the disease's progress. The numbness spread to her right calf. By evening, her right foot went numb, too, making it hard to walk.

On February 23, while trying to flex her numb right foot, she noted its range of motion was 2 inches less than that of her still-normal left foot. That morning, blood appeared in her sputum.

On February 24, Addie brought her more reading material: *The Habit of Being*, by Flannery O'Connor. This collection of the Southern novelist's letters recounts her own journey through lupus in the 1950s and '60s. O'Connor retired to her mother's farm in rural Georgia to raise peacocks and write stories, describing the course of her illness with candor and humor. Ruth focused on O'Connor's spirit, which seemed to grow stronger through repeated hospitalizations, even as her health failed.

Massage and floor exercises helped relax and tone Ruth's muscles. But the stomach pain flared with a vengeance. Her strength and coordination faltered. While trying to hold a cup in her numb left hand, she spilled her drink. In her mind, she scanned the events of years past for clues to the swiftly spreading disability. Years earlier, she'd had an episode of shingles when her skin had turned bright red. During her tai chi practice, she recalled awakening one morning with powerful leg cramps and foot pain. Were these episodes, she wondered, heralds of lupus? Probably not. But she had been so healthy for most of her life that her restless mind kept trying to connect the dots between rare bouts of sickness, which likely were unrelated to her current crisis.

Nerves in her numb leg would suddenly light up with a bolt of pain. At four in the morning on February 25, she passed blood and felt weak on her legs. That day, Dr. Feigenbaum started Cytoxan treatments and Dr. Perloff called for a neurology consult in March. Ruth's hair began to shed into her hairbrush, and Albert noticed strands in their bed.

All this was within the first week after diagnosis. Thinking back, Xavier said:

I probably didn't really realize how serious it was, or could have been. She's such a strong woman, you know? You always think she's going to come out of it. She never complained. Never whined, "I'm hurting" or "I'm tired." Nothing. That's remarkable.

Ruth relished Flannery O'Connor's spirited writing, spiked with unsparing descriptions of growing bald and "watermelon-faced" from steroid treatment, adjusting to crutches and prescriptions. The writer was treated with ACTH, a cortisol-stimulating hormone then extracted from the pituitary glands of pigs. Ruth had newer medicines and synthetic steroids. But she shared a bond with the writer, who received a grant from the Rockefeller family to help pay for her medicine. The Rockefellers were also patrons of Asawa, whose early sculptures they first purchased from the Peridot Gallery in Manhattan. Now the Rockefeller family called to offer help with her illness.

But where O'Connor, a practicing Catholic, went to Lourdes, Ruth went to Kaiser doctors and practiced her own brand of private spirituality. This involved not just the Zen view of life and suffering that was her heritage, but Ruth's singular view of her lupus ordeal not merely as a disease and its treatment, but as a challenge to her life as an artist:

This may not be an illness. It may be another dialogue with myself and the medication is helping thru it . . .

In her diary, Ruth noted O'Connor's belief that what a person does in spite of an illness is more important than the illness itself. The cortisone-based therapies that each woman took calmed their immune systems, but robbed their repose. Ruth copied O'Connor's reflection into her own diary: "Cortisone makes you think night and day until I suppose the mind dies of exhaustion if you are not rescued." Ruth's head buzzed around the clock with endless ideas about her art and life.

Xavier, who was a builder, came over to install a telephone answering machine for his mother. Gerri prepared a dinner of chicken, sweet potato, rice, salad, and cake. (Steroids tend to give patients a lumberjack's appetite.) The diminutive sculptor developed a moon face, a classic side effect of steroid treatment known as Cushing's syndrome.

Ruth noted in her diary that Dr. Feigenbaum explained lupus also triggers a dangerous condition known as vasculitis, in which the body attacks its own blood vessels, which can lead to lasting damage. The Cytoxan—for all its unpleasant side effects—aimed to reverse this situation.

Increasing tremors and shakiness inspired a note at two in the morning on February 28, when she tried to walk to the bathroom: "Need cane." Soon, she would be fitted for a foot brace to stabilize her weakened right foot.

One afternoon, as Mae Lee read her a passage from Mark Twain about dreams, Ruth snatched a rare thirty-minute nap, a precious taste of rest amid the sleepless nights. She had declined Dr. Feigenbaum's offer of sleeping pills because she had never experienced anything like the twelve nights of insomnia she would endure. Most of these nights, moments of sleep vibrated with artistic questions: Should she do a three-painting series titled *Systemic, Lupus,* and *Erythematosus*? She wrote in her diary that she needed rest in order to make a speech about a mural.

As flashes of pain struck her legs five minutes apart through one night, she envisioned her ravaged nerves as the network of wires of her sculpture. During her sleepless nights, Ruth also recalled and wrote down fragments of dreams. She awoke from "a rotating dream that looked like a film dissolve." Insomnia threatened to turn into delirium.

Ruth tried to fill her wakeful nights with automatic writing. First she attempted to write a fairy tale about an old man and woman, before impatiently breaking off after about a page: "Trying fantasy," she jotted in the margin, "don't like it."

Real events of her life story were more compelling than fiction: her childhood on the farm, her wartime experience in the camps, the discovery of art at Black Mountain, and finding love with Albert at age twenty-two. She filled page after page of yellow legal pads with episodes tumbling forth from her pen in a stream of consciousness. Her writings ranged from whimsical musings on natural remedies—*Some day I'm going to write a book on "How I Beat Lupus With Bok Choy."*—to dark reflections on the life-threatening journey of SLE:

> *. . . Sounds exotic mysterious, like*
> *an exotic flower*
> *A cane, sleeping pills, foot brace,*
> *massage, touch,*
> *A blue journey without travel within*
> *Assigned and unknown.*

Ruth engaged in furious debates on paper defending her values in art and life. She drafted an impassioned plea to Santa Rosa officials to use bronze for the courthouse square fountain. The beautiful metal would be lasting, although expensive. During the long, dark hours, she argued with herself. Her handwriting veered from her even, rounded script to the spidery scrawl of a body drained and disarticulated by autoimmune attack.

Ruth's written account gives voice to the pain and frustration her children never heard her speak aloud. But even in the small hours of near-despair, her notes are leavened by an affirmation of her love of family.

Raising children: More "Yeses" than "Nos"
I have six of the most wonderful gorgeous children
& 6 sweetheart babies. . . .

She had a boundless appetite for the company of friends and good food. Her diary records visits from children and friends bearing flowers and savory dishes. In the midst of the diary, she jotted down menus with diary notations about Mae Lee's egg custard, Addie's steamed fish and vegetables, Aiko's stews, and Adam's freshly caught salmon. Later, vowing to eat for nutrition rather than taste alone, she reverted to the clean Asian flavors of her youth: miso soup, tofu, and bok choy. Writing about food seemed to buoy her spirits.

Meticulous about acknowledging gifts, Asawa logged a staggering thirty pages of notes listing the bouquets, cards, and books her friends brought, along with the givers' names and when proper thank-you notes were sent.

As a compliant patient, Ruth not only took her medicines, but also conserved her energy and adopted a strategy for recovery. She declined speaking engagements and meetings. She canceled her involvement with a Soviet-American women's exchange group. She wrote to city officials in Santa Rosa, seeking an extension of her deadline for completing the courthouse square fountain due to her illness. She submitted an application for disability benefits, signed by Dr. Perloff.

Friends were stunned and bereft to learn that the catalyst of so many art and public service projects was sidelined by a debilitating condition. The Valley Girls, her colleagues from Alvarado Arts, gathered at each other's houses and held free-form prayer meetings where they sent healing thoughts for her recovery.

Ruth briefed her longtime patron William Matson Roth, the Ghirardelli Square developer. Roth had backed her vision for the mermaid fountain against attacks. Now, she laid out her health crisis in stark terms:

Dear Bill,
How are you? Me? Not so good. I have just been diagnosed as having Systemic

Lupus Erythematosus, an autoimmune disease which has pretty much affected my whole body. Little is known about the disease, but it is a permanent/chronic illness. With medication, diet, rest and avoiding stressful situations, it can be controlled and will go into remission. It is not contagious but can be inherited. People have lived normal lives for 10-20+ years. I am reading Flannery O'Connor's letters "The Habit of Being," where she refers to her lupus, treatment and physical deterioration of her hips. Her father died of it when she was 15 years old. Today, there is 90% success in controlling the disease. My medication is cortisone/prednisone and Cytoxan which is given to cancer patients.

On top of that I have two commissions. Both just started. The contract for my last one was signed in January. I am requesting an extension. The other one is a fountain already designed, but must be fabricated by September. I am excited by this one because it will be in stainless steel, and I have the great fortune of working with Mai Arbegast, landscape architect, and Ed Tower, architect. It is at Howard and Embarcadero, the starting point of the Bay to Breakers. I put the runners in the last panel of the Ramada wall relief.

At last, I will go into my garden and paint the flowers, tomatoes, lettuce and bok choy. I once told Albers that even if I studied with him I would rather paint flowers than abstract paintings. His reply: "Good. Be sure they are Asawa flowers."

Albert is making a beautiful garden of kiwi vines, Babcock peach, pear, artichokes, cosmos, Mexican sunflower, daisies, nasturtiums, and on and on. I might learn their Latin names.

My doctors are reassuring. I was tested for ulcers, tumor, occupational chemical and metal poisoning, all negative. It has taken four months to come to this conclusion. Reflecting back, I had warning signs. If this is really my last large work, I have an idea which will cap all my ideas into one. I feel it's full circle as though this was willed. I need your advice so hope you will have some time for me (lunch will be served) when you are next in San Francisco, plus one hour to plaster cast your face.

You have always been willing to risk with me. Remember when you came to the foundry and said, "Don't worry Ruth. If the mermaids don't work, I'll put them in my bathtub. Keep going."

. . .

Give Joan a hug for us.
Love,
Ruth

Actor Peter Coyote was devastated by Ruth's illness. The sight of Asawa sketching had inspired him to resume his acting career. As a student of Zen, Coyote held as a fundamental truth that suffering is part of the human condition. Still, her ordeal upset his worldview:

> *I was very sorry to hear of your illness and found it hard to understand because I have always believed that fundamentally healthy people—mentally healthy, alive, selfless, committed—don't get sick. Another prejudice bites the dust . . .*

As the disease advanced, with her coughing and the blood in her sputum, Ruth was admitted to Kaiser Hospital for a biopsy of lung nodules that had appeared on X-rays and CT scans. A biopsy would analyze cells from her airways to determine the extent of the lupus inflammation. Chief of vascular surgery Dr. Douglas Grey, who performed the procedure, marveled at the will of his diminutive patent.

"She was tiny but a force of nature," he said.

Ruth, who sketched every bouquet sent by well-wishers, had also brought origami papers, practicing her craft with fingers that now were numb. In a trick that delighted visitors, Ruth folded an origami paper camera, concealing inside a tiny sketch of her visitor. When they came to her bedside she would pretend to take their picture, and—click—out came the "photo."

She greeted Dr. Grey during the week with a new paper animal every morning. When he brought his young daughters, Emily and Maggie, on hospital rounds on the weekend, Ruth demonstrated paper-folding techniques for them. Emily, eight years old, took those techniques back to her school to teach her fellow second graders what the artist had taught her.

"She was a sweetheart," said Dr. Grey. "A unique person. We had long conversations about art, and how to stimulate children's interest in it."

After Ruth's discharge, Dr. Grey made house calls on his patient. The artist led the surgeon on a tour of her studio. She gave his family a print and painted their portrait in miniature on an eggshell ornament for Christmas.

"You outdid yourself with Emily and Maggie, who are now 'origami addicts' and wonder why their father can't do the same," the surgeon wrote her. While glad for her recovery, he added that after she was discharged, he missed her presence on rounds.

As long as treatment lowered her immune defenses, Ruth remained at risk of contracting infections that would worsen her lupus. Keeping her recovery on track and reducing stress was a delicate balance. It meant keeping visitors to a minimum and imposing a ban on unnecessary kissing, according to a note she jotted in the margin of a medical journal article. Even family members were held at bay. Hudson's wife, Terry, wrote her mother-in-law newsy updates on the family, from apricot picking and Hudson's building business to their son Max's acceptance in a Japanese bilingual kindergarten:

> *Dear Ruthie,*
> *Even though I can't come see you, I've been thinking of you and getting daily reports from Aiko or Albert. When this is all over and you're back to health, we'll remember this like a bad dream, but something that made us all stronger and wiser . . .*

For the first half of 1985, Ruth was disabled and bedridden much of the time. Even after medication damped the worst of the disease's inflammation, she remained weakened, and never fully regained her originally formidable strength. For a time, she couldn't lift heavy objects or walk unassisted by crutches or a foot brace. She was forced to focus on essential projects. She fortified herself with juices and greens from her garden. She worked her body with massage. She engaged the muscles of her hands in drawing, painting, and origami—reviewing the lessons of Black Mountain.

Slowly, lupus yielded to treatment. The worst of her symptoms abated. She steeled herself to resume work on major projects. Her mind churned with plans for the fountain in Santa Rosa's Courthouse Square.

Earlier, in her prednisone-fueled insomnia, she had drafted a handwritten memo to city officials, outlining her concerns about the project. She argued that the design of the art should precede setting a budget for the commission, not the other way around. To keep track of time, she headed each page with the hour: "2:59 a.m.," "4:10 a.m."

Ten or twelve days into her marathon of insomnia, Ruth wrote, "I was high as a kite, in an alpha state where the mind can almost leave the body. Yogis reach that state." Concerned, her family made her lie down on the sofa and close her eyes. She lay down. Euphoria would not yield.

After a massage, she finally slept. In a kind of dream, she sensed her spirit rise. She felt herself levitating, leaving her body and hovering above it. But soaring away was impossible with the Santa Rosa fountain and other projects incomplete.

"My God," she thought, "I can't leave yet, I haven't done the job."

CHAPTER 11

WOMAN WARRIOR

After her brief out-of-body experience, Ruth awoke back on her couch, thinking about how she would resume work on her sculptures-in-progress.

Recovery was slow, and she wasn't out of the woods yet. Her daughter-in-law Terry wished that lupus would dissolve like a bad dream. But then as now, lupus remained chronic and incurable. Under fire of steroids and chemo, the wolf may retreat and go into remission, only to return later like a stealth predator.

But Ruth was relentless. In 1985, the Pacific Asian American Women Bay Area Coalition named her its Woman Warrior in the arts. Long before the fifth-century folk heroine Mulan became the subject of a Disney cartoon, the figure of the female fighter in Asian culture had been explored by Maxine Hong Kingston in her 1976 book, *The Woman Warrior*. The figure of the righteous woman as a creative force for good in society likewise inspired the Woman Warrior Awards, which honored leaders in the arts, professional life, and social service.

Ruth was recognized for wielding wire, ink, paint, clay, cement, and bronze to make art, heedless of racial and gender barriers. The metaphor of a warrior was apt for Ruth in more ways than one. After soldiering through six months on high-dose steroids, Ruth's lupus symptoms had begun their ragged retreat.

Perhaps it was a coincidence, but after years during which Ruth reserved her comments on the past, the Woman Warrior honor opened a new chapter in which she slowly would become more outspoken.

By June 1985, she was at home in the house in Noe Valley, and strong enough to take short walks around the neighborhood with Mae Lee. She doggedly weaned herself off drugs over about six months. Rest and Shiatsu massage soothed her inflamed muscles. In her lupus diary, she stressed, "nutrition . . . need strength for mural . . ."

A daunting backlog of commissions faced her. She had to complete the design of the Santa Rosa Courthouse Square fountain, finish fabrication of the *Aurora* fountain on San Francisco's Embarcadero, and more.

Ruth also was designing a wall in bas-relief to help convert a vacant lot in the Tenderloin into a safe, welcoming playground for children. Named for Father Alfred Boeddeker, a priest who ran St. Anthony's Dining Room, the park would be an oasis for increasing numbers of children—many of them immigrants—living in the transitional neighborhood. With apologies for the delay, Ruth sent a final check to Lafayette Manufacturing Company for the concrete casting of her relief, which showed kids at play.

Photos taken just after lupus showed the normally trim Ruth round-cheeked as an apple doll from the steroids. She peered wanly from beneath a fringe of fine, silvery bangs. Strikingly open about her illness and her drive to bounce back, she granted an interview about lupus to a magazine published by St. Mary's Hospital in San Francisco.

Drug-induced episodes of sleeplessness and mania were "interesting to me as an artist," she told the magazine. She said she now focused on building herself up with carrot and orange juices made at home. The hospital communications director sent her the magazine's cover photo, depicting her with arms akimbo and a broad grin. Ruth wrote that her family appreciated the portrait because in the grip of the disease "I was too sick to smile."

The year of the lupus attack, Ruth had plans to visit Japan, and she wasn't about to give up the trip. Unlike her sisters, she'd missed a chance to study there as a girl. Now she was slated to help lead a group of garden, art, and architecture enthusiasts on a Japan in Autumn tour from October 20 to November 12. Landscape architect Mai Arbegast, her friend and collaborator on the *Aurora* sculpture, was the tour's garden expert; Albert, the architect; and Ruth, the artist leading travelers in sketching gardens. She and Albert still had the fall trip on their calendar. Lupus patients can travel once their symptoms are under control. And Ruth was now in remission. Aiko and her family bid them bon voyage with a hand-drawn card: "Sayonara, Ruthie and Al."

Ruth now embarked as a mature artist on a trip deferred since she was a nine-year-old schoolgirl. She took in the bullet trains and the commuters packed like sardines. She sketched terraced hillsides, a white cherry tree with crimson leaves, an ancient gnarled pine, a hand-tied bamboo trellis, and a stone garden path. She saw a five-story pagoda representing the five elements of the universe: earth, water, fire, air, and heaven. Her pencil captured everyday objects in a folkcraft museum: a teapot, a broom, a vase. She jotted notes about the Shinto worship of nature, which inspired in her a sense of awe and calm. On the road, she indulged in the silky soba and udon noodles she craved—since Albert wasn't a fan of the dishes at home.

While Ruth worked on restoring herself amid the autumn landscapes of Japan, her younger daughter Addie accepted the Woman Warrior award on her behalf.

On her return from Japan, Ruth resumed nurturing her seventh child, the School of the Arts. She plunged back into the fray of raising funds, planning curriculum, and recruiting artists in residence. The young school was ravenous for funding, and finding money would be a major challenge for the first decades of its life. When she wasn't wooing friends, artists, businesses, and foundations to sponsor the training of young artists, Ruth was thinking about workshops and designing craft items that students could produce and sell to benefit the school. In December 1985, partnering with the Embarcadero Center retail mall, Ruth helped students sculpt two thousand red and green clay poinsettia ornaments to give away to holiday shoppers. This initiative netted the school $10,000 from the Embarcadero Center. No craft project seemed too small to claim Ruth's time.

Art commissions delayed by lupus were now revived in what seems record time. For the *Aurora* fountain, Ruth had prepared a scale model in her backyard. Albert calculated the angles and made working drawings for the steel fabricators, who then bent and welded the metal facets into a giant, gleaming origami.

On March 19, 1986—just thirteen months after Ruth's diagnosis—the steel sunburst of *Aurora* was hoisted into position. The fountain stood in a courtyard facing the Bay Bridge and the sunrise over the East Bay hills. Its 120 stainless steel triangles, replicating the planes of a folded origami piece, reflected the sun's rays through the water that bathed its surfaces.

Ruth wanted to use the *Aurora* installation to benefit the School of the Arts. The corporate sponsors agreed that coins tossed into the fountain could be fished out and donated to the school. To kick off the coin campaign, the building's developer and leasing agent presented Ruth with one hundred dollars in silver. Mayor Dianne Feinstein issued a proclamation honoring Asawa. Ruth wrote:

> *Thank you for ordering good weather for the dedication. . . . I also want to thank you for your contribution to the School of the Arts Foundation with the donation of the coins tossed into the fountain. Please advise me on how to go about collecting the coins.*

Restarting the Santa Rosa fountain commission was more complicated. It was hard for Ruth to give up her grand vision for redesigning the whole courthouse square, and casting the fountain in enduring bronze. But she made her peace with economic constraints and settled for a fountain made of fiberglass-reinforced cast concrete.

The fountain's design—a historical tableau of Sonoma County—was collaborative. She consulted all the city's constituencies to ensure the subject matter would be backed by a consensus in the community. Figures in the tableau would include early Spanish governors, basket-weaving Indians, and Chinese farmers and railroad

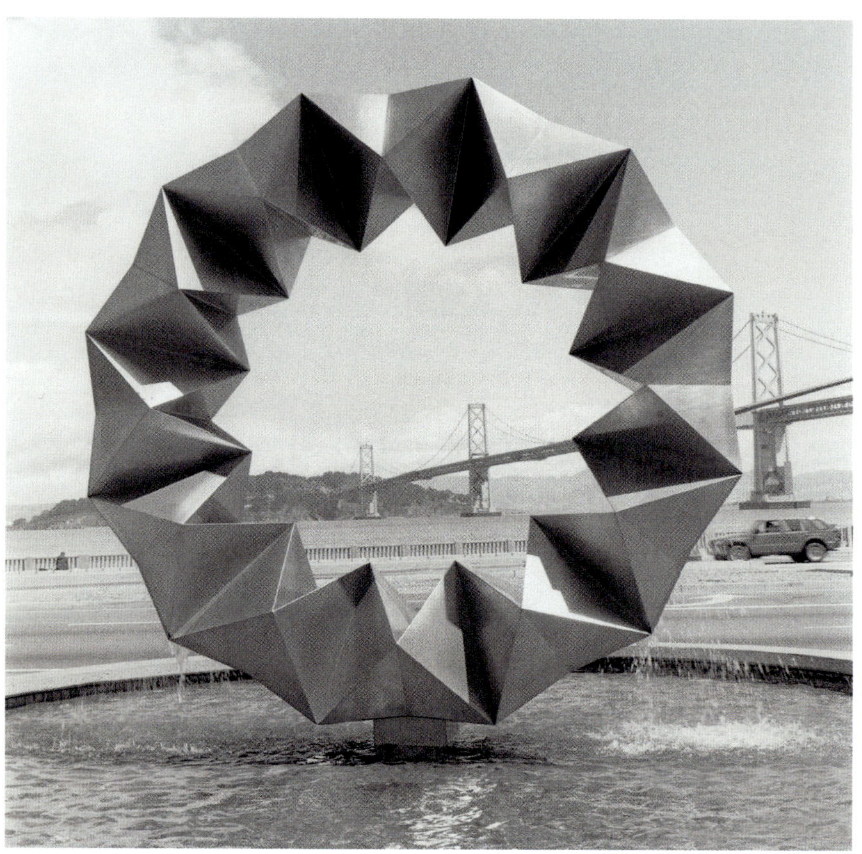

Aurora, Bayside Plaza, San Francisco, 1986
Stainless steel
144 x 144 x 39 in. (3.7 m x 3.7 m x 99 cm)
Photograph by Hudson Cuneo

workers. The horticulturist Luther Burbank had a spot. So did Snoopy, the canine hero of the cartoon strip *Peanuts*. The Sonoma Mission and Buena Vista Winery would figure on the sculpted walls wrapping around the fountain.

But it was the fountain's fourth wall that was the most collaborative and pleasurable for Ruth. The fourth wall, situated beneath the fountain's flow, would be a picture of the region's sea life, designed by the city's schoolchildren and viewed through a sheer curtain of fountain water spilling over it.

Eager for the experience of guiding children's hands again, Ruth enlisted pupils from kindergarten through sixth grade at Santa Rosa's Luther Burbank School to come to San Francisco for inspiration and planning. She organized buses to bring the kids south for a day trip. They would see her sculptures in the city, visit her home studio, and end up at the Steinhart Aquarium in Golden Gate Park to study and sketch the fish they would be modeling in baker's clay for the fountain.

After ushering the children around the city, she brought them to her home studio, to view her ceiling full of woven wire sculptures and the walls peopled with life masks of her family, friends, and colleagues.

The kids were incredulous: Did she do all that?

"If any of you want to become an artist, I'll tell you it's a lot of work. But it's fun all the time," said Asawa, casual in a cardigan and beads, peering through oversize glasses at the rapt young faces. Then they headed off to the aquarium to draw fish.

"I want to make a swordfish," one boy piped up. "And I want to make a sand shark," another said.

In all, 318 children modeled baker's clay figures of lobster, squid, salmon, and more for the fountain's seascape. Ruth and her team of artists, including Nancy Thompson and her son Paul, incorporated their individual fish into the scene.

The city of Santa Rosa had granted Ruth an extension on the project due to her illness. But lupus returned. Whether it was her rush back to work, the intensity of community collaboration, or the commutes back and forth to Santa Rosa, Ruth's work through 1986 on the design and construction of the Courthouse Square Fountain was too much. Just before the fountain's slated installation in early 1987, Ruth relapsed and was hospitalized again. Her Kaiser doctors treated her and quelled the flare-up in time for her to attend the installation and dedication. Such episodes were a sobering reminder that the condition was chronic. It could—and would—flare again.

In January 1987, the four cast concrete fountain walls were gently lowered into place. A reporter for the local newspaper, the *News Herald*, stood by in Santa Rosa Courtyard Square to watch schoolchildren file past the fountain to see their handiwork on the wall depicting marine life. The artist was there too, and she spent time thanking the installation workers.

"Asawa, in her typical populist manner," wrote the reporter, "collected autographs from the workers who gave her one-ton panels such tender loving care."

To celebrate the 1987 installation of the Santa Rosa fountain so wholeheartedly, Asawa must have made her peace with the city's use of an economical material. But if she could have peered into the future, she would have been pleased to know that nearly four decades later, when the fountain was due for restoration, the city would decide to remake the fountain using bronze just as she originally wished.

She was back, firing on all cylinders again, with her studio and the School of the Arts in high gear. She kept finding new ways to embed her art into her public school service.

The school system gained a new collaborator in Jacques d'Amboise, formerly of the New York City Ballet. D'Amboise had founded the National Dance Institute, which ran workshops for schoolchildren culminating in a show called *The Event of the Year* in venues like Madison Square Garden. The event let average kids—not just elite dance students—experience the joy of performance.

Ruth met d'Amboise through Eric Hoffer, the longshoreman-philosopher whose book *True Believer* won acclaim in the 1970s. Hoffer served with Ruth on the San Francisco Art Commission. School of the Arts executive director Fred Sonenberg arranged for d'Amboise to bring *The Event of the Year* to San Francisco. He flew out west to help set up four months of dance training before a performance on April 30 at the San Francisco Opera House.

D'Amboise auditioned around 700 kids and selected about 250 for the training and performance, including not just trained dancers and those with perfect physiques, but a rogue's gallery of tall and short, lean and stout, graceful and enthusiastic.

Boys and girls leaped and boogied to Whoopi Goldberg's reading of Gwendolyn Brooks's jazz-inflected poem, "We Real Cool." They donned tiger suits to claw and growl their way through "Little Big Top," a circus number featuring props designed by Aiko. Aiko's son Ken danced in the ensemble. Comedian Robin Williams had a cameo, as did the San Francisco 49ers football team.

Corporations like the Bank of America contributed $150,000 to mount the show. The fundraising was on a scale unusual for a public school benefit performance. Eventually, San Francisco's *Event of the Year* grew too costly to both cover expenses and yield a surplus for the School of the Arts. But d'Amboise and Ruth's friendship continued to flourish, with correspondence and visits to San Francisco, where Jacques and his wife dined with Ruth and Albert. In photo shoots, he swept Ruth's diminutive figure into his arms and led her in dance steps.

"She was original, really unique," d'Amboise reflected in an interview. He recalled visiting her sculptures and school gardens, and having her cast his life mask. He exclaimed at seeing his perfect clay likeness on her wall: "Bizarre!" He wrote her from his travels all over the world—from teaching dance in China to hiking the Appalachian Trail, always signing off with a heart as, "Your Jacques."

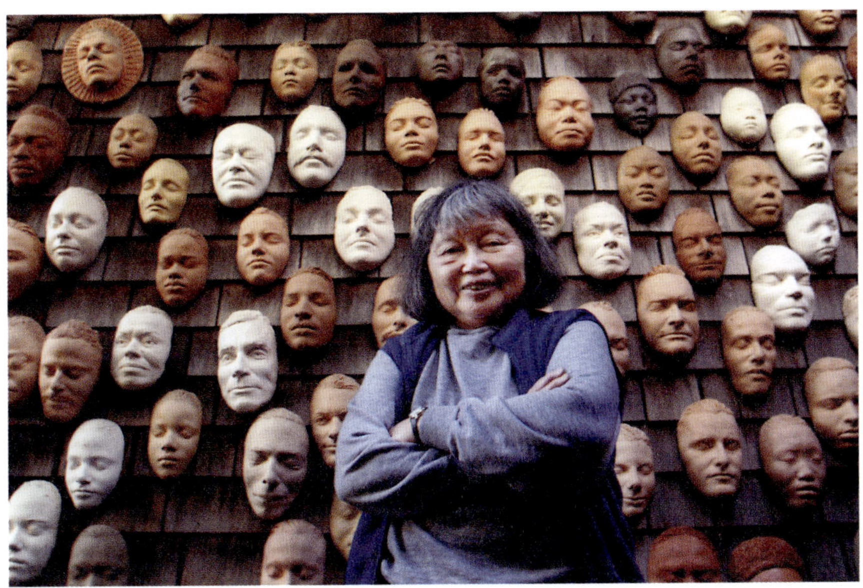

Ruth with life masks on the exterior wall of her house, 1988. Photograph by Terry Schmitt.

Now in her woman warrior phase, after forty years as a practicing artist, Ruth started speaking out for the right of artists to benefit from the resale value of their work. Fountain sculpture commissions, as she'd experienced them, were split among the artist, fabricators, installers, and makers of the base, pumps, and lighting, plus insurance. The artist's share usually was modest; sometimes she broke even. But when a work of art was later resold, the dealers, agents, and investors reaped the financial gains from a work's appreciation in value—a windfall the artist didn't share.

California lawmakers had earlier led the way by passing the California Resale Royalty Act in 1976, granting artists a share in the resale value of their work when it changed hands. Now, in the late 1980s, Ruth worked with Artists Equity Association to push for a national law. Making common cause with Senator Edward M. Kennedy, she submitted testimony to federal hearings, arguing that visual artists should have the same copyright protection as writers, musicians, and filmmakers. To make the case, Ruth shared figures:

In San Francisco, I have five fountains. One of these is the mermaid fountain I designed for Ghirardelli Square in 1968. When Ghirardelli Square was sold in the

The Visual Artists Rights Act, cosponsored by Senator Kennedy and Massachusetts Representative Edward Markey, tried to mend the inequity by letting visual artists share in the resale profits from rising valuation of their work. In the end, however, Congress cut out the provision for resale royalties for artists. The federal act passed in 1990 focused instead on protecting artists' "moral rights" not to have their names misappropriated or their creations defaced. (In July 2018, a California appeals court ruled that even the state's law granting resale royalties was incompatible with federal copyright law and should be struck down.)

The campaign fell short of securing financial equity for visual artists after all. But it provided a platform for Ruth to sound her voice on issues far beyond the schoolyard fence. She and Albert had for a long time quietly supported a basket of progressive causes—from peace candidates and a nuclear freeze to liberal elected officials who backed arts education. As they moved through middle age, they gave to a number of causes, including the Gray Panthers, which worked to expand seniors' political power, and Kimochi, an agency providing services for Japanese American elders.

Among Japanese Americans, an old cause had been gaining new life through the 1970s and '80s: the push to reconsider the cases of three young Japanese American men who had resisted what they believed was an injustice. The resisters included Minoru Yasui of Oregon, Gordon Hirabayashi of Washington, and Fred Korematsu of California. Their wartime cases had all challenged the United States's imposition of curfews on, and exclusion of, Japanese Americans without due process. They served time and fought all the way to the Supreme Court, which upheld their convictions in 1943 and 1944 per Executive Order 9066, authorizing the roundup of Japanese Americans into prison camps.

The injustice festered for decades following the war. But in 1982, Peter Irons, a law professor from the University of California at San Diego, began researching a book on Korematsu and the resistance. In a box of old papers, Irons found a "smoking gun"—documents showing that the War Department had withheld or destroyed evidence undermining the government's claim that disloyalty and espionage had dictated its actions. In an unusual move, a team of young Japanese American lawyers filed cases to reconsider the convictions of Korematsu and the other resisters, based on these new findings. From 1983 to 1987, the convictions of all three men were vacated—rendered legally void.

Central to the vindication of the resisters were revelations by an official Ruth had written to as a teenager: former assistant U.S. attorney general Edward Ennis, who served in the Justice Department during World War II. Ennis was one of the officials who received letters from incarcerated families—including the teenaged Ruth, petitioning for her father's release from alien enemy camp in New Mexico. Ennis, who had gone on to work for the American Civil Liberties Union (ACLU), testified that the government relied on false claims of treason against Japanese Americans in pressing its case against the resisters. It's unknown whether Ruth, as an adult, knew the recipient of her letters played a role in righting history.

Meanwhile Congress had passed a law creating the Commission on Wartime Relocation and Internment of Civilians, signed by President Jimmy Carter in 1980. From coast to coast, public hearings took testimony from 750 witnesses. The Civil Liberties Act of 1987, signed by President Ronald Reagan in 1988, called for reparations to be paid, citing the commission's findings that the roundups and incarcerations weren't required by national security or military necessity, but were the result of "race prejudice, war hysteria, and a failure of political leadership."

Umakichi Asawa didn't live to see this movement gain momentum. But Ruth and Albert quietly supported the National Council for Japanese American Redress. In 1989, Ruth also began filling out the forms to claim her share of reparations. She listed herself and her mother, Haru, as potential recipients.

The process probed old wounds, as the government questionnaire asked details of her wartime status, her family's addresses, and their movements from 1942 to 1945. Some of the questions highlighted the varied forms of incarceration: the distinction between her father, seized by FBI agents in the fields, and the rest of the family, ordered to report to Santa Anita Racetrack and Rohwer, Arkansas.

On the government questionnaire, a Japanese American's obedience to government's early suggestion that they leave their homes—before Executive Order 9066 made it mandatory—was described as "voluntary evacuation."

Question Number 8 read: "If individual was a voluntary evacuee, approximate date of evacuation and place of resettlement."

Ruth wrote: "May 1942—Question unclear."

On a deeper level, what could really be voluntary after Pearl Harbor? Anyone answering the questionnaire to obtain reparations would face such existential questions about whether free will could exist in wartime for Japanese Americans who were grouped into "aliens" and "non-aliens" (the double-negative term for the two-thirds of people driven from their homes who were citizens).

Meanwhile, the Lanier children planned a treat to honor their parents' fortieth anniversary in July 1989. Aiko created a card with a photo of the young Ruth and Albert holding a baby in front of the vivid red and green tomatoes sign they'd painted for the Asawa's farm stand. Inside, Albert had composed a casual welcome in his Southern style:

You are cordially (how else?) invited
to help Albert and Ruth
Celebrate their 40th wedding anniversary at a picnic
(since it has been nothing but a picnic) in their garden . . .
Come on time or the barbecued oysters will be gone.
Do not bring or send gifts.
They want for nothing. They just want to see you old timers and feed you.
If you don't come, see if we ever invite you to a 40th anniversary again!

Haru's wish that Ruth be lucky in her marriage seemed fulfilled. In 1990, just a year before restitution payments were to begin, Haru died at the age of ninety-five. As a picture bride, she had sailed to America, wed a hardworking farmer, and worked the fields with her babies on her back. Like many an Issei woman who survived the camps, her stoicism sustained a family fractured by war. But like her husband, she did not live to see the benefits of her country's reparations.

Ruth's brother George wrote a eulogy that recalled both the hardships and the happy times Haru had created for seven children before the war:

How can we children forget the memorable moments?—when we climbed into our parents' bed on Saturday mornings and Mama told us so many stories . . .

"Mukashi, mukashi . . . atta do. . . . "

Once upon a time . . .

Ruth's friends in San Francisco knew Haru as the tiny, sparrow-like lady who worked alongside her daughter in the studio, smiling and quietly sculpting plants and grasses for the Hyatt fountain. Ruth herself preserved indelible images of her parents' sacrifices: her father arrested in his strawberry fields, her mother enduring separation and confinement in Arkansas. All these images of a life disrupted, she stored away.

In April 1991, nearly a half century after her family was rounded up, Ruth received a check for $2857.14, the first installment of $20,000 in reparations, to be paid out to camp survivors over the next decade. Six months later, in October 1991, Ruth received a letter on White House stationery:

A monetary sum and words alone cannot restore lost years or erase painful memories; neither can they fully convey our Nation's resolve to rectify injustice and to uphold the rights of individuals. We can never fully right the wrongs of the past. But we can take a clear stand for justice and recognize that serious injustices were done to Japanese Americans during World War II.

In enacting a law calling for restitution and offering a sincere apology, your fellow Americans have, in a very real sense, renewed their traditional commitment to the ideals of freedom, equality, and justice. You and your family have our best wishes for the future.

Sincerely,
George Bush

All of this—the vindication of the resisters, the payment of reparations, and the apology of a president—were pieces of a partial victory that Ruth quietly absorbed. But the Supreme Court's 1944 decision upholding the legality of Executive Order 9066 lived on for decades. Not until 2018 would Chief Justice John Roberts strike it down. Ironically, he did so as a sidelight of his opinion upholding a similar act: President Donald Trump's Muslim travel ban. It was a decision that, according to dissenting Justice Sonia Sotomayor, "merely replaces one grave injustice with another."

CHAPTER 12:

TRUST ME

Ruth's work in art and public service was a continual leap of faith. She asked patrons and supporters to trust her—whether sculpting a mermaid, modeling a fountain out of dough, or starting a school.

In 1990, she accepted the San Francisco Chamber of Commerce's Cyril Magnin Award, named for the city's legendary retailer and philanthropist. Ruth used the moment to ask the city to trust her again by giving the School of the Arts a home of its own:

> *Since I was 42 years old, I have been brewing a pot of stone soup—with teachers, principals, parents, foundations, corporations and artists all contributing, and the stock is now very rich. I believe we finally have the right chemistry to make a free-standing, public arts high school happen in San Francisco . . . Trust me.*

Through the 1990s, that would be her quest. But it was also during this decade that she wove all the strands of her cultural DNA together: her Black Mountain legacy, her drive to share it with schools and museums, and, finally, a chance to tell her World War II story—not in words, but in bronze.

Ruth also started the '90s by serving as the first artist ever named to the Fine Arts Museums of San Francisco's board of trustees. Appointed in late 1989, she served through 1997 at the invitation of Director Harry S. Parker III, a Harvard-trained art historian who shared her belief in the primacy of arts education in the museums' mission. After stints at New York's Metropolitan Museum and the Dallas Museum of Art, Parker was determined to expand the board beyond what he called its usual complement of "bankers and debutantes." Ruth applied herself to the board's classic work of developing its audiences and collections, stabilizing its finances, and maintaining facilities—a job that included a seismic overhaul of the Palace of the Legion of Honor and a complete rebuilding of the de Young Museum due to earthquake damage. As a working sculptor and painter, she also brought fresh eyes and agile fingertips to the board—in a way that surprised fellow trustees.

During one otherwise routine meeting, Ruth passed out squares of paper for an impromptu origami lesson in folding cranes, a symbol of peace. She had recently made a poster for the film *Sadako and the Thousand Paper Cranes*, about a young

Hiroshima survivor who dies of leukemia while racing to fold a thousand paper cranes. In her design, Ruth spelled out each letter of the girl's name with an origami paper fold. The trustees found it challenging to complete even one, but the mood in the boardroom was playful, childlike.

"That was very novel, believe me, to have heads of corporations and socialites doing origami," recalled Florence Wong, trustee emerita.

Protests of clumsiness arose. Longtime president of the board of trustees, Diane B. Wilsey, said she and Director Parker were "the two biggest klutzes on the board" in the origami workshop. "I said: 'Harry and I fail.'" Wilsey recalled. "I wanted to bang the gavel and call time out."

Instead of a bird, one trustee folded a fan. "Very Mary McFadden," Wilsey said.

"There is no right or wrong," Ruth told the trustees.

"She was a jolly person," said Wilsey. And so they folded.

As a trustee and as an alumna of Black Mountain College, Ruth worked with the de Young on plans to host a Black Mountain College reunion in 1992, bringing together artists who, as students, helped define what it meant to be young and modern at mid-century. Over a weekend of lectures, music, poetry, and dance, the alumni would reconnect and remember a magical time.

Formerly the golden youth of mid-century art, the Mountaineers were now silver-haired. Ruth, the once shy young farm girl, had just turned sixty-six. For their gathering, she worked with the museum's education director Lois Gordon and staffer Tish Brown, planning the program and writing letters to alumni asking them to share their remembrances of what Black Mountain had taught them.

Her Milwaukee friend, Elaine Schmitt Urbain, now a New York painter and mother of two, recalled how Josef Albers strode around the class, indicating student projects with a stick. Elaine's sister, Elizabeth Schmitt Jennerjahn, remembered the sound of chamber music floating across campus, and her job of sweeping the dining room floor to make room for dance performances. Albert reflected on the collapse of Fuller's "Supine Dome." Movie director Arthur Penn recalled the heady freedom of what he called "those bountiful days."

Ruth herself, recalling how she'd been assigned to analyze her classmates' solutions to Albers's color and design problems, acknowledged, "No one had asked me to think before. . . . I felt so simple-minded. I was a country girl and they were asking you to express yourself."

Not all memories were idyllic. While others spoke of Black Mountain's efforts to integrate, Ruth recalled the academic turmoil and faculty defections of 1949. "When I left Black Mountain College," she said, "I swore that I would never come to a place like this again." Her last term serving as student moderator had been spent soothing disputes prior to the departure of Albers and other instructors. "I had been through the ringer," she said. "But then in the memories that I had when I began to raise a family . . . I began to realize the relevance of everything that I had learned there," she added. "So for the last twenty-five years I have been trying to get the school district to use artists in the schools."

The reunion ended with a brunch at Ruth and Albert's home, with photos and farewells—all of which revived memories of that Black Mountain magic. The gathering of the school's collective creativity refreshed Ruth's mission for the arts education she now wanted to replicate for San Francisco children.

Ruth had made a key new ally in her fight to bring first-class arts training into public schools: Susan Stauter, head of American Conservatory Theater's Young Conservatory training program. Before they were formally introduced, they'd sat side by side through School of the Arts task force meetings. Stauter was intrigued by the earthy older woman in jeans, a sweater, and "beads that looked like children had made them," who passed around a jar of homemade kosher dill pickles to share.

"I *like* you," the older woman volunteered one night, after Stauter had made a spirited defense of using art to help teach math. Friends called Stauter the next day to ask if she knew whom her ally at the meeting that night was.

"It's a good thing I didn't know who she was. I'd have been too intimidated," Stauter recalled. The next day someone sent a book on Black Mountain to her ACT Young Conservatory office. She connected the dots. Soon she and Ruth joined forces in support of the high school of the arts, and Stauter adopted Ruth as a mentor, almost a surrogate mother.

"You're a hot pepper," Ruth told Stauter after a particularly heated debate. She sealed the friendship by giving Stauter a sculpture and a watercolor study of a red pepper. Stauter sent her Valentine's Day and Mother's Day cards every year.

Now, in March 1992, in the afterglow of the Black Mountain College reunion, Ruth found herself again going before the Board of Education, asking for trust in her vision and renewing her plea to make the School of the Arts an independent and autonomous campus by moving it to a home of its own.

There were compelling reasons for failure. Superintendent Ramon C. Cortines expressed opposition to the move on two grounds. For one thing, the district could not afford the millions of dollars it would take to move the high school and refurbish a separate campus. For another, keeping the largely white arts school within the heavily minority campus of McAteer High helped maintain the court-ordered racial balance at the site. Moving it would upset the balance.

"... [U]ntil the District is in much better financial shape and there is relief from the court on desegregation, I do not see how the District can afford a stand-alone School of the Arts," Cortines wrote in a memo. It seemed like a double deal-breaker.

But fiscal or legal obstacles had never stopped Ruth before. The more daunting the obstacles appeared, the more resolute she became.

First she sought—and won—support from the school board's curriculum commission, led by teacher and rising politician Tom Ammiano. Ruth next faced the full board on March 24, citing donations raised as well as support rallied from the symphony, ballet, opera, and museum communities. She promised to deliver the student body growth, continued financial backing, and ethnic balance needed to make it an autonomous arts magnet school.

None of it was yet in place. But on the strength of Ruth's promise, that evening the board voted six to one in favor of giving the arts high school a home of its own.

Unlike McAteer's sprawling hilltop campus, the new site—Louise Lombard Elementary School—was tucked inconspicuously behind San Francisco State University, on Font Boulevard. The school was even farther away than was McAteer from Ruth's dream location near the performing arts hub. But it was the School of the Arts' first independent site, albeit a pint-size campus. Louise Lombard had been an elementary school that also served as a lab school for college students to practice teaching with small children. The site's former use was still visible in its tiny desks and low countertops. It had no lockers, no science lab, no cafeteria, no theater, and no library. The heating system was broken and full of asbestos, and the campus was choked with weeds.

A new superintendent, Waldemar "Bill" Rojas, declared his support for the School of the Arts while promising "not one dime" of taxpayer money would be spent on the experiment. When school secretaries complained it was so cold they had to work with their hands in their pockets, Rojas was quoted in the media saying, "So put on your coat."

All this only seemed to energize Ruth. Adversity never posed an obstacle to her art; it heightened the challenge. She invited parents and students to join her every Saturday during the summer for "workdays." She summoned all hands to scrub, prime, and paint classrooms. She dug in to mulch, water, and plant the courtyard by the opening day of September 9. Volunteers brought potluck lunches to share; food was the fuel for sweat equity from the early days of Alvarado Arts.

Ruth pushed a broom with the rest of the volunteers. Ever the farmer's daughter, she supplied cornmeal to feed the worm boxes that would enrich the mulch. She weeded and then sculpted the rich black mulch into professionally rounded furrows to ensure seedlings would get the best possible start.

Amid endless rounds of fix-ups, a loss brought her thoughts back to Black Mountain. The composer John Cage died in mid-August. Two days later, she wrote to her classmate Robert Rauschenberg in a rare minor key, acknowledging that life is finite and the School of the Arts was her great unfinished symphony:

> *I expected John Cage to go on living forever. It was a shock and a realization that we're all getting older.*
>
> *I'm in the middle of this project that has taken more of my energy and attention in the past ten years than makes sense. . . .*
>
> *I wanted to make a formal request to your foundation to establish the Robert Rauschenberg Chair in the Visual Arts at (the School of the Arts). Would you be willing to help us do this?*

There would be no Rauschenberg chair; the painter was busy launching his own foundation in Captiva, Florida. But Ruth tapped a corps of reliable donors for her arts projects, led by her stalwarts at the San Francisco Foundation, the Philanthropic Ventures Fund, the Miranda Lux Foundation, and a host of old San Francisco family philanthropies including the Fleishhacker Foundation, the Walter and Elise Haas Foundation, the Richard and Rhoda Goldman Fund, the Zellerbach Family Foundation, the Louise and Claude Rosenberg Jr. Family Foundation, and many more too numerous to mention.

Philanthropic Ventures was a young foundation started by Bill Somerville, who said: "It always perplexed me. Here you have a living legend, struggling for money and gigs! I would think there'd be a line a mile long to her office." Somerville would end up giving Ruth's projects several hundreds of thousands in grants. He was drawn to Ruth's "homegirl" quality: "You always came in through the kitchen door, never the front door."

Ken Blum, executive director of the Miranda Lux Foundation, said of the Asawa appeal: "Ruth . . . was shrewd but very elf-like, like a cloud. Razor-sharp perception about what was real and what was phony. . . . She would bounce around, graceful, joyous, innocent but not innocent. She wore her heart on her shoulder, but if anything was out of line she'd call it. She knew who she was."

The last remaining hurdle was a legal challenge. The school found itself on the wrong side of a lawsuit brought by the National Association for the Advancement of Colored People (NAACP). The organization, which was ever-vigilant about ensuring compliance with the federal desegregation order, charged that the art school's move to the new site would upset racial balance at the McAteer campus. Middle-class white students had made up the bulk of the arts school's student body during its first decade. When the School of the Arts shared the hilltop campus of McAteer, whose regular student body was largely Latino, African American, and Asian Pacific Islander, the combined student bodies at the site were jointly able to meet the letter of the integration order.

Now, just two weeks before the start of school, a meeting was to be convened before U.S. District Court Judge William H. Orrick Jr. to determine whether the move would violate court-ordered desegregation, which stated that no ethnic group could exceed 40 percent of the student body.

Ruth's team had been on an intensified summer recruitment blitz to enroll more minority students for the School of the Arts, making the rounds of schools and churches in every minority enclave, from Chinatown to Japantown, from the Latino Mission District to Glide Memorial Church, a diverse Tenderloin congregation. Recruiters also invited more McAteer students to come over to the arts high school—fighting the notion that art school was only for rich white kids who could afford a violin. In a couple months, the school felt it had secured enough new enrollees of color to ensure a balance on its standalone campus. The judge would decide.

In an eleventh-hour ruling, the judge declined to issue a restraining order against the School of the Arts move. The school could open at its new site. The miniature campus—now painted, planted, and stocked with high school books on its tiny shelves—was as ready as it could be.

On the first day of school, when 350 students arrived, chaos reigned. Bells rang out of sync. Students showed up as much as 20 minutes late to their classes. A class with 31 chairs drew 44 students. Teens towered over the miniature toilets and counters. The campus lacked the basic infrastructure for a high school, not to mention an art school—with no studio, dance floor, or stage. But what it had was a heady autonomy. Reporters who visited on opening day found that the hallway buzz was infused with a new sense of ownership.

"Shall we go to our courtyard?" said Estrella Esparza, a junior in overalls. "We own it," answered sophomore Jon Bailey. "Let's christen it."

Victory was more one of principle than practicality. It was clearly a temporary fix. Without a science lab, library, cafeteria, or lockers, the site was too small to accommodate growing demand. At an open house, 200 prospective families came to inquire about fewer than 65 openings for the following fall.

Cramped quarters only fueled Ruth's determination to make Font Boulevard an interim step toward her desired move downtown to 135 Van Ness, the former high-school-turned-administrative-building next door to the Civic Center arts hub, which includes the symphony, ballet, and opera house. There, her students might be matched with working artists and performers as professional mentors. Hardly had one victory been won, than the next battle was joined.

She kept stirring the pot for funding. She wrote her reliable patrons, the Rosenbergs, a note of gratitude, foreshadowed by a sense of the long battle ahead:

> *Dear Louise and Claude,*
> *. . . Your check for $25,000 in March for the School of the Arts (SOTA) marks a new beginning for San Francisco Public Schools. . . . If we are successful in our future plans, the permanent site will be at 135 Van Ness and or 170 Fell, the former Commerce High School.*
> *. . . I hope I live to see it.*

But the '90s weren't totally consumed by school campaigns. Ruth's own art was energized too, and her studio was preparing for a huge new commission that would for the first time enable her to address World War II on her own terms, in art.

Half a century after the war, the city of San Jose, south of San Francisco, was working with its local Japanese American community on a multiyear program to document the toll of internment on city residents, and to plan a memorial. It was to stand in the shadow of the Federal Courthouse, just steps from the site of the World War II–era War Relocation Authority (WRA) office that administered the roundup and incarceration of Japanese Americans. The city's fine arts commissioner wrote to Ruth in July 1989 to announce her selection for the project. Ruth began the research she needed to tell the story of her generation in bronze.

Long discreet about her wartime ordeal, Ruth prepared quietly for that commission from 1990 on, documenting and mapping out scenes depicting the community before and during the war. By 1991, San Jose sent Ruth a draft agreement outlining terms of the commission, involving four years of design and fabrication of a bronze bas-relief that would tell the whole story. The price tag—about $212,000—would not only cover labor of the artist and her studio, but also would include fabrication of the massive bronze wall by the Artworks Foundry in Berkeley and creation of a concrete base by Lafayette Manufacturing, along with transport, installation, and insurance. Ruth quickly assembled her team, tapping longtime studio collaborators—artist Nancy Thompson, her neighbor Mae Lee, and her children—in the effort. By 1992, the agreement had Ruth's signature.

Ruth knew her own family's story by heart. But for this commission, she would depict a broader narrative: the saga spanning the first-generation Issei immigrants, their children (the second-generation Nisei), their grandchildren (the third-generation Sansei), and beyond.

Ruth proposed a double-sided wall covered with scenes in bronze bas-relief. One side would portray the prewar culture of California's Japanese American communities, from the picture brides arriving on ships and the farmers tilling their fields to the other trades, crafts, and cultural traditions they practiced, and the schools and temples they attended.

The other side of the wall would depict the upheaval of World War II, from the arrests in the fields to the herding of families into stables and aboard camp-bound trains, taking "only what they could carry." She and her studio would sculpt tar-paper barracks, barbed wire fences, and gun towers with barrels pointed inward at the internees. The memorial would portray the Japanese American youth who served in the Army as members of the 442nd Regimental Combat Team. It would also show resisters like Fred Korematsu challenging Executive Order 9066 before the U.S. Supreme Court.

Ruth gingerly considered dredging up the past, telling one friend: "It is a very personal and somewhat painful past to re-create, but my biggest challenge to date."

As she prepared her preliminary design for presentation, she told members of the San Jose Commission on the Internment of Local Japanese Americans:

> *The process of designing this sculpture has forced me to recall my own experiences as a 16-year-old high school student, from having to face fellow students at a high school assembly on December 8, 1941, where our principal asked the student body to exercise tolerance and understanding to the removal of my father by the FBI and then our later removal to a camp that was hastily built over a cotton field in Rohwer, Arkansas. . . .*
>
> *The disruption and disorientation and novel experiences that my family went through from the end of 1941 to the end of the war is the story of almost every Japanese American family who lived and worked on the West Coast. . . .*
>
> *As a daughter of immigrant parents from Japan, I have deep and buried emotions and experiences that today are only memories . . .*
>
> *Facts are more fantastic [th]an fantasy.*

If the wire hanging sculptures were Ruth's most serious abstract art, the *Japanese American Internment Memorial* would be her most raw autobiographical work.

For decades, Ruth had told many people the camps were "the best thing that ever happened" because they exposed her to working artists from Disney Studios and relieved her of farm chores so she could paint. That wasn't untrue. But it wasn't the whole story. Now, for the first time, she could relate the full experience on her own terms.

Few had glimpsed Ruth's emotions about internment. One was Phyllis Matsuno, principal of Alvarado Elementary School, with whom Ruth worked on the school art project. They shared a past. Matsuno had been born in the desert camp in Gila, Arizona, and her family spent part of the war at Tule Lake. As Matsuno told Ruth about her parents' ordeal, she remembered that Ruth would say nothing, but would leave the room to get a tissue, silently weeping. Now Ruth confronted her own memories of half a century ago.

Some experts who study the experience speak of "community trauma." For those who grew up in a culture ruled by the values of *"gaman, nintai, enryo"*—bearing the unbearable with dignity—channeling their energy into professional achievement and community service were ways to sublimate the pain. In later years, the redress movement and reparations payments made it safer for some to speak out.

Ruth and Thompson gathered reams of reports, wartime records, newspaper articles, photos, and books. They plumbed historical records and archival photographs of immigrant life. While conducting their research, Ruth and Addie wondered why figures for how many were confined in the camps ranged from 110,000 to 120,000. San Jose officials told them that about 112,000 people were ordered into camps from the western United States, where they were joined by Japanese Americans from Hawaii, plus 5,000 babies born in captivity. All these additions account for the range, and the census has continued to be refined.

Ruth's son Paul was enlisted to work with his mother and Thompson building baker's clay models of the wall. They would first sketch and then model bas-relief scenes of life leading to up to war and imprisonment. The process opened up a new dialogue between mother and son.

"When we were growing up, we didn't hear many stories about the internment," Paul said. At thirty, he'd been told little of his mother's wartime experiences before he began work with her on the memorial. "But in working on this sculpture, I learned many of the stories of the suffering endured by many families. These events were part of my family's history."

"It's really autobiographical," Ruth told a reporter, gesturing with hands encrusted with flour and salt dough. She paused as her hands came to rest on her face. "It is personal," she said. "But . . . very generic too."

The city of San Jose's contract for $212,000 had to cover four years of preparation, paperwork, applications, payments to assistants, the design prospectus, mock-ups, materials, labor, and fabrication.

Once again, bronze casting would be intricate and costly. It involved making latex rubber molds, wax models, and ceramic molds; pouring molten bronze; welding panels together; and chasing, finishing, and applying a patina. Out of her commission, the artist had to pay for the bronze work by Artworks Foundry, plus the manufacture of the granite and concrete base by Lafayette Construction.

Ruth, Paul, and Thompson set up shop on the ground of Artworks Foundry. In a diary of intense eight- to twelve-hour days there and in Ruth's studio in San Francisco, the team logged its daily progress and setbacks while working to give form to Ruth's evolving vision.

On September 14, 1992, as Ruth's sons Paul and Hudson brought wooden forms for building the base of the two-sided sculptured wall, Ruth grappled with a practical quandary. How do you design a sculptured wall so pigeons can't roost, or loiterers

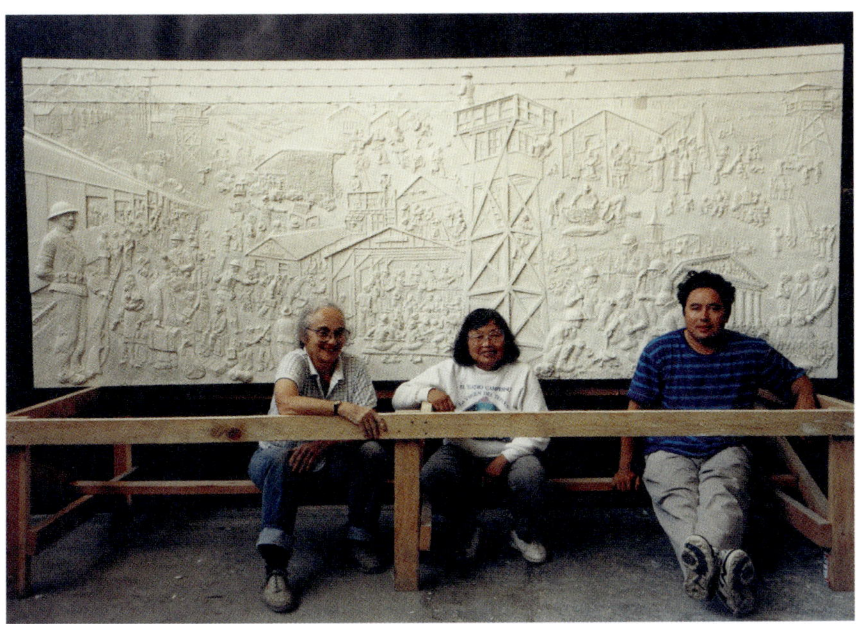

Nancy Thompson, Ruth, and Paul Lanier with the original baker's clay relief of the Japanese American Internment Memorial *before it was cast in bronze. Photograph by Terry Schmitt.*

leave beer bottles on top of it? The answer: Foundry owner Piero Mussi advised Ruth to make the top edge slope inward with an internal drain so debris couldn't collect.

On September 16, Ruth drove to the foundry with nearly double her weight in raw materials: 150 pounds of flour and over 80 pounds of salt to mix the baker's clay. Five days later, the team began arranging drawings of scenes to fit the wall's 5-by-14-foot dimensions. Side One, facing north, would depict early immigrant life before World War II. Side Two, facing south, would portray war and internment.

Air-drying the baker's clay dough proved to be nearly impossible, given the foundry's site in the south Berkeley flatlands, where a damp chill seeps in off the bay. Drying lamps presented a risk of fire. But they took that chance, and luckily avoided a conflagration.

Thompson and Paul—two headstrong artists—butted heads over how to get the work done by spring. But Paul trusted Thompson's draftsmanship and eye for nature. "You could ask her the difference between a cougar and a mountain lion's paw," he said, "and she would know."

Figures materialized through September, and the prewar immigrant community took shape: a Buddhist temple here, a fruit orchard there. Dominating the tableau was the prow of a transpacific ship from Japan bringing picture brides—like Haru—to wed immigrant farmers—like Umakichi—working the fields.

They ate and slept art. Even a pasta lunch break turned into a design meeting. Strands of spaghetti might be used to replicate twists of barbed wire surrounding the camps. They reserved a few strands to observe how it dried.

In mid-October, Ruth worked on a scene with personal resonance: a farmer being arrested in his strawberry fields by FBI agents flashing their badges. It was the story of her father's seizure and imprisonment.

As modeling proceeded, the team stayed some evenings to organize research files, listening to the political debates between George Bush and Bill Clinton in the run-up to the presidential election of November 1992.

The end of Daylight Saving Time brought early darkness. Paul worried that the team was behind schedule. Worse still, heavy winter rains raised concerns that leaks and water could dampen the flour and salt needed for the dough. Paul hung tarps over their work to shield the sculpture in progress.

In the first week of November, Ruth brought an old photograph of her family on the farm, and Thompson jotted down hopes that the team could include them on the panel. The day after Election Day, with a plurality declared for President–Elect Clinton, Thompson was sculpting strawberry plants around the feet of FBI agents seizing the Japanese farmer.

Thompson and Paul worked on immigration scenes of Angel Island in San Francisco Bay, the Ellis Island of the West Coast. The team consulted a reference book on birds to ensure an accurate design of the seagulls soaring overhead.

Mid-November sharpened the cold seeping into the foundry, as Thompson, Ruth, and Paul worked on scenes of agriculture. They welcomed a field trip group of sixty high school students from the School of the Arts, who bused over to watch the foundry workers perform their Wednesday morning "dance of the pour."

Ruth still adored the slow-motion ballet of foundrymen in silver fireproof suits, tilting the crucible to pour molten bronze heated to 4,000 degrees Fahrenheit into ceramic molds. After the shimmering heat cooled, and the bronze relief was cleaned of impurities, a rich coppery brown patina was applied and waxed for luster. The ancient art mesmerized Ruth, and she photographed the foundry's most spectacular display—the annual midnight pour, illuminated only by the glowing bronze as it spilled from the crucible.

Before Thanksgiving, Ruth finished the picture brides and immigration scenes, as well as swallows flitting above farmlands. Her friend, photographer Terry Schmitt, came to make photos of the memorial for a book that Ruth wanted to show to students.

One fine detail, making the texture of rope on the ship's hawser, was achieved by recycling a piece of old macramé from the SCRAP art supplies. Smooth progress seemed assured.

Then, in December, downpours soaked through the team's protective barriers, saturating the scene of a large soldier. The salt in the dough made the clay hydrophilic—soaking up water. The scene nearly disintegrated. A gas heater was quickly installed. Paul rigged a plastic tent with fans to dry out the clay.

With the holiday work breaks looming, the foundry crew held a potluck Christmas party. But Thompson stayed on task, modeling a last-minute addition to the scene of internees being shipped off. It was a true-life vignette of a young Japanese American college student from University of California at Berkeley expressing school spirit. As he left for the assembly center at Tanforan Racetrack, he held a sign out the window of the "special" bus with a message for his classmates: "Good Luck & Beat U.S.C."

The normally quiet week between Christmas and New Year's found the artists patching and waxing their clay models to fill in imperfections. They worked late into the evenings to light the sculpted panels for photos of their work in progress.

After a brief break, the team rang in the 1993 New Year on January 4 with discussions about how to help the foundry crew make rubber molds. For casting, they needed to divide the wall into eight sections. After casting the bronze wall in sections, the crew would need to weld the pieces together and polish it to conceal the seams. Mussi told the team not to worry.

"For Ruth, I would do anything," said Mussi, a bearded bronze artisan from Piacenza, Italy. He said he was struck by how unassuming and workmanlike Ruth was on the project, feeding his foundry crew and sharing artistic credit with everyone on his team.

She was very humble. She was very friendly. We did a couple monuments, pretty big size that wouldn't fit in her studio so she did it here. At lunchtime, she'd play with paper, play with wire, her hands were always moving, always making something. . . . She gave credit to everybody who touched her work.

She was simple. Afraid of taking my time. Showed me a drawing once out in the parking lot—a structural engineering drawing—she opened it up outside and I had to open the truck. It was so funny. . . . Some artists don't want to share their art. She was never afraid to give away anything.

As the first panel moved to the next stage—the making of a latex mold at the foundry—Ruth, Paul, and Thompson moved their work from the Berkeley foundry back to Ruth's studio to work on drawings for the second side of the wall, because it was warmer there than at the foundry.

After drawing Side Two's scenes of camp life in wartime, the team returned to the foundry to roll out dough for a panel to dry. The heaters warmed and dried the sculpted figures while warding off chill as the artists worked.

On January 20, Thompson noted in her journal, heavy rains inundated San Francisco while Washington marked the inauguration of President Clinton.

In the first week in February, humidity was causing the clay model to crack alarmingly. But with much vigilance and careful patching, they reached a major milestone. Thompson noted:

First wax section is poured. Bronze this afternoon!

During the second week of February, they tackled pivotal wartime scenes: Thompson modeled the Santa Anita Racetrack guard tower, and Ruth sculpted the prisoners sewing military camouflage nets for the troops—a scene she'd witnessed as a sixteen-year-old. Paul constructed the big gun tower of the Manzanar camp.

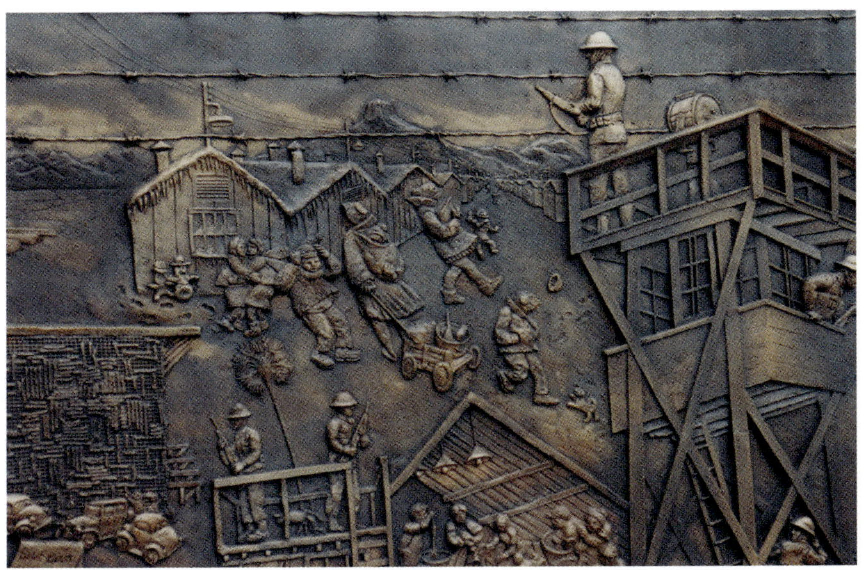

Japanese American Internment Memorial *(detail), San Jose, California, 1994. Photograph by Terry Schmitt.*

March 3 brought a string of bad luck. On the road to the foundry, Ruth got in a car accident. Unhurt, she soldiered on and got to work late. Then, as foundry workers poured molten bronze, a section of the first panel flamed out and burned—something that can be triggered by impurities in the mold. "Short day today," Thompson jotted.

Through March, Paul labored over the train to the camp, while his mother modeled another scene she had lived: imprisoned families who were made to stuff their own mattress ticking with straw.

While patching cracks in scenes of Tule Lake and Manzanar, the artists decided to add a more lighthearted scene of the inmates' baseball teams that were a feature of camp life. Ruth revealed she'd played shortstop on her camp softball team. "That's some mad skills," Paul marveled.

By March 22, Paul was sculpting the decorative ends of the wall with emblems of the San Jose Japanese American families. As a part of their research, Ruth and her daughter Addie had been writing letters to survivors' families to obtain pictures of crests representing the surnames of incarcerated families. In Japan, family surnames are represented by a crest known as a *mon*. Each family's *mon* bears a distinct design motif, often drawn from nature, such as a stylized flower, leaf, or feather. Every incarcerated family from the San Jose area who knew their family crest was invited to submit its design for inclusion on the memorial. All were documented by Addie and modeled in clay by Paul.

That month, the interiors of the camp barracks were modeled, along with a scene of Boy Scout troops meeting inside the camps.

In April, the 442nd Regimental Combat Team appeared around a campfire, cooking rice in helmets and sitting on an ammunition crate bearing the unit's motto, "Go for Broke." In the background, the artists placed a field of crosses.

They worked together on the scene of resisters—Korematsu, Yasui, and Hirabayashi—at the U.S. Supreme Court. Ruth handled portraits of the challengers, redoing them to get them just right.

Perhaps the most moving and personal scene was one that Thompson simply called "the Farewell." A young girl is shown bidding goodbye to her mother as she leaves camp for college, with her head bowed and her suitcase in hand, as Ruth had done:

I departed bowing to Mama, wondering what she was thinking . . .

By late May, only fine details were left to complete. But one final scene was added—almost as an afterthought—that would turn out to be many people's favorite detail. Schmitt returned to the foundry on May 28 to take photos of the work in progress. He'd just heard on the radio an interview with camp survivors, who told of children who made paper airplanes and sailed them over the barbed wire fences. It was a compelling symbol of the yearning of people in confinement for freedom.

"So a paper airplane was added," Thompson wrote.

On March 5, 1994, under a late winter sky, Japanese taiko drummers beat out rhythms that spectators could feel thudding in their chests, to open the dedication ceremonies of the *Japanese American Internment Memorial.*

Ruth, clad in a gray suit and long pink scarf, was almost dwarfed by a congratulatory chrysanthemum bouquet presented to her. The wall was wrapped and tied with red cord for the unveiling. Hundreds of spectators lined up to view it, elders pointing out scenes they'd lived, like a photo album in bronze. Among the dignitaries attending the dedication was Fred Korematsu, aged seventy-five, who saw his portrait in the Supreme Court scene. The encounter between two survivors who had suffered so much might have been overwhelming. But his daughter, Karen Korematsu, recalled the meeting between the resister and the artist as restrained:

He wasn't a hugger, not that generation. He shook her hand and was really
pleased with her work and thanked her for the education.

Later, at a reception at the San Jose Museum of Art, Ruth voiced a wish for the wall:

I hope we all are protected under the flag that waves above this memorial—[a]
reminder that we are all protected by our Constitution. . . .
We all worked to tell a story in a simple way so that I can take my grandchildren
and tell them my story. "Once upon a time when Grandma was a little girl . . ."

Ruth's friend Merry Renk Curtis braved the crowds at the opening of the memorial. She got in line to congratulate her friend. But the line was so long that she had to leave without saying hello. Instead, she later wrote Ruth a letter praising the piece, and acknowledging it had roiled turbulent emotions in her:

. . . [T]he portrayal of those memories in bronze stirred up such strong feelings in me
that I needed to write you.
I painfully realize that I had been similar to the German women who said that
they did not know what the Nazis were doing in Germany in the WAR. I became
aware of the internment in 1948 when I moved to California.
I do not approve or condone that government edict that interned Americans of
Japanese ancestry. The WAR gave our government permission for cruelty beyond
measure.
I hope that your sculpture will be photographed and reproduced in all the history texts of
the USA because you have created an indictment against WAR and the pain it causes.

Millions of Americans might have felt the same but lacked the nerve to admit it. Ruth and Curtis's friendship endured.

It had been a grueling, breakthrough year for Ruth, finally telling her history in bronze. She was approaching seventy. In a letter to her colleague Dottye Dean from Alvarado Arts, she mused about age and loss, and the unquenchable urge to create:

The mockingbirds have been particularly vocal at night on hot evenings. Our
granddaughter Sofia (Addie Laurie's) found a hummingbird's nest in our Burmese
honeysuckle hanging in our front yard with two little baby birds. We've watched them
grow and fly away. Our loquat tree was so loaded with fruit this year, celebrating the

end of our 4 year drought, that a huge limb cracked making it easy to reach the fruit. I made loquat chutney, and plum jam . . .

. . . I have worked for 9 months on the Japanese American Internment memorial sculpture during WWII. I had to dig deep into my past to find the common threads with other Japanese immigrants who endured the struggle and am glad I was part of it.

I also admire you for . . . balancing the day to day crises and keeping alive your personal, artistic flame lit. In a nutshell that was how the Alvarado Arts workshop evolved. Remember when the painters' union threatened to picket Alvarado if we put a brush stroke on "their" walls, or the P.E. department would not let us paint the hopscotch pink and red? It all had to be yellow.

We now have a high school for the arts near S.F. State . . . We begin our 2nd year hoping it will get better and better.

We gave our children our Guerneville place and now are their guests. . . . On July 3, Albert & I celebrate our 44th anniversary. How time flies. I am busier today than ever before working on my own work, and I am grateful to have lived to enjoy it.

Despite her elegiac tone, Ruth was far from done.

CHAPTER 13

THE FIGHTING YEARS

Fresh from installing her most personal work ever, Ruth started speaking out more publicly and more forcefully about the two forces that had driven her: her experience in wartime and the healing power of art.

In 1995, she accepted the Asian American Arts Foundation's Golden Ring award—honored alongside actor Joan Chen, writer Maxine Hong Kingston, and director Wayne Wang—by sharing parts of her life with a new candor:

> *As a teenager when I was interned with my family, it was art instruction by professional artists who were interned with us that kept our hope alive—saved us. There are many books written about the internment experience, but it is the paintings and artifacts that put a human face on the experience. . . . The arts saved us, and that experience will always be with us.*

Passing on that creative experience to youth was a way to sustain her connection with the regenerative power of art that had redeemed her life. But without a degree or credential—despite six years of college—Ruth didn't get to serve as a teaching artist in residence at the School of the Arts as her mentors at Black Mountain had done. Friends said she felt it keenly. She wanted working artists to teach art. But the district requires credentialed teachers not just for academic reasons, but also for reasons of legal liability, since teachers act in loco parentis.

But in 1995, Ruth's drive to expose students to working artists found a brand-new outlet: teaching a special, one-time class at the invitation of San Francisco State University. Her partner in the venture was Mark Johnson, director of SFSU's art gallery and a specialist in Asian American art. A tall, rangy Yale graduate who'd studied with Josef Albers, he helped her create a class—Zen, the Bauhaus and Public Art—woven from the threads of her own experience.

The class explored the intersection of her Zen heritage—humility, reverence for materials, respect for teachers—with the craft of her Bauhaus mentors. She coupled these two philosophy and design principles with tips on how to compete, win, and create public art commissions—all part of the unromantic but essential business of being a working artist who wants to eat and pay rent.

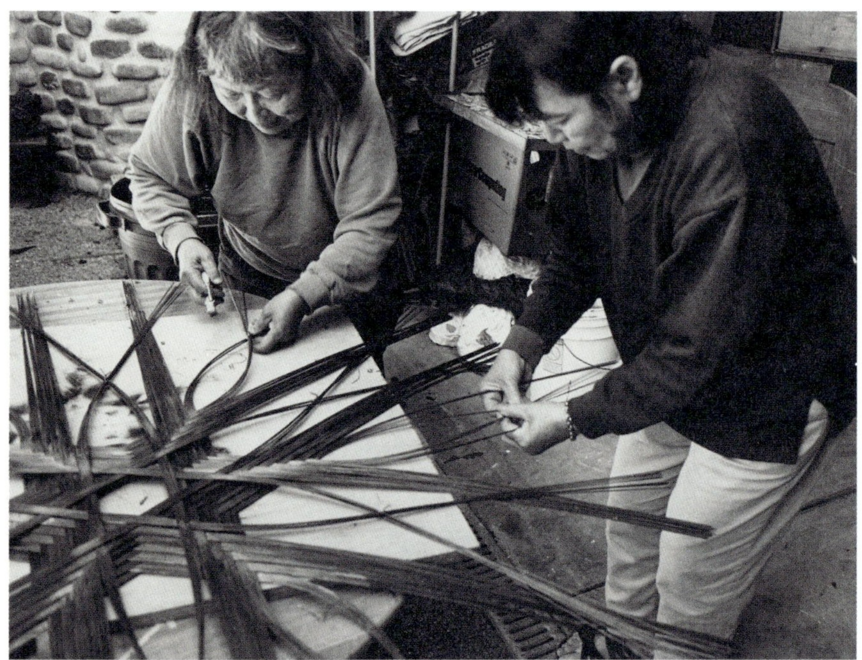

Ruth and Mae Lee working on a tied-wire sculpture, 1996.
Photograph by Laurence Cuneo.

Johnson had no trouble recruiting students for the class. "Ruth was grand dame artist-in-residence," he said. "Kids came and sat on the floor." He took signups in the hall. He videotaped Ruth telling the story of how her flared wire sculptures came from cutting open a mistake in the mesh. In a related anecdote, she told the students that one day, a bird flew in a window. It made its nest in one of the wire openings, and laid its eggs there. The sculptor was delighted.

As a bonus, she could bring together students from the School of the Arts with art graduate students at SFSU to work on an installation: two sculptured panels destined for window niches of the school's art gallery.

"She included everyone's vision," Johnson said. He added that Ruth would say, "That is where the Zen comes in."

Ruth oversaw students' sculpting of the two pendant metal sculptures from copper and nickel sheets—together weighing about 75 pounds. The heft of that raw material posed a challenge for Ruth's younger colleague.

"Ruth, I can help you," said the forty-two-year-old Johnson, when he saw Ruth, then nearly seventy, hauling those metal sheets up a steep hill toward class. She took him up on his offer and thrust half of the heavy load into his arms.

"My knees buckled," he said; he was stunned by the load she'd toted with such ease.

"I have always been strong," she explained with a sly smile.

The student sculptures, once finished, resembled burnished scrolls. Installed in the San Francisco State University art gallery lobby in 1997, they kept their pride of place for over two decades. Johnson proposed Ruth for an honorary doctorate in fine arts, and SFSU President Robert Corrigan finalized her selection in 1998.

It was half a century since she had been rejected for practice teaching and denied her first college degree back at Milwaukee State Teachers College. Now, at San Francisco State University's commencement, she said a life of adversity had given her unexpected gifts:

> *Had Milwaukee State not rejected me and forced me to the alternative of Black Mountain College, I would have quietly retired as an art teacher with retirement benefits in Sheboygan, Wisconsin. Instead, I am here today receiving the highest honor of this institution.*
>
> *I've spent my life making what was needed and what I wanted one and the same: in marriage, in raising a family, making fountains, or talking to a child.*
>
> *The investment has paid off for me: A loving husband of forty-nine years, my children and grandchildren living close to me, and I'm able to share my work with the community. What more can I ask?*

As it happened, 1998 brought another academic honor, this one fifty years overdue. A theater professor from the University of Wisconsin–Milwaukee had visited the School of the Arts and come to know Ruth. Support began to build for Wisconsin to offer Ruth an honorary doctorate there too. Upon receiving the offer, Ruth replied that she'd prefer the bachelor's degree denied by Milwaukee State Teachers College, now part of the University of Wisconsin. Fifty-two years later, the university honored her request.

On December 20, 1998, amidst Milwaukee's winter chill, Ruth donned a cap and gown over sensible black running shoes for her commencement. As she mounted the dais, her head, wearing the graduate's mortarboard, barely cleared the podium. Her daughter Aiko accompanied her mother to the ceremonies, where local newspapers photographed her grinning ear to ear. The cover story of the University of Wisconsin–Milwaukee Alumni Association magazine featured the story of Ruth getting her diploma a half century after being told "she would never be able to teach art in Wisconsin because of her Japanese ancestry."

Ruth was, to be sure, just one of thousands of students whose education was interrupted by wartime internment. Back at San Francisco State University, President Corrigan asked Ruth if she would design a memorial fountain for the campus to honor nineteen Japanese American students who were forced to withdraw from that school in 1942.

The university envisioned a tall, majestic fountain with a towering column of water to adorn the school's eastern entrance. The problem was that the wind off the Pacific Ocean would blow the fountain sideways, drenching students. Ruth told Johnson that she had a different memorial vision—one that was historical, yet peaceful and intimate.

She proposed a Garden of Remembrance, using natural elements of plants, rocks, and water. On a campus lawn with giant evergreens, she would place ten boulders, representing the ten main camps. Each stone would bear a plaque with the name and family crest of students interned there. A bronze scroll would tell the history of internment.

On a little hill overlooking the lawn, Ruth would design a Japanese-style garden, featuring flowering cherry trees and azaleas, divided by a waterfall flowing through rocks into a small tranquil pool.

"She selected every shrub," Johnson said. "Ruth wanted the tallest point in the garden to be the gingko tree that is just now coming into bud because in winter the leaves are golden."

Ruth was willful and irreverent during the planning process. On the lawn where she wanted to place the boulders, she wanted to clear all obstacles.

"There was an asymmetrical pine tree she said spoiled the view and that she wanted removed," Johnson remembered. He explained that was impossible because the pine was planted as a memorial, protecting it from removal under university rules.

"Pick me up at midnight," Ruth cracked in a conspiratorial tone. "I'll bring the poison." Johnson knew she was joking. The pine still stands.

For inspiration, Johnson and Ruth made a trip to Silicon Valley to view a Japanese garden on the estate of technology mogul Larry Ellison of Oracle Corporation. When Johnson came to pick up Ruth, he found her dressed for the studio, in a sweat suit covered in plaster and a folding bamboo sun hat, unfazed by her software tycoon host.

"I decided to dress down for Larry!" she explained. They toured the Ellison estate by golf cart, viewing the landscape designed by Isao Ogura and Shigeru Namba, who advised Ruth on the waterfall design and rock selection. She hoped to gather rocks from each of the ten main camp sites, but ended up using California river boulders to symbolize the remote and arid camps.

The garden was a meditation on contrasts—"deprivation and restoration, stillness and movement, isolation and community, rock and water, offense and forgiveness"—the university said when seeking a grant from the California Civil Liberties Education Project. The stones symbolized endurance, their dryness a reminder of the parched desert locales. The stream cascading down into a quiet pool represented the life-giving power of water. The garden's setting, near the gateway to the social hub of the student center, represented interned students returning to school, resuming their lives.

Groundbreaking for the memorial lawn and glade began in the fall of 2001. On September 10, the school issued a press release announcing that Ruth's monument to peace and reconciliation was under way. The garden's message would not be one of bitterness, nor would it be exclusively Japanese, she said. "It's a story about liberty and freedom."

The day after the university's statement went out, on September 11, terrorists hijacked four commercial jets that crashed into the World Trade Center in New York, the Pentagon in Virginia, and a field in rural Pennsylvania. The attacks by the extremist Islamic group al-Qaeda not only touched off a two-decade-long war on terrorism, but also spawned a violent backlash in the United States against anyone presumed to be Muslim.

Ruth was quick to call out hate crimes against Muslims after 9/11 as a throwback to the abuse of Japanese Americans she experienced after Pearl Harbor. In an interview with the SFSU student newspaper, she urged all Americans to remain on guard against abuse of minorities and fellow citizens in the chaos following an attack:

Discrimination [c]ould happen to any one of them. Now it's not Asians, but it's Middle-Easterners.

Her garden grew despite cataclysm in the wider world. Its soft tufts of green, ablaze with spring flowers, were nestled so subtly into a hill on campus that harried students often rushed by without pausing. Pointing out the saturated fuchsias, pinks, and purples, Johnson said the garden is a study on regeneration and persistence.

"She said the garden symbolizes renewal," Johnson said, "because 'we were not victims, but survivors.'"

By the time San Francisco State University dedicated the Garden of Remembrance in April 2002, Ruth had physically declined, going from hoisting stacks of metal sheets to needing a wheelchair to cross the campus.

Lupus had returned, affecting both her handwriting and walking, leaving her unsteady on her feet. She had started taking Coumadin, a blood-thinning drug that is used to prevent the formation of blood clots and that is sometimes prescribed for lupus patients. She wrote to an admirer:

I limit my activity now, and I am leaving the future up to you young people.

But the relapse didn't cloud her critical eye or soften her judgment.

With the new millennium, Ruth's work to help secure homes for two of the city's signature art centers took on a new urgency.

She intensified her campaign to move the School of the Arts—still cramped in the former elementary school on Font Boulevard—to the city's performing arts complex in the Civic Center, where students could walk to performances and learn from stars of music, dance, theater, and the visual arts.

She also worked to help rebuild the earthquake-damaged M. H. de Young Museum. Although retired from its board of trustees, she continued to serve on its education committee. The question was where to place the museum—on its historic site in Golden Gate Park, or a new site on the Embarcadero overlooking the Bay. Early on, Ruth declared her support for rebuilding the de Young in the park—at a time when its form, funds, and venue were all up for grabs. She was a populist who thought the museum's location was more central and accessible than the waterfront on the city's northern edge.

Both the School of the Arts and the de Young projects were complicated by seismic safety, spiraling costs, uncertain funding, and fractious city factions that fought over every detail—turning city dreams of high culture into epic battles.

Bond issues came and went, and voter support waxed and waned. Public opinion polls tested the sentiments of the San Francisco public. Scores of public hearings and endless discussions at the museum board of trustees and the school board drew Ruth, chipper and attentive, sketchpad in hand, ready to deliver sharp testimony with a smile. She invested years helping to create perfect settings for two civic jewels—a school for nurturing young artists near downtown stages; and a treasury of art and art education in its historical spot in the park. Both campaigns seemed overdue for success in the new millennium.

In a near miracle of can-do spirit, the School of the Arts' interim residence in the tiny Louise Lombard Elementary School hung on for nearly a decade as Ruth's downtown dreams got deferred again and again.

Many bond issues, which were earmarked for capital projects and which included a potential share for a new School of the Arts campus on Van Ness, came and went. The designated spot occupied nearly a square block of prime real estate just south of the city's opera house, symphony, and ballet. These institutions were founts of expertise that Ruth wanted to tap for city students.

The Spanish Colonial Revival building at 135 Van Ness had been a city high school in the 1920s; in later years it served the school district as administrative offices. The block also included a 1910 yellow brick high school structure around the corner at 170 Fell Street. But both were a shambles of deferred maintenance and seismic safety issues. Still, Ruth led walking tours to show how the bones of the old high schools could provide a foundation for the arts high school of Ruth's dreams. At her side throughout the campaign was Susan Stauter, who had left her theatrical position as conservatory director of ACT, believing she could do more good as artistic director for the San Francisco Unified School District. But like many dreams, theirs became entangled in money woes and bureaucratic inertia.

Both buildings were landmarks, which saved them from the wrecking ball. But their historic status complicated efforts to reach consensus about the best and most economical way to remodel them and to make seismic repairs. The project was mired in controversy from the start. Albert, whose instincts as an architect always favored conservation and rehabilitation over demolition, wanted to see the old structures preserved and remodeled sooner rather than later. But he grew weary of warring reports and estimates.

"We must not ask another generation of students to wait another four years to enter the promised land," he and Ruth wrote in a joint statement to the School of the Arts Move Task Force. He pored over blueprints and read fine print on every environmental impact report and cost projection. He objected when school administrators put their part of the transformation—a move to new headquarters at 555 Franklin Street—ahead of the School of the Arts renovation. When bond funds that had included monies for the School of the Arts were consumed by other school district needs, the school board voted to mothball 170 Fell—preserving it for a later seismic retrofit—and to shelve the entire School of the Arts question for a future date, when sufficient funds could be raised. Albert had had enough. He jotted a despairing note at the bottom of a Task Force letter:

I am tired. Ruth says we have to keep going.

Although the focus of her public campaign had shifted to the high school, and despite age and infirmity, Ruth still turned out for Saturday "workdays" at the Alvarado Elementary School gardens. Donning jeans and a straw hat, she got down on her hands and knees, pulling weeds, mulching, and planting flowers. She still created photo albums of the workdays.

Photographer Terry Schmitt recalled one day when Ruth insisted on doing yard work in spite of problems with balance:

> *Working later, the lupus took its toll. We were over at Alvarado pulling weeds, and she would pull some, then she'd sort of gently topple over. She'd lie there, lie on ground and pull all the weeds within reach and move to a new spot to topple over and pull weeds.*

Her friends knew better than to make a fuss, he recalled. She'd just right herself and keep weeding.

Meanwhile, funds from bond issues that designated some money for the School of the Arts' move downtown were spent on other needs—not an uncommon problem in fiscally challenged public school districts.

The projected prices of deferred mega projects tend to grow rather than shrink during years of delay. So it was that cost estimates for creating the School of the Arts at 135 Van Ness and 170 Fell ballooned from an early low of $23 million up to $143 million for Van Ness alone, or $172 million for the entire complex. Retrofitting an attached theater, the Nourse Auditorium, would by one estimate have added another $29 million to the grand total. In 2019 dollars, the remodeling and building project at the arts center without 170 Fell reached $300 million.

After all the bond issues and statements of support, the school district didn't have the money to transform the earthquake-fractured 135 Van Ness building into the new School of the Arts in 2002. Meanwhile, the old McAteer High School, dogged by dwindling enrollment and marginal performance, was dissolved to make way for other uses of the facility. To Ruth's dismay, the school board decided to return the School of the Arts from Font Boulevard to its old McAteer site. Back to square one.

Ruth wrote in a guest editorial for the *San Francisco Examiner*:

> *How ironic that the same week San Francisco hosts a forum on creativity touting the benefits of arts education, the Board of Education announces it will locate our*

*high school of the arts on the McAteer High School campus, not at the promised site
in the downtown Civic Center corridor—a part of town dedicated to civic life and
the arts.*

She never gave up the fight. But as she approached her late seventies, Ruth
acknowledged that time is finite, and that such battles took time away from her art. A
student of her former Black Mountain instructor M. C. Richards wrote Ruth to praise
her fountains and work with children. Ruth replied that she liked to read Richards's
"Old Age" essay, which "speaks to me in my old age, which I didn't expect." Then she
made an acknowledgment few had heard:

> *I am happy for the years of productive works, and the "fighting years."*
> *If I had it back I would fight less and do my work more.*
> *"Do it while you are able to." That's my advice to the young.*
> *Only you know what to do.*

Amid a season of fighting for her high school of the arts, Ruth suffered a series of
small strokes, affecting her speech and mobility. She cut back on her public appearances. Receiving a Local Heroes Award from the Asian American community, she got
a standing ovation and spoke candidly about her disability:

> *I have had two strokes, so my speech is a little funny. You wouldn't believe that last
> year I would be driving a truck and not getting any tickets . . . Now I can't do it. If
> there's somebody in the audience that could make me strong again, I would be very
> grateful.*

The years-long battle to rebuild the de Young Museum was nearing an end.
Environmentalists, joggers, cyclists, and skaters opposed rebuilding the de Young in
Golden Gate Park because they feared the museum would draw more car traffic. But
Ruth campaigned to keep the museum in the heart of the park. She also backed the
addition of an underground garage to allow auto access to the museum for people
with limited mobility—a group that now included Ruth herself. If the San Francisco
49ers could get a parking lot, she argued, the museum should too.

Two failed bond issues were followed at last by a successful funding measure.
Board of Trustees President Diane B. Wilsey said it took fifty-six public meetings and

endless debates before supporters of keeping the museum in the park won the day. Wilsey recalled:

> *[Ruth] helped us build the de Young, testified for us, made it clear to people who had their heads in sand why it's important and why you have to build the buildings. She was so warmhearted—everybody's mother—it would be hard not to embrace her thought or her desire. You were not going to argue with her.*

When the museum selected the Swiss architects Jacques Herzog and Pierre de Meuron to create its new design, Director Parker knew the firm liked to involve local artists to discuss a project. Herzog and de Meuron had invited Chinese artist Ai Weiwei to take part in plans for the Beijing National Stadium, known as the Bird's Nest. Parker knew whom to bring into the talks in San Francisco. Parker remembered:

> *When I met Pierre in Basel . . . I said you ought to get to know Ruth Asawa. She's not only an artist of reputation, she's a trustee and she lives near the museum, and you're going to love her house. I took him to Ruth's house and we sat down and had coffee outside on the terrace outside her living room, and we were looking at sculptures hanging from the rafters—maybe fifty or sixty. Pierre, who is a very sophisticated French Swiss man, fell in love with Ruth Asawa.*

Ruth lobbied for the museum to feature an education tower. The symbolism was powerful, because it devoted the highest point in the structure, not to the executive offices, but rather to learning spaces: research libraries, studios, and classrooms for city schoolchildren. After all, she argued, the de Young was less known for its collection than its support for youth arts festivals and workshops. With charm and steel, she made the case for the education tower. "It was an exciting idea—the only education tower in any American art museum," Parker said.

The architects' design—a copper-clad structure with its postmodern torqued tower piercing the tree line—would take time to grow on a very divided public, some of whom likened the design to a "huge shed," an "Internet start-up company," an "aircraft carrier," or a "Howard Johnson's of the future."

While Wilsey plied patrons to build a critical mass of multimillion-dollar donations, Parker said Ruth, a populist, set about doing the crucial social networking to build support among community constituencies. With her knack for public outreach, Ruth grew grassroots support. She engaged schoolchildren and their families in a piggy bank campaign. She enlisted the ceramics expertise of her son Paul in crafting one hundred white-glazed banks, modeled like the museum tower with a slot for coins. Distributing banks to public schools, she invited donations of any spare change students could offer. Parker said:

> *It was such an innocent, high-minded idea, and quite a contrast with the work of extracting millions. The student campaign went on. In the end, these tower banks were brought in. We emptied the coins. There was $686. It was a huge energizer with public relations value as well. We viewed it as a statement that the museum was really a popular museum, and always a destination for kids.*

As the de Young's new education tower was being topped off, Parker and Ruth donned green hard hats. After ascending in a construction elevator to the top of the tower, Parker steered the artist in a wheelchair to take in its sweeping views. What did she think? Would the space work? He wanted to know. It had been her vision all along. She peered at Parker with an elfin smile, and said it was up to him.

Parker wanted to open the new de Young with a massive retrospective exhibition of Ruth's work. She in turn made a major gift of her sculptures to be displayed permanently in the museum. She placed one restriction on the gift: If the museum ever deaccessioned—or stopped showing them—the sculptures would be returned to the family. Ruth carefully chose fifteen of her translucent wire hangings and spiky tied-wire sculptures for the museum. They were hung in an intimate gallery in the education tower lobby, a spot that resonated with Asawa's role as an advocate for art education. Despite her age and fragility, Ruth took a hands-on approach to their placement and lighting to ensure that all the sculptures were properly displayed and cast shadows to her liking on the walls.

"Many may take credit but it was completely Ruth," said Wilsey, referring to the look and feel of the small gallery, with its rough, putty-colored concrete walls. The brute material worked; it somehow highlighted the subtle colors of the wire used in each sculpture. "She knew what she was doing. She knew the tower, shape, light, material. Many tried to do it differently, but Ruth had the authority. You had an artist giving you these objects, saying this is the one that needs to be over there and over here. Who's going to argue with her?"

The little gallery's contents sparkled. Wilsey said Ruth's sculptures transformed "a cold, gray, difficult space" into a constellation. "They were stars," she said. "The color was different at different times of day." As the installation progressed, Wilsey said, museum staff "became quite enchanted. . . . It was the buzz."

The gallery remains one of the de Young's few spaces—along with the Wilsey Court, museum café, and sculpture garden—that were designed to be free at all times to the public.

It also turned out to be a bonus for the museum, Parker noted:

You know what's happened to the value of her work? Today, it's a $15 million to $20 million gift.

The museum's director of contemporary art projects, Daniell Cornell, took charge of mounting the expansive retrospective show, *The Sculpture of Ruth Asawa: Contours in the Air*. It comprised years of work by Cornell, Ruth, the Asawa family, and museum staff. Cornell curated the exhibition and lighted it like an underwater garden to give viewers the same sensual experience he had had when he first visited Ruth's house in Noe Valley, where her mesh sculptures hung from the rafters like garlands of seaweed, adrift in currents of air. He included works on paper, paintings, and lithographs as well.

As a gay man who came of age in the 1980s, Cornell said he felt a bond with Ruth and Albert over their shared experience of being marginalized. His writings on Ruth brought attention to her stature as a major American sculptor, balancing her place among the modernists with her roots in Japanese culture and Zen Buddhism.

The Asawa retrospective show was a family affair. It featured Ruth's daughter Aiko and granddaughter Lilli leading workshops in origami, plus demonstrations of her technique of winding wire for sculpture. It was one of the last wire workshops, which her family later stopped giving due to fears of plagiarism.

Albert was unable to attend the 2006 opening, and instead he had a private viewing with his wife. A longtime smoker who had struggled to quit, he had been on oxygen for years due to emphysema. Ruth's health, too, was challenged after lupus returned in 2001. From walker to wheelchair, moving about was more difficult for her.

Ruth's longtime friend and former Levi Strauss vice president Bud Johns was among the hundreds who attended the gala opening of her retrospective show. He bent his tall frame down over the artist, seated in a wheelchair, to speak a few words of private congratulations. Ruth gave way to tears.

Director Parker had planned his retirement to coincide with the museum's reopening, and would be returning with his wife, Ellen, to the family home on Fisher's Island in New York. As he set about packing up his office, he looked up to see the

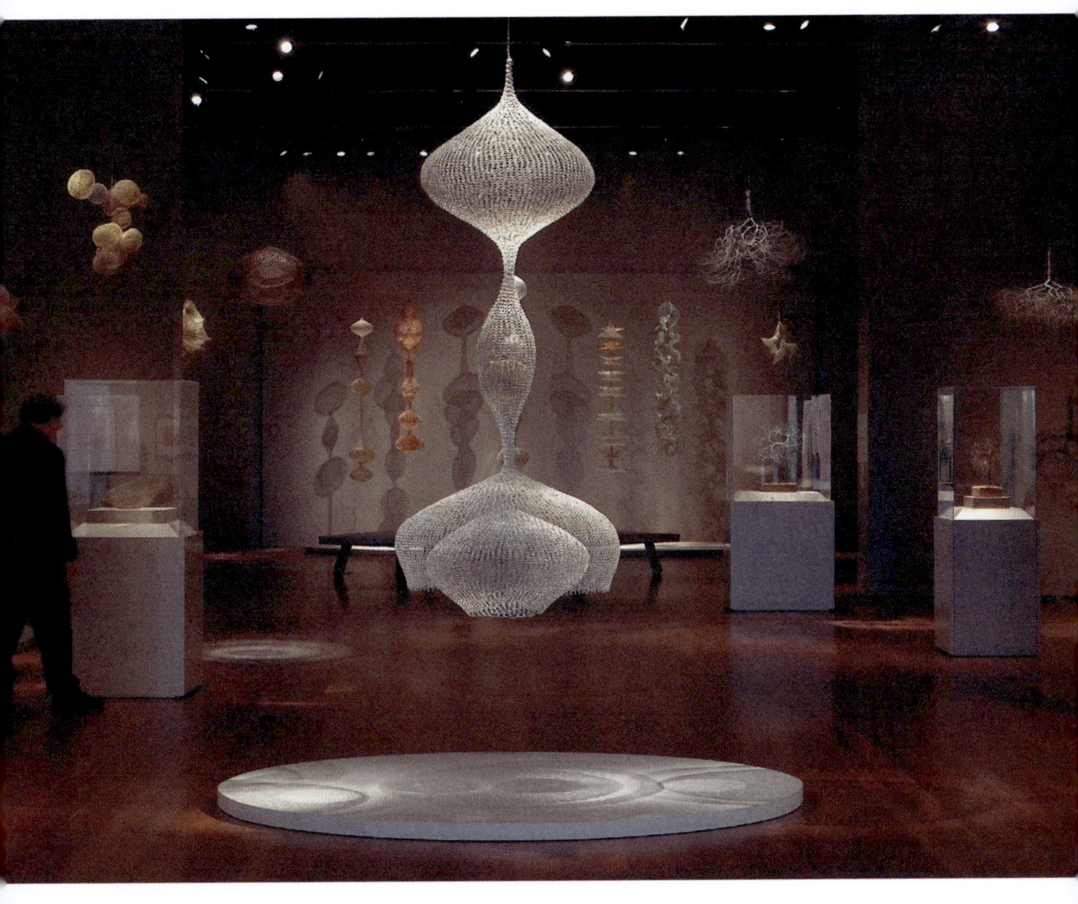

Installation view, The Sculpture of Ruth Asawa: Contours in the Air, *de Young Museum, San Francisco, 2006.*
Photograph by Laurence Cuneo.

Lanier family trooping in to say farewell, bearing a white box. As they chatted amid the chaos of packing, he postponed opening their gift and then lost track of the box in moving. He finally uncrated his gift at the New Year of 2007:

> *Dear Ruth,*
>
> *. . .*
>
> *Lo and behold, we found your wonderful sculpture in the beautiful white box that it arrived in at my office so many weeks ago. You must have wondered what happened—but we have just discovered it. Perhaps, it means more—now that things have settled down and we have time to contemplate all the excitement of the last few months.*
>
> *It was great to get the de Young finished (or almost), opened and celebrated. Then, came all the goodbyes and sentiment. It all blurs, but we can savor the high points. First among these is the Asawa family gift of such a beautiful sculpture. We spent sometime selecting the right location—hoping also for the incredible shadows that are such a feature of your Tower installation at the de Young. It is really true that more people comment on the Asawa installation than any other artwork at the new museum! I hope you are as pleased as I am with the success of that project.*
>
> *Well, Ruth, you and I—and Albert and Ellen—have lived through a lot and seen the good guys prevail! (at least, for awhile) . . .*
>
> *Love, Harry*

A COMPACT OF LOVE

When Ruth and Albert retired to the small suite downstairs that he had remodeled for their later years, their unmarried son Adam helped his siblings look after them. He was an avid gardener who competed fiercely with his father to see who could keep the most delicate roses alive. He was the most reliable worker in his brother Hudson's contracting business, and also a lone angler who'd go off on fishing trips, returning with an epic trout or salmon, which he presented to his mother for the grill. To his nieces and nephews, "Uncle Adam was the guy who took 'em fishing and played golf," architect Bill Bondy said.

Like his father, Adam liked to smoke. Although Albert had worked hard to quit—clipping smoking cessation articles and logging a "last cigarette on March 15, 1996"—he was in his later years homebound and tethered to an oxygen tank. Adam's vigorous life through his mid-forties, on the other hand, may have hidden a silent toll.

In May 2003, Adam suddenly collapsed on the job. Hudson's son Max found him and, in vain, the two tried to revive him. When Aiko got word, she raced to find Addie so they could be together to deliver the news to their parents.

It was too late. Hudson's client, the homeowner at the job site, rushed to call the Lanier home to offer his condolences—too soon. By the time the sisters arrived at home, their parents already knew that Adam, at 46, was gone.

A terrible quiet descended on the house. "Adam took such good care of Grandma and Grandpa," said Hudson's daughter Lilli. "It was the only time I saw Grandma cry."

Ruth, a great saver of cards and letters, left few traces in her archives of the void left by Adam's loss. One rare exception was correspondence from Adam's boyhood companion Jimmy Sanz, who shared Adam's sense of adventure. Jimmy had basked in the presence of Ruth and Albert, and the friendship of Adam.

I was aware that he was adopted in a compact that was underlined by love for that is how he left the world -- with love.

After Adam's death, Sanz sent Ruth and Albert a handmade card with pressed gingko leaves, sketches, and a memoir of his absent friend:

I remember warm summer days and campfire nights. I remember flour salt and water all over the place. Pulling weeds and planting gardens. Endless board games

*and Adam's messy room. I remember wire and tools & sun lighted rooms where we
as children lived out a magical childhood.*

*The long dinner tables—listening to Albert's stories and having good meals.
I remember art in every corner of the rooms. Riding the back of the truck—and
at night watching the stars, sleeping outside, trading monster stories with Adam.
Watching your example of Nature. And learning to respect it.*

*While the outside world changed and became harsh [it] seemed hardly visible
to me.*

*The many experiences help me remember—and retain a faith in nature and
vision of art the world does not always appreciate. I took for granted all people were
of this nature—as in the days of my childhood [with] Adam & family.*

. . . thanks for all that.

Five years after Adam's sudden cardiac death, Albert's own health struggles became
critical. He had suffered from emphysema and required oxygen—first intermittent
puffs and then a steady stream—to support his breathing for years. He was hospitalized in the fall of 2008 during an emphysema flare-up. There, the folksy, bearded
Southern gentleman who once received a letter addressed to "the Abe Lincoln" of
his Noe Valley neighborhood, died on October 31, at the age of eighty-one.

Ruth was at his bedside with her children and grandchildren as he passed. "We
rode home in the van with her," recalled Hudson's daughter Lilli. "She was just quiet."
Hudson's wife, Terry, remembers Ruth weeping, as she had for Adam.

Halloween long had been a holiday the family marked in grand style, decorating
their home as a haunted house with young and old in elaborate costume, and Ruth on
occasion stirring a witches' brew to welcome trick-or-treaters. From now on, whatever else happened, it was a somber anniversary.

Fragile in her grief, Ruth could not attend Albert's memorial service because her
health had grown so delicate. The family made a video of the service to show her at
home. But her love for Albert was very much a presence at his memorial in November
at the First Unitarian Universalist Church. The program bore her ink portrait of a
pensive Albert, his jaw fringed with the beard that—along with his trademark overall
suspenders—gave him the air of an Amish elder. Printed on the memorial was one of
Albert's favorite sayings:

*Children are like plants. If you feed them and water them, generally they'll grow.
Art is a very "iffy" occupation.*

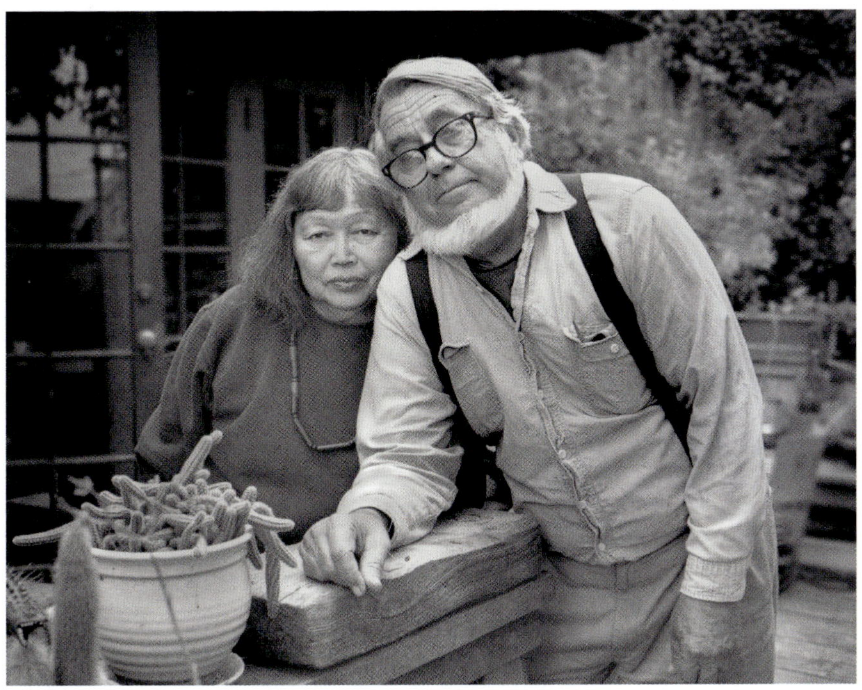

Albert and Ruth on the front deck of their home, 1998. Photograph by Laurence Cuneo.

In their eulogies, his children and friends celebrated him as an architect whose trademarks were sunlight and spare elegance; and a passionate preservationist, whose motto was: "Renovate, don't demolish. And if you demolish, compost." They remembered him as a Southern yarn spinner, whose tales made nobody laugh more than Albert himself.

Among memories that prompted a smile was Albert's story about the shopping habits of Miss Ruby Waters, who ordered the butcher to give her a Sunday chicken that embodied all the best attributes of the leading matrons of his hometown, Metter, Georgia:

She'd say, "Well, I want a chicken that's got a bosom like Miss Brunie Turner . . . and drumsticks like Sister Bird." And so on, describing every part of the chicken's body in terms of various matrons' body parts. They went through this ritual every Saturday because he always wanted to find out what outrageous comparison she wanted to make between the chickens and matrons of the town.

But he was much more than the wisecracking Georgia storyteller. He was a progressive man—especially by the standards of his generation—who backed Ruth's art and activism for six decades. He was her silent studio partner, doing the engineering drawings and mathematical calculations for the installation of many of her shows and large public commissions. He was her comrade in arms, fighting with her to bring the School of the Arts to the Civic Center arts hub, and sharing her bitter disappointment when their plans were frustrated. He had made her laugh behind her hands like a teenager, even at the end, after they moved into the twin hospital beds downstairs in the studio space he had presciently remodeled for their old age. Now Albert's death left an aching void.

"It was so quiet," Aiko said.

By 2008, Ruth had long since given up public speaking in the aftermath of her lupus relapse and strokes. Now even private speech became rarer, harder to decipher. She communicated with facial expressions, a personal sign language, and words that her children interpreted.

In a sad coincidence, her jeweler friend Merry Renk had lost her husband, Earle Curtis, on October 30, just a day before Albert died. They had been neighbors on Saturn Street, colleagues in art shows, and vacationers in the South of France. Merry and Earle had been at Ruth's bedside when she was stricken with lupus, bringing her a book on the impressionists that gave her the courage to pick up her paintbrush when her arms were too weak to sculpt. Now both women's partners were gone. Curtis made Ruth a card with a double portrait of Albert and Earle in January 2009, marking the first birthdays of their new widowhood:

> *Your 83rd birthday will be lonely like my 88th birthday this year—*
> *but what wonderful memories we have.*

Ruth was in a wheelchair when she received the first Mayor's Arts Award from Mayor Gavin Newsom and the San Francisco Arts Commission in October 2007. In a barely audible voice, she said:

> *Thank you, San Francisco, for all you have done for the arts. I hope you do more.*

It turned out to be her final public address.

Although Ruth saw few visitors, three like-minded women came to see her in 2010 concerning the School of the Arts. School board veteran Jill Wynns had spent a year studying at New York City's High School of Performing Arts, and had shared Ruth's passion for melding arts and academics. Wynns wanted to rename the School of the Arts in Ruth's honor. Susan Stauter, the school district's artistic director, got on board and joined the visit. Paul's wife, Sandra Halladey, a public education activist, came in a supporting role, enlisting Aiko's permission to make their special request at Ruth's bedside.

The trio faced a sensitive issue: seeking Ruth's blessing in their campaign to rename her school the Ruth Asawa San Francisco School of the Arts—even though it had not reached "the promised land" of a new home in the Civic Center arts hub.

"Trust us," they asked, echoing Ruth's refrain.

Ruth was skeptical of tributes. Despite twenty-eight years and half a dozen graduating classes, the arts high school was still a work in progress.

"I told her nothing's perfect," Wynns said.

There were many reasons why Ruth resisted the name change. She had never craved that tribute—an eponymous arts school—for herself. So much was left to do to fulfill her vision. Most painfully, her dream of an ideal arts campus downtown was unrealized. There was a history of private hurt, too, as Ruth hadn't been allowed to teach art in the classrooms of the school she founded. But the three women promised Ruth that, along with the name change, they would work to ensure the values of Black Mountain College would be preserved.

"I gave her my sacred word to make sure it was a good school," Stauter said.

The Board of Education and the wider school community approved the name change in February 2010, and the school was formally rechristened in 2011. On the windswept campus at the crest of Upper Market Street, at 555 Portola Drive, a modest sign reads: "Ruth Asawa School of the Arts."

Unable to attend the 2011 naming ceremony, Ruth remained at home as her youngest son accepted the honor. Paul said:

Our family is so proud to have this wonderful school named after our mother. It's her lifelong dream to have children work with, and be taught by, professional artists, and to have students pursue their dreams.

The current campus—the old McAteer High School site—remains remote from the Civic Center arts hub and far from the ideal school for which Ruth gave the last measure of her energy as a public citizen. Yet Ruth's spirit is palpable everywhere in the verve of the students, whose arts education would not exist without her. A huge portrait of the young Ruth at Black Mountain adorns a glass case in the main hallway. The photo, taken by her friend Hazel Larsen Archer (née Hazel-Frieda Larsen), shows Ruth in winter, gazing at the sky, snowflakes in her hair.

On a school tour, visitors can hear a voice class singing Cole Porter tunes, a taiko ensemble drumming, and the music of an Afro-Haitian dance class. They might spot a solo violinist playing an impromptu solo while walking down the hall with a friend. The counterpoint from class to class looks and sounds like a montage from the movie *Fame,* the 1980 feature film about gifted high school performers at New York City's High School of Performing Arts. The soundscape emanating from classrooms melds into a cheerful cacophony that swells like a Charles Ives composition.

Donn Harris, a former principal of the Ruth Asawa San Francisco School of the Arts and now the school district's executive director for creativity and the arts, said the new home Ruth wanted for the school is "more than a realistic hope. It's going to happen. There's only one barrier left, and it's money." Harris said creating the new campus at 135 Van Ness, near the Civic Center arts complex, is a $300 million project, of which roughly $150 million is available from previously approved funds.

"We'll succeed," predicted another supporter, former San Francisco mayor Willie L. Brown.

Others are less sanguine. "There aren't enough visionaries in the city to get the school moved," worried Ken Blum of the Miranda Lux Foundation, one of Ruth's sponsors. "People love to talk; they don't like to make action."

Decades of delay in building the perfect Civic Center venue didn't stop visual arts student Glory Rubio from working toward her 2017 graduation and college acceptance. Raised by a single mother and her grandmother, Rubio exemplifies the sort of gifted inner-city youth for whom the school was created. Introduced to art at the local Boys and Girls Club, Rubio found a mentor who urged her to apply to the Ruth Asawa San Francisco School of the Arts. Ruth's insistence that art not be elite, but egalitarian, made possible her training as a painter.

Rubio said she was inspired by the painter Kehinde Wiley, who depicts African Americans in scenes from classical myth and history. That sense of history infused her senior project, an ink painting of her mother, her sister, and herself as the Three Fates of Greek mythology. She shyly shows the picture of the three, dressed in urban street garb and holding the thread of life.

Ruth Asawa's art speaks to her too. "It's a sculpture . . . but when lighting is put on it, it becomes a shadow piece as well," she said. "It plays with the light."

Quite by chance, Ruth's work also spoke to a New York curator who has become one of her most influential champions in the twenty-first-century fine art marketplace. Schooled at the Chicago Art Institute and Pratt Institute in Brooklyn, Jonathan Laib is a painter who carved out his niche at Christie's auction house in New York for seventeen years, where he specialized in postwar and contemporary fine art, with a focus on Josef Albers.

In 2009, Laib took a cold call from Addie, who had phoned Christie's to explore the possible sale of an Albers color study in green belonging to her mother. Laib acknowledged in an interview:

> *I didn't know who [Ruth Asawa] was. We began by talking about the painting in her collection—a classic* Homage [to the Square] *painting.*

Laib learned that Ruth's children, like many families, were planning for their mother's home care, a costly need. They weren't rich, but they had art.

Addie inquired about selling Albers's green painting from his *Homage to the Square* series, painted in 1962. It was the piece given to Ruth by the painter, bypassing his gallery and asking her to keep the matter confidential, writing on a piece of white wrapping paper, *"Dear Ruthie, This is just for revenge . . ."* The 18-by-18-inch oil painting was signed and dated "A62" on the lower-right corner and inscribed on the reverse: "Study for Homage to the Square: 'Cool Reising' Albers 1962 For Ruth." For years it had hung in her house in Noe Valley, its squares of emerald, teal, and hunter green changing hues with the light of day, beguiling Ruth.

Laib was intrigued by the painting and its provenance. "I knew that, for a gift like that, she must have been pretty important to Josef," he said.

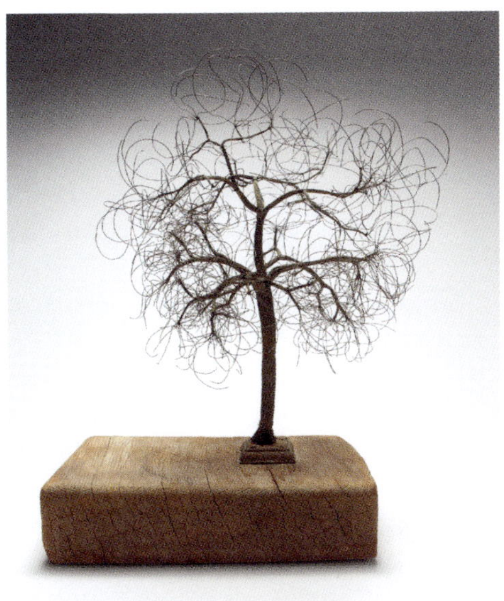

Untitled (S.058), 1962
*Naturally oxidized brass wire mounted on
a driftwood base*
18 x 13.75 x 12.25 in. (45.7 x 34.9 x 31.1 cm)
Photograph by Laurence Cuneo

The conversation became emotional, he said. Artists' children grow up surrounded by art. Any decision to sell a parent's treasure is freighted with family history and memories.

Laib said he'd handle the Albers sale, and gently inquired about its owner. "We talked about her mother's work. I asked if she'd send images," he said, acknowledging, "I didn't know Ruth's work." That soon changed.

Viewing pictures of Ruth's sculptures, he realized that if Ruth hadn't pulled out of the New York gallery world after 1958, she would have ranked among her contemporaries with a higher profile and market values to match. But creating a commercial sensation was never her priority. Laib said:

As soon as I saw the images, it clicked for me: This is an artist who is thought of as a regional Bay Area artist. That felt like a dilemma and something that needed to be corrected. Realizing its quality, I realized there was a larger audience.

He thought Ruth belonged among the major figures of the mid-twentieth century. "I started thinking of her contemporaries like [sculptor] Louise Bourgeois," Laib added, along with sculptor Louise Nevelson. Laib also saw some commonality with Eva Hesse and Yayoi Kusama, who carried out repetitive themes to the point of obsession. "With Asawa," he added, "it's a meditative process, also physically draining." Creatively, he mused that Ruth was as outrageous as other mid-century moderns, but after her all-night-long studio marathons, she chose to lead a life of modesty and responsibility to her community and her family.

"Her own commercial work was never at the top of her list," Laib acknowledged. Still, he saw both an opportunity and an obligation to restore Ruth's position on the world art market, and in his words, "relaunch her in the commercial sphere."

The sale of Ruth's green *Homage to the Square* painting yielded $116,500 for Ruth's living expenses—an amount that her own work wouldn't yet have garnered at auction. That felt wrong to Laib. So in summer 2010 he flew out to San Francisco to visit Ruth and her family.

"My first thought was, how do I go about building a larger audience?" he said. "Christie's as an international global platform could provide, perhaps, if handled in the right way, the right kind of visibility," he said. Where Ruth's most recent auction sales elsewhere had been in the category of "design auctions," a category reserved for decorative arts and crafts pieces, Laib said, "I knew her work didn't belong in the design sale category. Once placed along Louise Bourgeois, Josef Albers, Eva

Hesse, I knew people would see she stood right there in the postwar contemporary world."

Laib was planning a daytime auction of postwar and contemporary fine art to take place six months later, in November 2010. To show Ruth to advantage in the company of her contemporaries, he advised the family to offer one of Ruth's "super A-plus works," as a test case. They selected a 10½-foot copper and brass wire piece, *Untitled (S.044)*. The strand of six lobes enfolding smaller mesh spheres—a technique known as a "form-within-form"—casts soft layered shadows reflecting the densities of the nested forms within. Said Laib:

> *We were ready to push the limits of her market with an unprecedented $120,000 to $180,000 estimate. We would rather see it fail than sell for less than $120,000.*

With such an aggressive valuation, the piece might well have gone unsold. But he installed the sculpture prominently at Christie's, hanging it between two marble staircases so collectors and visitors couldn't miss it.

And far from dampening interest, the lofty estimate had a galvanizing effect.

> *Every one of my colleagues at Christie's was on the phone with a client who had an interest in this piece. For the longest time Ruth's works were available for the taking, but after the sale of this sculpture, that would no longer be the case.*

The winning bid was $578,500—almost quintuple the entry estimate, and nearly six times the previous record six months earlier for an Asawa sculpture at a different auction house. Laib's calculated bet paid off, and the price point affirmed Ruth's renaissance. It was a storybook ending because the proceeds supported her care. However, it wasn't simply about pushing the price point, but also about recognizing originality and genius. Laib said:

> *People bidding on Ruth weren't looking for trophy art, blue chip status, but people looking for integrity and authenticity.*

The sale established a momentum.

Laib flew out to San Francisco in 2010 and again in 2012 to meet with Ruth. He outlined plans for expanding her exposure with an exhibition of her work at Christie's—her first New York City show since she had left the Peridot Gallery more than a half century earlier, when her works became cramped by its 8-foot ceilings. Now the sky would be the limit.

Ruth listened to Laib's proposal. Despite her modest lifestyle and indifference to commercial success, she had always been a sharp judge of artistic merit. She would tell her daughters, as they tagged work for a show, which pieces should be in a museum. Now, with her mind alive but her speech impeded, his pitch was a one-sided conversation, with Ruth's end of the exchange conveyed mostly through facial expressions.

"She was in bed dealing with lupus," Laib said. "She could nod, and spoke with her smile." Her look indicated her consent for his plans.

Some figures in the art world didn't approve of an auction house managing Ruth's sculptures. Among these was Trish Bransten, Ruth's former representative at San Francisco's Rena Bransten Gallery. To Bransten, Ruth belonged in a gallery, which could gather, curate, and present her pieces to the world, rather than sell and disperse them into private hands, possibly losing them to public view. Understanding the family's need to move on, though, Bransten hoped to see Ruth's sculptures heading from Christie's to a big museum retrospective.

Laib credits local arts institutions like the Rena Bransten Gallery and the de Young Museum for upholding Ruth's stature in San Francisco over many decades, but he asserts that it was time to widen her horizons. He agreed it's unusual for auction houses like Christie's to represent artists like Ruth Asawa. The Andy Warhol Foundation was one of the rare exceptions, he said.

Untitled (S.044), 1968-72
Copper and brass wire
120 x 21 x 21 in. (304.8 cm x 53.34cm x 53.34 cm)
Photograph by Laurence Cuneo

But exhibiting Ruth and auctioning off selected pieces would restore her visibility in both the New York City and worldwide art markets.

Too long neglected due to implicit bias against female sculptors, women of color, and West Coast artists generally, Asawa sculpture was ripe for renewed consideration, according to Bransten:

> *There is still prejudice. Think about it. Think about how many Japanese American artists are nationally known. There is Noguchi, but he was from New York. Racism and sexism exist to such a strong degree in the art world. And regionalism completes that trilogy.*

But as the new millennium entered its second decade, buyers were hungry for originality.

"If being a Japanese woman sculptor from California hurt her in the global market, by 2008 it was doing the opposite," Bransten said. Today, of course, Japan's Yayoi Kusama has vaulted to the ranks of top-selling living artists worldwide, with her popular, polka-dotted "infinity nets." Viewers also have come to know the delicate traceries of fiber artist Kay Sekimachi, and to appreciate the startling modernity of Miné Okubo's graphic internment camp chronicle, *Citizen 13660*, and the work of other Japanese American innovators.

With the public's appetite whetted, and Ruth on board for her first one-woman gallery show in fifty years, Laib planned the exhibition, *Ruth Asawa: Objects and Apparitions*, for May 2013. The show included an auction of one of her most imposing looped-wire sculptures. Laconically labeled, like most of her works, *Untitled (S.108)* is a copper and brass wire garland of six translucent teardrops, enclosing smaller nested spheres. It measures almost 11½ feet long and 2 feet wide. The piece dates from the late 1960s, a period when her form reached full bloom.

The night of Christie's evening auction of postwar and contemporary art on May 15, 2013, finally arrived. Ruth's sculpture went to auction with an estimated value of $250,000 to $350,000. Again, Laib pushed the envelope—and again that guidance proved conservative. "The auction was quite exciting—it was personally quite gratifying to see that the strategy of a private selling exhibition and auction together could produce such a frenzy," Laib said. Bids rose higher, tripling and quadrupling the estimate. The hammer came down on a sale price of $1,443,750. It was a new world record for Asawa, and two and a half times Christie's prior record of $578,000 for her work at the 2010 auction. The price of the piece, now

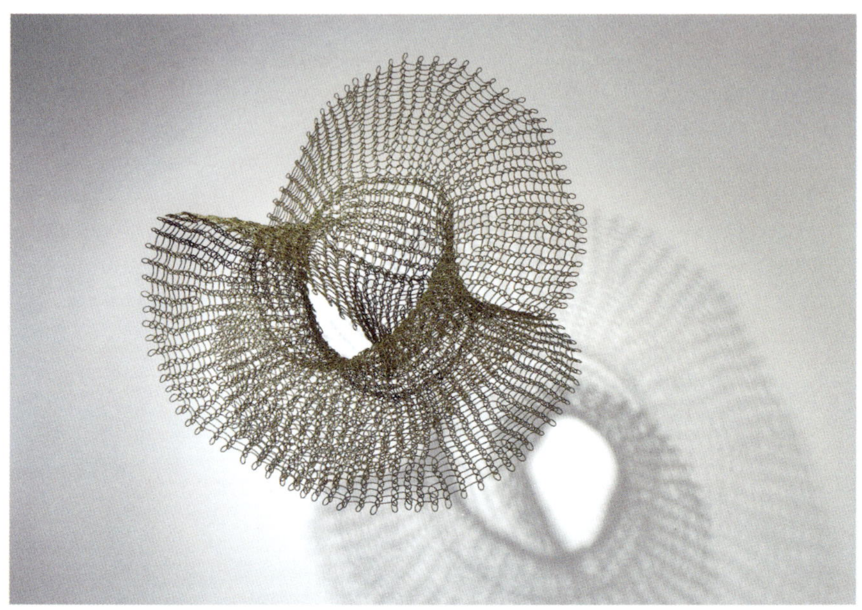

Untitled (S.049), *ca. 1962*
Naturally oxidized copper wire
23 x 18 x 14 in. (58.4 x 45.7 x 35.6 cm)
Photograph by Laurence Cuneo

also known as *Osaka*, has since been surpassed in private sales for undisclosed amounts, Laib said.

Far from the fray, in her quiet lookout over the garden, Ruth awaited the results of the sale. She greeted her daughters' news with a look of wonder and incredulity. More than mere commercial gain, Laib said that the sale confirmed that a slumbering art market was belatedly "waking up to her work."

Just when the New York art market came alive to Ruth's abstract sculptures, a San Francisco development threatened one of her most popular representational works. The Hyatt Union Square fountain—the bronze bas-relief of San Francisco city scenes—stood in the path of a new Apple Store on the corner of Post and Stockton Streets.

The fountain's place there, since 1973, seemed no match for Apple's retail development plans. The fountain was carted off and stored at Artworks Foundry in Berkeley for safekeeping during the store's construction. As the white-and-glass storefront was being completed, the fountain remained in storage, its return to the corner anything but certain.

Ruth's days of fiery speeches and letters to the editor now were past. But when *San Francisco Chronicle* writer John King reported her fountain's displacement by the Apple Store in May 2013, it galvanized editorial pages, columnists, and citizens. Among the outraged was Ruth's longtime friend Bud Johns, who wrote a letter to the editor of the *Chronicle* to protest the loss of a landmark:

> *Not only is Ruth one of the city's most important artists—for bronzes as well as her ethereal wire sculptures and work on paper—but she has a legacy for public art and education, especially of children. I hope that all the people . . . join to block this.*

With the fountain in limbo, and her fighting years behind her, the artist who entered the world with a yell in the winter of 1926 left it with scarcely a sigh in the predawn hours of August 6, 2013.

Ruth Asawa made a quiet exit, without fanfare. Her caregivers arrived at the home in Noe Valley, expecting a normal day. Her family gathered at her bedside. Her daughters went into the garden to pick small flowers to place around her body.

"She died where she wanted to die," her daughter Addie said, in the little room where she could look out the window and see the hummingbirds hovering and flitting about amid the greenery.

Three weeks later, on a cool Tuesday morning, hundreds of students, artists, teachers, and politicians gathered in Golden Gate Park, near the de Young Museum and the Japanese Tea Garden—two sites of Ruth's epic preservation battles. Colleagues, children, and grandchildren gave eulogies. The choir of the Ruth Asawa San Francisco School of the Arts sang "Make Our Garden Grow," from Leonard Bernstein's *Candide*.

Undone by grief, Susan Stauter quoted the Taoist philosopher Lao Tzu: "The spirit of the fountain dies not. It is the eternal feminine." She recounted scenes of Ruth in her fighting years, racing to three art education events a day in her old car, spicing up school board debates with homemade pickles, and fighting to preserve the lessons of Black Mountain for a new generation of students.

"Albers was her teacher," Stauter said, "and she was mine."

On a dais bedecked with bamboo and maple, Ruth's eldest son, Xavier, spoke about the essence of his mother: "Patience, passion, talking eyes, no complaining." She fed everyone and shunned fuss, he mused. "A brown bag lunch under the trees would have been fine with a sketchbook."

In a small mercy, on the very day of Ruth's memorial, reporter John King's story was published, disclosing that Apple had approved a revised design for its new store on Union Square, redrawing the building's footprint in a way that made room on the corner for reinstalling Ruth's circular bronze cityscape. "Apple spares beloved fountain," read a *San Francisco Chronicle* front-page headline. Now the fountain stands on the corner once again, its water splashing beneath a small group of trees—giving the bronze a backdrop of greenery that likely would have pleased its maker.

Laib left Christie's auction house as senior vice president and senior specialist in 2016, and joined the David Zwirner Gallery as a director in 2017. He took with him representation of Ruth Asawa works. The gallery also represents works of her mentor Josef Albers and his wife, Anni, leaving their posthumous legacies intertwined. Laib mounted an Asawa retrospective at the gallery in September 2017, prompting a fresh round of critical notice. Reviewers rediscovered Ruth. *New Yorker* critic Andrea K. Scott's review "Woman on Wire" said that Ruth's posthumous show was "upending the white male hit parade" and "rewriting art history."

Robert Storr, an artist, critic, curator, and professor of painting at Yale University, called Ruth's body of work "a topological poem to the universal capacity for metamorphosis." In an interview, he hailed her as "a master" of sculptural geometry—a medium that, whether rounded or angular, knows no gender.

Asked about Ruth's choice to sculpt with wire, the material of her prison camp's barbed wire fences, Storr gave a measured reply. "I don't see her work as a commentary in any straightforward way on the spatial markers of suffering," Storr said. "But it doesn't mean you can't take swords and make them into ploughshares. And I think that's what she did." Quite apart from her historical narrative, he stressed that in purely formal terms, "her work stands on its own."

Stanford University's Special Collections and University Archives Department in Palo Alto, California, now houses Ruth's archives at the Cecil H. Green Library, where students and researchers can study her life's work in 275 boxes bursting with documents and designs. Under the arched windows and soaring ceilings of the library's Field Reading Room, the life of the artist emerges from within the gray archival boxes. Her journey is recorded in thousands of pages of letters, speeches, sketches, and photos, each a puzzle piece of the whole.

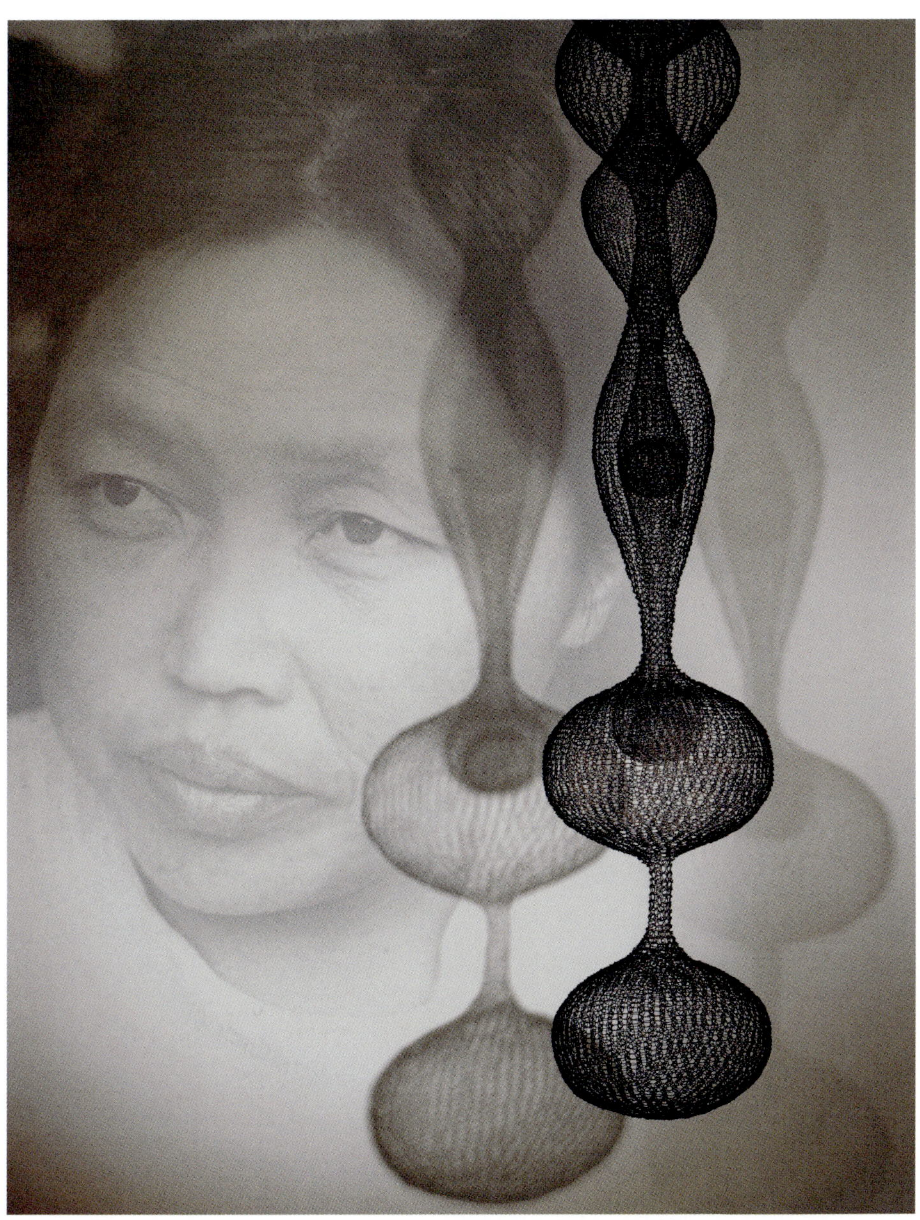

Photo composite of Ruth and sculpture detail, 1969 and 2006. Photographs by Xavier Lanier and Laurence Cuneo.

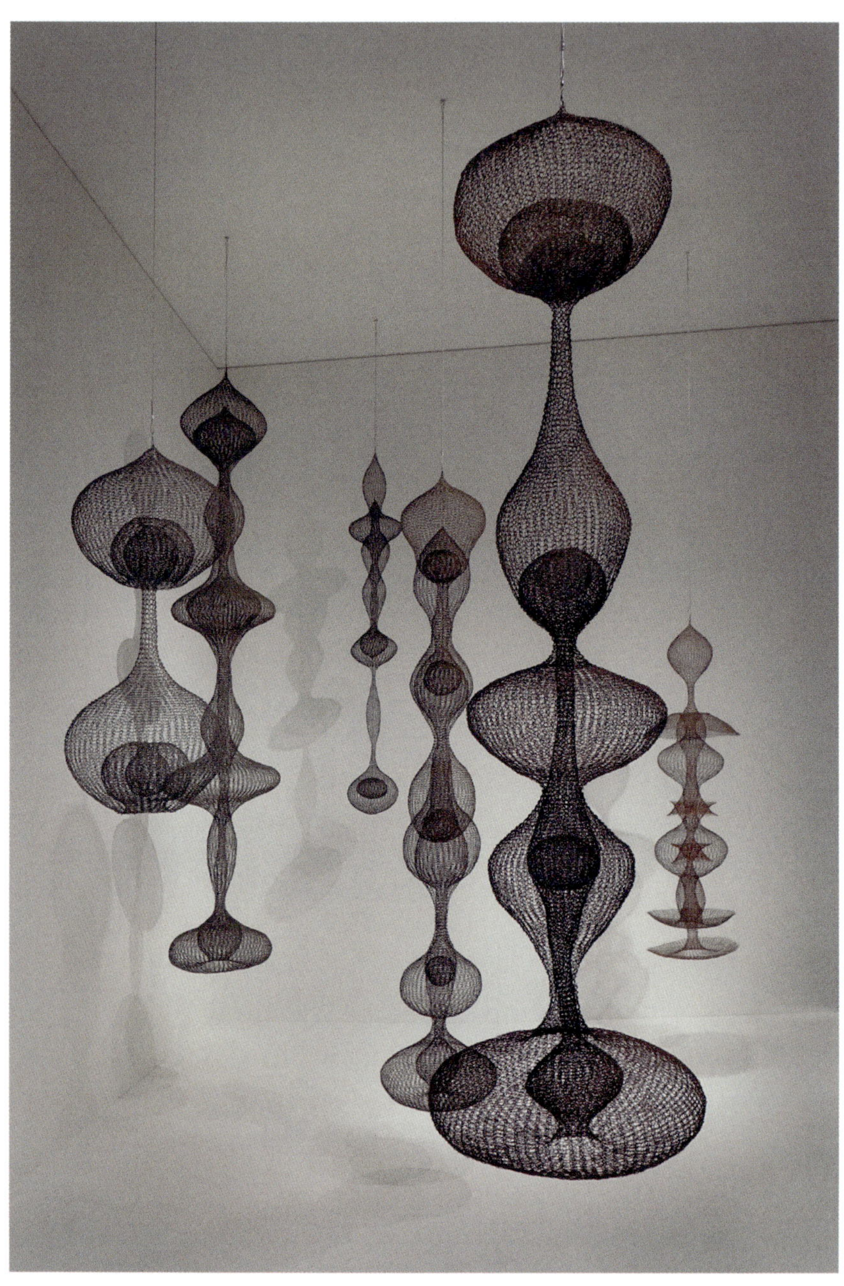

Installation view, Architecture of Life, *Berkeley Art Museum and Pacific Film Archive, University of California, Berkeley, 2016. Photograph by Laurence Cuneo.*

It seems an improbable life: her birth to immigrant farmers in 1926, near death from diphtheria at age three, imprisonment in war, deprivation of her art teaching degree, flowering at Black Mountain, fateful encounter with a Southern lad, and their barely legal union leading to a family bursting with children and art—all captured in black and white by Imogen Cunningham's camera.

In letters, one can hear Ruth's quiet, level voice growing into full-throated advocacy. Public service was interwoven with art in her life, like loops in her wire sculpture. If she hadn't worked in the schools, Ruth insisted, she would never have explored the baker's clay that she used to model her Union Square fountain and the *Internment Memorial*. Whatever the cost to her in time and energy, the artist and activist, the creator and citizen in Ruth were indivisible.

Art scholars like Mark Johnson of San Francisco State University believe that Ruth's sculptures of the 1950s and '60s are historically her most important creative work of her life. Yet late in life, when Ruth's daughter Aiko asked her what she considered her life's most important work, she paused and said, "the schools." Art and education were the warp and weave of her life.

Those who go looking for a monument to Ruth will find her spirit in the shimmer of wire sculptures at the de Young Museum, the light illuminating copper, brass, steel and gold hues, and casting voluptuous shadows. Her undulating forms take pride of place beside other mid-century modern masters in the collections of the Whitney Museum of American Art, the Museums of Modern Art in New York City and San Francisco, the Solomon R. Guggenheim Museum, the David Zwirner Gallery, and in shows and installations in a growing number of public and private venues. Her legacy resounds in the halls of the Ruth Asawa San Francisco School of the Arts, and in the fierce determination of her colleagues to finish the work she began by moving the school to the heart of the city's downtown arts center.

There is no public memorial marking Ruth's grave. She had other ideas. Following her wishes, her son Paul mingled Ruth and Albert's ashes together with those of their son Adam, and folded them into clay.

From that clay, Paul created a series of ceramic pieces, one for each of his siblings. Each is different. All are crafted in a simple, rustic style, respecting his mother's Japanese American roots. True to her teacher Albers, Ruth made sure her earthly matter was not destroyed but rather transformed until, in the end, Ruth Asawa herself became a work of art.

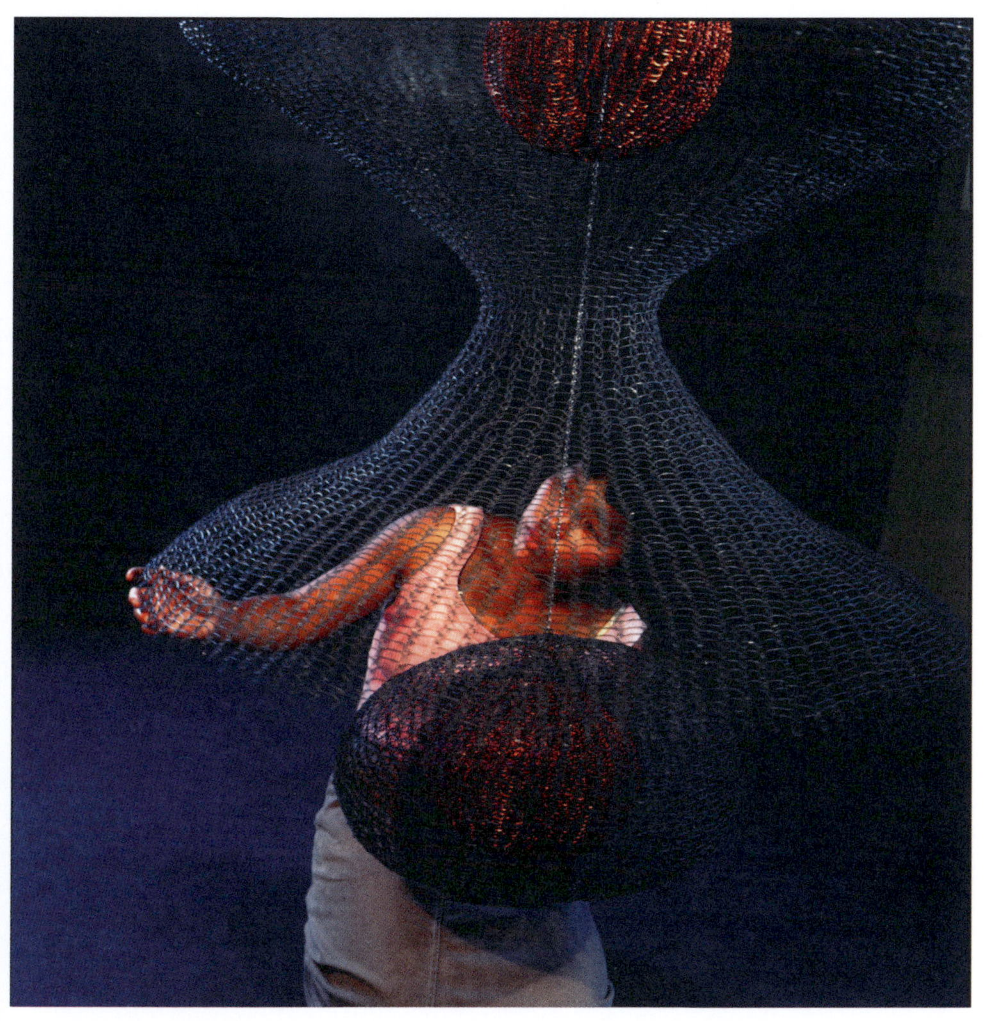

Ruth Asawa, kneeling inside a hanging looped-wire sculpture, 1957. Photograph by Imogen Cunningham.

ACKNOWLEDGMENTS

Research for this book was born of curiosity about an American hero: Ruth Asawa. In the summer of 2014, I learned this sculptor and survivor left her papers to Stanford University. A reporter finds it hard to resist a treasure trove in a library. The Field Reading Room of the Cecil H. Green Library at Stanford University, my alma mater, houses four million volumes and is the gateway to a world of archives in its Department of Special Collections. There I spent a year and a half reading and studying Asawa's life as it was captured in 275 boxes of papers that she and her family had the foresight and generosity to leave to history. Thanks are due to all the librarians and staffers—especially Tim Noakes, Larry Scott, and Nan Mehan—who hauled those boxes to the front desk, fulfilled my endless requests for photocopies, and tolerated my being so often the last to leave their sanctuary at closing time.

Writing the life story of sculptor Ruth Asawa was a risky proposition. It flew in the face of conventional book industry assumptions about readers' desire to read about the lives of artists. Many cautioned our project was not a safe bet commercially. So I'm indebted to the exquisite taste—and appetite for risk—shown by my agent, Carrie Hannigan, of the Hannigan Salky Getzler Agency. Carrie and her most excellent assistant, Ellen Goff, kept the faith.

My gratitude goes to Chronicle Books art editor Bridget Watson Payne and project editor Mirabelle Korn, for backing the project with their generous vision for the possibilities of art, and for their gimlet eyes for the prose style we needed to capture Ruth Asawa's essence without sentiment or sensationalism. Bouquets to designer Kristen Hewitt for weaving photos beautifully throughout the text. And to the rest of the Chronicle Books team: Michele Posner, Janine Sato, Steve Kim, Sarah Lin Go, and Diane Levinson.

Although this book is an independent book rather than an "authorized biography," the Asawa family gave gracious and patient access to their art, knowledge, archival materials, and family correspondence of Ruth Asawa and Albert Lanier. Although they shy away from thanks, they include: Aiko Cuneo, her husband, photographer Larry Cuneo, and their son Hudson Cuneo; Addie Lanier and her husband, Peter Weverka; Hudson Lanier, his wife, Terry, and daughter Lilli; Paul Lanier, his wife, Sandra Halladey, and daughter Emma; and Xavier Lanier and his wife, Gerri. Ruth's sisters Janet Davis and Kimiko Devadas shared memories of Ruth that only a sister can know.

Many members of the Japanese American community offered essential guidance about navigating the culturally sensitive ground of the World War II experience and its aftermath: Rosalyn Tonai of the National Japanese American Historical Society, Brian Niiya of Densho Encyclopedia, author and camp art scholar Delphine Hirasuna, and filmmaker and activist Dr. Satsuki Ina, among many others.

The former mayor of Rohwer, Arkansas, Rosalie Gould, and her filmmaker daughter, Vivienne "Lee" Schiffer, schooled me on the history and culture of the region where Ruth was confined in camp. Alice Imamoto Takemoto, Ruth's longtime friend from their Norwalk school days through their camp years, offered life lessons on the trauma and resilience of their generation.

I was blessed to speak with Ruth's Black Mountain College classmates, the artists Mary Parks Washington and Susan Weil; and to communicate with the children of her friends from Milwaukee and Black Mountain, Elaine Schmitt Urbain and Elizabeth Schmitt Jennerjahn.

The Ruth Asawa San Francisco School of the Arts and creative leaders of the San Francisco Unified School District, who shared their invaluable perspectives, include Donn Harris, Barnaby Payne, Jill Wynns, and Susan Stauter. Ruth Asawa's band of volunteers who led the Alvarado Arts Workshop—the Valley Girls—recounted stories of painting murals and planting daffodils on a shoestring. Anne Marie Theilen, the doyenne of SCRAP, told of salvaging art materials from the dump so small hands could create. Piero Mussi of the Artworks Foundry in Berkeley, California, let me in on the magic of molten bronze and the fiery "dance of the pour" that so mesmerized Ruth as her sculptures took form.

Museum, gallery, and university art experts began sharing knowledge from my lucky first interview with Harry S. Parker III, former director of the Fine Arts Museums of San Francisco. Daniell Cornell of the Palm Springs Museum of Art, Mark Johnson of San Francisco State University, and Robert Storr of Yale University offered elegant scholarly analyses. Trish Bransten of the Rena Bransten Gallery and Jonathan Laib of the David Zwirner Gallery enlightened me about the interplay of galleries, auction houses, and museums in an artist's career trajectory.

As a brave first reader, my friend and former colleague Carrie Dolan, a page one editor at the *Wall Street Journal*, was a fount of good cheer and infallible instincts. Academic colleagues and leaders Dean Ed Wasserman at the University of California, Berkeley, and Journalism Program Director Jay Hamilton of Stanford University offered encouragement and understanding during my book leave from classroom teaching.

My infinite thanks and love go to Randy Chase for accompanying me on this five-year journey.

A NOTE ON SOURCES, LANGUAGE, AND INTERVIEWS

This book draws from a wealth of documents, primary source works, eyewitness accounts, and interviews. The Ruth Asawa Papers, now housed at the Department of Special Collections in Stanford University's Cecil H. Green Library, encompasses 275 boxes of letters, photographs, sketches, plans for sculptures and fountains, school artwork and memorabilia, professional correspondence, family correspondence, contracts, fan mail, holiday greeting cards, calendars, datebooks, and personal effects. These artifacts range from a cast bronze hand of Buckminster Fuller to a quilt made by volunteers in the Alvarado Arts Workshop.

Among documents in this treasury were Ruth Asawa's writings, including the journals she kept during the long nights of insomnia endured during treatment for lupus in 1985. She gave several long conversational interviews including those with Harriet Nathan for the Oral History Office of the Bancroft Library of University of California, Berkeley; Mary Emma Harris of the Black Mountain College Project; and Joanne Iritani for the Florin Japanese American Citizens League and California State University, Sacramento.

The Asawa family's wartime journey from their farm to the camps is gathered from the artist's written memories, her sisters' accounts, and federal government documents, including the Ruth Asawa Evacuee Case File and Alien Enemy File of Umakichi Asawa, accessed by her granddaughter Aiko Sofia Weverka and independently by me from National Archives and Records Administration in Washington, D.C. Federal records include her father's arrest records, her camp health forms and letters, a high school autobiography written by the seventeen-year-old Ruth, and her correspondence with the U.S. Department of Justice arguing for her father's release from camp in Lordsburg, New Mexico, and reunion with his family, confined in a camp in Rohwer, Arkansas.

I was fortunate to be granted access to love letters between Ruth Asawa and her fiancé, Albert Lanier, from 1948 and '49 as they planned their life together, and worked out how to be true to their art and to each other in a world not yet ready for their interracial union. For this, I thank the family and the Estate of Ruth Asawa.

Although Asawa's eighty-seven years of abundant creativity ceased one year before my research began, I had the good fortune to mine extraordinary archives, and interview scores of her family, friends, artists, educators, and colleagues, along with art scholars, critics, and historians who shared insights into her character, her work, and the World War II era. While this is an independent work, and not an authorized biography, my deepest thanks go to members of the Asawa and Lanier families for their time, insights, and generous access to archival treasures.

Some visual artists like Ruth Asawa and members of the Black Mountain College community employ phonetic spellings. To avoid a thicket of "[sic]" notations, wherever possible I have simply let Ruth's spellings and words stand unchanged to preserve the flavor of both her formal writing and informal journal jottings. To do otherwise would seem pretentious and pedantic.

It is important to acknowledge that any writer attempting to tell the story of a life in wartime risks exacerbating the pain of old wounds by recounting suffering and searching for words to describe it. Wartime racism and hysteria were expressed not only in words of explicit hate speech such as "Jap," but in the vast array of euphemisms designed to mask and minimize the trauma inflicted, and to cloak the roundup and incarceration of 120,000 innocents with a sense of military necessity and bureaucratic routine, as if prison camps were hardy pioneer villages or boomtowns. They were not.

Words like *relocation* and *evacuation*—implying a rescue or a flight to safety—sought to conceal the malign aim of concentration camps: gathering and excluding from society fellow citizens who shared ethnic roots with an enemy. Even *internment*—while literally denoting imprisonment for political reasons—is falling out of use among historians and social critics as connoting a bland, official whitewash. *Internment* dodges the blunter truth of words like *seizure, roundup, imprisonment*, and *incarceration*. We need only recall that U.S. government officials themselves referred to these bleak barracks settlements as "concentration camps"—even before Pearl Harbor—in a label that acknowledged the heart of their purpose. Any use of that label quoting U.S. officials isn't meant to minimize the atrocities committed in Nazi death camps—which created evil of a different order—or to offend those who suffered there.

As a writer relating one artist's life journey through history, I have tried to stay in the moment, using the language of the era when needed, quoting official government titles for agencies and institutions when necessary, and also stepping outside it to use plainer language of detention, imprisonment, and incarceration in the authorial voice when I can. I'm indebted to Dr. Satsuki Ina, Brian Niiya, Delphine Hirasuna, and other members of the community for their candor and generosity in helping me navigate the sensitivities of a culture that is not my own. While thanking them, I acknowledge that any errors in this account are mine alone. I also thank art historian and author Mark Johnson for comments and insights about Ruth's place in the art world.

Following is a list of major interviews—done in person, by phone, or via e-mail or letters:

Joan Abrahamson, Jacques d'Amboise, Mary Baxter, Ken Blum, William Bondy, Jamie Bowles, Trish Bransten, Tish Brown, Willie L. Brown, Jr., Judy Burns, Sally Bylin, Milton Chen, Daniell Cornell, Ruth Cox, Peter Coyote, Aiko Cuneo, Belva Davis, Janet Asawa Davis, Nancy Kimiko Asawa Devadas, Sue Diekman, Dr. Paul Feigenbaum, Lawrence Ferlinghetti, Leah Forbes, Shinchi Linda Galijan, Judy Gough, Rosalie Gould, Dr. Douglas Grey, Sandra Halladey, Donn K. Harris, Kimi Kodani Hill, Delphine Hirasuna, Satsuki Ina, PhD, Andrea Jepson, Bud Johns, Fran Johns, Professor Mark Johnson, Geré Kavanaugh, Karen Korematsu, Jonathan Laib, Addie Lanier, Emma Lanier, Gerri Lanier, Hudson Lanier, Lilli Lanier, Paul Lanier, Terry Lanier, Xavier Lanier, Kathleen LaRusso, Gaye LeBaron, Mae Lee, Phyllis Matsuno, Pierre de Meuron, Janice Mirikitani, Piero Mussi, Howard Nemerovski, Brian Niiya, Harry S. Parker III, Barnaby Payne, Dr. Phillip Perloff, Sheila Pressley, Barbara Purcell, Glory Rubio, Jimmy Sanz, Sharon Savage Litzky, Vivienne Schiffer, Terry Schmitt, Kay Sekimachi, Bill Somerville, Gary Snyder, Susan Stauter, Professor Robert Storr, Alice Imamoto Takemoto, Anne-Marie Theilen, Rosalyn Tonai, Mary Parks Washington, Susan Weil, Diane B. Wilsey, Sally Woodbridge, Robin Woodland, Flo Oy Wong, Florence Wong, Jill Wynns, Jan Yanehiro

ENDNOTES

Prologue: Auction, 2013

Frenzied bidding . . . Jonathan Laib, interview with the author, February 6 and 9, 2017.

"Really?" . . . "Mama, you're playing with the big boys now!" Aiko Cuneo and Addie Lanier, private communications with the author, June 13, 2017.

Chapter 1: War

"Terror struck all of us . . . " Ruth Asawa Papers, M1585: Box 173, Folder 5. Department of Special Collections, Stanford University Libraries.

After the bombing, his family took down the emperor's picture . . . Oral History Interview with Ruth Asawa Lanier by Joanne Iritani, April 7, 2000, c. Florin Japanese American Citizens League and California State University, Sacramento, 25.

"To rid the house of any Japanese artifacts . . ." Ruth Asawa Papers, M1585: Box 173, Folder 5. Department of Special Collections, Stanford University Libraries.

Hoover who insisted . . . Richard Reeves, *Infamy: The Shocking Story of the Japanese American Internment in World War II* (New York: Henry Holt & Co., 2015), 39. Thanks for helpful analysis by Brian Niiya, content editor of Densho Encyclopedia, e-mail to the author, January 19, 2019.

"Prepare plans for concentration camps." Reeves, *Infamy,* 9.

President Roosevelt himself used the word (concentration camps) . . . Amid concern about Japan's naval buildup and suspicion that Japanese Americans might harbor loyalty to Tokyo, Roosevelt sent a memo to the Chief of Naval Operations on August 10, 1936 that read: "One obvious thought occurs to me—that every Japanese citizen or non-citizen on the Island of Oahu who meets these Japanese ships or has any connection with their officers or men should be secretly but definitely identified and his or her name placed on a special list of those who would be the first to be placed in a concentration camp in the event of trouble."

Peter Irons, *Justice at War: the Story of the Japanese American Internment Cases (New York: Oxford University Press, 1983),* 20.

"I am for immediate removal of every Japanese . . . " Reeves, *Infamy,* 35.

"Waiting for the Signal from Home." Reeves, *Infamy,* p. 21 and 5th page of photo insert between p. 136 and 137.

"All Japanese, whether citizens or not, must be placed in inland concentration camps . . . " Reeves, *Infamy,* 106.

"Japs in vicinity . . . " Reeves, *Infamy,* 55.

While a vigorous supporter of the Japanese exclusion . . . G. Edward White, "The Unacknowledged Lesson: Earl Warren and the Japanese Relocation Controversy," *The Virginia Quarterly Review* (Autumn 1979), https://www.vqronline.org/essay/unacknowledged-lesson-earl-warren-and-japanese-relocation-controversy. Accessed April 23, 2019.

First Lady Eleanor Roosevelt . . . Doris Kearns Goodwin, *No Ordinary Time: Franklin and Eleanor Roosevelt: The Home Front in World War II* (New York: Simon & Schuster, 1994), 323.

The American Civil Liberties Union . . . Goodwin, *No Ordinary Time,* 321.

"Without warning . . . two F.B.I agents appeared looking for Father . . . " Ruth Asawa Papers, M1585: Box 173, Folder 5. Department of Special Collections, Stanford University Libraries.

Umakichi was raised in a very poor family in Fukushima province. As a young boy, he peddled natto . . . Interviews with Ruth Asawa by Harriet Nathan, 1974–1976, Oral History Center, Bancroft Library, University of California, Berkeley, 17. The Ruth Asawa Papers, M1585: Box 127, Folder 4. Department of Special Collections, Stanford University Libraries, 3-4. Addie Lanier added historical nuances of the Asawas' samurai origin story.

Norwalk saw biplanes. . . Richard L. Kahanek, *A History of Norwalk, Los Angeles County, California* (Norwalk: Andrews Printing, 1968), 47–57. Stanford University Libraries, 3-4.

Japanese farmers produced . . . 40 percent . . . Goodwin, *No Ordinary Time,* 321.

Haru gave birth at home . . . Interview with Janet Asawa Davis, May 3, 2018. "I'm the youngest, and I was born at home. So I'm sure she (Ruth) was born at home. They usually had midwives in those days." Ruth's birth certificate lists no hospital.

"I, being a winter baby . . . " "My Autobiography," Ruth Asawa Evacuee Case File, National Archives and Records Administration. The use of midwives was confirmed by Asawa's sister, Janet Tomiko Asawa Davis, in an interview on May 3, 2018.

[T]he state passed the Alien Land Law of 1913 . . . Cherstin M. Lyon, "Alien land laws," Densho Encyclopedia, 23 May 2014, 22:40 PDT, 12 Nov 2018, 11:50, https://encyclopedia.densho.org/Alien%20land%20laws.

Depression vegetable prices and exploitation of Japanese American farmers . . . Interviews with Ruth Asawa by Harriet Nathan, 1974–1976, Oral History Center, Bancroft Library, University of California, Berkeley, 15–16. Ruth Asawa Papers, M1585: Box 12, Folder 4. Department of Special Collections, Stanford University Libraries.

For working the whole summer, the Asawa children each got ten dollars to buy shoes and clothes. Interviews with Ruth Asawa by Harriet Nathan, 1974–1976, Oral History Center, Bancroft Library, University of California, Berkeley, 17. The Ruth Asawa Papers, M1585: Box 127, Folder 4. Department of Special Collections, Stanford University Libraries, 17.

"They were fearless people." Ruth Asawa Papers, M1585: Box 125, Folder 5. Department of Special Collections, Stanford University Libraries.

"I was bossed and I was boss." Jacqueline Hoefer, "Ruth Asawa: A Working Life," *The Sculpture of Ruth Asawa: Contours in the Air*, Daniell Cornell, ed., Fine Arts Museums of San Francisco (Berkeley and Los Angeles: University of California Press, 2006), 11.

Diphtheria. . . Ruth Asawa Papers, M1585: Box 128, Folder 4. Department of Special Collections, Stanford University Libraries.

"Fortunately, Father drove me home from the hospital in our very best Model T . . ." "My Autobiography," Ruth Asawa Evacuee Case File, National Archives and Records Administration.

Exploding ketchup . . . Interview with Susan Stauter, March 9, 2017.

Her reception of the award was the only occasion Ruth remembered that her shy and hardworking parents visited the school. Oral History Interview with Ruth Asawa Lanier by Joanne Iritani, April 7, 2000, c. Florin Japanese American Citizens League and California State University, Sacramento, 13.

"People do not understand what it was like." Interview follow-up with Nancy Kimiko Asawa Devadas, via her daughter Mina Devadas, November 19, 2018.

National School Newspaper, Ruth Asawa Papers, M1585: Box 78, Folder 15, Current Events. Department of Special Collections, Stanford University Libraries.

". . . [A]s strong as ten thousand octopus suckers." "My Autobiography," Ruth Asawa Evacuee Case File, National Archives and Records Administration.

Ruth's school bus friendship was recounted in an interview with Alice Imamoto Takemoto, February 28, 2017.

It was drilled into her... Ruth Asawa Papers, M1585: Box 173, Folder 5. Department of Special Collections, Stanford University Libraries.

... Agriculture lobbying groups admitted they weren't sorry to see their rivals go. Cited by Doris Kearns Goodwin, *No Ordinary Time*, 321.

"April 14 was the last day in Norwalk... "*"My Autobiography," Ruth Asawa Evacuee Case File, National Archives and Records Administration.

"With tear-drenched eyes... "*"My Autobiography," Ruth Asawa Evacuee Case File, National Archives and Records Administration.

The palm tree-lined racetrack... sheltered nearly half of its eighteen thousand inmates in barracks in the infield and parking lot, while less fortunate families like the Asawas were assigned to horse stables... Brian Niiya, content editor of Densho Encyclopedia, e-mail to the author, January 19, 2019. (Niiya also notes not all Japanese Americans went to "assembly centers"—some went directly into camps.)

"Hairs from the horses['] mane & tail... "Handwritten speech notes. Ruth Asawa Papers, M1585: Box 173, Folder 5. Department of Special Collections, Stanford University Libraries.

Showers and details of facilities at Santa Anita Racetrack Assembly Center are recorded in the Densho Encyclopedia, https://encyclopedia.densho.org.

"Two of the worst things that happened... "Ruth Asawa Papers, M1585: Box 173, Folder 5. Department of Special Collections, Stanford University Libraries.

The eyes of the nation are upon us... Santa Anita Pacemaker, Ruth Asawa Papers, M1585: Box 174, Folder 4. Department of Special Collections, Stanford University Libraries.

"How lucky could a 16-year-old be... "Ruth Asawa Papers, M1585: Box 173, Folder 5. Department of Special Collections, Stanford University Libraries.

"We all knew that... 'Inu'" Ruth Asawa Papers. M1585: Box 173/Folder 5, Department of Special Collections, Stanford University Libraries.

"It must have been near September 15... "*"My Autobiography," Ruth Asawa Evacuee Case File, National Archives and Records Administration.

"It was near nightfall... "*"My Autobiography," Ruth Asawa Evacuee Case File, National Archives and Records Administration.

"Rohwer! Get ready to leave!" Details of the arrival at Rohwer Camp, *First Rohwer Reunion Booklet,* First Rohwer Reunion Committee, Los Angeles, July 1990. Ruth Asawa Papers, M1885: Box 173, Folder 3. Department of Special Collections, Stanford University Libraries. Additional details were offered by Brian Niiya of Densho Encyclopedia, in an e-mail to the author, January 19, 2019.

"Dismal, spooky air…" Interviews with Ruth Asawa by Harriet Nathan, 1974–1976, Oral History Center, Bancroft Library, University of California, Berkeley, 1980.

Chapter 2: The Camp

Inside the 10,000-acre site… Brian Niiya, content editor of Densho Encyclopedia, accessed May 22, 2018, https://encyclopedia.densho.org/Rohwer.

Arkansas Governor Homer Martin Adkins, a onetime member of the Ku Klux Klan… Arkansas Encyclopedia of History & Culture, accessed May 22, 2018, http://www.encyclopedia-ofarkansas.net.

"Jap!" First Rohwer Reunion Booklet, ibid.

"Even such barren quarters, Ruth decided, were 100 percent better…" "My Autobiography," Ruth Asawa Evacuee Case File, National Archives and Records Administration.

FBI documents tracked him… Umakichi Asawa, Alien Enemy File, RG60, Alien Enemy Internment Case File, A1 COR 146-13 Box 226(1).pdf, Department of Justice, National Archives and Records Administration.

"Decidedly evasive"… "potentially dangerous" Umakichi Asawa, Alien Enemy File, RG60, Alien Enemy Internment Case File, A1 COR 146-13, Box 226(1).pdf, Department of Justice, National Archives and Records Administration.

…[A] barren room with a pot-bellied stove measuring about 20 feet by 24 feet… Brian Niiya, content editor of Densho Encyclopedia, noted families like the Asawas in A-units were afforded a 20-by-24-foot room, rather than a 20-by-16-foot or a 20-by-20-foot space. E-mail to the author, January 19, 2019.

Internment camp furniture and crafts are documented by Delphine Hirasuna and Kit Hinrichs in *The Art of Gaman: Arts and Crafts from the Japanese American Internment Camps, 1942–1946* (Berkeley: Ten Speed Press, 2005).

"Perhaps our most prized commodity, SEEDS." Ruth Asawa Papers, M1585: Box 173, Folder 5, handwritten speech notes. Department of Special Collections, Stanford University Libraries.

Rohwer's thirty-seven-cents-a-day rations are cited by Densho Encyclopedia, accessed January 5, 2019, https://encyclopedia.densho.org/Rohwer.

[T]he "hey, at least they fed you people" syndrome. The Rohwer Outpost, First Rohwer Reunion Committee, Los Angeles, July 1990. Ruth Asawa Papers, M1585: Box 173, Folder 3. Department of Special Collections, Stanford University Libraries.

Rumors had it that some men either imported or built a sake still . . . First Rohwer Reunion Booklet, ibid.

L'il Dan'l cartoons . . . George Akimoto, *The Rohwer Outpost,* 1st ed., First Rohwer Reunion Committee, August 1989. Ruth Asawa Papers, M1585: Box 173, Folder 2. Department of Special Collections, Stanford University Libraries.

"[T]he mess gong clanging in the distance . . . " Akimoto, *Rohwer Outpost,* and Ruth Asawa Papers. Ibid.

Accounts of daily life at Rohwer camp drawn from the *First Rohwer Reunion Booklet,* ibid.

"[T]he first vacation they had really ever taken . . . " Interviews with Ruth Asawa by Harriet Nathan, 1974–1976, Oral History Center, Bancroft Library, University of California, Berkeley.

Assigned to a private plantation—to pick cotton . . . John Howard, *Concentration Camps on the Home Front: Japanese Americans in the House of Jim Crow* (Chicago: University of Chicago Press, 2008), 131.

"With liberty and justice for all . . . 'Except me.'" Oral History Interview with Ruth Asawa Lanier by Joanne Iritani, April 7, 2000, c. Florin Japanese American Citizens League and California State University, Sacramento, 35. Department of Special Collections, Stanford University Libraries.

"I can still see you in my mind's eye . . . " Sachi Fujikawa, letter to Ruth Asawa, April 10, 2007, Ruth Asawa Papers, M1585: Box 172, Folder 3. Department of Special Collections, Stanford University Libraries.

The habit of drawing students . . . Paul Lanier, e-mail to the author, February 14, 2019.

Lordsburg was a special internment camp . . . "Lordsburg (detention facility)," Densho Encyclopedia, https://encyclopedia.densho.org/Lordsburg%20(detention%20facility). Accessed July 15, 2015, and November 12, 2018.

"Dear Mr. Palmer. . ." Ruth's letters to free her father from Lordsburg, her father's interrogation by D.O.J. and F.B.I. investigators, and neighbors' affidavits in support of him are all drawn from the Umakichi Asawa, Alien Enemy File, RG60, Alien Enemy Internment Case File, A1 COR 146-13, Box 226(1).pdf, Department of Justice, National Archives and Records Administration.

Inmates replying "no" . . . The numbers of Rohwer inmates sent to Tule Lake for replying *"No . . . No"* to the loyalty questionnaire numbered 808 in the first transports in the fall of 1943, and eventually rose to 1,403, according to Brian Niiya, content editor of Densho Encyclopedia, e-mail to the author, January 19, 2019.

"Dearest Ruthie, Aw gee . . ." The Bayou Roundup (Rohwer High School Yearbook), Ruth Asawa Papers, M1585: Box 172, Folder 8. Department of Special Collections, Stanford University Libraries.

"To a little lady with lots of talent and a big heart . . ." The Bayou Roundup, Ruth Asawa Papers. ibid.

The most highly-decorated unit . . . U.S. Department of Defense, Know Your Military. "Go for Broke: Army Unit's Motto Now a National Day," April 4, 2019. Accessed April 23, 2019. https://www.defense.gov/explore/story/Article/1805390/go-for-broke-this-army-units-motto-is-now-a-national-day/.

"I thought I was in Dante's Inferno . . ." Angela Carella, interview with Sam Ichiba, "Personal Combat," *The Sunday Advocate* (Stamford, CT), June 5, 1994. page A9. Ruth Asawa papers, M1585.Box 172, Folder 2. Department of Special Collections, Stanford University Libraries.

"She gave us college catalogues to look through . . ." Ruth Asawa Papers, M1585: Box 127, Folder 5. Department of Special Collections, Stanford University Libraries.

"Imagine telling a 16-year-old not to be bitter . . ." Ruth Asawa Papers, M1585: Box 127, Folder 5. Department of Special Collections, Stanford University Libraries.

"I departed bowing to Mama . . ." Ruth Asawa Papers, M1585: Box 127, Folder 5. Department of Special Collections, Stanford University Libraries.

"A terrible injustice . . ." Ruth Asawa Papers, M1585: Box 173, Folder 5. Department of Special Collections, Stanford University Libraries.

"Mrs. Beasley took me to the train station . . ." Ruth Asawa Papers, M1585: Box 127, Folder 5. Department of Special Collections, Stanford University Libraries.

Chapter 3: Getting Up in the World

[S]he sat on duffel bags among soldiers heading to war . . . Ruth told her children this story about going off to college, according to Addie Lanier, private communication with author, February 2, 2019.

Yet Ruth's curiosity drew her too close to the lake . . . Hoefer, *The Sculpture of Ruth Asawa: Contours in the Air,* 14.

"For Ruth . . . Daddy." A photograph of this carved box is included in *All That Remains: The Legacy of the World War II Japanese American Internment Camps,* by Delphine Hirasuna, 46–47, published in conjunction with the *Art of Gaman Exhibition of Arts and Crafts,* which traveled throughout the United States and Japan from 2005 through 2015, with support of Tom and Gayle Hoshiuyama, the Japanese American Citizens League, San Francisco Chapter.

"Mrs. Beasely [sic] arranged . . . I ate my meals in the kitchen." Ruth Asawa Papers, M1585: Box 127, Folders 5 and 6. Department of Special Collections, Stanford University Libraries.

"Your Japanese inheritance . . ." Ethel R. Potts, letter to Ruth Asawa, March 6, 1944, courtesy of the Estate of Ruth Asawa.

Twick and Twack . . . Interview by the author with Mabel Galian's daughter, Shinchi Linda Galijan, June 2, 2017.

"I was all hot to go to Mexico . . ." Interviews with Ruth Asawa by Harriet Nathan, 1974-1976, Oral History Center, Bancroft Library, University of California, Berkeley, 30. Ruth Asawa Papers, M1585: Box 127, Folder 4. Department of Special Collections, Stanford University Libraries.

"[I]ncredible, unbelievable" smell . . . Asawa interview by Nathan, 32.

"I was getting up in the world . . ." Asawa interview by Nathan, 32.

"Lois and I didn't know what to do about the toilets . . . " Ruth Asawa Papers, M1585: Box 127, Folder 5. Department of Special Collections, Stanford University Libraries.

"Clara Porset . . . " Asawa interview by Nathan, 30. (Ruth called her by her nickname Clarita.)

Hiroshima and Nagasaki deaths . . . "U.S. Strategic Bombing Survey: The Effects of the Atomic Bombings of Hiroshima and Nagasaki," June 19, 1946. Truman Papers, President's Secretary's File. Atomic Bomb—Hiroshima. Accessed June 20, 2018, https://www .trumanlibrary.org.

Self-defense with bamboo sticks . . . Asawa interview by Nathan, 23.

An estimated 50 million deaths . . . Goodwin, *No Ordinary Time,* 621.

"While [we were] in Mexico, the Japanese surrendered." Ruth Asawa Papers, M1585: Box 127, Folder 5. Department of Special Collections, Stanford University Libraries.

Umakichi had been allowed to rejoin his wife in late 1943 . . . Addie Lanier, private communication with the author, February 2, 2019.

[N]earing retirement age at sixty-three and fifty-one . . . Addie Lanier, private communication with the author. Umakichi Asawa was born in 1882 and Haru in 1894.

"Pulled out morning glory vines . . . " Howard, *Concentration Camps on the Home Front,* 238.

A study would later suggest . . . Gwendolyn M. Jensen, "The Experience of Injustice: Health Consequences of the Japanese American Internment," University of Michigan Dissertation Service, Ann Arbor, MI, 1997. Cited by Satsuki Ina in *Children of the Camps,* accessed July 10, 2018. https://www.pbs.org/childofcamp/

A farewell ritual . . . Howard, *Concentration Camps on the Home Front,* 223.

" . . . I shall expect to be treated roughly . . . " Howard, *Concentration Camps on the Home Front,* 226. Thanks to Brian Niiya of Densho Encyclopedia for pointing out that Mr. Takeda was known by the first name of Bean.

"In my third year the college . . . " Ruth Asawa Papers, M1585: Box 127, Folder 5. Department of Special Collections, Stanford University Libraries.

"I decided to go to Black Mountain College." Ruth Asawa Papers, M1585: Box 127, Folder 5. Department of Special Collections, Stanford University Libraries.

"She bears hardships . . ." Reference of Elizabeth Christel, April 25, 1946. Black Mountain College, Western Regional Archives, North Carolina Department of Natural and Cultural Resources.

"I regard Ruth Asawa . . ." Reference of Cecelie Sieverts, May 5, 1946, Black Mountain College, Western Regional Archives, North Carolina Department of Natural and Cultural Resources. (Thanks to Mrs. Sieverts's daughter, Laurie Snyder, for background interview and historical context, November 18, 2018.)

Black Mountain's tuition and fees . . . F. A. Foster, "Black Mountain College," *Black Mountain College: Sprouted Seeds: An Anthology of Personal Accounts,* Mervin Lane, ed. (Knoxville: University of Tennessee Press, 1990), 95.

"I hope you have all your things packed . . ." Elaine Schmitt, letter to Ruth Asawa, April 11, 1946, courtesy of the Estate of Ruth Asawa.

She thought she might be good at this craft . . . Aiko Cuneo, private communication with the author, February 2, 2019.

Chapter 4: Climbing Black Mountain

Green cars with red and silver wheels. Dick Andrews, "A Few Vignettes," *Black Mountain College: Sprouted Seeds: An Anthology of Personal Accounts,* Mervin Lane, ed. (Knoxville: University of Tennessee Press, 1990), 71.

Black Mountain was founded in 1933 . . . For history of the college, see Mary Emma Harris, *The Arts at Black Mountain College* (Cambridge: MIT Press, 1987), 2–7. See also: Martin Duberman, *Black Mountain: An Exploration in Community* (Evanston, IL: Northwestern University Press, 1972), 1–10.

"Art knows nothing about graduation." "Ruth Asawa: Black Mountain Work," accessed July 25, 2018, https://www.ruthasawa.com/art/black-mountain-work.

"The magnet of Black Mountain was not luxurious living but the luxurious mind." John J. Reiss, "Behind the Silver Curtain," *Black Mountain College: Sprouted Seeds: An Anthology of Personal Accounts,* Mervin Lane, ed. (Knoxville: University of Tennessee Press, 1990), 138.

"Dungarees." Interview with Mary Parks Washington by the author, April 19, 2017.

[F]loor length frocks, sewn from dyed flour sacks . . . Elizabeth Jennerjahn, "Betty Schmitt, How Did You Ever Get Here?," *Black Mountain College: Sprouted Seeds: An Anthology of Personal Accounts,* Mervin Lane, ed. (Knoxville: University of Tennessee Press, 1990), 130.

"A very good soul. Talented but very unorderly . . ." J. Albers to Registrars Office, August 16, 1946, Ruth Asawa Student File, Black Mountain College, Western Regional Archives, North Carolina Department of National and Cultural Resources, © The Josef and Anni Albers Foundation.

". . . [A] monk's cell in austerity . . ." John Andrew Rice, "Black Mountain College Memoirs," *Black Mountain College: Sprouted Seeds: An Anthology of Personal Accounts,* Mervin Lane, ed. (Knoxville: University of Tennessee Press, 1990), 16.

"CLEAN IMMEDIATELY . . ." Ruth Asawa Papers, M1585: Box 175, Folder 1. Department of Special Collections, Stanford University Libraries.

"Picasso-itus, Matisse-somnia, Klee-tomania . . ." Josef Albers interview, Lane, ed., *Black Mountain College: Sprouted Seeds,* 34.

"I signed up for Josef Albers Basic Design . . ." Ruth Asawa Papers, M1585: Box 127, Folder 5. Department of Special Collections, Stanford University Libraries.

"Schwindle . . ." "Ruth Asawa: Black Mountain College," https://www.ruthasawa.com /life/black-mountain-college. Accessed April 23, 2019.

Dissident students once turned Albers's lesson . . . Duberman, *Black Mountain: An Exploration in Community,* 57.

"Matière momma . . ." Elaine Schmitt, letter to her family, undated. Ruth Asawa Papers, M1585: Box 25, Folder 7. Department of Special Collections, Stanford University Libraries. And with the permission of Catherine Urbain.

"Let the material express itself." Ruth Asawa, museum lecture on Albers, 1959, Ruth Asawa Papers, M1585: Box 127, Folder 1. Department of Special Collections, Stanford University Libraries.

"He was primarily interested in color and relativity of color . . ." Ruth Asawa interviews by Harriet Nathan, 1974–1976, Oral History Center, Bancroft Library, University of California, Berkeley, 130–131. Ruth Asawa Papers, M1585: Box 127, Folder 4. Department of Special Collections, Stanford University Libraries.

"I was a very obedient student . . . I followed directions." Duberman, *Black Mountain: An Exploration in Community,* 60.

"[A] beautiful teacher" . . . "an impossible person . . ." Robert Rauschenberg, statement on Josef Albers, undated, accessed August 6, 2018, https://www.rauschenbergfoundation. org/art/archive/albers.

"Who likes not discipline, let him leave soddenly!" Allan Sly, taped reminiscences, *Black Mountain College: Sprouted Seeds: An Anthology of Personal Accounts,* Mervin Lane, ed. (Knoxville: University of Tennessee Press, 1990), 65.

"Don't be proud of your work of 12 hours; I wait for your work of 12 weeks." Ruth Asawa Papers, M1585: Box 175, Folder 1. Department of Special Collections, Stanford University Libraries.

"Schön . . . " Peggy Loram Bailey, *Black Mountain College: Sprouted Seeds: An Anthology of Personal Accounts,* Mervin Lane, ed. (Knoxville: University of Tennessee Press, 1990), 45.

"Donnerwetter . . . " John J. Reiss, "Behind the Silver Curtain," *Black Mountain College: Sprouted Seeds: An Anthology of Personal Accounts,* Mervin Lane, ed. (Knoxville: University of Tennessee Press, 1990), 136.

"[A]n element of theater . . . " Jane Slater Marquis, "This Paradise Apart," *Black Mountain College: Sprouted Seeds: An Anthology of Personal Accounts,* Mervin Lane, ed. (Knoxville: University of Tennessee Press, 1990), 90–91.

"When he taught drawing, he wanted you to look at the figure . . . " Interview #189 with Ruth Asawa by Mary Emma Harris, February 17, 1998, Black Mountain College Project, Inc., New York, 9. Quoted with permission. Ruth Asawa Papers M1585: Box 35, Folder 8. Department of Special Collections, Stanford University Libraries.

"So the girls and the boys, they knew each other sweating . . . " Josef Albers, "1965 Interview," *Black Mountain College: Sprouted Seeds: An Anthology of Personal Accounts,* Mervin Lane, ed. (Knoxville: University of Tennessee Press, 1990), 37.

Black Mountain began early steps to integrate . . . Duberman, *Black Mountain: An Experiment in Community,* 180–181. See also Micah Wilford Wilkins, "Social Justice at BMC Before the Civil Rights Age: Desegregation, Racial Inclusion, and Racial Equality at BMC," Accessed online October 10, 2018, www.blackmountainstudiesjournal.org/volume-6.

For more on history of how Black Mountain addressed integration, see Harris, *The Arts at Black Mountain College,* 71.

"She was the sweetest girl . . . " Interview with Mary Parks Washington by the author, April 19, 2017.

"Ruth was a beautiful, quiet person . . . " Interview with Susan Weil by the author, July 19, 2017.

"[R]espectful" of Ruth . . . Interview with Susan Weil by the author, July 19, 2017. Weil said "I think he was respectful of [Asawa]. For the most part he didn't interact with students

on a personal level. He was very caring and loving with Anni. I just assumed they had a very good marriage and so on."

"I thought this would be my opportunity to repay these good people . . . " Ruth Asawa Papers, M1585: Box 127, Folder 5. Department of Special Collections, Stanford University Libraries.

"See, see, color is the most relative medium" . . . "He went into ecstasy while eating a whole one." Ruth Asawa Papers, M1585: Box 127, Folder 5. Department of Special Collections, Stanford University Libraries.

"[A] very interesting face . . . " "Well, it's just nonsense." Ruth Asawa interviews by Harriet Nathan, 1974–1976. Oral History Center, Bancroft Library, University of California, Berkeley, 31. Ruth Asawa Papers, M1585: Box 127, Folder 4. Department of Special Collections, Stanford University Libraries.

"Sleepito." Ruth Asawa Papers, M1585: Box 127, Folder 5. Department of Special Collections, Stanford University Libraries.

"Wire can play." "Black Mountain Notebooks," Ruth Asawa Papers, M1585: Box 175, Folder 5. Department of Special Collections, Stanford University Libraries.

On her course card . . . Ruth Asawa Student File, Black Mountain College, Western Regional Archives, North Carolina Department of Natural and Cultural Resources.

"I returned filled with ideas and excitement . . . " Ruth Asawa Papers, M1585: Box 127, Folder 5. Department of Special Collections, Stanford University Libraries.

William Albert Lanier was the son of lawyer and district attorney Weylud (cq) Hudson Lanier . . . Albert Lanier's family history and genealogy, recounted in an interview with Ruth Asawa interviews by Harriet Nathan, 1974–1976, Oral History Center, Bancroft Library, University of California, Berkeley, 31. Ruth Asawa Papers, M1585: Box 127, Folder 4. Department of Special Collections, Stanford University Libraries.

"It didn't work nearly as well for me . . ." and "to build beautiful buildings." Interview with Albert Lanier by Harriet Nathan, "Architecture, Gardens, and the Individual," 1979, Oral History Center, Bancroft Library, University of California, Berkeley, 4-5. Ruth Asawa Papers, M1585: Box 127, Folder 4. Department of Special Collections, Stanford University Libraries.

"I thought I'd never seen anything as exotic looking as this girl." Hoefer, *The Sculpture of Ruth Asawa: Contours in the Air,* 15.

"Sunday, Ruth Asawa, a Japanese girl . . . " Albert Lanier, letter to Mr. and Mrs. W. H. Lanier, April 22, 1947, courtesy of the Estate of Ruth Asawa.

"He thought she was the most beautiful thing . . . " Interview with Mary Parks Washington by the author, April 19, 2017.

"Bucky then whirled off into his talk . . . " Elaine de Kooning, Black Mountain College: *Sprouted Seeds: An Anthology of Personal Accounts,* Mervin Lane, ed. (Knoxville: University of Tennessee Press, 1990), 246-247.

"You succeed only when you stop failing." Alice Rawthorn, "The Prescient Vision of a Gentle Revolutionist," *New York Times,* May 12, 2013, accessed April 19, 2019.

. . . [F]emale nudity kills the mystery that feeds male desire . . . homosexuality . . . overpopulation. R. Buckminster Fuller, interview in *Playboy,* February 1972.

"An abstraction that looked like a diagram of ballet positions . . . " *Time,* August 16, 1948, 44, Ruth Asawa Papers, M1585: Box 243, Folder 2. Department of Special Collections, Stanford University Libraries.

Chapter 5: Love Letters

"It's the strangest looking car ever . . . " Albert Lanier, Letter to Mr. and Mrs. W. H. Lanier, September 1, 1948, courtesy of the Estate of Ruth Asawa.

Albert resorted to selling his blood . . . Interview with Sally Woodbridge by the author, March 1, 2017.

"Blood money . . . " Aiko Cuneo, e-mail communication with the author, August 1, 2018.

"I love you Albert . . . " Ruth Asawa, letter to Albert Lanier, September 17, 1948, courtesy of the Estate of Ruth Asawa.

Each thought the other would destroy such an intimate dialogue . . . Aiko Cuneo, private communication with the author, November 27, 2018. (Ruth had once written Albert to burn her letters. Neither did. Late in life, as her archives were being organized, Ruth agreed that their correspondence should be preserved for history.)

"It is again so good to be with people . . . " "Mama and I speak of marriage . . . " "We are crowded . . . " Ruth Asawa, letter to Albert Lanier, September 28, 1948, courtesy of the Estate of Ruth Asawa.

"This is Albert." Interview with Nancy Kimiko Asawa Devadas by Aiko Cuneo, April 13, 2015. Courtesy of the Estate of Ruth Asawa.

"Mrs. Asawa, you are so beautiful . . ." Interview with Nancy Kimiko Devadas by Aiko Cuneo, April 13, 2015. Courtesy of the Estate of Ruth Asawa.

"Ruth Asawa is of an unusual artistic talent . . ." Josef Albers, letter to Hobart Nichols, September 18, 1948, Ruth Asawa Student File, Black Mountain College, Western Regional Archives, North Carolina Department of Natural and Cultural Resources, © The Josef and Anni Albers Foundation.

"I passed as an Indian boy . . . it was thrilling." Ruth Asawa, postcard to Albert Lanier, October 18, 1948, courtesy of the Estate of Ruth Asawa.

"It was like spreading the wings of a dragonfly . . ." Ruth Asawa, postcard to Albert Lanier, October 9, 1948, courtesy of the Estate of Ruth Asawa.

". . . like a portrait of us looking towards the lake." Ruth Asawa, letter to Albert Lanier, October 23, 1948, courtesy of the Estate of Ruth Asawa.

"Thinking of you really keeps me going . . ." *"I love the quiet . . ."* *"Memories are beautiful . . ."* Ruth Asawa, ibid.

"I was surprised beyond words . . ." *"When they disapprove of a marriage to Ruth . . ."* Laurie Pearson, letter to Albert Lanier, November 1, 1948, courtesy of the Estate of Ruth Asawa.

"Dearest Albert, Hazel will walk again . . ." Ruth Asawa, letter to Albert Lanier, November 1, 1948, courtesy of the Estate of Ruth Asawa.

"I have begun to think more and more in terms of US . . ." Ruth Asawa, letter to Albert Lanier, November 11, 1948, courtesy of the Estate of Ruth Asawa.

"[D]ishonorable intentions . . . stupid carpentry class . . . [A]ll reserved for you . . ." Albert Lanier, letter to Ruth Asawa, November 22, 1948, courtesy of the Estate of Ruth Asawa.

"The life of the artist-scientist-explorer . . ." Lanier, November 22, 1948.

"[A] sensible attitude . . ." Lanier, November 22, 1948.

"Nomads going from one job . . ." Lanier, November 22, 1948.

"Next Christmas . . ." Lanier, November 22, 1948.

"I just can't drink hot chocolate . . ." Lanier, November 22, 1948.

"My love, love, and no more letters . . ." Lanier, November 22, 1948.

"Lois . . . hopes for a glorious beautiful journey . . ." Ruth Asawa, letter to Albert Lanier November 30, 1948, courtesy of the Estate of Ruth Asawa.

"We dance tomorrow . . . " Ruth Asawa, letter to Albert Lanier, December 16, 1948, courtesy of the Estate of Ruth Asawa.

"When I say that I want children . . . " Ruth Asawa, letter to Albert Lanier, December 23, 1948, courtesy of the Estate of Ruth Asawa.

"Much love to you! A wedding ring . . . " Buckminster Fuller, letter to Ruth Asawa, December 24, 1948, courtesy of the Estate of Ruth Asawa.

"I am sure Fuller is the one . . . " Ruth Asawa, letter to Albert Lanier, c. December 28, 1948, courtesy of the Estate of Ruth Asawa.

"I hope it is only the S.F. Bay . . . " Ruth Asawa, letter to Albert Lanier, c. December 28, 1948, courtesy of the Estate of Ruth Asawa.

"[L]ess sens[ible] and less rational." Ruth Asawa, letter to Albert Lanier, December 29, 1948, courtesy of the Estate of Ruth Asawa.

"They dare to be tolerant . . . " "You will have to look at me on streetcars . . . " Ruth Asawa, letter to Albert Lanier, December 29, 1948, courtesy of the Estate of Ruth Asawa.

"You painted me brown . . . " "I will take no more love . . . " Ruth Asawa, letter to Albert Lanier, December 29, 1948, courtesy of the Estate of Ruth Asawa.

"The increasing frequency with which you write about love versus work . . . " Albert Lanier, letter to Ruth Asawa, January 11, 1949, courtesy of the Estate of Ruth Asawa.

With pressure mounting for Dreier's ouster . . . Mary Emma Harris, *The Arts at Black Mountain College* (Cambridge, MA: MIT Press, 1987), 164–165.

"[T]he fatal blunder . . . heart and soul . . . " Harris, 165.

"Resignation of all definite . . ." Ruth Asawa, letter to Albert Lanier, undated, courtesy of the Estate of Ruth Asawa.

"There was a battle . . . " Si Sillman, letter to Albert Lanier, January 31, 1949, courtesy of the Estate of Ruth Asawa.

"Our Valentine party ended gay-drunk . . ." Ruth Asawa, letter to Albert Lanier, undated (c. February 15, 1949), courtesy of the Estate of Ruth Asawa.

New leadership was recruited from Swarthmore . . . Harris, 164–165.

Perez and Davis sued . . . Perez v. Sharp, 32 Cal.2d 711, accessed July 18, 2018, https://scocal .stanford.edu/opinion/perez-v-sharp-26107.

"Albert's mother cried. She had hoped that Albert would marry a sweet blue eyed girl from Metter . . ." Ruth Asawa Papers, M1585: Box 127, Folder 5. Department of Special Collections, Stanford University Libraries.

"That is how many Japanese express 'no'" . . . Ruth Asawa Papers, M1585: Box 127, Folder 5. Department of Special Collections, Stanford University Libraries.

"She is very beautiful . . ." Albert Lanier, letter to his parents, April 10, 1949, courtesy of the Estate of Ruth Asawa.

[N]o "hard-ugly things . . ." Laurie Pearson, letter to Albert Lanier, April 10, 1949, courtesy of the Estate of Ruth Asawa.

"I am Ruth Asawa . . ." Ruth Asawa, letter to Mr. and Mrs. W. H. Lanier, May 6, 1949, courtesy of the Estate of Ruth Asawa.

"You and Albert! . . ." Bernice Lanier, letter to Ruth Asawa, May 10, 1949, courtesy of the Estate of Ruth Asawa.

"Daddy, 'such marriages' . . ." Albert Lanier, letter to Mr. and Mrs. W. H. Lanier, April 23, 1949, courtesy of the Estate of Ruth Asawa.

"I love our city so much . . ." Albert Lanier, letter to Ruth Asawa, postmarked April 18, 1949, courtesy of the Estate of Ruth Asawa.

"San Francisco will make all of us happy . . ." "Please don't let anything come between us . . ." . . . "Oh I remember the pains of it . . ." "I dance all of the time . . ." Ruth Asawa, letter to Albert Lanier, April 4, 1949, courtesy of the Estate of Ruth Asawa.

"I begin to feel the loft is home . . ." Albert Lanier, letter to Ruth Asawa, May 10, 1949, courtesy of the Estate of Ruth Asawa.

Anni also designed and made Ruth a wedding hat. Mark Johnson regarding a conversation he had with Ruth Asawa, e-mail communication with author, February, 16, 2019.

"A beautiful dress . . ." Ruth Asawa, letter to Albert Lanier, May 20, 1949, courtesy of the estate of Ruth Asawa.

"What I really want to do now . . ." Albert Lanier, letter to his parents, June 20, 1949, courtesy of the Estate of Ruth Asawa.

"The world is your oyster . . ." Ruth Asawa Papers, M1585: Box 127, Folder 5. Department of Special Collections, Stanford University Libraries.

"Fine, just make sure they are Asawa flowers." "Come in Asawa . . ." "Ya, ya, you make babies . . ." Ruth Asawa Papers, M1585: Box 127, Folder 5. Department of Special Collections, Stanford University Libraries.

"Don't ever let her stop doing her work . . ." Interviews with Ruth Asawa by Harriet Nathan, 1974–1976, Oral History Center, Bancroft Library, University of California, Berkeley, c. 1980, 191.

Chapter 6: A Loft for a New Life

"Albert did not like diamonds . . ." Ruth Asawa Papers, M1585: Box 127, Folder 5. Department of Special Collections, Stanford University Libraries.

". . . [S]pring from the heart." Albert Lanier, "Our Wedding," Albert's Stories, 2003, courtesy of Aiko Cuneo and the Estate of Ruth Asawa.

"Talbert probably prayed . . ." Lanier, "Our Wedding." Ibid.

"Our honeymoon commenced . . ." Albert Lanier, "Our Wedding," Albert's Stories, 2003, courtesy of Aiko Cuneo and the Estate of Ruth Asawa.

"The Champagne tasted just as good." Ruth Asawa Papers, M1585: Box 127, Folder 5. Department of Special Collections, Stanford University Libraries.

"[N]ever ever let her work as a secretary . . ." Ruth Asawa Papers, M1585: Box 125, Folder 5. Department of Special Collections, Stanford University Libraries.

". . . [T]oo many nosey tourists buzzing about . . ." Ruth Asawa, letter to Mr. and Mrs. Lanier, September 19, 1949, courtesy of the Estate of Ruth Asawa.

". . . [A]warm enchanting city . . . Understand that Albert's silence . . ." Ruth Asawa, letter to Mr. and Mrs. Lanier, postmarked August 23, 1949, courtesy of the Estate of Ruth Asawa.

"Police would stop me . . ." Albert Lanier, "135 Jackson Street," Albert's Stories, 2003, courtesy of Aiko Cuneo and the Estate of Ruth Asawa.

She booked the stripper Tempest Storm . . . Ruth Asawa, letter to Saul Zaentz, Fantasy Films, Ruth Asawa Papers, M1585: Box 127, Folder 5. Department of Special Collections, Stanford University Libraries.

"We have selected 'Old Maryland' . . . " Albert Lanier, letter to Mr. and Mrs. W. H. Lanier (with handwritten postscript by Ruth Asawa), July 11, 1949, courtesy of the Estate of Ruth Asawa.

"With wallpaper spread on the floor . . . " Albert Lanier, letter to Mr. and Mrs. W. H. Lanier, August 6, 1949, courtesy of the Estate of Ruth Asawa.

"TOMATOES" . . . Albert Lanier, letter to Mr. and Mrs. W. H. Lanier, Aug. 6, 1949, courtesy of the Estate of Ruth Asawa. For color vibration theory, see: Joseph Albers, *Interaction of Color*, 50th Anniversary Edition (New Haven: Yale University Press;. 2013), 61–62, 182–183.

"Everything is fine now . . . " Ruth Asawa, letter to Mr. and Mrs. W. H. Lanier, February 24, 1950, courtesy of the Estate of Ruth Asawa.

"We have more news for you . . . " Ruth Asawa, letter to Mr. and Mrs. W. H. Lanier, April 12, 1950, courtesy of the Estate of Ruth Asawa.

"Aiko and Xavier are doing well . . . " Ruth Asawa, letter to Mr. and Mrs. W. H. Lanier, Dec. 1, 1950, courtesy the Estate of Ruth Asawa.

"We are beginning to wonder . . . " Ruth Asawa, ibid.

"Aiko's Red/Xavier's Green . . . " Ruth Asawa, Christmas card to Mr. and Mrs. W. H. Lanier and Helen, December 22, 1950, courtesy of the Estate of Ruth Asawa.

"Because he wants to ____ with her . . . " Ruth Asawa Papers, M1585: Box 6, Folder 7. "How Albert Met Imogen." Department of Special Collections, Stanford University Libraries. Note: the blank suggesting having sex isn't the author's self-censorship. It is the way the story is recounted in Ruth's records. According to her daughter Addie, Ruth declared, "Swearing shows a lack of imagination." Albert, for his part, never used "the F-word" in front of his kids, his strongest language being, "Damn it!" or "God Almighty knows," according to Aiko Cuneo, e-mails to the author April 23, 2019.

Brats . . . Ruth Asawa Papers, M1585: Box 6, Folder 1. Department of Special Collections, Stanford University Libraries.

" . . . I consider her as a most gifted art student . . . " Josef Albers, letter to Harry B. Green, San Francisco State College, October 24, 1951, Ruth Asawa Papers, M1585: Box 175, Folder 12. Department of Special Collections, Stanford University Libraries. © The Josef and Anni Albers Foundation.

"Insomnia is nothing more than a fear of losing time . . . " Ruth Asawa, letter to Albert Lanier, postmarked December 16, 1948, as quoted by Mary Emma Harris, "Black Mountain College," *The Sculpture of Ruth Asawa: Contours in the Air*, Daniell Cornell, ed., Fine Arts Museums of San Francisco (Berkeley and Los Angeles: University of California Press, 2006), 52.

"Is Ruth like you? . . . " Interview with Nancy Kimiko Asawa Devadas by Aiko Cuneo, January 31, 2017, courtesy of Aiko Cuneo and the Estate of Ruth Asawa.

"Aiko got into the paint . . . " Albert Lanier, letter to Mr. and Mrs. W. H. Lanier, February 12, 1952, courtesy of the Estate of Ruth Asawa.

"[L]eggerezza aerea," "tre bambini." Domus, July–August 1952, 34–35; Ruth Asawa Papers, M1585: Box 243, Folder 3. Department of Special Collections, Stanford University Libraries.

Preserving dogwoods . . . Mary Emma Harris, private email communication with the author, July 20, 2020.

Xavier's first recollection . . . Interview with Xavier Lanier by the author, August 2, 2017.

"[Ruth's] baskets are selling fairly well . . . " Albert Lanier, letter to Mr. and Mrs. W. H. Lanier, Sept. 27, 1952, courtesy of the Estate of Ruth Asawa.

"Miss Asawa's sculpture is perhaps the most remarkable . . . " "Some Roses and Some Barbs," Alfred Frankenstein, *San Francisco Chronicle,* April 11, 1954, Ruth Asawa Papers, M1585: Box 215, Folder 5. Department of Special Collections, Stanford University Libraries.

"We have no money." Albert Lanier, letter to Robert (Bob) Abell, Ruth Asawa Papers, M1585: Box 17, Folder 2. Department of Special Collections, Stanford University Libraries.

"Noguchi, 50, has long been recognized . . . " "Eastern Yeast," *Time* magazine, January 10, 1955, Ruth Asawa Papers, M1585: Box 243, Folder 4. Department of Special Collections, Stanford University Libraries.

Critics and juries still wrestled . . . Aiko Lanier Cuneo, note of April 7, 2005, from 1956 press clippings, Ruth Asawa Papers, M1585: Box 243, Folder 7. Department of Special Collections, Stanford University Libraries.

"Please do me a favor . . . " Ruth Asawa, letter to John Rawlings, November 11, 1954, Ruth Asawa Papers, M1585: Box 100, Folder 11. Department of Special Collections, Stanford University Libraries.

"[N]ews of another baby . . ." Ruth Asawa, letter to Louis Pollack, June 26, 1956, Ruth Asawa Papers, M1585: Box 101, Folder 1. Department of Special Collections, Stanford University Libraries.

Her new arrival, the infant son of a Japanese mother and Caucasian father . . . Aiko Cuneo, private communication with the author, November 28, 2018.

"He is 7 weeks old and a joy . . ." Ruth Asawa, letter to Elen (sic) and Hank, August 6, 1956, Ruth Asawa Papers, M1585: Box 101, Folder 3. Department of Special Collections, Stanford University Libraries.

"Ruth Asawa's sculptures . . ." "Displays at the Peridot," *New York Times*, March 14, 1956, Ruth Asawa Papers, M1585: Box 243, Folder 7. Department of Special Collections, Stanford University Libraries.

"Ruth Asawa's huge abstractions . . ." Alfred Frankenstein, *San Francisco Chronicle*, April 8, 1956, Ruth Asawa Papers, M1585: Box 243, Folder 7. Department of Special Collections, Stanford University Libraries.

Juries selecting pieces for art exhibitions . . . In a note Asawa appended to her 1956 reviews, Asawa's daughter Aiko Cuneo wrote: "The jury argued about whether Ruth's work was sculpture or not—Because it wasn't on a pedestal and didn't move in the air like a Calder—It moved on a single axis."

"The eye is actually dazzled . . ." *Arts*, April 1956, Ruth Asawa Papers, M1585: Box 243, Folder 7. Department of Special Collections, Stanford University Libraries.

"I've been meaning to tell you . . ." Louis Pollack, letter to Ruth Asawa, April 17, 1956, Ruth Asawa Papers, M1585: Box 101, Folder 1. Department of Special Collections, Stanford University Libraries.

"How nice to hear about Claude . . ." Ruth Asawa, letter to Louis Pollack, May 3, 1956, Ruth Asawa Papers, M1585: Box 101, Folder 1. Department of Special Collections, Stanford University Libraries.

A financial statement from her Spring 1956 . . . Peridot statement to Ruth Asawa, May 7, 1956, Ruth Asawa Papers, M1585: Box 101, Folder 1. Department of Special Collections, Stanford University Libraries.

"I apologize for the slow reply. I've been sick . . . " Ruth Asawa, letter to Lou Pollack, January 8, 1958, Ruth Asawa Papers, M1585: Box 101, Folder 7. Department of Special Collections, Stanford University Libraries.

"[T]oo busy to consider whether we are happy or not . . . " Ruth Asawa, letter to Laverne Originals, October 28, 1958, Ruth Asawa Papers: M1585: Box 101, Folder 6. Department of Special Collections, Stanford University Libraries.

"Dear Lou, the $500 is certainly encouraging . . . " Ruth Asawa, letter to Louis Pollock, November 26, 1958, Ruth Asawa Papers, M1585: Box 101, Folder 7. Department of Special Collections, Stanford University Libraries.

"Holidays and inertia . . . " John Hohnsbeen, letter to Ruth Asawa, January 2, 1959, Ruth Asawa Papers, M1585: Box 101, Folder 7. Department of Special Collections, Stanford University Libraries.

"Is that possible . . . ?" Ruth Asawa, letter to John Hohnsbeen, April 6, 1959, Ruth Asawa Papers, M1585: Box 101, Folder 7. Department of Special Collections, Stanford University Libraries.

"You should do an article on my photographer and friend, Imogen Cunningham . . . " Ruth Asawa, letter to Bernice S. Decker, February 26, 1959, Ruth Asawa Papers, M1585: Box 127, Folder 1. Department of Special Collections, Stanford University Libraries.

"I'm pregnant again . . . " Ruth Asawa, letter to John Hohnsbeen, May 13, 1959, Ruth Asawa Papers, M1585: Box 101, Folder 7. Department of Special Collections, Stanford University Libraries.

"Pore thang . . . He's gonna get 'er!" Interview with architect William "Bill" Bondy by the author, May 31, 2017.

Chapter 7: A Workshop in Noe Valley

"[A] rustic cabin . . . a gold miner's cabin, rustic . . . high ceilings, wood interior, with sculptures . . . it's magic." Interview with Harry S. Parker III by the author, January 4, 2017.

"The idea was to show us what work was." Interview with Xavier Lanier by the author, August 2, 2017.

"OK, we're not going to throw apples at the pigs" . . . *"Adam? Adam? ADAM??"* The story of the pig-pelting incident and leaving Adam in the apple orchard comes from a consensus of family sources, including interviews by the author with Hudson Lanier, March 9, 2018, and with Aiko Cuneo, February 2, 2019.

They would celebrate with a waltz . . . Interview with Paul Lanier and Aiko Cuneo by the author, November 1, 2017.

"We kept finding them for years after." Hoefer, *The Sculpture of Ruth Asawa: Contours in the Air*, 20.

He paid Hudson and Xavier $1.25 a weekend . . . Interview with Hudson Lanier by the author, March 9, 2018.

"Junk stores." Aiko Cuneo, private communication with the author, February 9, 2019.

"Ruth is a feeder." Interview with Susan Stauter by the author, March 9, 2017.

125 guests would come . . . Interview with Aiko Cuneo by the author, November 1, 2017.

"Albert had incredible space sensibilities." Interview with Bill Bondy by the author, May 31, 2017.

Lighted juke box or neon cocktail glass . . . Albert Lanier, letter to the editor of the *San Francisco Chronicle*, 1957, Ruth Asawa Papers, M1585: Box 163, Folder 2. Department of Special Collections, Stanford University Libraries.

Albert's design sense would get him invited . . . William Albert Lanier obituary, accessed September 11, 2018, https://www.legacy.com/obituaries/sfgate/obituary.aspx?n=william-albert-lanier&pid=119893038.

"We are moving to a bigger house so that could get all of our children in." Ruth Asawa, letter to Louis Pollock, February 4, 1961, Ruth Asawa Papers, M1585: Box 101, Folder 11. Department of Special Collections, Stanford University Libraries.

"Please, Mom, can't we have a normal American door . . . *"* Hudson Lanier, quoted in Hoefer, *The Sculpture of Ruth Asawa: Contours in the Air*, 21.

"As a child, I wanted to be called Linda or Kathy . . . *"* Aiko Cuneo, speech to National Japanese American Historical Society Film Series, March 10, 2018, and private communication with the author, February 9, 2019.

"Bucky used to visit us . . . *"* Interview with Hudson Lanier by the author, March 19, 2018.

"I thought the guy was really out there . . . *"* Interview with Xavier Lanier by the author, August 2, 2017.

"I am touched by Mr. Albers's generous offer." Ruth Asawa, letter to Sidney Janis Gallery, February 28, 1957, Ruth Asawa Papers, M1585: Box 1, Folder 3. Department of Special Collections, Stanford University Libraries.

"Dear Ruthie, This is just for revenge . . ." Josef Albers, note on wrapping paper to Ruth Asawa, undated, Ruth Asawa Papers, M1585: Box 1, Folder 1. Department of Special Collections, Stanford University Libraries. © The Josef and Anni Albers Foundation.

"Dear Ruthie, Sometime ~~I want~~ I hope to exchange . . ." Josef Albers, note to Ruth Asawa, undated, Ruth Asawa Papers, M1585: Box 1, Folder 1. Department of Special Collections, Stanford University Libraries. © The Josef and Anni Albers Foundation.

"Dear Mr. & Mrs. Albers: This painting is magical . . ." Ruth Asawa, letter to Josef Albers, January 5, 1965, Ruth Asawa Papers, M1585: Box 1, Folder 5. Department of Special Collections, Stanford University Libraries.

"At our return from abroad," . . . "Dear Ruthie, I am so pleased . . ." Anni and Josef Albers, letter to Ruth Asawa, January 23, 1960, Ruth Asawa Papers, M1585: Box 101, Folder 9. Department of Special Collections, Stanford University Libraries. © The Josef and Anni Albers Foundation.

"Returned Carbondale last week . . ." Anne and Buckminster Fuller, telegram to Ruth Asawa, October 15, 1961, Ruth Asawa Papers, M1585: Box 3, Folder 3. Department of Special Collections, Stanford University Libraries.

"[T]he fact remains . . ." Louis Pollock, letter to Ruth Asawa, April 18, 1961, Ruth Asawa Papers, M1585: Box 101, Folder 111. Department of Special Collections, Stanford University Libraries.

"I think that's what Albers was saying . . ." Interview #189 with Ruth Asawa by Mary Emma Harris, February 17, 1998, Black Mountain College Project, Inc., New York, 21–22. Quoted with permission. Ruth Asawa Papers, M1585: Box 35, Folder 8. Department of Special Collections, Stanford University Libraries.

"Overwhelmed . . ." Louis Pollock, letter to Ruth Asawa, March 20, 1962, Ruth Asawa Papers, M1585: Box 101, Folder 13. Department of Special Collections, Stanford University Libraries.

"Breathing elegantly." Lorna Blaine Halper, letter to Ruth Asawa, postmarked May 5, 1962, Ruth Asawa Papers, M1585: Box 101, Folder 15. Department of Special Collections, Stanford University Libraries.

"I decided that I wasn't interested in sending things to New York . . ." Interviews with Ruth Asawa by Harriet Nathan, 1974-1976, Oral History Center, Bancroft Library, University of California, Berkeley, c. 1980, 129.

"Ruth Asawa's webs of wonder . . ." Miriam Dungan Cross, undated excerpt, Ruth Asawa Papers, M1585: Box 99, Folder Portfolio. Department of Special Collections, Stanford University Libraries.

"Miss Asawa possesses one of the most original and unprecedented styles . . ." Alfred Frankenstein, *San Francisco Chronicle,* 1960 review of de Young Museum show, reprinted in exhibition announcements from de Young, San Francisco Museum of Art, Rental gallery, Ruth Asawa Papers, M1585: Box 110, Folder 5. Department of Special Collections, Stanford University Libraries.

"Oriental . . ." Alfred Frankenstein, Art review, *San Francisco Chronicle,* August 18, 1963. Ruth Asawa Papers, M1585: Box 99, Folder Portfolio. Department of Special Collections, Stanford University Libraries.

"[T]he dented can store . . . we always ate well." Xavier Lanier, interview with the author, Aug. 2, 2017.

"You know how, in the winter, how the water hangs loose on pine needles . . ." Interviews with Ruth Asawa by Harriet Nathan, 1974-1976, Oral History Center, Bancroft Library, University of California, Berkeley, c. 1980, 132. Ruth Asawa Papers, M1585: Box 127, Folder 4, Department of Special Collections, Stanford Libraries.

"I made a presentation and was so enthralled with Ruth's work . . ." Interview with Geré Kavanaugh by the author, May 22, 2017.

"They said, 'You've gone commercial.' . . . They were jealous." Interview with Geré Kavanaugh by the author, May 22, 2017.

In 1962, she was audited . . . Ruth Asawa Papers, M1585: Box 101, Folder 15. Department of Special Collections, Stanford University Libraries.

"I've been very busy with our new house." Ruth Asawa, letter to Lou Pollack, March 20, 1962, Ruth Asawa Papers, M1585: Box 101, Folder 13. Department of Special Collections, Stanford University Libraries.

"[S]mall, feminine, bland and decorative." Imogen Cunningham, partial clip of 1962 review, Ruth Asawa Papers, M1585: Box 243, Folder 13. Department of Special Collections, Stanford University Libraries.

"Her gently turning shapes . . ." Henry J. Seldis, *Los Angeles Times,* April 20, 1962, Ruth Asawa Papers, M1585: Box 243, Folder 13. Department of Special Collections, Stanford University Libraries.

"[S]urely among the most original and satisfying new sculpture . . ." Gerald Nordland, *Art Forum,* June 1962, Ruth Asawa Papers, M1585: Box 243, Folder 13. Department of Special Collections, Stanford University Libraries.

"[E]nchanted with your sculptures . . ." "the most beautiful doors he has seen anywhere in the world." Joan Ankrum, Letter to Ruth Asawa and Albert Lanier, May 4, 1962, Ruth Asawa Papers, M1585: Box 101, Folder 14. Department of Special Collections, Stanford University Libraries.

"We were always excited to go to the farm and ride the tractor . . ." "The Japanese ones couldn't speak English. My grandfather had a pipe. We always remember the smell of his pipe. He smiled a lot. Without words." Interview with Xavier Lanier by the author, August 2, 2017, and e-mail communication, December 11, 2018.

"We did laundry, changing diapers . . ." "She was teaching us all the time . . ." Interview with Xavier Lanier by the author, August 2, 2017.

"I remember people calling her Jap" . . . "Don't you even say that!" Interview with Xavier Lanier by the author. August 2, 2017.

"If we hurt someone's feelings . . ." Interview with Aiko Cuneo by the author, November 1, 2017.

David Rockefeller acquired an Asawa . . . E. C. Bassett, letter to Ruth Asawa, January 27, 1961, Ruth Asawa Papers, M1585: Box 101, Folder 12. Department of Special Collections, Stanford University Libraries.

"Dearest Asawa, It was awfully kind of you to send me the excellent photos . . ." Josef Albers, letter to Ruth Asawa, June 20, 1969, Ruth Asawa Papers, M1585: Box 1, Folder 5. Department of Special Collections, Stanford University Libraries. © The Josef and Anni Albers Foundation.

"Dear Ruthie, Yes of course I should be glad to recommend you . . ." Josef Albers, letter to Ruth Asawa, September 4, 1971, Ruth Asawa Papers, M1585: Box 1, Folder 6. Department of Special Collections, Stanford University Libraries. © The Josef and Anni Albers Foundation.

Asawa's quest for Guggenheim support . . . disappointment only made her work harder. Aiko Cuneo, private communication with author, August 17, 2018.

"Dear Ruth, I sense the symptoms of long distance maternal concern," Sally Woodbridge, letter to Ruth Asawa, September 18, 1965, Ruth Asawa Papers, M1585: Box 30, Folder 3. Department of Special Collections, Stanford University Libraries.

"To this day, I feel guilty . . . " Interview with Nancy Kimiko Asawa Devadas by Aiko Cuneo, April 13, 2015, courtesy of the Estate of Ruth Asawa.

"It was a joy to have you . . . [A] love affair between Tamarind and Asawa. " June Wayne, letter to Ruth Asawa, November 10, 1965, Tamarind Institute Records, Collection 574: Box 3, Folder 48. Courtesy of the Center for Southwest Research and Special Collections, University Libraries, University of New Mexico.

"Anything she touches . . . " June Wayne, "Confidential Report on Candidate for Fellowship," Simon Guggenheim Memorial Foundation, December 1, 1971, Tamarind Institute Records, Collection 574: Box 3, Folder 48. Courtesy of the Center for Southwest Research and Special Collections, University Libraries, University of New Mexico.

Chapter 8: Gamble with the Young

"Taught Adam to iron; drew daffodils." Ruth Asawa Papers, M1585: Box 179, Folder 2. Department of Special Collections, Stanford University Libraries.

". . . [T]here was such confusion of children coming and going . . . " Ruth Asawa, letter to Marilyn Fischbach, February 16, 1965, Ruth Asawa Papers, M1585: Box 102. Department of Special Collections, Stanford University Libraries.

"Her chicken, her roast pork . . . " Interview with Hudson Lanier by the author, March 9, 2018.

One weekend morning, Addie confused plaster of Paris for flour . . . Addie Lanier, private communication with the author, February 2, 2019.

"Beneficial chaos . . . " Interview with Sally Woodbridge by the author, March 1, 2017.

4 cups flour . . . Recipe for baker's clay, accessed August 28, 2018, https://www.ruthasawa.com/resources/bakers-clay-recipe.

"I remember Ruth saying . . . " Interview with Kathleen LaRusso by the author, July 10, 2017.

"She was a quiet mover . . ." Interview with Judy Burns by the author, July 10, 2017.

"His alternative service will benefit many." "I hope my country can accept his offer . . ." Ruth Asawa and Albert Lanier, letters to Local Draft Board Number 40, 1971–1972, Ruth Asawa Papers, M1585: Box 30, Folder 6. Department of Special Collections, Stanford University Libraries.

"Ruth had a lot of energy . . . You couldn't say no to her." Interview with Andrea Jepson by the author, February 28, 2017.

"[A] minority of one." Ruth Asawa Papers, M1585: Box 127, Folder 5. San Francisco Art Institute, First Multi-Cultural Symposium, c. 1988. Department of Special Collections, Stanford University Libraries.

"Teachers have a lot to do and we were on some level disruptive . . ." Interview with Andrea Jepson by the author, February 28, 2017.

"Dear Mrs. Maillard, Thank you for inviting me to your quake party . . ." Ruth Asawa, letter to Charlotte Maillard, April 25, 1969, Ruth Asawa Papers, M1585: Box 30, Folder 5. Department of Special Collections, Stanford University Libraries.

"My dear Mrs. Asawa . . ." Charlotte Maillard, letter to Ruth Asawa, April 23, 1969, Ruth Asawa Papers, M1585: Box 30, Folder 5. Department of Special Collections, Stanford University Libraries.

"She drew all through the meetings . . ." Interview with Andrea Jepson by the author, February 28, 2017.

"What has been accomplished is nothing short of a miracle, more so, since your allotment for art is only 2½ cents per day . . ." Ruth Asawa, letter to E. D. Goldman, February 6, 1970, Ruth Asawa Papers, M1585: Box 134, Folder 5. Department of Special Collections, Stanford University Libraries.

"Dear Ruth, . . . [T]hirty-five thou. WOW!" Jack Whisman, note to Ruth Asawa, September 28, year undated (c. 1972–1973), Ruth Asawa Papers, M1585: Box 134, Folder 9. Department of Special Collections, Stanford University Libraries.

"She opened the door behind the kitchen . . ." Interviews with Joan Abrahamson by the author, April 12 and July 14, 2017.

"How do you deal with six kids?" Interviews with Joan Abrahamson by the author, April 12 and July 14, 2017.

"Often those things didn't work." Interview with Andrea Jepson by the author, August 28, 2018.

"He was hard of hearing so we were yelling at him." Interview with Andrea Jepson by the author, August 28, 2018.

". . . I got those sad old weary blues . . ." Ruth Asawa Papers, M1585: Box 136, Folder 6. Department of Special Collections, Stanford University Libraries.

"And as every class came out, they'd claim: 'There's mine!'" Interview with Jacques d'Amboise by the author, April 5, 2017.

"She listened . . . you felt acknowledged." Interview with Kathleen LaRusso by the author, July 10, 2017.

"Buy bulbs . . ." Interview with Sharon Savage (formerly Litzky) by the author, July 10, 2017.

In 1969, a black father named David Johnson sued . . . Heather Knight, "The Resegregation of San Francisco Public Schools," *San Francisco Chronicle,* May 18, 2015, accessed December 11, 2018, https://www.kqed.org/news/10527348/is-desegregation-dead.

By 1971, a federal court ordered the city to bus students . . . "Is Desegregation Dead?," accessed September 28, 2018, https://www.sfchronicle.com/schools-desegregation.

In a letter to the editor, she would later charge busing failed . . . Letters to the editor, *San Francisco Examiner,* December 25, 1991, Ruth Asawa Papers, M1585: Box 248, Folder 5. Department of Special Collections, Stanford University Libraries.

"Kids loved to sing . . ." Interview with Kathleen LaRusso by the author, July 10, 2017.

"Somehow we got started planting flowers . . . We planted two thousand daffodil bulbs . . ." Interview with Kathleen LaRusso by the author, July 10, 2017.

"The first thing I noticed, she was never without a pad . . ." Interview with Peter Coyote by the author, January 12, 2017.

"[T]he only sober man in the neighborhood . . ." "Tommy's Gift—a Five-Finger Exercise," Mildred Hamilton, *San Francisco Examiner,* November 16, 1976. Ruth Asawa Papers, M1585: Box 28, Folder 1. Department of Special Collections, Stanford University Libraries.

Ruth Asawa—the little giant towers a million miles . . . Tommy Roberts, "Thoughts After Your Exhibition," September 22, 1976, Ruth Asawa Papers, M1585: Box 28, Folder 1. Department of Special Collections, Stanford University Libraries.

"We had an orange truck called Maude." Interview with Anne-Marie Theilen by the author, March 17, 2017.

"Nice day but extremely windy . . . But we persevere . . . " Nancy Thompson's journal, *The Alvarado Experience,* Andrea I. Jepson and Sharon S. Litzky (San Francisco: Alvarado School Workshop, 1978), 34–36.

"[O]ne of the most vital and successful programs." Remarks of the Hon. John Brademas of Indiana in the House of Representatives, November 19, 1974, Congressional Record, Ruth Asawa Papers, M1585: Box 98, Folder 2. Department of Special Collections, Stanford University Libraries.

"San Francisco with the arts is building a city of gold." John Hoare Kerr, National Endowment for the Arts, "Profile: The Alvarado Arts Workshop," May 1975, Ruth Asawa Papers, M1585: Box 136, Folder 1. Department of Special Collections, Stanford University Libraries.

"Ribs in the oven. Spaghetti on the stove . . . " Ruth Asawa Papers, M1585: Box 182, Folder 2. Department of Special Collections, Stanford University Libraries.

Chapter 9: The Fountain Lady

The meeting of with Ruth and Albert with shipping heir William Matson Roth was recounted in an interview with Ruth Asawa by Aiko Cuneo, in memo to Alison Isenberg, August 19, 2005, Ruth Asawa Papers, M1585: Box 117, Folder 6. Department of Special Collections, Stanford University Libraries. (In a note by Isenberg, Aiko added Ruth was not the San Francisco artist wearing Marimekko because "it was too pricey.")

"The most cited success story of the 1960s was Ghirardelli Square . . . " Alison Isenberg, *Downtown America: A History of the Place and the People Who Made It* (Chicago: University of Chicago Press, 2004), 283. Ruth Asawa Papers, M1585: Box 117, Folder 6. Department of Special Collections, Stanford University Libraries.

When Roth Properties opened talks . . . Warren Lemmon, memo to W. M. Roth, September 21, 1965, Ruth Asawa Papers, M1585: Box 117, Folder 4. Department of Special Collections, Stanford University Libraries.

"I wasn't up for that . . . " "The baby would cry . . . skin like Marie Antoinette." Interview with Andrea Jepson by the author, February 28, 2017.

"Ruth what are people saying . . . " Interview with Andrea Jepson by the author, February 28, 2017.

"[Y]ou should go ahead and have the lady cast, and if it didn't work out it might end up in my bathtub." William M. Roth, letter to Ruth Asawa, July 31, 1967, Ruth Asawa Papers, M1585: Box 117, Folder 4. Department of Special Collections, Stanford University Libraries.

"[C]ute and Disneyesque," . . . "camp." Lawrence Halprin, letters to William Matson Roth, February 10 and November 27, 1967, Ruth Asawa Papers, M1585: Box 117, Folder 4. Department of Special Collections, Stanford University Libraries.

"We are violently opposed to it!" Lawrence Halprin on the new sculpture in the fountain at Ghirardelli Square, Ruth Asawa Papers, M1585: Box 131, Folder 5. Department of Special Collections, Stanford University Libraries.

"Something everybody can enjoy . . . " "Fuss Over Mermaid in City Fountain Grows," *San Francisco Examiner,* March 26, 1968, Ruth Asawa Papers, M1585: Box 117, Folder 7. Department of Special Collections, Stanford University Libraries.

"For the old it would bring back the fantasy . . . " Andrea fountain, National Registry of Historic Places Inventory Nomination, 21, January 1982, courtesy of the Estate of Ruth Asawa.

"Ruth Asawa, you messed it . . . " W. Merle Weidman, letter to Ruth Asawa, March 27, 1968, Ruth Asawa Papers, M1585: Box 117, Folder 5. Department of Special Collections, Stanford University Libraries.

"Hope you retain Ruth Asawa's charming fountain . . . " D. Douglas, letter to W. M. Roth, March 29, 1968, Ruth Asawa Papers, M1585: Box 117, Folder 5. Department of Special Collections, Stanford University Libraries.

"May I suggest . . . " Jean Fahey Crother, letter to Ruth Asawa, March 26, 1968, Ruth Asawa Papers, M1585: Folder 117, Box 5. Department of Special Collections, Stanford University Libraries.

"Dear Bill, This is to clear myself . . . " Ruth Asawa, letter to William Matson Roth, March 28, 1968, Ruth Asawa Papers, M1585: Folder 117, Box 5. Department of Special Collections, Stanford University Libraries.

"I don't agree with Mr. Halprin . . . I think that Miss Asawa's work is in complete harmony . . . " "Art Row Spreads: Ghirardelli Mermaid Praised by Alioto," *San Francisco Examiner,* April 8,

1968, Ruth Asawa Papers, M1585: Box 117, Folder 7. Department of Special Collections, Stanford University Libraries.

"Friends said to me, 'This is child's play…'" "Ruth Asawa: Fountainhead," *San Francisco Examiner and Chronicle,* May 9, 1971, Ruth Asawa Papers, M1585: Box 118, Folder 6. Department of Special Collections, Stanford University Libraries.

"Mr. Pritzker agreed to gamble on Chuck's crazy idea." Ruth Asawa, dedication notes, Hyatt Union Square Fountain, February 14, 1973, Ruth Asawa Papers, M1585: Box 118, Folder 1. Department of Special Collections, Stanford University Libraries.

"[F]or the gods…" Hannah Koler, letter to Ruth Asawa, June 24, 1971, Ruth Asawa Papers, M1585: Box 30, Folder 6. Department of Special Collections, Stanford University Libraries.

It was a logistical challenge to take a technique originally designed for school crafts… Sally B. Woodbridge, Ruth Asawa, Laurence Cuneo, "Ruth Asawa's San Francisco Fountain," 1973.

Hyatt Hotels President Donald Pritzker died suddenly of a heart attack… "Hyatt Chief: Donald Pritzker Is Dead at 39," *San Francisco Chronicle,* May 8, 1972.

"It has the shiniest snout in Italy…" Herman Mueller Associates, undated press release for Hyatt Corporation, Ruth Asawa Papers, M1585: Box 118, Folder 6. Department of Special Collections, Stanford University Libraries.

Ruth ended up offering to pay thousands of dollars out of pocket… The financial aspects of the Hyatt Union Square Fountain are documented in the Ruth Asawa Papers, M1585: Box 118, Folders 1–5. Department of Special Collections, Stanford University Libraries.

"The artist always pays for the privilege of doing it." Interviews with Ruth Asawa by Harriet Nathan, 1974–1976, Oral History Center, Bancroft Library, University of California, Berkeley, c. 1980, 137.

"Mom always lost her shirt…" Interview with Aiko Cuneo and Addie Laurie Lanier by the author, February 23, 2017.

"My best wishes to you all for the holidays." Josef Albers, letter to Ruth Asawa, March 28, 1975, Ruth Asawa Papers. M1585: Box 1, Folder 6. Department of Special Collections, Stanford University Libraries. © The Josef and Anni Albers Foundation.

"Just putting colors together…" "Josef Albers, Artist and Teacher, Dies," *New York Times,* March 26, 1976, accessed on July 16, 2019, https://www.nytimes.com.

The image was so beautiful, she wrote Albers's widow, she couldn't bear to use the stamps . . . Ruth Asawa, letter to Anni Albers, March 17, 1990, Ruth Asawa Papers, M1585: Box 2, Folder 1. Department of Special Collections, Stanford University Libraries.

. . . I remember Imogen most for being able to turn frugality . . . Ruth Asawa, Statements 1990–1993, Ruth Asawa Papers, M1585: Box 127, Folder 6. Department of Special Collections, Stanford University Libraries.

In cherry blossom season . . . Ruth Asawa, letter to Dianne Feinstein, February 14, 1974, Ruth Asawa Papers, M1585: Box 118, Folders 8 and 9. Department of Special Collections, Stanford University Libraries. Asawa worked with Raymond H. Clary, Golden Gate Park historian, and the John McLaren Society and others in this effort.

Architect and planner Rai Okamoto asked Ruth Asawa to submit a design . . . Asawa's undated notes on Nihonmachi (Japantown) Origami sculpture, Ruth Asawa Papers, M1585: Box 119, Folder 1. Department of Special Collections, Stanford University Libraries.

Over the years of drought . . . The Japantown fountain rehabilitation issues are detailed by Fran Johns, "Japantown Fountains in Limbo," accessed August 24, 2018, https://newfillmore.com/2016/09/30/japantown-fountains-in-limbo.

"My reason for leaving . . . *"* Ruth Asawa, letter to Harold Zellerbach, December 2, 1975, Ruth Asawa Papers, M1585: Box 87, Folder 3. Department of Special Collections, Stanford University Libraries.

". . . *I had her and Peter Coyote to my house* . . . *"* Gary Snyder, letter to the author, March 7, 2017.

"The Axe Handle pencil drawing you gave me is a treasure!" Gary Snyder, letter to Ruth Asawa, undated (noted by recipient received on January 11, 1994), Ruth Asawa Papers, M1585: Box 29, Folder 7. Department of Special Collections, Stanford University Libraries.

She couldn't bear to use them . . . Ruth Asawa, letter to Anni Albers, March 17, 1990, Ruth Asawa Papers, M1585: Box 2, Folder 1. Department of Special Collections, Stanford University Libraries.

In September 1982, San Francisco's School of the Arts welcomed . . . The history of the Ruth Asawa San Francisco School of the Arts requires a separate book; it is impossible to chronicle within the bounds of this biography. Documents occupy fifteen boxes in the Ruth Asawa Papers, M1585, Boxes 138–152. Department of Special Collections, Stanford University Libraries.

Chapter 10: The Wolf at the Door

Ruth and Albert's thirty-fourth anniversary . . . The journal of their European trip is found in Ruth Asawa Papers, M1585: Box 127, Folder 5. Department of Special Collections, Stanford University Libraries.

"We arrived home on July 4th . . . *"* Ruth Asawa Papers M1585: Box 186, Folder 1. Department of Special Collections, Stanford University Libraries.

The Santa Rosa Courthouse Square Fountain history, design, and sculptor selection process is documented in the *Santa Rosa Press-Democrat,* including the columns of Gaye LeBaron, 1984–1987, Ruth Asawa Papers, M1585: Boxes 247 and 248; in letters and contracts in Boxes 121 and 209; and in notebooks in Box 187. Department of Special Collections, Stanford University Libraries.

"She's better than Grandma Moses." "New hotel's mural gets ceremonial unveiling," *San Francisco Examiner,* October 5, 1984, Ruth Asawa Papers, M1585, Box 247, Folder 3. Department of Special Collections, Stanford University Libraries.

"Darling Ruth, Am deeply concerned over your allergy . . . *"* Buckminster Fuller, letter to Ruth Asawa, May 30, 1982, Ruth Asawa Papers. M1585: Box 4, Folder 1. Department of Special Collections, Stanford University Libraries.

"I know she's squeezing my hand . . . *"* Allegra Fuller Snyder, "Notes on Anne and Bucky Fuller's Deaths," Buckminster Fuller Institute. Accessed September 21, 2018, https://www.bfi.org/about-fuller/biography/notes-anne-and-bucky-fullers-deaths.

Ruth's specific diagnosis was systemic lupus erythematosus (SLE), or lupus . . . Ruth Asawa Papers, M1585: Box 187, Folder 1, Notebooks & Planners. Department of Special Collections, Stanford University Libraries.

The condition affects women more than men . . . Lupus Detailed Fact Sheet, U.S. Centers for Disease Control and Prevention, accessed August 27, 2018, https://www.cdc.gov/lupus/facts/detailed.html.

Acute acetone poisoning . . . National Library of Medicine Toxicology Data Network, accessed August 27, 2018, https://toxnet.nlm.nih.gov/cgi-bin/sis/search/a?dbs+hsdb:@term+@DOCNO+41.

"Most of us were not surprised . . . *"* Interview with Andrea Jepson by the author, February 28, 2017.

"2/20/85 Beautiful spring day. 1st pill . . . *"* Ruth Asawa Papers, M1585: Box 187, Folder 1. Department of Special Collections, Stanford University Libraries.

"Their visit today is subconsciously gearing me up . . . " Ruth Asawa Papers, M1585: Box 187, Folder 1. Department of Special Collections, Stanford University Libraries.

"Still not steady on my feet . . . " Ruth Asawa Papers, M1585: Box 187, Folder 1. Department of Special Collections, Stanford University Libraries.

Ruth focused on O'Connor's spirit, which seemed to grow stronger through repeated hospitalizations . . . The Habit of Being: Letters of Flannery O'Connor, Sally Fitzgerald, ed. (New York: Farrar, Straus and Giroux, 1979).

"I probably didn't really realize . . . " Interview with Xavier Lanier by the author, August 2, 2017.

Now the Rockefeller family called to offer help with her illness. Ruth Asawa Papers, M1585: Box 187, Folder 1. Department of Special Collections, Stanford University Libraries.

"This may not be an illness. It may be another dialogue with myself . . . " Ruth Asawa Papers, M1585: Box 187, Folder 1. Department of Special Collections, Stanford University Libraries.

"'Cortisone makes you think night and day . . . '" Ruth Asawa Papers, M1585: Box 187, Folder 1. Department of Special Collections, Stanford University Libraries.

"Need cane . . . " Ruth Asawa Papers, M1585: Box 187, Folder 1. Department of Special Collections, Stanford University Libraries.

"[A] rotating dream that looked like a film dissolve." Ruth Asawa Papers, M1585: Box 187, Folder 1. Department of Special Collections, Stanford University Libraries.

"Trying fantasy . . . don't like it." Ruth Asawa Papers, M1585: Box 127, Folder 5. Department of Special Collections, Stanford University Libraries.

Some day I'm going to write a book . . . Ruth Asawa Papers, M1585: Box 127, Folder 5. Department of Special Collections, Stanford University Libraries.

Sounds exotic, mysterious . . . Ruth Asawa Papers, M1585: Box 127, Folder 5. Department of Special Collections, Stanford University Libraries.

"Raising children: More 'Yeses' than 'Nos'. . . " Ruth Asawa Papers, M1585: Box 127, Folder 5. Department of Special Collections, Stanford University Libraries.

The Valley Girls, her colleagues from Alvarado Arts, gathered at each other's houses and held free-form prayer meetings . . . , interview with Judy Burns by the author, July 10, 2017.

"Dear Bill, How are you? Me? Not so good . . ." Ruth Asawa, letter to William Matson Roth, Ruth Asawa Papers, M1585: Box 105, Folder 3. Department of Special Collections, Stanford University Libraries.

The sight of Asawa sketching had inspired him to resume his acting career . . . Interview with Peter Coyote by the author, January 12, 2017.

"I was very sorry . . ." Peter Coyote, letter to Ruth Asawa, August 26, 1985, Ruth Asawa Papers, M1585: Box 177, Folder 1. Department of Special Collections, Stanford University Libraries.

"She was tiny but a force of nature." Interview with Douglas Grey, M.D., by the author, September 26, 2017.

"She was a sweetheart . . ." Interview with Douglas Grey, M.D., by the author, September 26, 2017.

"You outdid yourself . . ." Douglas Grey M.D., letters to Ruth Asawa, April 29 and May 16, 1985, Ruth Asawa Papers, M1585: Box 31, Folder 1. Department of Special Collections, Stanford University Libraries.

"Dear Ruthie, Even though I can't come to see you . . ." Terry Lanier, letter to Ruth Asawa, March 29, 1985, Ruth Asawa Papers, Lupus Letters, M1585: Box 175, Folder 19. Department of Special Collections, Stanford University Libraries.

"I was high as a kite . . . My God I can't leave yet . . ." Ruth Asawa, draft letter to Steve Burke, March 17, 1985, Ruth Asawa Papers, M1585: Box 187, Folder 2, and Box 121, Folder 4. Department of Special Collections, Stanford University Libraries.

Chapter 11: Woman Warrior

Asawa landed back in the hospital . . . Aiko Cuneo, e-mail communication to the author, October 5, 2017.

Asawa named Woman Warrior. . . Asian Week, October 11, 1985, Ruth Asawa Papers, M1585: Box 247, Folder 4. Department of Special Collections, Stanford University Libraries.

Father Alfred Boeddeker Park aimed to provide an oasis for children . . . Ruth Asawa Papers, M1585: Box 120, Folder 5. Department of Special Collections, Stanford University Libraries.

"[I]nteresting to me as an artist." ... *"I was too sick to smile."* Ruth Asawa, letter to Margaret Smetana, January 24, 1986, Ruth Asawa Papers, M1585: Box 165, Folder 2. Department of Special Collections, Stanford University Libraries.

... Ruth was now in remission. Interviews by the author during 2017 through 2019 with Asawa's Kaiser physicians and her daughter Aiko about the general course of her lupus.

Scenes of Japan ... Ruth Asawa, spiral notebook of autumn trip to Japan, October–November 1985, courtesy of the Estate of Ruth Asawa.

Ruth's determination to use the installation of Aurora to benefit her School of the Arts ... "Asawa's Tribute to the Goddess of the Dawn," Mildred Hamilton, *San Francisco Examiner,* January 2, 1986, Ruth Asawa Papers, M1585: Box 247, Folder 5. Department of Special Collections, Stanford University Libraries.

Aurora installation. San Francisco Progress, March 21, 1986, photo caption "Aurora by the Bay," Ruth Asawa Papers, M1585: Box 247, Folder 5. Department of Special Collections, Stanford University Libraries.

"Thank you for ordering good weather for the dedication." Ruth Asawa, letter to John Buss, March 28, 1986, Ruth Asawa Papers, M1585: Box 121, Folder 1. Department of Special Collections, Stanford University Libraries.

"If any of you want to become an artist ..." ... *"I want to make a swordfish."* ... *"And I want to make a sand shark."* "Planning a Fountain for Santa Rosa," Mildred Hamilton, *San Francisco Examiner,* March 1, 1986, Ruth Asawa Papers, M1585: Box 247, Folder 5. Department of Special Collections, Stanford University Libraries.

"Asawa in her typical populist manner ..." *News Herald,* Santa Rosa, California, January 13, 1987, Ruth Asawa Papers, M:1585: Box 248, Folder 1, Department of Special Collections, Stanford University Libraries.

"Event of the Year." San Francisco Examiner, May 2, 1986, and *Noe Valley Voice,* April 1986, Ruth Asawa Papers, M1585: Box 247, Folder 5.Department of Special Collections, Stanford University Libraries.

"She was original, really unique." Interview with Jacques d'Amboise by the author, April 5, 2017.

"Your Jacques." Jacques d'Amboise, letter to Ruth Asawa, Ruth Asawa Papers, M1585: Box 177, Folder 2. Department of Special Collections, Stanford University Libraries.

"In San Francisco, I have five fountains . . ." Ruth Asawa speech in support of legislation providing artists resale royalties, Ruth Asawa Papers, M1585: Box 168, Folder 4. Department of Special Collections, Stanford University Libraries.

In the end, however, Congress cut out the provision . . . "Resale Royalties, An Updated Analysis," U.S. Copyright Office, 2013, accessed October 9, 2017, https://www.copyright.gov/docs/resaleroyalty/usco-resaleroyalty.pdf.

In July 2018, a California appeals court ruled . . . "Should Artists Get Royalties If Their Work Is Resold? Europe Says Yes, US Says No," Daniel Grant, *Observer*, July 13, 2018, accessed September 13, 2018, https://observer.com/2018/07/california-court-ruling-kills-resale-royalties-for-artists-in-u-s.

The resisters . . . challenged the United States' imposition of curfews and the exclusion of Japanese Americans . . . Thanks for Brian Niiya, content editor of Densho Encyclopedia (https://densho.org), for clarifying distinctions between the resisters' specific challenges to government curfew and exclusion.

"Smoking gun . . ." Peter Irons, Interview II, Segment 12, 2000, Densho Encyclopedia, accessed September 24, 2018, http://encyclopedia.densho.org/coram_nobis_cases.

Convictions of all three men were vacated, rendered legally void . . . For detailed background on the resisters and their court cases, see Densho Encyclopedia (https://densho.org) and Richard Reeves, *Infamy: The Shocking Story of the Japanese American Internment in World War II* (New York: Henry Holt & Co., 2015), 93–97, 273–284.

"[R]ace prejudice, war hysteria and a failure of political leadership." "Personal Justice Denied: Report of the Commission on Wartime relocation and Internment of Civilians," U.S. Government Printing Office (Washington, D.C., 1982–83), Civil Liberties Public Education Fund and University of Washington Press, 1997, 18.

But Ruth and Albert quietly supported the National Council for Japanese American Redress . . . Ruth Asawa Papers, M1585: Box 165, Folder 2. Department of Special Collections, Stanford University Libraries.

Question Number 8: "If individual was a voluntary evacuee . . ." "Question unclear." Ruth Asawa Papers, M1585: Box 173, Folder 6. Department of Special Collections, Stanford University Libraries. Brian Niiya, content editor of Densho Encyclopedia, believes the term "voluntary evacuee" interprets this government question to refer to persons who, at the urging of the U.S. government, left the restricted western regions prior to the mass roundup and incarceration of Japanese Americans.

You are cordially (how else?) invited . . . Ruth Asawa Papers, M:1585: Box 175, Folder 13. Department of Special Collections, Stanford University Libraries.

"How can we children forget . . . ?" "Our Mother, Haru," George Asawa, courtesy of Aiko Cuneo and the Estate of Ruth Asawa.

"A monetary sum and words alone . . . " George H. W. Bush, letter on reparations to survivors of internment, Ruth Asawa Papers, M1585: Box 173, Folder 6. Department of Special Collections, Stanford University Libraries.

"[M]erely replaces one 'gravely wrong' decision with another." "Korematsu, Notorious Supreme Court Ruling on Japanese Internment, Is Finally Tossed Out," Charlie Savage, *New York Times,* June 26, 2018, accessed December 15, 2018, https://www.nytimes.com/2018/06/26/us/korematsu-supreme-court-ruling.html.

Chapter 12: Trust Me

"Since I was 42 years old, I have been brewing a pot of stone soup . . . " Ruth Asawa, Cyril Magnin Award Acceptance Speech, Ruth Asawa Papers, M1585: Box127, Folder 6, Statements. Department of Special Collections, Stanford University Libraries.

Ruth also started the '90s by serving as the first artist ever named to Fine Arts Museums of San Francisco's Board of Trustees. Interviews with the author and e-mails from Harry S. Parker III, former director, Fine Arts Museums of San Francisco, and Diane B. Wilsey, president board of trustees of FAMS.

"[B]ankers and debutantes . . . " Interview with Harry S. Parker III by the author, January 4, 2017.

"That was very novel, believe me . . . " Interview with FAMSF Trustee Emerita Florence Wong by the author, January 14, 2017.

"[T]he two biggest klutzes on the board . . . Harry and I fail," Interview with Diane B. Wilsey by the author, April 26, 2017.

"There is no right or wrong . . . She was a jolly person," Interview with Wilsey, April 26, 2017.

"No one had asked me to think before . . . I felt so simple-minded. I was a country girl . . . " "Although College Died, Students Really Lived," *New York Times,* March 14, 1992, Ruth Asawa Papers, M1585: Box 23, Folders 1 and 2. Department of Special Collections, Stanford University Libraries.

"When I left Black Mountain College I swore that I would never . . . " Black Mountain Reunion Statements, Ruth Asawa Papers, M1585: Box 23, Folders 1 and 2. Department of Special Collections, Stanford University Libraries.

"But then in the memories . . ." Black Mountain Reunion Statements, Ruth Asawa Statements of Elaine Urbain and Betty Jennerjahn, Pete Jennerjahn, Mary Park Washington, and M. C. Richards, Ruth Asawa Papers, M1585: Box 23, Folders 1 and 2. Department of Special Collections, Stanford University Libraries.

"[H]eavy ceramic beads that looked like children had made them." . . . "I like you . . ." Eulogy for Ruth Asawa by Susan Stauter, August, 2013.

"It's a good thing I didn't know who she was . . ." . . . "You're a hot pepper." Susan Stauter, interview by the author, March 9, 2017.

" . . . [U]ntil the District is in much better financial shape and there is relief from the court on desegregation . . ." Ramon Cortines, memo to Commissioner Tom Ammiano, Ruth Asawa, et al., January 16, 1992, Ruth Asawa Papers, M1585: Box 142, Folder 1. Department of Special Collections, Stanford University Libraries.

"Not one dime . . ." . . . "So put on your coat." "Arts School Poses Challenge to New Superintendent in S.F.," Nanette Asimov, *San Francisco Chronicle,* August 25, 1992, Ruth Asawa Papers, M1585: Box 146, Folder 1. Department of Special Collections, Stanford University Libraries.

"I expected John Cage to go on living forever . . ." Ruth Asawa, letter to Robert Rauschenberg, August 14, 1992, Ruth Asawa Papers, M1585: Box 145, Folder 2. Department of Special Collections, Stanford University Libraries.

"It always perplexed me." Bill Somerville, interview by the author, June 16, 2017.

"Ruth was very shrewd." Ken Blum, interview by the author, November 10, 2017.

"Shall we go to our courtyard?" "Arts High School Finds a Campus to Call Its Own," Diana Walsh, *San Francisco Examiner,* September 10, 1992, Ruth Asawa Papers, M1585: Box 146, Folder 1. Department of Special Collections, Stanford University Libraries.

"Dear Louise and Claude . . . Your check for $25,000. . . ." Ruth Asawa, letter to Claude and Louise Rosenberg, March 1993, Ruth Asawa Papers, M1585: Box 145, Folder 2. Department of Special Collections, Stanford University Libraries.

"It is a very personal and somewhat painful past to re-create . . ." Ruth Asawa, letter to Mary, June 1, 1990, Ruth Asawa Papers, M1585: Box 31, Folder 5. Department of Special Collections, Stanford University Libraries.

"The process of designing this sculpture . . ." Ruth Asawa, undated handwritten remarks on being selected to design *Internment Memorial* sculpture, Ruth Asawa Papers, M1585: Box 122, Folder 3. Department of Special Collections, Stanford University Libraries.

Listening to Matsuno's experiences, Asawa would weep silently . . . Interview with Phyllis Matsuno by the author, November 7, 2017.

Some experts who study the internment speak of community trauma . . . Interview with Dr. Satsuki Ina by the author, July 26, 2017. Therapist, filmmaker, and professor emerita of California State University, Sacramento, Ina was born in the Tule Lake internment camp and built her research, activism, and filmmaking around the subject of the internment.

While conducting their research . . . The population of internment camps, often expressed as a range of 110,000 to 120,000 people, is derived beginning with the 1940 U.S. Census, listing 127,000 persons of Japanese ancestry, 112,000 of whom lived in the Western areas designated for removal. These interned people were increased by about 5,000 births in the camps, plus people sent from Hawaii and other venues for a total figure of about 120,000 in ten camps. Clifford Uyeda of the National Japanese American Historical Society, letter to Ruth Asawa and Addie Lanier, August 24, 1993, Ruth Asawa Papers, M1585: Box 122, Folder 6. Department of Special Collections, Stanford University Libraries.

(Note: Camp census numbers continue to be refined: "There were just under 6,000 babies born in WRA camps; in addition to the group from Hawaii, the other large group to arrive in the WRA camps later were men 'paroled' from INS/Justice Department camps allowed to rejoin their families." Brian Niiya, content editor of Densho Encyclopedia, e-mail to the author, January 19, 2019.)

"When we were growing up, we didn't hear many stories about the internment . . ." Paul Lanier, quoted in *"Japanese American Internment Memorial Unveiled in S.J.,"* Barbara Hiura, *Hokubei Mainichi,* Mar. 9, 1994, Ruth Asawa Papers, M1585, Box 124, Folder 4. Department of Special Collections, Stanford University Libraries.

"It's really autobiographical . . ." Ruth Asawa, quoted in "Memorial Tells Story of Internment," *Dallas Morning News,* January 5, 1994, Ruth Asawa Papers, M1585: Box 249, Folder 1. Department of Special Collections, Stanford University Libraries.

In a daily diary of intense 8-to-12-hour-days . . . Ruth Asawa and Nancy Thompson's journal of making *Internment Memorial,* September 14, 1992–March 19, 1993, Ruth Asawa Papers, M1585: Box 124, Folder 2. Department of Special Collections, Stanford University Libraries.

"For Ruth, I would do anything . . ." Interview with Piero Mussi by the author, February 8, 2017.

When photographer Terry Schmitt came to the foundry . . . Interview with Terry Schmitt by the author, May 3, 2017.

"So a paper airplane was added." Nancy Thompson, in Ruth Asawa and Nancy Thompson's journal of making *Internment Memorial,* September 14, 1992–March 19, 1993, Ruth

Asawa Papers, M1585: Box 124, Folder 2. Department of Special Collections, Stanford University Libraries.

"He wasn't a hugger . . . " Interview with Karen Korematsu by the author, May 23, 2018.

"I hope we all are protected under the flag . . . " Ruth Asawa, speech following San Jose *Internment Memorial* dedication, March 5, 1994, Ruth Asawa Papers, M1585: Box 127, Folder 7. Department of Special Collections, Stanford University Libraries.

" . . . [T]he portrayal of those memories in bronze . . . " Merry Renk Curtis, letter to Ruth Asawa, Ruth Asawa Papers, M1585: Box 14, Folder 8. Department of Special Collections, Stanford University Libraries.

"The mockingbirds have been particularly vocal . . . " Ruth Asawa, letter to Dottye Dean, undated, c. 1993. Ruth Asawa Papers, M1585: Box 127, Folder 6. Department of Special Collections, Stanford University Libraries.

Chapter 13: The Fighting Years

"The arts saved us . . . " Ruth Asawa Papers, M1585: Box 97, Folder 3. Department of Special Collections, Stanford University Libraries.

"When I was a teenager . . . that experience will always be with us." Ruth Asawa Papers M1585: Box 97, Folder 3. Courtesy of the Department of Special Collections, Stanford University Libraries.

"Ruth never had a classroom of her own . . . and she felt it." Interview with Donn Harris by the author, June 6, 2017.

School districts are required to have credentialed teachers for academic and also liability reasons [because you are acting] in loco parentis. That's how districts operate . . . Interview with Donn Harris by the author, June 6, 2017.

"Ruth, I can help you . . . " Interview with Mark Johnson by the author, April 4, 2017.

"My knees buckled," Mark Johnson, e-mail to the author, February 16, 2019.

"Ruth was the grand dame artist . . . " Interview with Mark Johnson by the author, April 4, 2017.

"Had Milwaukee State not rejected me . . . " Ruth Asawa, Ruth Asawa Papers, M1585: Box 250, Folder 1. Department of Special Collections, Stanford University Libraries.

On December 20, 1998, amidst Milwaukee's winter chill . . . Ruth Asawa Papers, M1585: Box 235, Folder 3. Department of Special Collections, Stanford University Libraries. Box 250, Folder 1—Clippings, *Milwaukee Journal Sentinel,* December 18, 1998.

"[S]he would never be able to teach art in Wisconsin . . ." *UWM Today,* Spring '99, University of Wisconsin-Milwaukee Alumni Association, April 1999, Ruth Asawa Papers, M1585: Box 250, Folder 3. Department of Special Collections, Stanford University Libraries.

"She selected every shrub." Interview with Mark Johnson by the author, April 4, 2017, and amended in an e-mail on February 16, 2019, regarding Ruth's choice of the gingko tree, with its golden leaves.

"There was an asymmetrical pine tree." Interview with Mark Johnson by the author, April 4, 2017.

"I decided to dress down for Larry!" Interview with Mark Johnson by the author, April 4, 2017.

"Deprivation and restoration, stillness and movement . . ." Robert Corrigan, 2000–2001 CCL-PEP Grant Application, Ruth Asawa Papers M1585: Box 127, Folder 5. Department of Special Collections, Stanford University Libraries.

"Discrimination [c]ould happen to any one of them . . ." "Waterfall to Honor Interned Students," M. Watanabe, Golden Gate [X]Press, September 27, 2001, Ruth Asawa Papers, M1585: Box 125, Folder 7. Department of Special Collections, Stanford University Libraries.

"[A] poetic metaphor about renewal . . ." Interview with Mark Johnson by the author, April 4, 2017.

"I limit my activity now," Ruth Asawa, professional correspondence, August 29, 2001, Ruth Asawa Papers, M1585: Box 107, Folder 2. Department of Special Collections, Stanford University Libraries.

"You dare to give your administration a pay raise . . ." Ruth Asawa, letter to Dr. Arlene Ackerman, April 12, 2001, Ruth Asawa Papers, M1585: Box 107, Folder 2. Department of Special Collections, Stanford University Libraries.

"We must not ask another generation of students to wait another four years to enter the promised land." Ruth Asawa and Albert Lanier, statement to School of the Arts Move Task Force, Ruth Asawa Papers, M1585: Box 148, Folder 4. Department of Special Collections, Stanford University Libraries.

"I am tired. Ruth says we have to keep going." Albert Lanier, letter to School of the Arts Move Task Force, Ruth Asawa Papers, M1585: Box 148, Folder 5. Department of Special Collections, Stanford University Libraries.

"Working later, the lupus took its toll." Interview with Terry Schmitt by the author, May 3, 2017.

Deferred mega projects . . . "Being Propositioned by the San Francisco Unified School District," SOTA 2001–2012, Ruth Asawa Papers, M1585: Box 144, Folder 1. Department of Special Collections, Stanford University Libraries.

"How ironic . . . " Opinion, *San Francisco Examiner,* February 1, 2002, Ruth Asawa Papers, M1585: Box 250, Folder 6. Department of Special Collections, Stanford University Libraries.

"I am happy for the years of productive works, and the 'fighting years.'" Ruth Asawa, letter to Julia O'Connor, Ruth Asawa Papers, M 1585: Box 14, Folder 6. Department of Special Collections, Stanford University Libraries.

"I have had two strokes . . . " "Bay Area Asian American 'Local Heroes' Honored," Hokubei Mainichi, July 2, 2002, Ruth Asawa Papers, M1585: Box 250, Folder 6. Department of Special Collections, Stanford University Libraries.

"She helped us build the de Young . . . " Interview with Diane B. Wilsey by the author, April 26, 2017.

"When I met Pierre in Basel . . . " "I took him to Ruth's house . . . " Interview with Harry S. Parker III by the author, January 4, 2017.

A "huge shed" . . . "De Young's Rebirth," Julian Guthrie, October 15, 2005, accessed August 31, 2018, https://www.sfgate.com/news/article/De-Young-s-rebirth-It-had-to-overcome-design-2564985.php.

"It was such an innocent, high-minded idea." Interview with Harry S. Parker III by the author, February 11, 2019.

"It was an exciting idea—the only education tower . . . " Interview with Harry S. Parker III by the author, January 4, 2017.

"'Harry, how much would it cost . . . ?'" Interview with Harry S. Parker III by the author, January 4, 2017.

"You know what's happened to the value of her work?" Interview with Harry S. Parker III by the author, January 4, 2017.

"Today, it's a $15 million to $20 million gift." Interview with Harry S. Parker III by the author, February 11, 2019.

As a gay man who came of age in the 1980s . . . Interview with Daniell Cornell by the author, April 18, 2017.

The risk of plagiarism is too great. Aiko Cuneo, private communication with author.

"A cold, gray, difficult space" . . . "They were stars" Interview with Diane B. Wilsey by the author, April 26, 2017.

Ruth gave way to tears. Interview with Bud Johns by the author, March 7, 2017.

"Dear Ruth, Lo and behold . . . " Harry S. Parker III, letter to Ruth Asawa, January 19, 2006, Ruth Asawa Papers, M1585: Box 95, Folder 4. Department of Special Collections, Stanford University Libraries.

Epilogue: A Compact of Love

"Uncle Adam was the guy who took 'em fishing . . . " Bill Bondy, interview by the author, May 31, 2017.

"[L]ast cigarette on March 15, 1996 . . . " Albert Lanier's notebook, 1996, Ruth Asawa Papers, M1585: Box 175, Folder 13. Department of Special Collections, Stanford University Libraries.

It was too late . . . Interview with Hudson Lanier by the author, March 9, 2018.

"Adam took such good care of Grandma . . . " Lilli Lanier, March 9, 2018.

"I was aware that he was adopted in a compact that was underlined by love for that is how he left the world — with love. Jimmy Sanz (a.k.a. Henry Trout), letter to Ruth Asawa and Albert Lanier, postmarked October 14, 2011, Ruth Asawa Papers, M1585: Box 34, Folder 2011. Department of Special Collections, Stanford University Libraries.

I remember warm summer days and campfire nights . . . thanks for all that. Jimmy Sanz (a.k.a. Henry Trout), undated birthday card to Ruth Asawa, cited with permission, Ruth Asawa Papers, M1585: Box 38, Folder 1. Department of Special Collections, Stanford University Libraries.

"Abe Lincoln . . . " Albert Lanier, "Architecture, Gardens, and the Individual," interview with Harriet Nathan, 1979, Oral History Center, Bancroft Library, University of California,

Berkeley, accessed in Ruth Asawa Papers, M1585: Box 127, Folder 4. Department of Special Collections, Stanford University Libraries.

"We rode home in the van with her . . . She was just quiet." Interview with Lilli Lanier by the author, March 9, 2018.

"Children are like plants . . . " Albert Lanier Memorial Program, Ruth Asawa Papers, M1585: Box 175, Folder 13. Department of Special Collections, Stanford University Libraries.

"Renovate, don't demolish. And if you demolish, compost." William Albert Lanier obituary, November 11, 2008, accessed December 22, 2018, https://www.legacy.com/obituaries /SFGate/obituary.aspx?page=lifestory&pid=119893038.

She'd say, "Well, I want a chicken that's got a bosom like Miss Brunie . . . " Albert's Stories, William Albert Lanier, September 2003, courtesy of Aiko Cuneo and the Estate of Ruth Asawa.

He had made her laugh behind her hands like a teenager . . . Interview with Barbara Purcell by the author, July 5, 2017.

"It was so quiet . . . " Interview with Aiko Cuneo by the author, November 1, 2017.

"Your 83rd birthday will be lonely like my 88th birthday . . . " Merry Renk Curtis, card to Ruth Asawa, January 21, 2009, Ruth Asawa Papers, M1585: Box 14, Folder 8. Department of Special Collections, Stanford University Libraries.

"Thank you, San Francisco . . . " Ruth Asawa, quoted by Leah Garchik, *San Francisco Chronicle,* October 4, 2007, accessed online February 17, 2019.

"I told her nothing's perfect . . . " Interview with Jill Wynns by the author, October 23, 2017.

"I gave her my sacred word to make sure it was a good school . . . " Interview with Susan Stauter by the author, March 9, 2017.

"Our family is so proud to have this wonderful school named after our mother." Paul Lanier, "Ruth Asawa San Francisco School of the Arts," *Noe Valley Voice,* September 2011, Ruth Asawa Papers, M1585, Box 252, Folder 3. Department of Special Collections, Stanford University Libraries.

"[M]ore than a realistic hope. It's going to happen." Interview with Donn Harris by the author, June 16, 2017.

"We'll succeed." Interview with Willie L. Brown by the author, March 10, 2017.

"There aren't enough visionaries in the city . . ." Interview with Ken Blum by the author, November 10, 2017.

"It's a sculpture . . . It plays with the light." Interview with Glory Rubio by the author, May 16, 2017.

"I didn't know who [Ruth Asawa] was." Interview with Jonathan Laib by the author, February 6, 2017.

"Dear Ruthie, This is just for revenge . . ." Josef Albers, note on wrapping paper to Ruth Asawa (undated), Ruth Asawa Papers, M1585: Box 1, Folder 1. Department of Special Collections, Stanford University Libraries. © The Josef and Anni Albers Foundation.

"The 18-by-18-inch oil painting was signed and dated A62 . . ." Jonathan Laib, e-mail to the author, January 2, 2019.

"Cool Reising . . ." This title of Albers's green *Homage to the Square* study given to Asawa likely reflects a phonetic misspelling—reverting to the German dipthong "ei" for the long "I" sound—made in haste by the painter. Albers most probably meant the title to be "Cool Rising," according to an e-mail to the author on January 14, 2019, from Jeannette Redensek, who is cataloguing Albers's paintings at the Josef and Anni Albers Foundation.

"We talked about her mother's work . . ." *"As soon as I saw the images . . ."* Interview with Jonathan Laib by the author, February 6, 2017.

". . . I started thinking of her contemporaries . . ." Interview with Jonathan Laib by the author, February 6, 2017.

"[I]t's a meditative process . . ." Interview with Jonathan Laib by the author, February 6, 2017.

"Her own commercial work was never at the top of her list" . . . *"Relaunch her in the commercial sphere."* Interview with Jonathan Laib by the author, February 6, 2017.

"My first thought was, how do I go about building a larger audience?" Interview with Jonathan Laib by the author, January 4, 2019.

"I knew her work didn't belong in the design sale category. Once placed along Louise Bourgeois, Josef Albers, Eva Hesse . . ." Interview with Jonathan Laib by the author, January 4, 2019.

"We were ready to push the limits . . ." Jonathan Laib, e-mail to the author, August 1, 2017.

"Every one of my colleagues at Christie's was on the phone . . ." Jonathan Laib, email to the author, August 1, 2017.

"It was a storybook ending . . ." Jonathan Laib, e-mail to the author, August 1, 2017.

"People bidding on Ruth weren't looking for trophy art, blue chip status, but people looking for integrity and authenticity. . . ." Interview with Jonathan Laib by the author, February 6, 2017.

"She was in bed dealing with lupus . . ." Interview with Jonathan Laib by the author, February 6, 2017.

"There is still prejudice . . ." Interview with Trish Bransten by the author, April 4, 2017.

"The auction was quite exciting ... such a frenzy." Jonathan Laib, e-mail to the author, August 1, 2017.

But when San Francisco Chronicle *writer John King reported her fountain's displacement . . .* John King, "Plans for shiny new Apple store could mean farewell for fountain," *San Francisco Chronicle,* May 28, 2013; "Moving Asawa art for Apple 'wouldn't make sense,'" May 31, 2013; accessed online February 18, 2019.

Not only is Ruth one of the city's most important artists . . . Bud Johns, letter to the editor, *San Francisco Chronicle,* May 31, 2013, Ruth Asawa Papers, M1585: Box 252, Folder 5. Department of Special Collections, Stanford University Libraries.

She died where she wanted to die . . . "Farewell to Ruth Asawa," Steve Steinberg, *Noe Valley Voice,* September 2013, Ruth Asawa Papers, M1585: Box 252, Folder 5. Department of Special Collections, Stanford University Libraries.

"The spirit of the fountain dies not. It is the eternal feminine . . ." Susan Stauter, eulogy for Ruth Asawa.

"Albers was her teacher and she was mine." Interview with Susan Stauter by the author, March 9, 2017.

"Patience, passion, talking eyes . . ." Xavier Lanier, notes for a eulogy for Ruth Asawa.

"Apple spares beloved fountain." "Architecture: Apple spares beloved fountain," John King, *San Francisco Chronicle,* August 27, 2013, Ruth Asawa Papers, M1585: Box 252, Folder 5. Department of Special Collections, Stanford University Libraries.

Laib left Christie's auction house . . . "David Zwirner Poaches Postwar Senior Specialist From Christie's, Now Represents Ruth Asawa Estate," *ARTnews,* Nate Freeman, January 6, 2017, accessed December 22, 2018, http://www.artnews.com/2017/01/06/david-zwirner-poaches-postwar-senior-specialist-from-christies-now-represents-ruth-asawa-estate.

"[R]ewriting art history." "Ruth Asawa Reshapes Art History," Andrea K. Scott, *New Yorker,* October 9, 2017, accessed January 1, 2019, https://www.newyorker.com/magazine/2017/10/09/ruth-asawa-reshapes-art-history.

"[A] topological poem to the universal capacity for metamorphosis." Robert Storr, "Ruth Asawa: Sketches of the Cosmos," in *Ruth Asawa*, Anne Wehr, ed. (New York: David Zwirner Books, 2018).

"I don't see her work as a commentary in any straightforward way on the spatial markers of suffering . . . " Interview with Robert Storr by the author, February 7, 2017.

Ruth's wire sculptures of the 1950s and 1960s are historically her most important creative works . . . Mark Johnson, e-mail to the author, February 16, 2019.

"The schools." Aiko Cuneo, e-mail to the author, February 17, 2019.

Asawa's youngest son, Paul, mingled Ruth and Albert's ashes into clay . . . Interview with Paul Lanier by the author, April 18, 2018.

SELECTED BIBLIOGRAPHY

Albers, Josef. *Interaction of Color: 50th Anniversary Edition.* Edited by Nicholas Fox Weber. New Haven, CT, and London: Yale University Press, 2013.

Bannai, Lorraine K. *Enduring Conviction: Fred Korematsu and His Quest for Justice.* Seattle: University of Washington Press, 2015.

Chang, Gordon H., Mark Johnson, Paul Karlstrom, eds. *Asian American Art: A History, 1850–1970.* Stanford, CA: Stanford University Press, 2008.

The Civil Liberties Public Education Fund, *Personal Justice Denied: Report of the Commission on Wartime Relocation and Internment of Civilians.* Seattle and London: University of Washington Press, 1997.

Cornell, Daniell. *The Sculpture of Ruth Asawa: Contours in the Air.* Fine Arts Museums of San Francisco. Berkeley and Los Angeles, CA: University of California Press, 2006.

Dempster, Brian Komei. *From Our Side of the Fence: Growing Up in America's Concentration Camps.* Produced by Japanese Cultural and Community Center of Northern California. San Francisco: Kearny Street Workshop, 2001.

Duberman, Martin. *Black Mountain: An Exploration in Community.* Evanston, IL: Northwestern University Press, 2009.

Fitzgerald, Sally. *The Habit of Being: Letters of Flannery O'Connor.* New York: Farrar, Straus and Giroux, 1979.

Fuller, R. Buckminster. *Nine Chains to the Moon.* New York: Anchor Books, Doubleday & Co. Inc., 1971.

Goodwin, Doris Kearns. *No Ordinary Time: Franklin and Eleanor Roosevelt: The Home Front in World War II.* New York: Simon & Schuster, 1994.

Harris, Mary Emma. *The Arts at Black Mountain College.* Cambridge, MA: MIT Press, 1987.

Hill, Kimi Kodani. *Topaz Moon: Chiura Obata's Art of the Internment.* Berkeley, CA: Heyday, 2000.

Hirasuna, Delphine. *The Art of Gaman: Arts and Crafts from the Japanese American Internment Camps 1942–1946.* Berkeley, CA: Ten Speed Press, 2005.

Howard, John. *Concentration Camps on the Home Front: Japanese Americans in the House of Jim Crow.* Chicago: University of Chicago Press, 2008.

Inada, Lawson Fusao. *Only What We Could Carry: The Japanese American Internment Experience.* Berkeley, CA: Heyday Books, 2000.

Iritani, Joanne. Oral History Interview with Ruth Asawa Lanier, April 7, 2000, c. Florin Japanese American Citizens League and California State University, Sacramento.

Irons, Peter. *Justice at War: The Story of the Japanese American Internment Cases.* New York and Oxford: Oxford University Press, 1983.

Jepson, Andrea I., and Sharon S. Litzky. *The Alvarado Experience: Ten Years of a School-Community Art Program.* San Francisco: Alvarado School Art Workshop Inc., 1978.

Katz, Vincent, ed. *Black Mountain College: Experiment in Art.* Cambridge, MA: MIT Press, 2013.

Laib, Jonathan. *Ruth Asawa: Line by Line.* New York: Christie's, 2015.

Laib, Jonathan, Charlotte Perrrotey, Charlie Adamski. *Ruth Asawa: Objects and Apparitions.* New York: Christie's, 2013.

Lane, Mervin. *Black Mountain College: Sprouted Seeds: An Anthology of Personal Accounts.* Knoxville: University of Tennessee Press, 1990.

Molesworth, Helen. *Leap Before You Look: Black Mountain College, 1933–1957.* New Haven, CT: Yale University Press, 2015.

Nathanson, Harriet. *Oral History with Ruth Asawa and Albert Lanier.* Oral History Center, Bancroft Library, University of California, Berkeley, c. 1980.

Niiya, Brian. *Densho Encyclopedia.* https://encyclopedia.densho.org.

Niiya, Brian. *Japanese American History: An A-to-Z Reference from 1868 to the Present.* New York: Facts on File, 1993.

Okubo, Miné. *Citizen 13660.* Seattle: University of Washington Press, 2014. (Originally published New York: Columbia University Press, 1946.)

Otsuka, Julie. *The Buddha in the Attic.* New York: Anchor Books, 2012.

Poon, Irene. *Leading the Way: Asian American Artists of the Older Generation.* Seattle: University of Washington Press, 2001.

Reeves, Richard. *Infamy: The Shocking Story of the Japanese American Internment in World War II.* New York: Henry Holt & Co., 2015.

Rountree, Cathleen. *On Women Turning Seventy: Honoring the Voices of Wisdom.* San Francisco: Jossey-Bass, 1999.

Rubinstein, Charlotte Streifer. *American Women Sculptors: A History of Women Working in Three Dimensions.* Boston: G.K. Hall & Co., 1990.

Sato, Kiyo. *Kiyo's Story: A Japanese-American Family's Quest for the American Dream.* New York: Soho Press, 2007.

Schiffer, Vivienne. *Camp Nine.* Fayetteville, AR: University of Arkansas Press, 2011.

Weher, Anne, ed. *Ruth Asawa.* New York: David Zwirner Books, 2018.

Document Collections:

Mary Emma Harris, The Black Mountain College Project, Inc., New York, NY.

Ruth Aiko Asawa, War Evacuee Case File.pdf. QO1—308506115, digital file reproduced at National Archives and Records Administration, Washington, D.C.

Ruth Asawa Papers, M1585. Department of Special Collections and University Archives, Stanford University Libraries, Stanford, CA.

Ruth Asawa Student File. Black Mountain College. Western Regional Archives, North Carolina Department of National and Cultural Resources, Asheville, NC.

Umakichi Asawa, Alien Enemy File, RG60, Alien Enemy Internment Case File, A1 COR 146-13 Box 226(1).pdf. National Archives and Records Administration, Washington, D.C.

Film:

Ruth Asawa: Of Forms and Growth. Robert Snyder. Masters & Masterworks Productions, 1978.

IMAGE CREDITS

Photographs by Imogen Cunningham, © 2019 Imogen Cunningham Trust. www.imogencunningham.com. Cover, 2, 109, 118, 123, 130, 133, 139, 147, 149, 256, 328

Photograph © 2013 Christie's Images Limited, 11

Photographs courtesy of Estate of Ruth Asawa, 15, 16, 23, 33, 45, 50, 69, 71, 93, 104, 105

Photographs by Laurence Cuneo, © Estate of Ruth Asawa, 95, 99, 115, 116, 119, 135, 140, 160, 163, 171, 173, 179 (top), 226, 237, 241, 245, 248, 250, 253, 254

Photographs by Aiko Cuneo, © Estate of Ruth Asawa, 156, 165, 179 (bottom)

Photographs by Hudson Cuneo, © Estate of Ruth Asawa, 143, 200

Photographs by Xavier Lanier, © Estate of Ruth Asawa, 174, 253

Photograph by Mary Parks Washington, courtesy of Estate of Ruth Asawa, 61

Photograph by Mabel Rose Jamison, courtesy of Estate of Ruth Asawa, 36 (top)

Photograph courtesy of the National Japanese American Historical Society, 31

Photograph courtesy of National Portrait Gallery, Smithsonian Institution. Gift of the Children of Ruth Asawa, 48

Photographs courtesy of the Estate of Hazel Larsen Archer and the Black Mountain College Museum + Arts Center, 63, 75

Photograph courtesy of the Estate of Hazel Larsen Archer, by permission of Erika Archer-Zarow, 85, 90

Photograph by Nat Farbman/The LIFE Picture Collection/Getty Images, 107

Photograph by Paul Hassell, courtesy of Estate of Ruth Asawa, 127

Photograph by Phiz Mezey, courtesy of the Phiz Mezey Trust, 187

Photograph by Allen Nomura, © Allen Nomura, 184

Photographs by Terry Schmitt, © Terry Schmitt, 203, 217, 221

Facsimile from Umakichi Asawa, Alien Enemy File. RG 60, Alien Enemy Internment Case File. A1 COR 146-13, Box 226(1).pdf. Asawa FBI Files, courtesy of the National Archives and Records Administration, 40, 41

Images © Estate of Ruth Asawa, courtesy of the Fine Arts Museums of San Francisco, 76, 82

Wynns, Jill, 243

Y

Yasada, Ura, 16
Yasuda, Haru. *See* Asawa, Haru
Yasui, Minoru, 204, 222

Z

Zellerbach, Harold, 152, 161, 179
Zuckerberg, Mark, 126

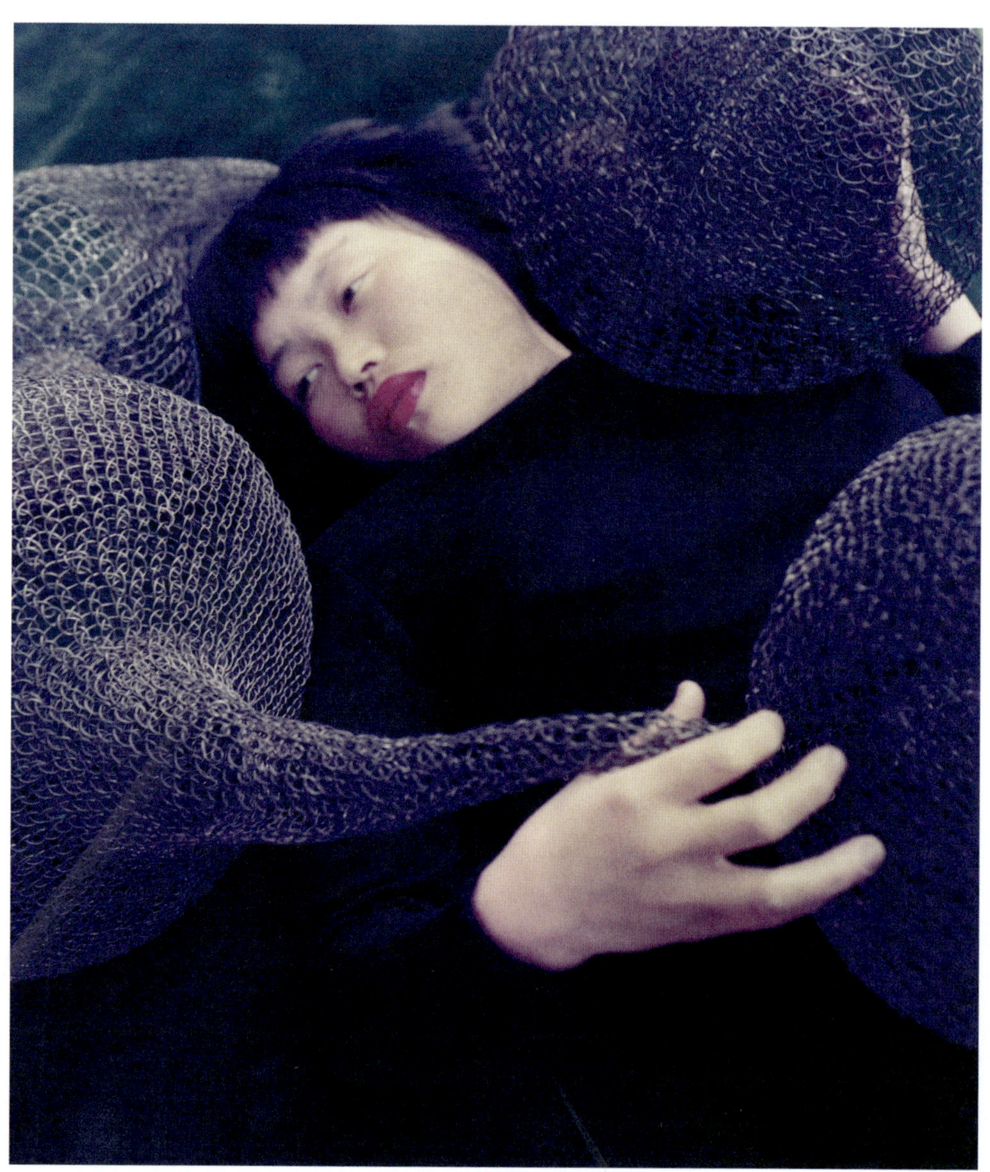

Ruth reclining and encircled by a looped-wire sculpture, 1951. Photograph by Imogen Cunningham.